François-X. Garneau

History of Canada

from the time of its discovery till the union year - 1840-1 - Vol. 2

François-X. Garneau

History of Canada
from the time of its discovery till the union year - 1840-1 - Vol. 2

ISBN/EAN: 9783337186357

Printed in Europe, USA, Canada, Australia, Japan

Cover: Foto ©ninafisch / pixelio.de

More available books at **www.hansebooks.com**

HISTORY OF CANADA,

FROM

THE TIME OF ITS DISCOVERY

TILL THE UNION YEAR (1840-1):

TRANSLATED FROM

"L'HISTOIRE DU CANADA" OF F.-X. GARNEAU, Esq.

AND ACCOMPANIED WITH

ILLUSTRATIVE NOTES,

ETC., ETC.

BY ANDREW BELL.

IN THREE VOLUMES.

VOL. II.

Montreal:
PRINTED AND PUBLISHED BY JOHN LOVELL,
ST. NICHOLAS STREET.
1860.

HISTORY OF CANADA.

BOOK SIXTH.

CHAPTER I.

ESTABLISHMENT OF LOUISIANA

1683–1712.

Province of Louisiana.—Louis XIV puts several vessels at the disposal of La Sale to found a Settlement there.—His departure with a squadron; and misunderstandings with his colleague, M. de Beaujeu.—He misses the sea-entry of the Mississippi, and is landed in Matagorda bay, Texas.—Shameful conduct of Beaujeu, who leaves La Sale and the colonists to their fate.—La Sale builds two fortlets, and calls one St. Louis.—He explores several parts of the country, to no good purpose, during several months, and loses many of his men.—Despairing of finding the Mississippi, he sets out for the Illinois, in view of obtaining succour from France.—Part of his companions murder him and his nephew.—His assassins fall out; and two of their number killed by the others.—Joutel and six of the party, leaving the conspirators behind, reach the Illinois.—Sad fate of most of the party left in the Texas territory.—D'Iberville undertakes to re-colonise Louisiana, and settles a colony at Biloxi (1698-8).—Appearance of the British on the Mississippi.—The Huguenots ask leave to settle in Louisiana, but are refused.—D'Iberville demands free trade for his colony.—Illusive metallic riches of the country.—The Biloxians removed to Mobile in 1701.—The colony progresses apace.—Death of M. d'Iberville.—An intendancy appointed, and its evil results.—Louisiana ceded to M. de Crozat. (1712).

The name LOUISIANA was given, in days past, to all the countries situated on the Gulf of Mexico, and which extends from the bay of Mobile: *i. e.* eastward, up to the sources of the rivers which fall into the Mississippi; to the westward, as far as to

New Mexico and to the ancient kingdom of Leon. Now-a-days, this vast territory is divided into several States: viz., Texas, to the west, from the Rio del Norte up to the Sabine; Louisiana, properly so called, in the centre, from the latter stream as far as Pearl River; and the Mississippi, at the east, from Pearl River till some distance from the bay of Mobile; the interspace remaining, as far as that bay, forms a part of Alabama. To the north of these States, there are besides those of Arkansas, Missouri, Illinois, &c. At the epoch we have now reached in this History, all these countries were almost unknown. Ferdinand de Soto, a Spanish voyager, once a companion of Pizarro, traversed, but did not explore this region in 1539-40, when in search of a new Perou. Having set out from Holy-Spirit bay in Florida, with fully 1000 soldiers, he proceeded northward as far as the Apalachians; thence turning westward, he followed the lower line of that mountain range in a southerly direction, and arrived at and crossed the river Tombeckbee, near its junction with the Alabama. Afterwards he turned to the north-west, and crossed the Mississippi above the Arkansas. Turning again to the south, he crossed the Red River; which became the term of his course, as he died in 1542, near thereto, without having found what he sought. Moscosa, his lieutenant, heading the expedition, directed it towards Mexico, but, stopped by the intervening heights, he retraced his steps, and proceeded to the sea, on which he re-embarked with about 350 men, all that remained alive.* Of this enterprise, and of other voyages undertaken at wide intervals, by Spanish adventurers, to the northern coasts of the Gulf, only vague accounts have reached us.†

We have already noticed the gracious reception of La Sale by Louis XIV in 1683, when he returned to France and reported his discovery of the embouchure of the Mississippi. La Sale proposed to the king that the territory through which that great river flows should be appropriated as a part of New France; the suggestion was adopted, and La Sale himself commissioned to begin a colonization

---

* Jared Sparks: *Amer. Biog.* xi.

† *Carte de la Louisiana*, &c., 1782, by G. Delisle, in the *Itinéraire de la Louisiane*; GARCILASSO DE LA VEGA; *History of the Conquest of Florida*, by Ferdinand de Soto.

of Louisiana.—To effect this design, four vessels were put at his disposition: two ships of war, one of 40 and one of 6 guns; with a hired privateer ship and a trading vessel. The number of persons embarked did not reach 500 in all, including the crews; and among the passengers were eight missionaries and several gentlemen. The squadron, which was commanded by M. de Beaujeu, sailed from La Rochelle, July 24, 1684. As it proceeded, quarrels began between the commodore and La Sale, subsiding into a mutual aversion, perilous to the expedition. One of the ships was captured by the Spaniards of San Domingo. The others, led away by uncomprehended currents, and having faulty nautical instruments on board, overpassed their destination by many leagues. La Sale suspecting that the embouchure of the Mississippi was some way behind, would have turned helm; but Beaujeu, a vain and jealous man, impatient of La Sale's authority over him, refused to obey; and continued his western course, as blindly as obstinately.

On the 14th February, the squadron reached Matagorda bay, Texas; when La Sale, who knew not that he was 120 leagues distant from the Mississippi, ordered the captain of the privateer to disembark the people under his charge. Pretending to do so, he ran his vessel upon reefs,* where it was wrecked, and part of the cargo lost, including the warlike and other stores of the expedition.

Instead of censuring the privateer's-man, Beaujeu took him on board his own vessel, to screen him from La Sale's vengeance; and when asked to supply as many stores as he had on board, for partially replacing those lost, he refused to do so under frivolous pretexts; finally, on the 14th of March, he stood out to sea, leaving the colonists to their fate, on an unknown and desert shore.

La Sale, thus put to his shifts, set some of his people to cultivate the ground to obtain subsistence for all; and, along with a few artisans, began to construct a fortlet for defence against the savages. When near completion, he began to form another, on a height, two leagues higher up a stream afterwards known as the rivière des Vaches. This fastness he called Fort St. Louis. But

---

* Joutel (one of the colonists): *Journal historique.*

his handicraftsmen, being ill selected in France, proved inferior to their pretensions, and the work proceeded slowly. Worse still, the seed sown by his men, was, as it came, up trodden down by wild animals, or perished in the ground. Other mischances occurred; a mutinous spirit arose, and when this was severely checked by La Sale, his people desponded. Illness followed, under which 30 victims sank. The aborigines also manifested hostile intentions towards the luckless party, to whom they became all the more formidable as many of them rode bitted horses, and of course could not be followed across the prairies when their attacks were repulsed.

The country itself was agreeable enough, being free from bush, perfectly level, and well watered; the air was dry and pure, the temperature mild. But savage and venomous animals formed a considerable part of animated nature in this wilderness; including tiger-cats; caïmans (alligators), rattlesnakes, &c.

La Sale, despairing of forming a proper settlement, set out in search of the Mississippi; wandering, for some months, in the direction of the Colorado. At one place, the party was assailed by the savages and several persons killed. *La Belle*, a vessel of 6 guns, the only one remaining to him, was wrecked, and the people in her drowned. A second exploration he made, was as bootless as the first. Of a score of men composing it, but eight returned. Meanwhile those left at the bay of St. Bernard (Matagorda, in Texas) were dwindling away from illness and privation. La Sale's case was bad indeed. He had intended to despatch the vessel lately lost to the French Antilles, for succour; and that obtained, she was afterwards to coast the Gulf seaboard in search of the Mississippian embouchure.

The means of effecting this being now lost, it was needful to look to other quarters for aid, as the provisions of the party were now almost all consumed. La Sale determined to seek assistance from France; but to make his situation known, it was needful to go to Canada. He was a man of decision, and he resolved to go thither himself. By this time his people were reduced from 80 to 37 men; twenty of whom he left at St. Louis, under M. le Barbier; and with the seventeen others he set out for the Illinois country in January 1687.

The journey was painful, and its progression slow. Mid-March was over, and as yet only one of the tributaries of Trinity river * reached, when some of the men mutinied, murdered M. Moraguet, La Sale's nephew, and sought to kill him also. The latter hid himself, but was sought out and mortally wounded, in presence of Père Anastasius, a missionary who was of the party.—A few handfuls of earth, with a rude cross to mark the place, set up by the missionary, amid a vast wilderness, now covered all that could die of the discoverer of Louisiana.

The murderers, after despoiling the dead, resumed their march, but a dispute soon arose, about their several shares of the booty; when they rose upon two of their own number, who had been their leaders in the mutiny, and shot them both. The surviving conspirators then took to the woods; while the rest, seven in number, including a brother of La Sale, Joutel, and Père Anastasius, continued their way towards the Illinois, and reached St. Louis in mid-September.

The remanent party at Matagorda Bay, meanwhile, had sped yet worse. Shortly after La Sale left, the savages suddenly attacked them, and killed all but five, who being delivered to the Spaniards, then jealous of French intrusion, they inhumanly sent three of these captives to slave in the mines of New Mexico; two more, sons of a Canadian named Talon, were taken care of by the Mexican viceroy, and finally entered the Spanish marine service.†

Such was the unprosperous issue of a hopeful expedition, and which would have probably been even fortuitously successful, if the French had but remained in the locality where they first pitched their tent, for Texas is one of the finest and most fertile countries in the world. But La Sale then committed the same error which marked and marred his Canadian explorations: he took too many men with him to the interior. Being, besides, of a restless temperament, he was always for going *ahead;* while he ought to have stuck to the foundations he laid in Texas, and attended to agricultural pursuits.‡

---

* Mr. Jared Sparks fixes this tragedy at the river Brasos : most others place it as above.

† *Universal History,* xi, 278.

‡ "For force of will, and vast conceptions; for various knowledge,

During the years of war immediately preceding the peace of Ryswick, Louisianian colonisation was quite lost sight of by the French ministry; but the country being attractive, several of the Canadians who visited it at intervals on their own account, were induced to stay; and by degrees they formed two trading settlements; one near the embouchure of the Mississippi, the other on the Mobile: thence they commerced with the French Antilles.

Probably the reports reaching France that these settlers were thriving, now induced the court to take up the dropped project of systematically colonising the country. The Spaniards, who had exulted over the failure of La Sale, and assuming that the whole southern territory of North America was theirs, got the start of the French authorities; and, after taking or re-taking possession of it, with the accustomed ceremonials in their king's name, practically vindicated their claim by founding a colony on the Bay of Pensacola, at the western extremity of Florida. But they had not long settled in that locality, when M. d'Iberville appeared upon the scene.

After his return from Hudson's Bay in 1697, this navigator earnestly applied to the French ministry to be employed in an expedition to Louisiana; upon which two ships were put at his disposition, with orders to search for and chart the sea-outlets of the Mississippi. Accompanied by Messrs. de Sauvole and de Bienville, he sailed from La Rochelle, in September 1698; driven into Brest by contrary winds, he set out again late in October, and reached San Domingo early in December. Leaving that island, Jan. 1, 1699, he reached the shores of Florida in 26 days. He essayed to anchor at Pensacola, but being repelled, he passed

---

and quiet adaptation of his genius to untried circumstances; for a sublime magnanimity, that resigned itself to the will of Heaven, and yet triumphed over affliction by energy of purpose and unfaltering hope, he had no superior among his countrymen. He had won the affection of the governor of Canada, the esteem of Colbert, the confidence of his son (marquis de Seignelai), the favour of Louis the Fourteenth. After beginning the colonization of Upper Canada, he perfected the discovery of the Mississippi, from the Falls of St. Anthony to its mouth; and he will be remembered, through all time, as the Father of Colonization in the great central Valley of the West."—BANCROFT: *History of the United States*, iii, 173-4.—*B.*

on to Mobile bay. Returning to San Domingo again (why, does not appear, unless it were to obtain information to direct him in his researches), he coasted the seaboard of the Mississippi territory, till he found the embouchure of its great river, which he ascended for some distance, and landed at one or more native villages near either of its banks. After descending the stream, erecting a fort at Biloxi Bay, between the Mississippi and the Mobile river, and leaving M. de Sauvole in command there, he set sail for France.

He was well received at court, being created a knight of St. Louis, and soon afterwards nominated governor-general of Louisiana. Late in 1699, he set out with a body of colonials, almost all Canadians; and arrived at Biloxi in January 1700. The site of this post was ill adapted for a settlement, except in view of a trade with the isles and Europe, the country being arid, and the heat of the climate intense. It was nevertheless well peopled with aborigines of various tribes. Numbers of these people came to welcome D'Iberville, whose face they rubbed with white clay, in token of their esteem; they also presented him with the calumet of peace, and feasted the French for several days.

Upon his return to Europe, D'Iberville learned that a British vessel had been seen on the Mississippi; and that a number of Carolinian colonists had advanced to the river Yasous, in the Chickasaw territory. English attention had been drawn towards this country by Père Hennepin,* who to a new edition of his " Description of Louisiana " prefixed a dedication to William III, inviting him to appropriate the country, and cause the gospel to be preached to its heathen people. That king, accepting the proposal, sent three vessels, with a body of Huguenots embarked in them, to found a protestant colony on the Mississippi. These people proceeded as far as the province of Panuco, intending to form an alliance with the Spaniards, and induce them to expel the French catholics from Biloxi:† but their project was not relished, or likely to be, jealous as the Spaniards were of all the

---

* Louis XIV gave orders to arrest this monk if he ever came to Canada. *Official Correspondence.*

† *Universal History*, xi, n. 78.

French as colonists. Still the court of the Escurial made complaints to that of Versailles against the colonisation of any part of what was called the "Spanish Indies"; but the family relations between the two royal families becoming closer, no further notice was taken of the alleged encroachments.

A great number of Huguenots (so were the French Protestants nicknamed by their catholic fellow-countrymen) had settled in Virginia, Carolina, &c., after their expulsion or flight from France. They were received, as they deserved to be, for valuable colonists. In Massachusetts, they were allowed to send members to Assembly. They founded several cities, now flourishing. Others of them, preferring to live among their compatriots, even in enforced exile, petitioned Louis XIV to let them settle in Louisiana, intimating that they would be submissive to his will in all things else, if their religious rights were not interfered with; but His Majesty, in answer to M. de Pontchartrain, said, he "had not driven the Protestants out of his kingdom with an intent that they should form a republic in America." They renewed their request, during the Orleans regency, and the refusal was repeated.

Meanwhile, D'Iberville ascended the Mississippi as far as the Natchez' country, where he intended to build a town. While he was with the Tinssas' tribe (neighbours of the Natchez) a violent storm arose. A thunderbolt struck the idol temple of the Tinssas and set it on fire. Forthwith the savages howled dismally, tore their hair, rubbed their faces and bodies with clay, invoking the Great Spirit the while. Mothers brought their babes, strangled them, and threw the bodies into the flames. Seventeen of those innocents were thus sacrificed, despite the efforts of the French to prevent it.*

After a short stay in the country, D'Iberville returned to Biloxi, where he fixed his head-quarters. He wrote to Paris, to ask that freedom of trade should prevail in the colony. The country was reported to abound in the precious metals, which turned out to be an illusion. A vein of copper was discovered, but it was found too far off to be profitably worked. Parties ascended the Red

---

* *Relation, ou Annale véritable*, &c., 1699-1721, by Penicaut: Paris Documents, Series 2.

River, the Arkansas, and the Missouri, nearly to the Rocky Mountains, in search of gold, but found no sure signs of any.

D'Iberville having revisited France, late in 1701, got command of three ships of war, in which he returned to Biloxi, with orders to strengthen and extend the settlements already formed, and labour to prevent the British from entering the country. A four-bastioned fort was erected at Mobile. After a survey of the territory, D'Iberville sent a report to Paris, and recommended that emigrants should be sent in numbers, husbandmen especially. Finding that he had made a bad choice for his trading capital, he cused the settlers at Biloxi to remove to Mobile.

By degrees the French population increased, under the fostering care of D'Iberville; but their protector's career was now near its close. A life of incessant toils, in peace and war, had worn out his constitution. He fell ill of yellow fever in 1702; and, when convalescing, had to return to Europe. Ever restless, he proposed, to the king, to attack the fleets of Virginia and Newfoundland. The means of doing so were assigned to him at first, and then diverted to other purposes. He fell seriously ill again, and had not quite recovered when he offered to capture Barbadoes, with other West India Islands, and sweep from the American waters all British trade. M. Ducape had previously offered to take Jamaica: the plans of the two were now conjoined. They were tried in 1706, but proved abortive. D'Iberville, indeed, captured Nevis, took prisoner and carried away the governor and the colonists, 7000 negroes, and a great booty, landing the whole in Martinique, to the great enrichment of that French island.

When about to seek out the British convoys according to promise, he was smitten a second time with yellow fever and died, July 9, 1706, aged 44 years. This hero, as redoubtable a captain on sea as on land, was born at Montreal in 1662, being one of several sons, all more or less distinguished, of Charles le Moyne, Seigneur of Longueuil, near that city. The family was of Norman extraction.

Two years after D'Iberville's death, M. Dion d'Artaguette came to Louisiana as a kind of royal intendant, his prescribed duty being to labour for the advancement of the industry of the colony. Under his superintendence, all things retrograded; yet, all the while, the people of France were wished to believe that the colony was in the most flourishing state. In 1711, the Isle Dauphine was ravaged by corsairs; causing a loss to the crown of property valued at 80,000 francs. The colony was founded on unsound bases, observes Raynal, and could not long prosper. " Going on from bad to worse," says he, " there remained in it but 28 impoverished families; when the public was surprised to learn, in 1712, that M. Crozat * had asked and obtained for himself a 16 years' lease of the whole trade of Louisiana."—But before proceeding with the annals of this colony, it is time to return to the affairs of Canada, our more immediate subject.

---

* In the original printed 1742, by mistake. Antoine Crozat, marquis du Châtel, was a rich financier, probably one of the farmers-general.—*B.*

CHAPTER II.

TREATY OF UTRECHT.

1701‒713.

A French colony settled at Detroit.—Four years' peace.—" War of the Succession."—Operations in America.—Neutrality in the western region: hostilities confined to the maritime provinces.—Trinal state of Acadia.—Quarrels among the western savages.—Raids in New England by the French and the Abenaquis.—Destruction of Deerfield and Haverhill (1708).—Colonel Schuyler's remonstrances on these acts, and M. de Vaudreuil's defence of them.—Captain Church ravages Acadia (1704).—Colonel Marck's two sieges of Port-Royal; is repulsed in both (1707).—Notices of Newfoundland: hostilities in that island; M. de Subercase fails to take Fort St. John (1705).—M. de St. Ovide captures St. John (1709).—Further hostilities in Newfoundland.—The Anglo-American colonists call on the British government to aid them to conquer Canada: promises made in 1709, and again in 1710, to send the required aid, but none arrives.—General Nicholson besieges and takes Port-Royal.—The articles of its capitulation diversely interpreted. Resumption and termination of hostilities in Acadia.—Third attack meditated on Quebec, and double invasion of Canada; the Iroquois arm again.—Disasters of the British maritime expedition.—The Outagamis at Detroit; savages' intents against that settlement; their defeat, and destruction.—Re-establishment of Michilimackinac.—Sudden change of ministry in England, its consequences.—Treaty of Utrecht; stipulations in it regarding New France.—Reflections on the comparative strength of France at this time and at the death of Louis XIII.

M. de Callière, forecasting the advantages which would attend the possession of a fortified port on the shore of the *détroit*, or strait between the farthest great lakes, sent one of his officers, named la Mothe-Cadillac, with 100 Canadians and a jesuit missionary, to form a settlement, in June 1701, near the lower end of Lake St. Clair, where its waters pass into lake Erie. The important American city of DETROIT, which has, for part of its site, that of the post established in the first year of the 18th century, now contains at least 40,000 inhabitants, many of whom are of French descent. It was taken by the British in 1760, by the Americans in 1812. Its early annals, like those of all the frontier towns of North America during past ages, are replete with the incidents of war. It was harassed, in turn, by the aborigines and by the British, and sometimes attacked by both. But its earliest and worst enemies were famine and disease,* which stunted the early growth of a settlement located in one of the finest regions of America, enjoying a position inferior to none for all the purposes of internal trade.

The intriguers for Louis XIV in Spain, having, Oct. 2, 1700, persuaded its moribund king, Charles II, to appoint Philip duke of Anjou, second son of the dauphin of France, as his successor, shortly thereafter the young prince ascended the Spanish throne as Philip II; whereupon great umbrage was taken by politic sticklers for the " balance of power " in Europe. Alien discontents increasing, a treaty, offensive as against France and Spain, was signed Sept. 7, 1701, by the plenipotentiaries of Great Britain, the Emperor of Germany, and the Dutch States; in which afterwards conjoined Portugal, Savoy, and the kingdom of Prussia,— [the latter a regality then only a few months old.] Hostilities immediately followed, taking the name of " The War of Succession." With these European troubles Canada had no earthly concern; but the extension of the war thither cannot have been unwelcome, since its people forthwith proposed to essay the conquest of New England. They were admonished by the French ministry to lie quiet; that, for the present at least, their neutrality was desirable, and even necessary; and that their governor-general ought to do his best to maintain it intact. D'Iberville asked only 400 French regulars and 1000 Canadian militia for the capture of New York and Boston, which he proposed to reach, in winter, by the river Chaudière; but he was told that such a force, small as it was, could not be spared. Deferring, for the present, an attempt to obtain a portion of the coveted Atlantic seaboard by force, the Canadian authorities set about strengthening their positions in the interior. The lately-formed settlement at Detroit, could it be maintained, was a great acquisition; but it was viewed with jealous eyes by the

---

* This was the small-pox, which ravaged Canada in 1703, and reduced the population of Quebec 25 per cent.

British. With respect to the native populations, there was little cause for inquietude. By the treaty of Montreal, the neutrality at least, of the most formidable tribes, those of the Iroquois, was assured. The Canadian authorities had obtained a moral hold upon numbers of that people, through the conversions made by the missionaries they sent among them. Envoys from New York had tried, but in vain, to obtain their expulsion.

The first hostilities between the French and English colonists took place in Newfoundland and Acadia; they were unimportant. Before any operation of consequence was entered upon, New France lost its governor-general; M. de Callières dying May 26, 1703, after administering the colony four years and a half. The marquis de Vaudreuil, governor of Montreal, was nominated his successor, at the instance of the people of the province; but this appointment was conceded with some hesitation, because his countess was a native-born Canadian! *

The leaders of the Iroquois confederation, not understanding what the French and British had to war about, proposed to mediate between them, to bring about an accommodation! one of them observing that "the Europeans must be of ill-conditioned mind, to wage war, or to make peace, for causes which Iroquois right reason could not sanction." They spoke of the British colonists as their allies, not their protectors; recommending, or rather ordaining that the Canadians should not attack them. This being reported to the French king, he wrote to M. de Vaudreuil, that if successful war could be levied against the British possessions, *at little cost*, it might be ventured on; but if not, that the Iroquois mediation should be accepted. † His minister, meantime, recommended the governor to avoid invasions of the Anglo-American territory for the present, and to do his utmost to secure the alliance of all the native tribes.

But besides the danger arising from British influence among

---

* This intimation was given incidentally to M. de Vaudreuil in 1706, in a letter from the minister reproving him for licensing, in favour of his connexions, traffic prohibited by royal ordinances.

† Louis XIV, the haughtiest of monarchs, here manifested the inconsistent qualities of Pope's *Sporus*: "a wit that creeps, a pride that licks the dust."—*B.*

the savage nations, to French disadvantage, they were often on the verge of the deadliest war. Thus at this time, while the Hurons were evincing British tendencies, the Ottawas and the Miâmis, conjointly, fell upon some bands of the Iroquois at Cataracoui. The savages of the interlacunar Straits (*le Détroit*), had sent deputies to Albany; and colonel Schuyler was moving heaven and earth, as it were, to alienate the Iroquois from Canada. But for the Abenaquis, he would have already gained some of the Iroquois converts of Sault St. Louis and La Montagne. His intrigues against the French were incessant, and not always overscrupulous. In 1704, he instigated savages to set fire to the Detroit settlement in order to force the people to abandon it. In a word, so long as the British and French were at war, it was almost impossible for the aborigines to be compelled, or persuaded, to observe neutrality.

When matters were already tending to a crisis, in 1706, a war was precipitated through the mismanagement of La Mothe, governor of Detroit. The Miâmis had killed, thereabouts, some of the Ottawas; the relations of the deceased called on La Mothe to be their avenger. He promised to make inquiry, and act accordingly; but instead, set out for Quebec,—possibly to take counsel of the authorities there. The Ottawas of the locality, in no good humour at this evasion, which they mistook as an intended snare for their total destruction, had their feelings outraged by a brutal act of a French officer, who killed an Ottawa for striking his dog, the animal having previously bitten the man. They now took the law in their own hands, and attacked the Miâmis; who fled before them and took refuge at the fort, the guns of which had to be played upon their pursuers to drive them off. Numbers of the savages, on both sides, were killed; also some of the French, including Père Constantine, a missionary.

This untoward event much grieved M. de Vaudreuil; who was also perplexed greatly when a deputation from the Iroquois tribes arrived, demanding that the "perfidious Ottawas" should be rendered up to them for punishment. This he refused to do; but he called on the Ottawas to give up to him the parties implicated. Impatient at delayed justice, which they mainly imputed to the double-dealing of M. la Mothe, who had let their enemies go free intermediately, the Miâmis, in savage-like reprisal, killed all the

French in their horde. Cadillac was preparing to avenge their murders; but his hand was stayed, on learning that the Hurons and the Iroquois had concerted to fall suddenly upon all the French then in the Detroit territory. He entered into a treaty with the Miâmis, instead of punishing them; and when the Hurons and Iroquois returned from the scene of contention, he fell upon the Miâmis with 400 men and obliged the survivors to submit to such terms as he chose to prescribe.

While M. de Vaudreuil was firmly and skilfully holding in leash the forest "dogs of war," ever ready to fly at friend or foe, he ascertained that the Abenaquis had been tampered with by the New Englanders, and might turn against the French. To forestall the former, he found means to persuade the Abenaquis to take the field against those who thus sought their alliance. This was an extreme measure certainly; but the security, the existence even, of the French in Canada, then imperilled, was an imperious reason which silenced all others. When war re-commenced, the Bostonians had obtained a treaty of peace with a section of the Abenaquis. In order to break this paction, a body of Abenaquis warriors not comprehended in it were joined to some Canadians, and the united corps, commanded by M. Beaubassin, were let loose, early in 1703, upon the country between the French south-eastern frontiers and Boston; which they ravaged with fire and steel from Casco to Wells.* The Massachusetts people, unprepared as they were for this barbarous onslaught, made little efficient resistance for some time; but at length (in autumn) turned upon their invaders, and gave no quarter to any of the Abenaquis whom they overcame. M. de Vaudreuil, finding his savage bands hard pressed in turn, sent to their aid, during the winter, 350 Canadians, under Hertel de Rouville. This corps, traversing the Alleghanies, arrived at Deerfield, late in the evening of the last day of February, 1704. Here, as at Schenectady on a former occasion,† the Canadians

---

* Mr. Bancroft gives a touching account of the sufferings of the colonists of Massachusetts at this time, victims of the alleged defensive policy of their fell enemies across the lines.—*B.*

† We are willing to trust the assurances of M. Garneau,—for they are needful as a set off against the discredit attaching to what he calls " the cruel mode of war followed at that epoch"—that "the children and young

VOL. II.—B

found the unsuspecting inhabitants in their beds, whence they were similarly dragged,—many of them killed, and the survivors made captive.

In the same year, another attack on New England was concerted at Montreal, in an assembly of the christened chiefs of tribes. An expedition was formed, of as many savages as could be persuaded to join it, with a corps of Canadians over 100 strong; intending to assault Portsmouth, in New Hampshire. Finding the force insufficient, the invaders stopped short at Haverhill, on the Merrimac. M. Hertel de Rouville, their commander, either considering the enterprize perilous (for the colonists were on their guard this time) or else to give a pious example to his "savage Christians," exhorted any of his followers who had mutual enmities to forget them and fall upon their knees with him in prayer. This done, they rushed upon the defenders of the place, who made a stout resistance, but were finally overcome, numbers of them killed and many of the chief inhabitants carried off, after their dwellings had been pillaged and burnt.* A hue-and-cry being raised in the surrounding country, the victors were not allowed to retire unscathed with their booty. Intercepted in their retreat, they were nearly defeated, and some of their best men left dead behind.

The attacks of these Canadian bands plunged the New Englanders into despondency. Colonel Schuyler, in their name, remon-

---

people taken prisoners were tenderly treated by the resident Canadians, who were always kind to the unfortunate." He adds that, become adult, such prisoners often embraced catholicism, and were adopted as naturalised French; adding, "the registers of the superior council contain many pages of English names of parties taking out letters of naturalisation."—*B.*

* The author must have mistaken the year of this exploit:—" In 1708, Haverhill in Massachusetts was burned by the Indians, about 100 persons killed, and many more carried into captivity. Similar incursions were made along the whole northern border, from the river Ste. Croix to the great lakes; and the history of those times abounds with stories of scalping and plundering parties of Indians attacking the defenceless villages, burning the houses, killing numbers of helpless inhabitants, without distinction of age or sex; and then hurrying back to Canada with a handful of captives, before a force could be raised sufficient to resist or to punish the aggression." FROST's *Hist. U. States*, p. 84.—*B.*

strated with M. de Vaudreuil on the subject; saying, "I have thought it my own duty towards God and man to prevent, as far as possible, the infliction of such cruelties as have been too often committed on the unfortunate colonists." But, while lifting up a testimony against such excesses, he was himself intriguing with the Iroquois and other native allies of the French, to break off their relations with them; in other words, to repeat the like scenes in Canada, as those already acted in New England. It was such inimical polity as Schuyler's which had reduced Canada to the sad necessity of launching savages against its enemies. He knew of the horrors committed at British instigation, by the Iroquois, on the Canadians during the former war; that, in Boston itself, the French and Abenaquis taken were treated with a cruelty, equalling the at least barbarities he denounced; he was aware of the fact, that the British had more than once violated the law of nations by revoking accorded capitulations. Finally, he knew that while French prisoners were so unworthily used, British captives were always well treated by Canadians and their savages allies.*

We now turn a passing glance on Acadian affairs.—M. de Brouillon, governor at Placentia, had replaced M. de Villebon, who died in July 1700. The former was ordered to strengthen the fortifications of La Hève, and to extend the colony's trading operations, by driving away fishermen of British blood from its coasts. Obtaining no aid to carry out these directions from France, he encouraged corsairs to make a refuge of La Hève. The people of the place thereby became so flush of cash, that they were enabled to recompense the savages for their raids in New England, entered upon to avenge damage done to the seaboard Acadians by British ships. The Bostonians, in reprisal for the Deerfield massacre, equipped an expedition to attack Acadia.† The armament was composed of

---

* During these wars the French appear to have acted with the greatest barbarity towards their prisoners; fully equalling, in that respect, the conduct of the Indians themselves." W. H. SMITH.—*B*.

† "The brave colonists were by no means passive under their injuries. Believing that the French were the instigators of all the Indian hostilities, they were constantly raising large fleets and armies for the purpose of depriving them of their American possessions. Expeditions were repeatedly fitted out for Nova Scotia (Acadia), at the sole expense of

three ships of war, 14 transports, and 30 barges; the land force was 550 strong, commanded by captain Church, a veteran officer, who volunteered his services on the occasion. The posts on the Penobscot and Passamaquoddy rivers were first attacked, and put to fire and sword. The turn of Port-Royal was to come next, but the assailants were repulsed by a handful of defenders. They attacked Les Mines, and were thence also driven away. At Beaubassin they suffered great loss. Church spent part of the summer in descents on divers parts of the seaboard, taking about fifty prisoners, but no spoil.

A second expedition, for nothing less than the conquest of Acadia this time, was got up by the New Englanders in 1707. The land force, 2000 strong, led by colonel Marck, was embarked in 23 transports, convoyed by two ships of war. June 6, the squadron appeared before Port-Royal. The works of the town, then an insignificant place, were dilapidated, the garrison weak; but M. de St. Castin, with 60 Canadians, who arrived some hours before the enemy, were a great help to M. de Subercase, the successor of M. de Brouillon, who died in 1706. The fortifications were hastily repaired under fire of the besiegers, and were so well defended, that, after making an unsuccessful assault on the evening of the sixth day, they retired early on the next.

Great was the public mortification, or rather indignation, at this signal discomfiture. Marck, as fearing to show face, remained with the fleet at Kaskébé. Advice was sent to him to remain there; whither three vessels more were despatched, having 500 or 600 fresh soldiers on board. Thus reinforced, Marck again appeared before Port-Royal, August 20. The New Englanders were once more repulsed, and with greater loss than before; being obliged to re-embark in great haste. Thus ended an enterprise, which abased the self-love of the men of Massachusetts, and exhausted the colonial finances.

We pass next, for a moment, to contemporary affairs in Newfoundland. When the existing war began, the British made hostile

---

New England. The British Government was too much occupied in humbling Louis XIV, to render more than occasional and insufficient aid to the colonists in their arduous struggle." FROST'S *Hist.* p. 84.—*B.*

descents on the coasts where the French were settled; and it was not till the year 1703 that the latter could make reprisals. Their first feat was the capture of the British post of Fourillon, where they burnt several ships also. In winter succeeding, the French colonists did much damage to British commerce in the Newfoundland waters; but this was little compared with what followed.

M. de Subercase, then governor of the island, at the head of 450 men, including 112 Canadians under M. de Beaucourt, took the field Feb. 15, 1704, and marched towards St. John's. Feb. 26, he reached Rebon, which was yielded up. March 1-2, St. John's was taken without resistance and burnt. But the garrisons of two forts, erected for its defence, stood out successfully. The French and their savage allies burnt Fourillon and every other British establishment in the country, except that in Carbonnière island, then inaccessible; and ravaged all their plantations in the open country.

Late in 1708, M. de St. Ovide, king's lieutenant at Plaisance, volunteered to take the forts of St. John's, which covered the trade in the island, without cost to the government. The offer was accepted. Assembling 170 men, he set out Dec. 14, and arrived near the place Jan. 1, 1709, which he recognised by moonlight, and determined to assault at once. A third fort had been erected for better defence of the place. The two the French failed to take before, were carried in half an hour. The other, much stronger, was surrendered 24 hours afterwards. M. de Costebelle, governor at Plaisance, sent orders to blow up the works of St. John's, which was done.

The sole remaining British possession in Newfoundland was Carbonnière. A sea and land force, led by Gaspard Bertram, a corsair of Plaisance, was despatched against it soon afterwards, but failed to take it. Bertram was killed; but his men made prize of a well-laden British ship. With this exception, the French had now the mastery in all Newfoundland, but cannot be said to have possessed it with their few forces.

The British colonists, thus baffled in their own invasive projects against New France, turned to the mother country for aid. The house of assembly of New York, in 1709, sent a petition *

---

* Either M. Garneau or Mr. Bancroft must be mistaken as to the date

to Queen Anne, craving that she would accord the people of her American plantations such assistance as would enable them to expel the French from the country. Colonel Vetch, who was the inspirer of this application, had already proposed to the British ministry a plan for making an assured conquest of Canada, by a simultaneous assault of Quebec, and an invasion of the colony across Lake Champlain territory. It was promised that five regiments of the line should be embarked in England, and despatched to Boston. With these were to be conjoined 1200 militia-men, brigaded in Massachusetts and Rhode Island. These troops formed the land force intended to besiege Quebec. A second corps, 4,000 strong, a moiety being savages, were to advance against Montreal. Schuyler had succeeded, by this time, in securing the co-operation of four out of the Five Nations in the war. To support it, the provinces of Connecticut, New York, and New Jersey issued their earliest paper-money.

The place of rendezvous for the integral portions of the second corps above mentioned was on the banks of Lake Champlain, as aforesaid. When collected, in July, Governor Nicholson set to work constructing a camp, forming magazines of provisions and munitions of war, preparing means of transport, &c.

The Canadian authorities, at the same time, were making preparations to repel the invasion. The defensive works of Quebec were put in order, and other precautionary measures adopted.

---

of the above-mentioned address. In the *Hist. U. States* of the latter (vol. iii), the incident is thus entered:—

"In 1710, the legislature of New York unanimously addressed the queen on the dangerous progress of French domination at the West; observing, 'It is well known that the French can go by water from Quebec to Montreal. From thence they can do the like, through rivers and lakes, at the back of all your Majesty's plantations on this continent, as far as Carolina; and in this large tract of country live several nations of Indians who are vastly numerous. Among those they constantly send emissaries and priests, with toys and trifles, to insinuate themselves into their favour. Afterwards they send traders, then soldiers, and at last build forts among them; and the garrisons are encouraged to intermarry, cohabit, and incorporate among them: and it may easily be concluded that, upon a general peace, many of the disbanded soldiers will be sent thither for that purpose.'"—*B*.

The whole armed force in the colony was but 4,150 men, besides 700 sailors and savages.

The New England colonists, who had executed their part of the scheme for invasion with completeness and despatch, had made no allowance for the proverbial tardiness of the British government officials. When the regulars were ready to embark, months after the time, it was found convenient to employ them in Spain.— Meantime discontent, followed by disease, the consequences of incertitude and inaction, abated the martial ardour of the army encamped at Lake Champlain, and the militia-men yearned to revisit their homesteads.

The Iroquois, probably imputing the inaction of the Anglo-Americans to fear of the French, began to vacillate; and during the winter, deputations from the Onnontaguez and Agniers nations came to sound the views of the Canadian authorities: doubtless in view of selling their services to the highest bidder. They returned, it is said, " well pleased with their reception :" [meaning, it is presumable, that they did not leave the gubernatorial presence empty-handed].

In a grand council which was held at Onnondago, one of the chief orators remarked that their independence was only maintained by the mutual jealousy of the two European nations; and as it would be impolitic to let either quite prevail over the other, it was inexpedient to join in the present British expedition against the French. In consequence, most of the warriors assembled at Lake Champlain withdrew. The commanders there, already discouraged, burnt their blockhouses, &c., and gave up the enterprize for the present.

Contemporaneously, governor Nicholson speeded to England to obtain information regarding the intents of the British ministry, and to urge upon its members the importance of the ends in view, and deprecate the dangers of farther delay in carrying them out. He returned with a few ships-of-war, and a regiment of marines; and it was promised that a squadron should be sent early in the spring. Summer passed, autumn arrived, and none appeared. Not to let the season pass idly by, he proposed to employ the force he had in hand against the French possessions in Canada, and his suggestion was adopted by the provincial assemblies. An expedition was promptly got up, of fifty vessels, in which were embarked five regiments of militia, about 3,500 men in all, which sailed from Boston Sept. 18, 1710, and arrived at Port-Royal Sept. 24.

The land force was disembarked without resistance, and proceeded to invest the place. Governor Subercase sustained bombardment till October 16, when he capitulated, his poor garrison of 156 famished soldiers "marching out with the honours of war." [Their proud monarch's magazines had been so poorly stored, that the victors had to deal immediate rations to his starving soldiers.] The garrison and people of the town, 480 persons in all, were, in virtue of a stipulation in the capitulation, transported to La Rochelle. The conquerors of this miserable place (with a vainglorious name) re-christened it "Annapolis," out of compliment to the queen-regnant. A garrison, 450 strong, was left in possession, with Colonel Vetch as commandant. The British parliament afterwards voted £23,000 to defray the cost of the expedition.

A misunderstanding arose with respect to the capitulation of Port-Royal. As Nicholson understood its terms, the cession of all French Acadia as well as the capital was to follow. As this interpretation was repudiated by Subercase, Colonel Livingston was sent to Quebec to remonstrate with the governor-general on the subject, who asserted that Subercase had taken a right view of the case. Livingston took occasion also to denounce the cruelties committed by the savages in French pay; and said that if they were continued, the British would retaliate upon the chief inhabitants of Acadia. M. de Vaudreuil replied, that he was not responsible for what the savages did; that the odium of the war lay upon those who had refused to ratify the proposed neutrality; and that, if such a threat were realised, certain reprisals would follow on British prisoners. This reply, however, he did not make to Livingston, but to the governor of Massachusetts, directing Messrs. de Rouville and Dupuy to deliver it in Boston; and to take heedful note of the localities they passed through in going thither and returning, for the direction of the leader of any invasion of it by the French, at a future time.

The Baron St. Castin (a half breed), appointed French governor of Acadia, issuing from his head-quarters at Pentagoët, for some time greatly harassed the British in the country, even sending a force to invest Port-Royal. The latter, on their part, retaliated on the French inhabitants; most of whom were constrained, from fear of starvation, to submit to their domination. A party of British, on one of their roving expeditions, was massacred by the natives, in a place which thence was called "Bloody Cove."

The loss of Acadia was sensibly felt in France. M. de Pontchartrain (Jérôme), successor of his father, deceased in 1699, as minister of marine, wrote to M. de Beauharnais: "I impressed upon you how important it is that Acadia be retaken before the enemy have time to colonise that country. The conservation of New France and our fisheries alike demand its re-possession by us." Yet no force was sent to effect that object so much desiderated; although all that M. de Vaudreuil asked, in order to make the attempt, was two transports to bear his Canadians thither. The minister, instead, devised a plan for colonising the country by a company, at no cost to the king; but no one was found willing to embark in such an enterprise.

General Nicholson paid a second visit to England to press the suit Colonel Schuyler made in person the year before to the British ministry, that Canada should be taken possession of. Five sachems or chiefs, of the Iroquois natives, accompanied him, who, having been presented to Queen Anne by the Duke of Shrewsbury,* were much caressed in London society; and this the rather, because they expressed much affection for the British colonists, and an aversion to the French.†

---

* One of these sachems, it is said, was grandfather to Thayendanegea, *alias* Captain Joseph Brant. W. H. SMITH.—They were carried in two of the royal coaches to St. James's palace; WADE.—*B.*

† M. Garneau prints here, that "Mr. St. John, afterwards Viscount Bolingbroke, a statesman of more imagination than judgment, then minister, promised to do all that was asked (by the British colonists). He interested himself in the enterprise as if he had been its author, and boasted of having planned it." Henry St. John was not then in power, had never as yet been, and was not at that time likely to be. The camarilla intrigue which made him second minister of state did not take place till late in September; the Iroquois were presented April 18, and they left, along with Nicholson, in spring.—*B.*

The Tory party in Britain, whose leaders had been kept in the background for many years by the Whigs, and whose cause reposed on the military talents of the Duke of Marlborough and the influence of his duchess, were now too much occupied with their own selfish interests to find time to attend to those of the nation either at home or abroad. Accordingly, the project for invading Canada, entertained by their predecessors, lay in abeyance till next year. In spring 1711, an expedition was got up to act in conjunction with such forces as the plantations could supply, for the invasion of Canada. The fleet, under the orders of Admiral Sir Hovenden Walker, had companies of seven regiments of regulars on board, draughted from the army Marlborough was leading from victory to victory.* The force was put under the charge of brigadier-general Hill.

Walker arrived in Boston harbor, June 25; where his presence was impatiently expected. The land force was now augmented by the junction of the militias of New York, New Jersey, Connecticut, &c., which raised it to a total of 6,500 infantry. The fleet now consisted of 88 ships and transports. The army, which was intended to act simultaneously with the ascent to Quebec by an advance on Montreal, and was now re-constituted, got ready to act, under the orders of general Nicholson, as before. It was composed of 4,000 Massachusetts' and other militia men, and 600 Iroquois. Having moved his corps to the banks of lake George, Nicholson there awaited the event of the attack on Quebec! Meantime, the invading fleet sailed from Boston, July 30.

The opposing force of the Canadians was proportionally small, in number at least. It did not exceed 5,000 men of all ages between 15 and 70, and included at the most 500 savages. But Quebec was now in a better state for defence than ever it had been before, there being more than 100 cannons mounted on the works. The banks of the St. Lawrence immediately below the city were

---

* M. Garneau designates these soldiers as "veterans drawn from the army of Marlborough then under the orders of general Hill, brother of Madame Masham" [Abigail Hill, afterwards Lady Masham]. The Duke was not superseded till December 30, 1711, when the Duke of Ormond, not General Hill, took the chief command. The British continental corps were not broken up till some time afterwards.—B.

so well guarded, that it would have been perilous to an enemy to land anywhere; above it, the invaders would hardly adventure. The garrison was carefully marshalled, and every man assigned to an appointed place, with orders to repair to it as soon as the enemy's fleet appeared.

But the elements were now the best defenders of Canada, which Providence seemed to have taken under his special protection. During the night of August 22, a storm from the south-west arose, accompanied by a dense fog, in the gulf of St. Lawrence; and the hostile fleet was put in imminent jeopardy for a time. The admiral's ship barely escaped wreck upon breakers. Eight of the transports were driven ashore on the Ile-aux-Œufs, one of the seven Islands, and 900 out of 1,700 persons on board perished in the waves. Among the corpses strewed on the beach afterwards, were found the bodies of a number of emigrants from Scotland, intended colonists for Anglicised Canada; and among other waifs found at the same time were copies of a proclamation to the Canadians, in Queen Anne's name, asserting the suzerainty of Britain, in right of the discovery of their country by Cabot.*

Admiral Walker now altered his course and rendezvoused with his scattered fleet, as soon as it could be collected, at Cape Breton; where he called a council of war, in which it was decided to renounce the enterprize. The British division of the fleet left for England, and the colonial vessels returned to Boston. But disasters ceased not to attend this ill-starred expedition; for the *Feversham*, an English frigate of 36 guns, and three transports, were lost when still in the Laurentian gulf; while the *Edgar*, of 70 guns, Walker's flag-ship, was blown up at Portsmouth, October 15, with 400 men on board.†

---

* This document (authentic or not) is given at length by Père Charlevoix.—*B.*

† The admiral, who returned to port Oct. 7, was ashore with all the other officers at the time of the accident. WADE's *British History*- "This expedition was ill managed, and the British fleet, owing to tempestuous weather and ignorance of the coasts, met with many disasters; losing by shipwreck, August 22, eight transports with 884 officers soldiers, and seamen." M. MARTIN's *British Colonies.*—B.

M. de Vaudreuil, as soon as he ascertained that Quebec was safe from present attack, formed a corps, 3,000 strong, at Chambly, to oppose general Nicholson, should the advance on Montreal be persevered in; but none was attempted. On the contrary, though the provincial militia were still kept embodied, and the frontier posts strengthened, these precautions were taken in expectation of a counter-invasion by the Canadians. The latter, about this time, had a dangerous thorn planted in their side through an incursion of the Outagamis, a brave but truculent nation, frequenting the savannahs beyond lake Michigan. At the instigation of the Iroquois, the latter—themselves impelled by British influence—induced parties of the Outagamis to move eastward, and squat in the region around Detroit; some of them taking a position close to the French settlement there; that savage people having undertaken to burn the settlement, and kill all the Canadians in or near it. The Detroit Ottawas, allies of the French, had aroused the vengeance of the Mascoutins, by murdering 240 of their people at the river St. Joseph; the latter were therefore in the plot, (as also the Kikapous), against the Detroit people. The latter, on the other hand, had in their favour at this time, not only the Ottawas, but roving parties of Hurons, Illinois, Missouris, Osages, Sauteurs, Poutouatamis, Sakis, Malhouimes, &c., who all banded together, to the number of 600 warriors, for defence of the settlement. The Outagamis and Mascoutins took refuge in an intrenched camp they had formed near the French fort. M. Dubuisson, the governor, finding that they presented so imposing a front, was willing that they should retire peacefully to their villages on seeing that their hostile intents were anticipated and provided against; but his native allies would not allow of this, and proceeded to invest their fastness. This was so well defended, however, that the assailants became dispirited, and wished to retire from the contest; but Dubuisson, now encouraging them to remain, turned the siege into a blockade. In a short time provisions, even water, failed the besieged; and when any of them issued from the enclosure to procure the latter, they were set on by their foes, killed on the spot, or burnt alive to make a savage holiday.

The beleaguered tried, by every means, to detach the native auxiliaries present from the French interest; but all in vain.

They then sent envoys to the governor to crave a truce of two days, to enable their foragers to procure food. This singular request was refused, but had better been accorded; for in revenge the Outagamis shot fire-arrows against the straw-roofed houses of the village, which were thereby entirely consumed. The cannon of the fort avenged this act of desperation. Already from three to four score of the besieged were dead of hunger and thirst, and the air was tainted with putrefaction. A third deputation came to implore quarter. Pemousa, a chief, who brought with him his wife and children as hostages, adjured the governor to "take pity on his flesh" and on the other women and children about to be put at French discretion. Some of the allied chiefs present at this piteous scene, instead of being moved by it, coolly proposed to Dubuisson to cut down four of the envoys, who, they alleged, were the chief defenders of the place. This much, at least, was refused.

The besieged, despairing of success, and hopeless of quarter if they surrendered, prepared to take advantage of any moment of relaxed vigilance in their besiegers, and try to escape. One stormy night they succeeded in this attempt; but exhausted by the privations they had undergone, halted on peninsular ground near St. Clair, whither they were soon followed. They intrenched themselves again, stood a siege of four days more, and then gave in. Not one of the men escaped, and it is very doubtful whether any of the women were spared; but the contemporary reports of what passed at that time, are in disaccord on this point.*

This abortive attempt, by whomsoever conceived or howsoever

---

* Report of M. Dubuisson dated June 15, 1715, of the attack on Detroit by the Mascoutins and Ottogamies; detailed relation of the same in the national archives of France, published in a number of the *Moniteur* of Paris, published in 1853.

["Notwithstanding their repulse at Detroit, the Outagamies continued the war whenever they had the opportunity of doing so without much risk to themselves, and made fierce attacks upon all the tribes in alliance with the French. Their watchful activity rendered the routes between the frontier posts of Canada, and the more distant ones on the Mississippi dangerous and almost impassable." W. H. SMITH, *Canada*, &c. I. lxi-ii.—*B.*]

terminated, sufficiently demonstrated that the Anglo-Americans could have no hope of ruining French interests in the north-west, by alliances with the native tribes of that region. On the other hand, it was a point of capital importance for New France to sustain the mastery over the country intermediating with Canada and the territories of the lower Mississippi. For this reason, therefore, the important site of Detroit at last being now secure, the fort at Michilimakinac, abandoned during late years, was, by order of the governor-general, put in a proper state of defence. He also strove, and effectually, to bring the savages of the western country into general concord, under his immediate protection or through his mediation.

The Tory ministry of Britain for a moment inclined to send an expedition to attack New France, hoping to retrieve the national disappointment following the last. But the project was never seriously taken up; a pacification with France, overtures for which had been previously made, being now determined upon. Meantime, intelligence of the momentary danger having reached Quebec, the merchants of that city raised a patriotic subscription of 50,000 crowns (*écus*) for strengthening its fortifications.

[Various reasons, public and private, moved the leaders of the Tory party to offer terms of peace to the French king. Among the former was that arising from their inability to find a competent successor to the duke of Marlborough in carrying on the war with effect. Among the occult and unpatriotic motives imputed to them by the Whigs, was a submission to an alleged desire of the queen that they should restore the older branch of the Stuarts at her demise.—By this time, " the balance of power," for the nice adjustment of which the war was ostensibly begun, had been re-deranged by the accession of the Austrian archduke Charles, titular king of Spain, to the throne of the German empire. A Bourbon king, who had made himself agreeable to a majority of the Spaniards, seemed no longer so prejudicial to the general well being of Europe. Besides, by the turn hostilities had lastly taken among the continental powers still engaged in combating France-British interests were little regarded by those belligerents. This was instinctively perceived by the people of England; and peace, although it did not involve the complete abasement of the French empire, was yet not so unacceptable to a majority of the nation as the whig party leaders—eager for carrying on the war against Louis, if only for his protection of the Pretender—were willing to admit.]

All preliminaries being arranged, a treaty of peace was signed at Utrecht, March 30, (O. S.) 1713, by the plenipotentiaries of France, Great Britain, Savoy, Portugal, Prussia, and the States-general of Holland. The articles in it regarding the French possessions in North America, provided that [the whole of] Acadia the Hudson's Bay territory, and Newfoundland, should be ceded to Britain; with a reserved right to French fishermen to dry their fish on a part of the seaboard of the latter island. Louis further renounced all claims to suzerainty over the Iroquois country; [which thus, by inference if not direct recognition, became an appurtenance of the British north-eastern plantations.]

Britain could well afford to be moderate in demanding conditions which the proud stomach of Louis could ill digest; nevertheless, in regard of American colonial possessions, French domination was considerably abridged. Excepting Canada, she had now left her in North America only Cape Breton and the other islands in the Laurentian gulf, with freedom of access, by sea, to her settlements on the Bay of Mexico; whereas, in Colbert's time, her American possessions extended from Hudson's Bay to Mexico, following the valleys of St. Lawrence and the Mississippi; including within their limits five of the greatest lakes and two of the noblest rivers in the world.

[The relative condition of Britain and France at the close of the reign of Louis the Fourteenth (now very near), forms a striking contrast to their state at its commencement. " In the chief elements of national strength, France was at the latter period equal, in many points superior, to her rival. In commerce, manufactures, and naval power, she was equal; in public revenue, vastly superior; and her (home) population doubled that of England. At the termination of the war between the two powers concluded by the peace of Utrecht,—which found her miserably exhausted, rather than beaten,—her revenue had greatly fallen off; her currency was depreciated 30 per cent.; the choicest of her people had been carried away, like malefactors, to recruit the armies: while her merchants and industrious artisans were weighed to the ground by heavy imposts, aggravated by the exemption of the nobility and clergy from taxation. France never completely recovered, under the Bourbons, the ruinous effects of her wars during the reigns of king William and queen Anne, sovereigns of Great Britain."*]

* *British History*, &c., by John Wade, p. 300. London, 1839.—*B.*

CHAPTER III.

COLONIZATION OF CAPE BRETON.

1713-1744.

Motives of the French Government for founding an establishment at Cape Breton.—Description of that island; its name changed to "Isle-Royale."—British jealousies excited.—Plans of Messrs. Raudot, for colonizing the island and making it a trading entrepôt (1706).—Foundation of Louisbourg.—Notices of the island's later colonization; its trade, &c.—M. de St. Ovide succeeds M. de Costebelle.—The Acadians, being aggrieved, threaten to emigrate to l'Isle-Royale.—Abortive attempt, in 1619, to colonize St. John's (Prince Edward's) Island.—A few notices of that isle.

The treaty of Utrecht tore from the failing hands of the moribund Louis XIV the two portals of Canada: Acadia and Newfoundland. That too-famous treaty marked the commencing decline of the French monarchy, ending in its fall in fourscore years thereafter. The nation which it humiliated, appeared, however, inclined to make a last effort to resume in America the advantageous position lately lost; and in this view a greater colonial system than ever was projected, the seat of which was to be in the region of the Mississippi,—a country made known entirely by Frenchmen. But the power or inclination of the government was not equal to the adventurous spirit of the people. Besides, had not the king, by the treaty of Utrecht, bought the throne of Spain for his descendant, the price being the sacrifice of the colonies; that is, at the cost of dismembering the French Empire?

By the cession of the two provinces* of the Laurentian Gulf, Canada was laid bare on its seaboard sides; and the alien power

---

* It was provided, in article 12 of the treaty of Utrecht, that "the whole of Nova Scotia, otherwise called Acadia, with its *ancient limits*, and *all its dependencies*, is hereby ceded to the crown of Great Britain." We shall see by and by how the French interpreted this article as regards Acadia, peninsular and continental.—*B*.

whose possessions were closely contiguous, could thereby, at any hostile moment, hinder succours from reaching the province, and cut off Quebec entirely from access to the sea. It became, therefore, essential for the protection of the colony, and the safety of the fisheries, that a new bulwark should be substituted, for the outer defences, now lost, in the north-eastern American waters. There still remained in French hands, Cape Breton and St. John's, situated between Acadia and Newfoundland; and the former of these, if properly turned to account, might become a double-pointed thorn in the flanks of the latter possessions, newly acquired by Britain. Accordingly, the flag of France was planted on the shores of an insular possession hitherto unregarded, and the construction of fortifications was begun on a site in Cape Breton, afterwards known to fame as LOUISBOURG. This proceeding manifested an intent to protect efficaciously the entry of the St. Lawrence; and the posts simultaneously formed in the Mississippi valley, equally signified that the security of the opposite region of New France was being anxiously cared for. The works in progress on Cape Breton, and the importance ascribed to that island in Old France, soon drew the alarmed attention of the Anglo-American colonists, who had thought, through wrenching, from the French, Nova Scotia and Newfoundland, that a mortal blow had been dealt to their rivals. They now saw with astonishment rising around them, from the rocks of Cape Breton, to the sands of Biloxi in Louisiana, a girdle of forts, the cannon of which menaced every point of their own frontiers. France, mistress of the two greatest floods of North America, the Mississippi and the St. Lawrence, possessed also two fertile valleys of a thousand leagues' extent, in which the productions of all climates grew. With so great a territory, commanding such water-ways, she might, in a few years, acquire inexpugnable force on the American continent! But to realize this, an energy and a management were needed, which it would have been vain to expect from the government. To begin with, an abundant immigration was wanted, both in Canada and Louisiana; but Louis XV sent no colonists. He thought that high walls, raised on a desert straud at the entry of the Laurentian Gulf, within cannon-shot of hostile ships, would be sufficient for all purposes. This was repeating the faults of the preceding century; viz. first inviting Britain and her colonies to unite their efforts against the new outpost, and, that once taken, they would be sure to use it as a stepping-stone for the conquest of all the other possessions of France in North America.

CAPE BRETON [the island thus inappropriately named] is situated N. E. of Nova Scotia, from which it is separated for 20 miles by a strait about a mile wide, called the Gut of Canso. To the N. W. lies Prince Edward's Island* (Isle de St. Jean); to the N. E. Newfoundland; the former 30, the latter about 50 miles distant. Cape Breton is of no definable configuration, but its nearest approach to any regular form is that of a triangle; which, from base to apex, or S. to N., is about 100 miles in a direct line, and a line run across the broadest part, S. to W. would measure 85 miles. Superficial area of land, about two million acres. The island, strangely indented in many places, is almost cut in two by an inlet of the N. E. seaboard called the Bras d'Or, which is separated from St. Peter's Bay, another inlet, entering from the opposite seaboard, by an isthmus only 850 yards across. The Bras d'Or is entered by two channels, formed by Boulardin island, which lies between the harbours of St. Anne and Sidney (Port des Espagnols). Two other harbours, are those of Miroy and Louisbourg. The latter (once important, but now deserted) has a circuit of 12 miles, and is entered by a very narrow strait. St. Peter's is situated on Toulouse bay; Sidney, on the N. E. coast, is the seat of the government, and had about 500 inhabitants at a recent date.

The climate is milder than that of Lower Canada, and not less salubrious, though the air is more humid. The soil is moderately fertile, and the farming produce raised includes the common cereals. Most of the population is agricultural. The southern slopes of the highland regions are tillable to the summit.† The natural wood found on the island, in early times, comprised oak, pine, maple, plane-tree, cedar, aspen—growths all yielding constructive material;

---

* Thus first named in 1779, in honour of Edward, duke of Kent, father of Queen Victoria.—B.

† "Let the poor emigrant pass not by neglected Cape Breton, where God has given him good soil to cultivate; coal for his fuel; fish for his food, and salt to cure it." Judge HALIBURTON.—B.

and at present ship-building is much carried on. There are several coal-mines, with gypsum and iron-stone quarries. Some salt-springs exist near the Bras d'Or, the most considerable of several sea-lakes in the island, but which contains no navigable stream. Most of the urban settlements lie along the shores of the Bras d'Or, which affords great facilities for trade. At a recent date, the population of the island was about 30,000; and the people are under the jurisdiction of the authorities of Nova Scotia, their territory forming a county in itself.

Cape Breton, anterior to the 18th century, was frequented only by fur-traders and fishermen. Towards the year 1706, Messrs. Raudot, father and son, the former being then intendant of New France, sent to Paris a memorial proposing to make the island a commercial entrepôt for all French America. In this document, which manifested the sagacity of its writers, it was urged that the fur-trade, almost the only commerce Canada possessed, was becoming less and less important yearly; and that, whilst it had become little profitable, it had vicious tendencies about it, as leading the population to trust to gambler-like chances of uncertain gain; invited men to lead a loitering, vagabond life; inspired dislike of tillage, and an aversion to continuous employment of any kind. "The Anglo-Americans," they said, "not leaving their homes as most of our people do, till their ground, establish manufactories, open mines, build ships, &c., and have never yet looked upon the peltry traffic but as a subordinate branch of their trade. Let us take an example from them, and encourage the exportation of salted provisions, lumber, pitch, tar, oils, fish, hemp, flax, iron, copper, &c. In proportion as exports increase, so will imports augment. Everybody will find employment; provisions and foreign commodities will come in abundantly, and consequently fall in price: a busy commerce will attract immigration, will hasten land-clearing, extend the fisheries, and in a word, give new life to the enterprise of this country, now so languishing." In many other passages, the Raudots pointed out, in particular, what ought to be done to make Cape Breton the emporium they said it might be, placed as it was between France and French settlements in Canada, Acadia, and Newfoundland; but, above all, they urged the necessity, if any thing effectual were to be done, to encourage a large immigration to it; and this not by any company or association of individuals, who always held monopolies which they worked for their own narrow purposes, but directly by the home government. Little or no notice seems to have been taken of this patriotic project, though most ably developed; but it was taken into serious consideration, at least, about the period now under our review.

The ministry, to mark the estimation in which France now held Cape Breton, re-named it Royal Island (l'Isle-Royale), by which appellation it was known as long afterward as French domination lasted in North America. The seat of government was fixed at English-haven (*hâvre à l'Anglais*), which was re-named "Louisbourg," in honour of the king. Its port could be fortified only at great cost, the needful materials of construction being far off. The harbour of Ste. Anne would have been far preferable in that respect and most others. M. de Costebelle, who had been ousted from his governorship at Plaisance by the place passing under British rule, was charged to superintend the colony, and lay the foundations of Louisbourg.

Instead of sending colonists from France, the inhabitants of the ceded settlements in Acadia and Newfoundland were invited to repair to Cape Breton, it being understood that they were impatient of British sway, and yearning to join their compatriots, even if they lost, in a material point of view, by the exchange. But in this the home authorities reckoned without their host; for the French settlers, who at first threatened to emigrate to other parts of New France, were getting reconciled to their new masters, who for the time treated them well; just as the Canadians were cajoled to repel the advances of the revolted Anglo-American provincials in 1774. What we have said now, refers to the majority; but a few did emigrate, not having any property to lose thereby, to Isle-Royale, wherein they formed some petty villages. In default of more eligible inhabitants, the government invited some of the Abenaquis savages to take up their abode in the island.

The town of Louisbourg was built on a tongue of land jutting into the sea, and in its palmiest days was fully a mile long. The houses were nearly all of wood, the chief state edifices being the only exceptions. Wharfs were constructed on the sea-frontage, at which vessels loaded and unloaded. As the great object of the government was to make the place a maritime arsenal, a series of fortifications, intended to be impregnable, were commenced in 1720. Before they were finished, more than 30 millions were expended upon them.

Fishing was the chief employment of the Cape-Bretons, whose numbers gradually increased to a total of 4,000 souls; and these were mostly congregated at Louisbourg. The island being little more than one great fishing-station, this amount might be doubled, perhaps, in summer by the arrival of fishers from all parts of Europe, who repaired to the coasts of the island to dry their produce.

The islanders trusted to the mother country and the French Antilles for the chief necessaries and all the luxuries of life. They imported, from France, provisions, beverages, tissues, and even furniture; for which they exchanged cod-fish. They sent annually to the West-Indies from twenty to twenty-five vessels, each of 70 to 140 tons burden, laden with lumber, staves, pit-coal, salmon, cod, mackerel, and fish-oil; thence importing sugar, coffee, rum, &c. There was a considerable excess of imports from the Antilles beyond the wants of the islanders; these were taken up, in part by the Canadians, and the rest bartered for other commodities with the New-Englanders. From the details thus given of the ordinary traffic of Isle-Royale, it may be imagined that the people enjoyed a considerable amount of material comfort: such was not the case. Most of them lived a life of constant penury. Those of them who strove to better their condition by plying extended industry, became the victims of usury, owing to the advances made to them in bad seasons, or when their floating ventures suffered wreck or other miscarriages, or salt was scarce as well as dear. Industrials who have to pay ordinarily from 20 to 25 per cent. a year for advances, must ever be on the verge of absolute insolvency; and thus he who loans as well as he who borrows, may be involved at last in common ruin.

The civil government of Isle-Royale and of St. John's Island (Prince Edward's) was modelled on that of Canada. The commandant, like the governor of Louisiana, was subordinate to the governor-general, resident at Quebec. Feudality was never introduced to Isle-Royale, as the king refused to constitute any seigniories there.

The re-founder of Isle-Royale was succeeded as commandant by M. St. Ovide. In 1620, Mr. Richard was nominated British governor of Acadia and Newfoundland. Jealous of the intercourse of his subjects with the people of Isle-Royale, he issued an arbitrary edict against it. He also required the men of French race under his jurisdiction to take an oath of allegiance to the British king within four months. M. St. Ovide interposed, and admonished the parties thus put under compulsion, that if they conformed, they would soon be obliged to forego their religion, and that their children would be taught to renounce it. The British, he further told them, would enslave those who yielded; adding, that even French huguenots were shunned by British protestants, &c. The inhabitants (wiser than their adviser) contented themselves with reminding Mr. Richard, that they had decided to remain in the country only on condition of having their nationality respected; that their presence in the island was advantageous to its new masters, in this respect, if for no other, that it was out of regard for the French residents that the Mic-Macs and other aborigines let the English live in repose, they being allies of the French only, and averse to English ways: finally, that if these two antipathies, civilized and savage, conjoined against British domination, it might be imperilled by them some day. Mr. Richard, moved or not by these considerations, took alarm on hearing that M. de St. Ovide had made arrangements to receive all deserters from Acadia and Newfoundland in St. John's Isle, and gave up his project of enforced *Anglification*.

The island just named, discovered in 1497 by Cabot, lies in the gulf of St. Lawrence; it extends, from E. to W. in a somewhat curvilinear shape and is about 134 miles long; its area 2160 square miles; in breadth it varies, from 1 mile only to 34 miles. It is separated from Nova Scotia and New Brunswick by Northumberland Strait, which in the narrowest parts is hardly more than ten miles wide. Its soil is fertile, and there are good pasture-lands in it. Till times posterior to that of the treaty of Utrecht, its merits had been overlooked. In 1719, a company was formed in France, in view of clearing the interior and establishing fisheries on the coasts. This project was born of John Law's speculations, when the Mississippi bubble was blown so disastrously for France. The count de St. Pierre, premier groom of the chamber to the duchess of Orleans, was at the head of the enterprise. The king conceded to him, along with the isle of St. John, the Magdalen group, and Miscou. Unhappily, personal interest, which had first brought the associates together, getting misdirected, all the parties wanting to be directors without needful experience in business, a fall out took place, and the project fell to the ground. St. John's Isle then fell into the oblivion whence it had been drawn momentarily; and therein remained till the year 1749, when a number of Acadians, evading the British yoke, began to settle there.*

---

* " This island contains 965,000 acres of excellent land, so free from stone as not to yield sufficient for building purposes. It contains 67 townships, with about 70,000 inhabitants. It forms a separate government. The whole area of the island exceeds 1,000,000 acres; and as there are no very lofty mountains, there are abundance of wood and many little lakes and streams; it is fertile and inhabitable throughout. The climate is softer and milder than that of Canada, without the fogs of Newfoundland and Nova Scotia; and the health and longevity of the inhabitants are remarkable." Judge HALIBURTON.—B.

BOOK SEVENTH.

CHAPTER I.

LAW'S SYSTEM—CONSPIRACY OF THE NATCHEZ.

1712–1731.

Notices of Louisiana and its inhabitants.—M. Crozat's monopoly.—Civil government re-constituted.—*La Coutume de Paris* introduced as a legal code.—Abortive attempts to originate a trade with New Mexico.—Traffic among the aboriginal tribes, shared with the British colonists.—The Natchez tribe exterminated by the French.—M. Crozat throws up his trading privileges in disgust; they are transferred to the Western Company, as re-instituted in favour of John Law and others.—Notices of this adventurer; rise, progress, and fall of his banking and colonizing schemes, known as the Mississippi System.—Personal changes in the colonial administration.—New Orleans founded, in 1718, by M. de Bienville.—New organization of the provincial government.—Immigration of the West India Company's colonists; the miserable fate of most of them.—Notices of divers French settlements.—War between France and Spain; its origin and course.—Capture and re-capture of Pensacola.—At the peace, the latter restored to Spain.—Recompenses to the Louisianian military and naval officers.—Treaties with the Chickasaws and Natchez.—Hurricane of Sept. 12, 1722.—Charlevoix recommends missions, and his advice is adopted.—Louisianian trade transferred to the Company of the Indies, after the collapse of Law's company.—M. Perrier, a naval lieutenant, appointed governor of the province.—Most of the aboriginal tribes conspire to exterminate all the French colonists.—The Natchez perform the first act of this tragedy, with savage dissimulation and barbarity, but too precipitately, happily for the remainder of the intended victims.—Stern reprisals of the French.—A few concluding words on the polity of the West India Company in Louisiana; which is fain to render up its modern privileges therein to the king.

Whilst France was engaged in fortifying Cape Breton, the most adventurous of her people were extending the colonization of those immense regions through which the lower Mississippi flows. As the fame of her name was first sounded in the far west of New France by born Canadians, the most conspicuous personages who now figured on the scene in Louisiana were also natives of the Laurentian provinces.

The second site chosen for a head settlement of Louisiana, served its purpose no better than the first. Mobile was soon found to be as unsuitable as Biloxi; and the colonists were removed from the latter to the Isle-Dauphine, which D'Iberville had named Massacre Island, owing to the number of human bones he found there, scattered about. This hapless island is little more than a large sand-bank, but it was selected for its seaward position, and from its containing a good haven.

We had occasion to mention, incidentally, in one of our preceding pages, the name of Antoine Crozat.* He had been a successful merchant, and now held a high office in the department of finances at Paris. In 1712, he obtained from the court a patent for exclusive mining in Louisiana, with a monopoly for sixteen years of the whole trade of that colony, the king reserving to himself its civil and military government. M. de la Mothe had just been nominated governor, in place of the deceased M. de Mays; M. Duclos, present *commissaire-ordonnateur*, replacing M. d'Arteguette, who had returned to France. A "superior council," of two members and a recorder (*greffier*), with power to add to its numbers, was constituted for three years, with jurisdiction civil and criminal. Its jurisprudence was to be that known as the *Coutume de Paris*, no other being then recognised in New France.

M. de la Mothe-Cadillac, whom M. Crozat had conjoined with him in carrying out his trading enterprises, did not reach the colony till 1713. The double duties he had undertaken to perform were inconsistent in nature with each other; and their conjunction was of evil augury for the colony. On his arrival he found the inhabitants leading a wretched existence in one of the

---

* This millionnaire was ennobled afterwards, as Marquis du Châtel. There is an elementary work on geography, compiled expressly for the use of a daughter of that financier, by the abbé Le François, and known to most French academies, in former times, as the "Géographie de Crozat." *Dict. des Dates.*—B.

finest countries in the world, for want of a circulating medium, and means for disposing of their produce. The governor turned his first attention to the formation of commercial relations with the neighbouring American settlements, especially those belonging to Spain. With this view, he despatched a vessel, laden with merchandize, to Vera Cruz. The viceroy of Mexico, faithful to the exclusive system of his nation and the times, ordered the vessel away. Cadillac, not discouraged, made a second attempt by means of M. Juchereau de St. Denis, one of the hardiest Canadian adventurers of the day, and a resident of Louisiana during fourteen previous years.

While thus seeking a trade with Mexico, the governor courted a traffic in peltry with the Natchez and other tribes of the Mississippi, among whom his agents found Virginians already resorting, partly for the same purpose, partly for courting alliances of the savages for British interests. The French, on their side, pursued the like policy; and a perilous rivalry of the two races of colonists, temporarily convenient but permanently hurtful, forthwith arose in the southern colonies of France and Britain, such as had long existed in other parts of the continent. Thus the Alabamans-the Choctas, and other tribes, become inimical to the Carolinians, fell upon their settlements and committed great ravages; while the Natchez, in 1716, spirited against the French, were on the point of exterminating them by a suddenly inflicted blow. Detected in their plot, M. de Bienville entered their country and forced them to be so submissive as to build, under his orders, a fortress for a French garrison, intended as a post of observation. This post, called Fort Rosalie, in compliment to Madame Pontchartrain, was erected on a bluff of the Mississippi.

In 1715, M. de Tisné laid the foundations of Nachitoches, on the right bank of the Red River. At this time, Louisianian trade was anything but flourishing in the hands of Crozat and his agents. Before his monopoly began, the inhabitants of Mobile and Isle-Dauphine exported provisions, wood, and peltry, to France, Pensacola, Martinique, and St. Domingo; receiving in return articles for barter with the natives, with other needful commodities and luxuries. Crozat's monopoly put a stop to this unshackled intercourse.

Ships from the Antilles ceased to frequent the port. Private ships were prohibited from going to Pensacola, whence the colonists had derived all their specie: whatever overplus produce they had, they were obliged to sell to Crozat's agents at such prices as the latter chose to put upon them. The rates of their tariff for peltry were fixed so low, that the hunters preferred to send them to Canada, or to the British colonies. Instead of imputing the evil plight of his affairs, the necessary result of such injustice, to his own purblind policy, M. Crozat complained to the ministry against other parties, as the cause of it all; but finding that no attention was paid to him, and that he was not able to form an arrangement with the Mexicans to take his goods for supplies of the precious metals, he threw up his patent in disgust, and it was soon afterwards handed over to the chief director of the renovated company of the French West Indies. [This was the famous John Law, of Lauriston.*]

From the time of Ferdinand de Soto, who visited the Mississippian region in 1539, it had become a fond tradition that its subsoil abounded in gold and silver. D'Iberville's reports had latterly tended to confirm these time-honoured illusions. Law, confiding in the reality of Louisianian wealth or not, now determined to turn the popular belief to account. He began by forming a bank of circulation in Paris (the first known to France), with a capital of forty million livres. Having ingratiated himself with the regent duke of Orleans (being an accomplished man, of courtly manners), he obtained the privilege, for twenty years, by edicts dated May 2nd and 10th, 1716, of issuing notes to be cashed at sight with specie. A sound system of credit, much wanted in France, would have resulted from this enterprise, had its opera-

---

* In much of this chapter, the editor has had recourse to various authorities for most of the particulars in it regarding Law's Bank and the Mississippi scheme. This is stated, if only in justice to M. Garneau. Law, who was one of the most able, and not the least honest financiers of his time, aspired to the honour of founding a national bank in France; thus rivalling his countryman, William Paterson, the projector of the Bank of England and the Bank of Scotland. Law, born in 1681, was son of a goldsmith in Edinburgh. He died poor, at Venice, in 1729.—B.

tions been kept within the prescribed bounds; but this does not seem to have been the intention of its projector, or of his patrons at court. It was but a pilot-balloon for what was to follow.

At this time the finances of France were in a deplorable state. Bills on the royal treasury were negotiable at only half their nominal value. The regent, by way of raising funds, created, in an edict dated March 12, 1716, a chamber of inquest for the prosecution of peculating farmers-general and others suspected of having become too rich at the expense of the state. Several of these were condemned, arbitrarily, to make restitutions; but, by dexterous evasions or collusions with their prosecutors, only a small sum was realized from an act of extra-legal procedure, bearing the discredit of being totally opposed to legitimate jurisprudence. This odious device having thus practically failed, the regent was well disposed to further Law's projects, as part of his plan was to take in exchange for the actions of his bank when extended, the government "promises to pay," not depreciated by 50 per cent., but at par. Next year, Law obtained, as we have intimated above, titles to the trading and mining monopoly in Louisiana renounced by Crozat, also the dormant privileges of the " Castor " or Canada Company, formed in 1710, of the St. Domingo association (1698), of the Senegal and Guinea Companies, of the Chinese Company (1700), and of the old West India Company. Whatever advantages might accrue from a monopoly of trade with those countries were hypothecated for the security of those who took shares in an association called the " Mississippi Company," with a capital of 100 millions of livres, which was made an adjunct of the bank.

By an edict dated Dec. 4, 1718, the regent erected his two-fold establishment as the *Banque Royale*, or State Bank of France. Dec. 27, an edict (*arrêt*) prohibited any re-payment of more than 600 livres in silver. This made paper that was out all the more needful for circulation, and occasioned further emissions. Yet people were so infatuated as to continue depositing their coined money, receiving shares and bank-paper in exchange. By Dec. 1, 1719, there were 640 million livres of the latter in the hands of the public. Dec. 11, an edict was issued, prohibiting the bank officers from re-paying more than 300 livres in gold, or ten in silver, at one time. Public confidence now began to give way.

By way of restoring it, the chief director, Law, was nominated controller-general of the royal finances: he having been naturalized on renouncing protestantism.

At one time, when public madness was at the highest, the stock of the Mississippi Company rose in price to 2050 per cent.; and 150 million livres were added to its capital. But, when the tide turned, their nominal value sank almost as rapidly as it rose.

In 1719-20, several foreign merchants having obtained large quantities of the "royal bank" paper, at a depreciated rate, contrived to obtain specie for them at the institution, and thus stripped France of a large amount of its coin. Public discontent was now rife, and the regent, to appease it, deprived Law of his post in the finances, but continued him in his situation as head of the Bank and West India Company. The device was now resorted to, of selling parcels of land in Louisiana, delivery guaranteed by the company. A tract of one square league was rated at 3000 livres. A few French capitalists thus acquired illusory right to enormous expanses of wilderness. To people these, all the vagabonds who then infested Paris were taken up, and placed in ward; the streets were also cleared of public women, who were put in prison; both species of *colonists* were thus detained till they could be shipped. By and by the archers (armed police) began to impress honest burgesses and respectable artisans, in view of obtaining ransoms for their release. Their friends rose upon the archers, killed some, and maltreated others. Impressment of the citizens thereupon ceased.

An edict dated May 21, 1720, ordained, that a monthly reduction should take place of the shares and notes of the West India Company and Royal Bank. This edict was recalled 24 hours afterwards, but too late to prevent a panic and a run. The regent dismissed Law, and put the bank under the direction of the duke d'Antin and some councillors of the parliament of Paris. This transference did not still the storm of public indignation against Law, who took refuge in the Palais-Royal, where the regent resided. Crowds broke into its courts, demanding the death of "the impostor who had ruined France." The people being driven out by force, three persons were crushed in the passages. Those in the streets, seeing Law's carriage pass by, rushed upon it, thinking he might be within; but finding it empty, they demolished the innocent vehicle.*

The regent rightly thinking Law's life not safe if he remained any longer in Paris, sent him to one of the royal seats in the country. Some of the many courtiers who were enriched by obtaining bank shares from him and selling out in time, were grateful enough to find means for getting him across the eastern frontiers, whereupon he found an asylum at Brussels, leaving a nation beggared which he had pretended to enrich. Shortly thereafter, a council of regency was holden, in which it was ascertained, that 2,700,000,000 livres in bank-bills had been issued, 1,200,000,000 of which amount were unsanctioned by any royal ordinance; but which the regent had privately empowered Law to issue, (ostensibly,) to retrieve the credit of the state.*

While these disastrous speculations, for which Louisiana was made a nominal handle, were going on, a change of administration took place in the colony; M. de la Mothe-Cadillac being superseded by M. de Bienville, now appointed commandant general of the province; while M. Hubert superseded M. Duclos as *commissaire-ordonnateur.* The settlements now established were Biloxi (once more the capital), Mobile, Natchez, and Nachitoches. The Isle-Dauphine was abandoned perforce, its haven having been silted up by the action of the waves, for l'Isle-aux-Vaisseaux. It now began to be thought that a site for a river-port, rather than a sea-haven, would be advantageous; and M. de Bienville found what he considered a suitable place about 100 miles up the Mississippi. In 1718, he went thither with some carpenters and smuggling salters, and laid the first planks of a

---

* The premier president of parliament was the first to announce this act of popular vengeance in his court, which he did in the following impromptu couplet:—

" Messieurs, messieurs! bonne nouvelle;
Le carrosse de Law est réduit en cannelle."

(Good news, my friends! Law's cozening tricks
Have made his coach be smashed in sticks.)

Whereupon all the members rose, in great joy; one of them asking, " Have they indeed torn Law in pieces?" J.-A. DULAURE: *Histoire de Paris.*—B.

village in marshy ground,—a Canadian thus founding the western capital of the United States. He named the place NEW ORLEANS, in honour of the regent of France, and appointed M. de Pailloux to take charge of it; but the seat of government was not transferred thither till the year 1723.

When the re-constituted West India Company (Law's) took possession of the colony, Bienville was continued in office, and constituted the company's resident director; and other appointments were made. In spring 1718, eight hundred persons, including the impressed colonists mentioned above, were embarked in three ships at La Rochelle, and despatched to Louisiana. Several gentlemen (*gentilshommes*) and retired military officers came along with this rabble ; the regent having promised to invest them with colonial dukedoms, marquisates, countships, &c. To Law himself was assigned an estate, four square leagues in extent, at Arkansas, which was constituted as a duchy, for peopling which he gathered 1,500 Germans and Provençals as his vassals. He intended to send 6,000 more, but was prevented by the sudden collapse of his "system." Of the first-mentioned band, numbers dispersed before the time of embarkation at Lorient; and the rest were not shipped till the year 1721, when they were despatched by the other directors of the West India Company.* Packed in the transports pell-mell, they were disgorged from them on the strand at Biloxi, where no preparation had been made to receive them. There were no proper means of transport there, to convey them up the river or elsewhere; provisions failed; some found means to support life by gathering shell-fish, but in the end, more than 500 perished of hunger. A company of Swiss soldiers, with its officers, escaped the general calamity by marching off bodily to Carolina.

Although the West India Company had exerted a disturbing, not a quickening influence on the colony, it still used the exorbitant powers granted to its expelled chief. The monopoly had

---

* The above account of the "Mississippi Scheme," which preluded the "South-Sea bubble," blown in England nearly at the same time, is taken partly from DULAURE's History of Paris, and other well-accredited French sources.—*B.*

already cost 25 millions. "The company's administrators," says Raynal, "who made those enormous advances, had the silly pretension to direct in Paris enterprises which could rightly be shaped in the New World only. From their bureaus they laid out the course to be followed by every colonist, in a way subservient to their own monopoly, and to that only. To hide the deplorable state of the settlements from the public eye, they made no scruple to intercept letters sent home by the sufferers."

The resident authorities had demanded a large immigration of agricultural settlers; but besides that France was not over populated after the exhausting wars it had gone through, its feudal system put obstacles in the way of such a transfer of human muscles and sinews. The nobility, landed gentry, and clergy, whose hierarchs were chiefs in the government, and principal lords of the soil, were noways inclined to make a present to the New World of those rural vassals who made their possessions worth the having. Neither, at any time, were the peasantry of France inclined to leave their native country for America.

Nevertheless, the ill-directed attempts at extended colonization in recent years were not entirely without some favorable results; and from this time forward, the possession of Louisiana was secured to the mother country. Besides the five chief settlements already enumerated, the foundations of others were laid at Yasous, Bâton-Rouge, Bayagoulas, Ecores-Blancs, Pointe-Coupée, the Rivière-Noire, Paska-Ogoulas, and some even towards the Illinois. These nuclei of as many colonies were widely spread, but most of them attained prosperity.

While the projects of Law were draining France of the "sinews of war," hostilities suddenly broke out with Spain in an unexpected manner. This was occasioned through a conspiracy, got up by Cardinal Alberoni, prime-minister of Spain, the abbé Porto-Carrero, and some French intriguers, including the Cardinal de Polignac and the Duc de Maine, a bastard son of Louis XIV. The object in view was to deprive the duke of Orleans of the regency of France, and confer it on Philip V, Bourbon king of Spain. Its detection was followed by a revolt of some of the nobles in Brittany; five of whom were capitally punished, and others exiled.

VOL. II—D

The regent, early in 1719, declared war against Spain, which had not a single ally, and had both France and Britain to encounter as enemies, on land and sea. Marshal Berwick (illegitimate son of James II) invaded Spain with a French army; the British beat the Spanish fleets at sea; and an expedition, commanded by M. de Châteauguay, with a land-force of French soldiers, Canadians, and savages, aided by three ships of war, under M. de Sérigny, invested and took Pensacola, after an obstinate resistance. But in June, the same year, the Spaniards sent sufficient forces to re-take the place, and M. de Châteauguay had to deliver it up.

The viceroy of Mexico, encouraged by this re-capture, resolved to expel the French from the seaboard of the Gulf. Accordingly, he despatched Don Carascora, who had re-taken Pensacola, to attack the French at l'Isle-Dauphine and Mobile; but he was repulsed in both places by Messrs. Vilinville and Sérigny.

The colonists once more turned their eyes on Pensacola, the permanent possession of which they had long coveted. Commodore Desnots arriving with five ships of war at the Isle-Dauphine, a council of war was called, and it was decided to attack that settlement by sea and land. September 17, 1719, Desnots forced a passage into the harbour, and captured the Spanish vessels moored inside. M. de Bienville, with a land-force, assailing the defensive works of the town, it was surrendered next day. The French took 1200 to 1500 prisoners, and dismantled the works all but the chief fort, leaving in it a small garrison.

After this exploit, the ministry accorded honours and promotions to those who had distinguished themselves (chiefly Canadians) in the wars of the colony. As Louisiana owed its foundation to them at first, so to them was its conservation due. Messrs. Bienville, Sérigny, Saint-Denis, Vilinville, and Châteauguay, were the chief parties whose merits were thus practically acknowledged.

The Spanish government soon grew tired of causeless hostilities, by which the nation gained no credit and reaped no advantage. As peace was signed February 17, 1720, and France declared war January 2, 1719, it was well that what ought to have had no beginning, had so prompt an ending. Alberoni, the causer

LAW'S SYSTEM—CONSPIRACY OF THE NATCHEZ. 51

of all the mischief, was expelled from Spain. In terms of a stipulation in the treaty, Pensacola was restored to the Spaniards.

Shortly thereafter, the colonists constrained the Chickasaws and the Natchez, who had taken advantage of the armed force being absent to commit depredations, into terms of peace.

On the 12th September, 1722, a hurricane passed over the colony, leaving death and desolation behind it. The waves of the seaboard, driven inland to an immense distance, flooded the country, and washed away most of Biloxi and New Orleans.

Up to this time, no proper provision had been made for the cure of souls in Louisiana. The pious Charlevoix, after visiting the colony, and remarking this want, called the attention of the court to it in 1723; urging upon the ministry, that " the conversion of the American aborigines was always the chief motive of the kings of France, for extending their domination in the New World; while the experience of nearly two centuries had proved, that the surest means of securing native attachment to the French was to impart to the savages with whom they had to do the Gospel of Christ. Independent of the spiritual fruit thence resulting, it was important for worldly polity's sake that the presence of a missionary among each of the tribes, whose character the natives must needs respect, to watch and report any intrigues against the French going on, was as effective as a garrison of observation, and far cheaper to the state." This last consideration was doubtless that which had most weight with the irreligious majority of the Regent's cabinet, which responded forthwith to the call made upon it, by sending out a number of Capucins and Jesuits to " evangelize the savages," (*and* dispose them to be regardful of French interests.)

M. Perrier, nominated to supersede M. de Bienville, arrived in October, 1726. The colony was then in a tranquil state, both as to its interior and exterior relations; but in the latter regard a storm against it was arising. The aborigines of the Mississippi valley, who in general received the first visits of the Europeans with favour or in a neutral spirit, finding that in proportion as they extended their settlement the former paid less and less regard to native rights or pretensions—the tribes of the regions between the Ohio and the Gulf of Mexico were now all ready, we say, at short notice or none, to take up arms against those whom they looked upon as interloping usurpers. Add to this feeling of enmity to Europeans in general among the several tribes, the chances presented of finally overcoming in detail the common enemy, with present advantages superadded, through the political and trading rivalries of the men of British and French race settled in or frequenting a country which was not theirs by natural right. For reasons good or bad, we repeat, the Chickasaws had become in the south-west, relatively to the French and British colonists, what the Iroquois were in the north-east of the upper continent of America. The result was, at the present time, a conspiracy to fall unawares upon the French, and massacre them all at a preconcerted signal given. The Chickasaws, the only people of the Louisianian tribes whom the French had not been able to render favourable, if prime movers in the plot were not to be alone in carrying it out, for all the other tribes, with the exception of the Arkansas, the Illinois, and the Tonicas, (friends of the French, and not let into the secret) were in league with the Chickasaws, to compass the perdition of the province.

The colonists were felicitating themselves on the calm that reigned around them, when a selfish demonstration of the Natchez, in rash anticipation of the intended catastrophe, became the means of averting it, but only to a limited extent. A barge, filled with provisions and merchandize for the use of the people at the principal colonial establishment among these savages, was eagerly coveted by them on its arrival. To pave the way to its seizure, they got up a hunting party pretending that they wanted to procure game for M. de Chepar, the governor, to feast the party who had come with the stores for his people. Having procured from the latter guns and amunition for the use alleged, early in the morning of the 28th day of November, 1729, they were swarming about the place, preparing as they said to take to the woods; but previously sounding a chaunt, in affected honour of the governor's guests, which proved to be a song of death. At a signal given by the chief of the Natchez, who called himself a descendant of the Sun, three shots were fired, as a preliminary; and then his men, scattered about the town, fell upon the French nearest to them, and in a few minutes' time two hundred men were butchered in the fort or near their dwellings. Only about a score of the male colonists, with a few of their negroes, several of the former more or less seriously hurt, contrived to escape. Sixty women, 150 children, and most of the blacks, were made captive. Several of the prisoners were afterwards tortured to death.

While the slaughter was in progress, the Natchez chief was seated under the Company's tobacco-shed, taking things very coolly. The head of M. de Chepar—who during life reposed unlimited faith in his murderers—was brought in; also, in succession, those of his officers, and set in a ghastly row. The heads of the commonalty were pitched into a pile indiscriminately. The first onslaught over, refugees were sought out from their hiding-places. Pregnant women were ripped up; and the cries of children stilled with the hatchet, as being importunate and troublesome to the slayers of their parents. The persons of some of the female victims were abused previously to their immolation. The Natchez butchers were encouraged to proceed with predictions that the victims would not be avenged by their compatriots, the chief assuring his men that the French in all parts of the country where they were settled, had been subjected to the same treatment already; *and that the British were about to take their place.**

---

* The foregoing narration of the "plot of the Natchez," is translated textually. M. Garneau, in summing up his statements, makes the following strictures, which, even if deserved, are certainly out of place, as there were no "English colonists" located within several hundred miles of the Louisianian French or of the aborigines of the Mississippi, so early as the year 1729: "We have seen with what jealousy the English colonists saw the French settlements extending along the St. Lawrence to the great lakes; this jealousy had no bounds when they saw the French take possession of the great Mississippi valley. They infused distrust and hatred of the French in the savage mind; they depicted them as greedy traders, who would soon seize the whole territory, and expel the natives. By degrees, fear and wrath entered the hearts of the natives, naturally proud and ferocious; and they resolved to rid themselves of encroaching aliens, who were daily extending their settlements." M. Garneau has omitted to state what were the colonies which indulged in the above nefarious diplomacy; also, who were the agents employed in it on the present occasion. He has also overlooked a passage germane to the subject in the inaugural discourse delivered before the "Historical Society" of Louisina by the President, H. A. Bullard, Esq., Jan. 13, 1836; which was couched in these few pregnant words: "The massacre of the French by the Natchez, which led to the extermination

The news of this massacre reached New Orleans, December 2nd. The governor, M. Perrier, immediately sent an officer to warn the colonists on both sides of the Mississippi of their danger; and to observe the movements of the natives in the surrounding country. But the precipitation of the Natchez had probably retarded rather than hastened the consummation of the general massacre. The Chactas, who had joined in the plot only for the sake of the spoil expected to accrue by pillaging the colonial establishments, would not come forward; or, rather, they inclined to join the French in avenging it on their common enemies, the Natchez. Other tribes implicated, finding the colonists on their guard, also held back. The Yasous, not so prudent, attacked the fort erected in their territory, and killed all within, 17 persons. The entire tribe was, in consequence, exterminated. The Arkansas, a potent nation, always attached to the French, fell upon the Corrois and the Sioux, both parties to the conspiracy, and massacred them to the last man. These reprisals, the presence of a corps of armed men, and the intrenchment of the concessions of land, re-assured the colonists of their future safety; and enabled the governor to send Major Loubois, with a colonial corps, to wage war on the Natchez territory; he would have gone thither himself, but for doubts he had of the fidelity of the blacks at New Orleans. He was now secure of the alliance of the Illinois, the Arkansas, the Offagoulas, the Tonicas, the Nachitoches, and the aid, as auxilia-

---

of that tribe, was provoked by the atrocious attempt, by the commandant, to destroy their village at St. Catherine's, *in order to annex the land to his own plantation.*" Mr. Bullard added, that "Neither the French nor the Spanish government recognized in the Indians any primitive title to the land over which they hunted, nor even to the spot on which their permanent dwellings were fixed. They were often grantees of lands for very limited extents, not exceeding a league square, covering their village. They were sometimes permitted to sell out their ancient possessions, and had a new locality assigned them. Many titles of that kind exist at the present time, and have been subjects of judicial decision; but the policy of extinguishing the primitive Indian title, as it is called, by purchase, which prevailed universally among the English colonists, appears to have been wholly unknown to the French and Spaniards in Louisiana." *Historical Collections of Louisiana,* Part I, p. 20, New York, 1846.—*B.*

ries, of the Chactas. Louisiana was not only safe, but in a condition to turn the tables upon its enemy. Unfortunately, Loubois' soldiers were an undisciplined and disorderly band, and could not form a junction with M. Lesueur at a time and place appointed. In consequence, the latter, at the head of 700 Chactas, advanced without waiting for Loubois, attacked the Natchez, and defeated them. The surviving Natchez took refuge in two palisaded posts, wherein they were beleaguered by Loubois, who had brought four cannon with him; but they were so poorly worked, that little impression was made upon the Natchez' defences. The Chactas, wearied with the siege, threatened to withdraw; and as it could not be carried on without their aid, the colonists consented to raise it, upon the besieged delivering up the women and children of the colony whom they had kept as prisoners. This termination of a campaign intended to wreak signal vengeance on their captors, who had also made them widows and orphans, was looked upon as little better than a defeat by the men of the colony; but it was chiefly due to the inefficiency of the soldiery sent, added to the impatience and self-sufficiency of the Chactas. The governor had to explain this at head-quarters, justifying what had been done and left undone, by the critical circumstances of the case. Add to all, that the Chickasaws were still dangerously inimical, though as yet covertly only, to the colonists, striving to detach other tribes from the French alliance; while, on the other hand, the Chactas, although earnestly solicited by the British, whose overtures were accompanied by rich presents, refused to change sides, and swore inviolable fidelity to M. Perrier.

The retreat of Loubois greatly emboldened the Natchez tribes; but the insolence they manifested in consequence led to their ruin. The governor, in Dec. 1730, formed a corps 600 strong, at Bayagoulas, composed of soldiers from France and colonial militiamen; with which he ascended the river in barges, and appeared, Jan. 20, 1731, before the two forts Loubois had failed to take. Alarmed at their appearance, the Natchez being thus taken unawares, and few in number at the time, asked for terms of surrender; Perrier detained their envoy. The besieged then offered to leave the place unarmed if their lives were spared. This was agreed to; but they were detained as prisoners, all but twenty who escaped; and afterwards, along with "the descendant of the Sun," sent to St. Domingo as slaves. This chief, who had long governed the Natchez nation, died at Cape Français a few months afterwards. The fate of a personage they regarded as a kind of divinity so exasperated his subjects, that they flew to arms, and they fought the French with a persevering courage which they had never evinced before. After some minor combats in which they had the worst of it, M. St. Denis signally defeated them, all their chiefs being among the killed. Those who escaped this rout took refuge with the Chickasaws; who, in adopting them, became heirs of the hatred of their nation to the French, and vindicators of their wrongs.

Thus finished a war which led to a revolution in the affairs of the association then monopolising the trade of the province of Louisiana. The West India Company, long defunct, was succeeded, in 1723, by the Company of the Indies, with the duke of Orleans for governor, and a jurisdiction extending over all the colonies of France, whether in Asia, Africa, or America. The latter association, become discredited as well as impoverished by the insurrection of the savage tribes,—suppressed without much of its aid, thanks to the energy and talent of M. Perrot,—in 1731 gave up to the king its chartered privileges in Louisiana and the Illinois country. The policy of the Company while suzerain in the colony, may be judged of by the fact, that in order to put in its interest the governor and the intendant, it granted to both yearly gratuities (entered in their books, still extant), also allowed them a percentage on whatever produce was sent to France. Such a corrupt system could not work well either for the association or the state; but least of all, for colonial benefit.

CHAPTER II.
DISCOVERY OF THE ROCKY MOUNTAINS.
1713-1744.

State of Canada; reforms effected and projected by M. de Vaudreuil.—Rivalry of France and Britain in America.—The frontier question; uncertain limits of Acadia.—The Abenaquis' territories.—Hostilities between that tribe and the New-Englanders.—Murder of Père Rasle.—Frontiers of western New France.—Encroachments on the Indian territories.—Plans of Messrs. Hunter and Burnet.—Establishments, one at Niagara by the French, one at Oswego by the British, are followed by complaints from the former, protests from the latter,—Fort St. Frederick erected at Crown-Point; a deputation from New England vainly remonstrates against this step.—Loss of the *Chameau*, French passage-ship, in the Laurentian waters.—Death of M. de Vaudrenil; his character.—M. de Beauharnais appointed governor-general, with M. Dupuis as intendant.—Death of M. de St. Vallier, second bishop of Quebec; dissensions among his clergy about the interment of his corpse, which lead to a complication of troubles, in which the civil authorities take part; the governor betraying his duty to the state, the clergy come off with flying colours.—Recal of M. Dupuy, who is thus made a scape-goat by the French ministry.—M. Hocquart nominated intendant.—Intolerance of the clergy of the cathedral of Quebec.—Mutations in the episcopate for several years; nomination of Messrs. de Mornay, Dosquet, de l'Aube-Rivière, as third, fourth, and fifth bishops; appointment and settlement of M. Pontbriant as sixth prelate.—The Outagamis' hostilities avenged on their allies.—Travels and discoveries of the Messrs. Vérendrye, in search of a route to the Pacific Ocean :—they discover the Rocky Mountain range.—Unworthy treatment experienced by the family.—Appearances of war being imminent, M. de Beauharnais takes precautionary measures, and recommends more to be adopted by the home authorities: the latter (as usual) repel or neglect his warnings.—Anecdote, affecting the reputation of M. Van Renselaer, of Albany.

We now resume the annals of Canada proper, recommencing A. D. 1713. Under the sage administration of the marquis de Vaudreuil, the country was enjoying a state of peace and security at least, if not such a full measure of prosperity as he was always endeavouring to obtain for it. In 1714, he went to France, leaving those whom he could depend upon in charge of his office, and did not return till after the demise of Louis XIV,* an event the news of which he was the first to announce; while his first public act after he arrived was to proclaim the nominal accession of the child-king, Louis XV, and the formation of a regency.

The accession of a new monarch always gives rise to hopes of benefits to accrue from the change; and we may reasonably suppose that the colonists of New France may have had their expectations raised that their interests would be better attended to by the new rulers than the old: this the rather, because their governor-general had personal interest at court. M. de Vaudreuil, evidently believing himself that a new era was about to dawn, earnestly set about improving the governmental institutions of his province, and putting new life into its trading and civil relations. The state of the currency first called for his attention. He had been able to procure a financial composition with the home government, so that the state paper-money in the province (a kind of exchequer-bills drawn, at various times, on the royal treasury) should be redeemed forthwith in specie,—the holders submitting to a loss of 5-8ths of its nominal value. He next vindicated his own paramount authority by ordaining that military subalterns should send regular reports to him; while law subalterns were to communicate, thenceforth, directly with the royal intendant, not with the Supreme Council as thithertofore. The extension of public education, up to this period supplied gratuitously by the Jesuits and Recollets brethren, was an object of the governor's special solicitude at this time; but it was not till the year 1722, that he was able to conjoin eight secular schoolmasters with the ecclesiastical teachers already at work in different parts of the country, engaged in imparting elementary instruction to the children of the humbler colonists.

The imperfect means of defence at command, in case the colony were invaded by sea, also engaged the serious attention of its governor-general. In 1716, he pressed this point strongly on

---

* Sept. 1, 1716. He was succeeded by his great-grandson, then five years old.—B.

the attention of the heedless regent Orleans; intimating, that, Quebec once taken, Canada were lost to France. No regular system of fortification for that city had been entered upon till the year 1702, when some works were begun, after a plan traced by M. Levasseur. In 1711-12, other defences, planned by M. de Beaucourt, were added: but still the line of defence was of an imperfect character; and this it was which made M. de Vaudreuil so earnest that the works should be improved and extended. At length, in 1720, the home government having approved of the plan for further fortifying Quebec, by M. Chaussegros de Léry, the needful works were proceeded with. Two years afterwards, it was ordained that the city of Montreal should be walled and bastioned; but this had to be done at the expense of the residents, the home government pleading inability to defray the cost.

At this date, the colony was already divided into three distinct governments; namely, those of Quebec, Trois-Rivières, and Montreal; but no regular subdivisions, civil or parochial, had been properly fixed. The whole colonial territory was at length (1721-2) parcelled into 82 parishes: 48 of which were ascribed to the northern side of the St. Lawrence, and 34 to its southern side. Bay St. Paul and Kamouraska were the easternmost; l'Isle du Pads, the most western parish of the whole. This arrangement was ratified by an edict (*arrêt*) of the royal council of state, duly registered at Quebec.

A kind of census was drawn up, giving an approximative idea of the actual population of the colony.* In 1679, it was estimated that the entire people of New France numbered 10,000 souls; 1-20th of the whole was assigned to Acadia. In 1697, the total was increased by 2,300. M. de Vaudreuil proposed that a statement of the colonial population, the amount of cultured lands, live-stock, &c., should be drawn up annually, beginning with the year 1721.—The returns, or rather estimations at this time, made the whole population of Canada to be only 25,000; of which number 7000 were located in Quebec, and 3000 in Montreal.

---

* Exact statisticians always distrust round numbers, and consider an "estimation" as a plausible *guess* at best.—B.

Acres (*arpents*) of land under tillage, 62,000; acres of land in grass, 12,000. The cereal produce for the year was thus estimated, in bushels (*minots*):—Breadstuffs (*bled*) 282,700; maize, 7,200; pulse (*pois*), 57,400; oats, 64,000; barley or rye (*orge*), 4,500. Tobacco grown, 48,000 lbs.; flax, 54,600 lbs.; hemp, 2,100 lbs. The amount of edible produce raised, per acre, therefore, was considerable, relatively; being 6¾ bushels per acre: with the addition of 1⅞ lb. per acre of tobacco, flax, or hemp.— Live-stock total, 59,000 head, including 5,600 horses.

There was little to encourage so patriotic a colonial chief as De Vaudreuil in conning over these meagre returns. The low state of the province, as compared with almost any separate plantation of British America, had long disquieted his mind. Thus, in 1714, he wrote to M. de Portchartrain, that "Canada contained but 4,484 inhabitants capable of bearing arms for its defence (males aged 14 to 60 years), in addition to 620 colonial troops (28 *compagnies des troupes de la marine*); and this scanty force spread over 100 leagues of territory. The British colonies have 60,000 males fit for war; and it is not to be doubted that as soon as war supervenes, an attempt will be made by them to achieve the conquest of Canada." The governor's applications for increased immigration were incessant; and at one time, as most of his demands were met by deplorations of the diminished population of the mother country, kept down by past just wars, and scarcely able to confront new, he proposed, upon one occasion, to receive convicts; but this suggestion, as we know, was not adopted.* In a general way, scarcely any emigrants came to Canada from France, but now and then a band of broken soldiers, the very worst species of settlers for any but a military colony. When such were sent, it was on condition that they should marry and remain in the country. Each was allowed a year's pay, when discharged.†—Of the miscellaneous immigrants

---

* Neither was it likely to turn out well in the semi-nomade communities sparsely, and nowhere very fixedly, located in New France.—*B.*

† Letters of Messrs. de Frontenac and de Champigny, in 1698, second series. [A year's pay of a French soldier, at any time, was and is a very small sum; and would, in most instances, be soon and uselessly spent. Such a careless way of *setting up* colonists marks the unregardful polity of the time.—*B.*]

to Canada who came voluntarily at their own cost, were men fond of adventure,—cadets or castaways of families of mark; travellers sailors, &c.; also, on one occasion or more, parties of French catholics from provinces (such as Poiton) where the neighbourhood of Protestant communities, it seemed, was irksome to them.*

The fortification of Quebec, according to the latest plan adverted to, appears to have been suspended; for we find, in 1728, the minister, in reply to the governor-general, who had advised that a regular citadel should be reared for the protection of his capital, asserting that " the Canadians liked not to fight behind walls;" and that besides, "the state could not support the expense such a construction would incur:" lastly it was intimated, that "it would be difficult to invest Quebec in regular form, so as to ensure its being taken." [The second reason might have sufficed, for the first was a hollow plausibility; while the third assumption was signally disproved by after experience.]

The vexed question of the frontier lines between New France, the Indian territories, the Spanish colonies, but, above all, the rapidly extending British possessions in North America, was becoming every year more and more difficult to deal with. The few attempts which had hitherto been made to define intelligibly, on either side, the limits of French and British territory in America, had always come to nothing. Commissioners were appointed, indeed, by a stipulation of the treaty of Utrecht: they met, long conferred, parted, and left the matter as they found it.†

---

* M. Garneau, in order to refute a prevailing opinion, that the Gallo-Canadian race had an almost entirely Norman origin—an assumption first made by Charlevoix—took the trouble to examine notarial records, still extant, for 1700 and some anterior years, which prove that the population of Quebec, at the close of the 17th century, was derived from a wide surface of the mother country. Out of 2002 entries affecting residenters in Quebec, only 26 refer to aliens; and among these are only four English, 1 Scotch, and 2 Irish individuals.—B.

† The rights assumed by Europeans over foreign lands uninhabited or peopled by savages, were founded upon: 1. discovery; 2. nominal possession taken; 3. colonization, general or partial. If the nations of Europe, when parcelling out the two Americas, had come to an agreement, that no power should be allowed to assert a claim it had not turned to account by forming regular settlements in a territory, within, say, ten years of

Disputes concerning boundaries between national possessions are proverbially the most difficult to terminate, by any other arbitrament than that of war. For many years past the British had striven to make French colonization miscarry in America. They controverted our ancestors' territorial rights, their participation in the peltry traffic, even their influences, political and religious, over the native tribes. At every fresh demonstration of this enmity on the part of the British provincials, the colonial authorities made representations to the home authorities, desiring their interposition with those of Britain, that an arrangement might be come to regarding the boundaries of the possessions of the respective nations; but this was either never done, or not properly followed up.

When the British, in terms of the treaty of Utrecht, reclaimed Acadia, they did not define what they understood to be its limits, or take any note of the settlements formed along the neighbouring continental seaboard, and the northern shore of Fundy bay, from the Kennebec to the peninsula. The French remained in possession of the St. John's river, and fortified their settlements upon it; they were left undisturbed, also, on the Etchemins' coast up to the St. Lawrence.

---

the time it was first proclaimed such had taken place and could be proved by records, printed, written, or graven, then all pretensions, falling within the first and second categories, above noted, would have become invalid. We have an instance, somewhat parallel, arising out of international laws, that neutrals are not bound to respect the " paper blockades" of belligerents. But a case more in point, may be deduced from the patent laws of every country, which ordain that patents become null if inventors do not practically avail themselves of the exclusive rights accorded to them within a prescribed time.

With respect to the pretensions of Louis XIV and Louis XV to have and to hold most of the continent of North America, it is difficult to say where New France began, or where it ended. A claim was latterly made, not only to the valley of the Mississippi, but to the lands watered by everyone of its tributaries ; the Missouri, the Ohio, &c., of course included. When we thinkof the enormity of this territorial grasp and of the equally exorbitant pretensions to an appropriation of the whole Laurentian valley, with the uncolonized lake regions beyond, we smile grimly as we own " la grandeur des projets sur l'Amérique qui effrayait l'Angleterre," to cite textually M. Garneau.—B.

By way of detaching the natives of the country (Maine) from French interests, the Bostonians sent a protestant missionary to preach to them, and deride catholic observances. This theologian met his overmatch in Père Rasle, a missionary resident in the Kenneebc territory for many years. The protestant's hackneyed diatribes against the imputed idol-worship of catholics were lost upon the perception of the Abenaquis; for savages comprehend better a religion which speaks to the soul by its symbols, than one of an abstract kind, which confines itself to a few prayers, without sacrifices or penitential acts. The Jesuit easily gained the victory in the controversy; and his discomfited opponent soon returned to Boston.

The British, ever better traders than religious disputants, having obtained permission, on certain conditions, to establish a factory on the Kennebec, took advantage of the concession, to found settlements and to erect fortified posts on different points of that river. The aborigines (Abenaquis), beginning to feel uneasiness at their encroachments, questioned them as to their rights thus to possess themselves of the country. The answer was, that the French government had given it up to them. The Abenaquis, repressing their indignation for the time, sent a deputation to Quebec, to consult M. de Vaudreuil, who assured the envoys that the treaty of Utrecht made no mention whatever of the territory in question. The Abenaquis then resolved to expel the intruders by force, if they would not consent to leave peacefully.

A negotiation was now entered into between the aggrieved Abenaquis and the New England authorities. Its governor * promised to meet the Abenaquis tribe in conference, and demanded that they should send hostages as a security for his personal safety. He failed to come, yet retained the hostages. The betrayed Abenaquis would have taken up arms at once but for Père Rasle, and Père de la Chasse; the latter, superior-general of the missions in that country. These missionaries advised the wronged savages to cause a double demand to be made on the Bostonians; namely, that they should at once release the hostages, and engage to quit the country in two months' time. No reply being sent

---

* If Massachusetts is referred to here, it was governor Dudley.—*B.*

to this summons, the Abenaquis were so enraged, that M. de Vaudreuil had to use all his influence over them to prevent a war. This happened in 1721.*

At this time, as all others, the Anglo-Americans having a bitter hatred for the Jesuits, attributed to the missionaries the general enmity of the natives to themselves. In particular, the New-Englanders doubted not that Père Rasle had caused the Abenaquis to assume their present hostile attitude; and although that Jesuit actually exerted all his influence to avert open war, the Americans set a price upon his head, and sent 200 men to seize him in the village he most frequented; but, this time, he escaped. They were more successful in getting hold of the chief of the Abenaquis, baron de St. Castin, who lived near the seaboard. One day in January 1721, a known vessel appeared on the coast. The baron went on board, to see the captain, as he had done many times before; when he was now put in ward, treated as a criminal, kept for several months, and released only after repeated demands by M. de Vaudreuil. Meanwhile the Abenaquis, not waiting for his release, avenged his capture by firing all the American settlements on the Kennebec, but without otherwise harming any of the people in them. The latter always ascribing the Abenaquis' enmity to the evil counsel of Père Rasle, sent a force, 1100 strong, to make reprisals on Narantaonak, a considerable native horde, grouped around the hated Jesuit's chapel. To reduce that edifice to ashes with all its environage of brushwood, was the work of a few minutes. The assailants, as soon as they perceived the venerable missionary, made his person a target for their balls; seven savages who tried to protect him, were killed also. Not satisfied with mere homicide, the Americans afterwards mangled the Jesuit's body in a shocking manner. The war, thus begun on both sides, was continued; but, in general, to the advantage of the Abenaquis.

In 1725, colonel Schuyler, and three deputies from New England, came to Montreal to treat for peace with a number of the chiefs of tribes then assembled in that city. The conferences took place in presence of M. de Vaudreuil. The Abenaquis demanded that

---

* This date, or that which follows, would seem to be inexact.—*B.*

they alone should remain masters of the country between Saco and Port-Royal; the governor laying no claim, for the French, to the lands on the northern Fundy seaboard, out of regard to the Abenaquis' rights ; just as the independence of the Iroquois territory was now respected by French and British alike. The Abenaquis also demanded that the murder of Père Rasle, and the damage done during the war by the Americans, should be "covered with presents." The envoys said they could only report these demands to their principals on their return. Meantime, they complained of the encouragement the French had given the Abenaquis in their recent hostilities against the British colonists, as a breach of the existing peace; and finished by demanding the release of certain prisoners retained in Canada.*

The British colonial authorities not consenting to such exorbitant conditions, which they doubtless believed the Abenaquis chiefs had been spirited to propose, preferred to brave their hostilities. At length, in 1727, a treaty was concluded with those savages at Kaskébé, recognizing their territorial rights, and freedom of choice to side with French or English in any future war. When news of this peace reached Paris, M. de Maurepas, the minister of marine, expressed much regret, as foreseeing the increased risks Canada would thenceforth incur, when attacked by sea. He added an earnest monition that the missionaries should, at whatever cost, preserve their influence over those savages, whose country formed a barrier towards Acadia. Another advice of the minister, at this time, was "to people the country below Montreal rather than that beyond; for numbers were more wanted in the lower region of the valley than the upper, to resist (British) invasion."

In the year 1725, a war-ship, of the French royal navy, called

---

* There is no question that the intimation of M. de Vaudreuil's having "rather excited than restrained the savages" was justified by the facts of the case; for the author owns in his text, that "the governor feared lest an accommodation should result from the conferences;" and his having "previously written to M. de Beauharnais that such a consummation was to be prevented by every means." This underhand dealing might be justified, perhaps, on unscrupulous political principles; for Père Charlevoix, in 1721, wrote that "the Abenaquis, though not a numerous nation, have formed, during the two last wars, the principal bulwark of New France against New England."—B.

Le Chameau, was fitted up as a passage vessel, to convey M. de Chazel, nominated intendant of Canada to replace M. Bégon; also M. de Louvigny, governor of Trois-Rivières, along with several officers, ecclesiastics, traders, six schoolmasters, and a number of intending colonists. Arrived in American waters, a tempest overtook the ship and drove her upon reefs near Cape-Breton. Every one on board perished.

While the colonists were mourning over this disaster, their governor-general's last hour was near. M. de Vaudreuil expired October 10, 1725, after ruling New France for 21 years. After passing 53 years in the royal service, he tardily received the cross of St. Louis. He was much and deservedly esteemed by all, and his death greatly lamented. His administration was tranquil, and his measures, whether civil or warlike, were usually crowned with success. Louis XV nominated as his successor, the Marquis de Beauharnais, a commodore (*chef d'escarde*) in the royal navy, in which he had gained distinction during bygone years, and had filled some important posts afterwards. Upon hearing the fate of M. de Chazel, the king nominated M. Dupuis as successor to M. Bégon, ex-intendant. These high functionaries arrived at Quebec in 1726.

No attempt was made at any time, between 1718-19 and 1748, to mark out the limits of Acadia. At the former date, French and British commissioners met in view of settling the frontier lines, but left the matter as uncertain as they found it. As matters now stood, the British left the French colonists in quiet possession (without changing allegiance) of their posts on the St. John's river, along the side of the Etchemins, and thence to the river St. Lawrence, even the inhabitants of the Mines, those of the Acadian isthmus, &c.

In the upper regions of the Laurentian valley, and in the lower basin of the Mississippi, the French maintained their positions and their traffic almost entirely by alliances with the native tribes; for the British ever disputed in principle, and often in act, the rightful extent of New France, as propounded by its governors-general. Every year almost, the British plantations, extending westwardly, were trenching, more or less, on territories claimed for the French of Louisiana, which extended as far eastward as the Alleghany mountains. As early as the year 1718, governor Hunter of New York wrote to the home authorities, that if the French were allowed to settle undisturbed in the Mississippi valley and the great lake countries, the British plantations would not only be limited in territory, but be exposed to constant incursions; and that, in the end, they might thus be entirely lost to the mother country. His successor, Mr. Burnet (son of the famous bishop of Sarum), adopting his views, recommended, in order to deaden French enterprise in America, that a passive war, in the shape of an act of non-intercourse between the colonists of the two nations, should be passed. Governor Burnet became early aware of the danger to be apprehended for the British settlements, if the French succeeded, in what was now evidently their aim, to establish a line of fortified posts, from the upper St. Lawrence to the lower Mississippi. It was this consideration which induced him to erect a fort at Oswego, on lake Ontario, as we shall presently see; thus hoping, by this practical demonstration of opposition to the plans of the French, to deter them from persevering in their execution.

By way of a counterpoise, M. de Vaudreuil obtained the consent of the Tsonnonthouans and Onnontaguez, to locate a factory, with defensive works, at the entrance of the Niagara river into lake Ontario; scheming that it should serve the double purpose of diverting part of the peltry traffic from Albany, and become a link in the chain of posts, intended to be formed, as above mentioned. Burnet, finding himself thus outgeneralled, wrote to the governor a letter of protestation against what had been done, denouncing it as a decided contravention of the treaty of Utrecht. The latter replied, that the Niagara territory had always formed an integral part of New France. Not being prepared to insist with effect that the French should relinquish their new holding, governor Burnet resolved to temporize; thus stating, meantime, in a despatch to the officials of the Board of Trade and Plantations, London, what course he intended to follow: "I shall do my endeavour," he wrote, "in the spring of next year, without committing overt hostility, to get our Indians to demolish the new settlement. The place is of great consequence, for two reasons: first, because it keeps the communication open between Canada and the Mississippi by way of the river Ohio, which else our Indians would be able to intercept at pleasure. And, second, if it should be made a fort with soldiers enough in it, the place will prevent our Indians from going over the narrow part of the lake Ontario, by this only pass of the natives, except by leave of the French; so that if it were once demolished, the far-removed Indians would depend on us."

It does not appear that any attempt was made to realise the plan laid out as above; although four out of the Five Nations of Iroquois were in alliance with the Anglo-Americans; the Tsonnonthouans not only refusing to expel the French, but demurring to any other colonial post being erected in their country. Burnet then cast about for a site whereon to erect a factory near the frontiers, and pitched on the outlet of the river Oswego to lake Ontario, midway between Niagara and Fort Frontenac.*

The demonstrations made on each side, more by acts than words, proved that the representative colonial chiefs of France and Britain would, neither of them, give way in the polity both had determined to carry out. When the proceedings of Messrs. de Vaudreuil and de Joncaire (the latter of whom had obtained the site of the factory at Niagara, and erected its defences), came under review at Court, Louis XV appended to a memorial regarding the subject, these words: "The post at Niagara is of the greatest importance, for preserving the trade of the upper country." His Majesty ordered, at the same time, that a stone fort should be built, at the outlet of Lake Ontario, replacing that formerly constructed by Denonville, and known as Fort Frontenac. The king also ordained that the liquor barter with the natives should be free to French traders, as it was already to the American traders; and that the sale of trading licences should be resumed, each trader to pay 250 livres for his licence. At the same time, M. de Beauharnais was ordered to prohibit all aliens to set foot in the colony under any pretext whatever; and as several Anglo-Americans had settled in Montreal, whose presence gave umbrage, they were ordered to leave that city within two days.

The duke of Newcastle, the British prime minister, complained

---

* *Documents de Paris.—Journal historique* of Charlevoix.

to the French ministry against the formation of the factory at Niagara, but in vain, as we may easily conceive. Burnet, who protested also against the same foundation, in a letter to M. de Longueuil, governor *pro tem.* of New France (M. de Vaudreuil having deceased), had of course no better success.

Burnet now caused the post at Oswego to be strengthened; and, after a summons to quit it had been sent him by M. de Beauharnais, in 1727, placed in it a numerous garrison. Fort Oswego was doubly important to the Americans: it was necessary for realising a project they had formed of monopolising the peltry traffic; and it served to protect their establishments situated between the river Hudson and lake Ontario.

These encroachments, on each part, gave rise to others. Beauharnais, seeing that Burnet was determined to maintain his position at Oswego, by way of reprisal, in 1731, erected a fort at la Pointe de la Chevelure on lake Champlain. M. de la Corne, an able Canadian officer, was the first to call the attention of the colonial government to the importance of such a locality, situated on a water-way opening a passage into the heart of the New York territory. As a military position, Crown-Point became a standing menace both to Oswego and Albany. The New Yorkers and New Englanders, foreboding the use that would be made of this post some day, to their disadvantage, sent a deputation to Canada to remonstrate against the erection of Fort Frederick.*

The royal intendant, M. Dupuy, who had filled high offices as a court lawyer, was a great formalist, and tried to introduce into

---

* The place was named in honour of the count de Maurepas (Jean-Frédéric Phélippeaux), minister of marine at that time. The Anglo-Americans had an exaggerated opinion of the natural strength of the place; for the site was ill chosen, and commanded by neighbouring heights. It could neither defend the navigation of the lake, nor the entry of the colony on that side. But it served well enough as a fastness, whence parties of Canadians and Indians could make raids upon the American settlements, to plunder, destroy, and kill. When the French garrison retired from Fort Frederick in 1749, General Amherst began to erect a new fort, on the site which the former would have occupied had the French engineer employed been fit for his task. It was never completed, yet it is said to have cost the British nation no less than two million pounds sterling!—*B.*

Canadian judicial process all that pedantic precision which characterised the organisation of the parliament of Paris; even endeavoured to exalt the supreme council into such public consideration as the former great body enjoyed in France. His attempts to reform irregularities among the judicial subordinates he found installed in office, and which had grown systematic, were resisted, and made his position uneasy. But any difficulties the rigid intendant had with his subalterns were trifling compared to the coming troubles he was destined to have through quarrels among the clergy of the diocese of Quebec.

The latter difficulties, hitherto ignored by all previous historians, originated at the decease, Dec. 1725, of M. de St. Vallier, who succeeded M. de Laval, in 1688, as bishop of the province. The defunct prelate's corpse was taken in charge, for interment, with all funereal rites befitting, by M. de Lotbinière, archdeacon of the diocese. Hereupon the other members of the chapter, with M. Boulard at their head, intimated that as the functions of M. de Mornay (then in France) as grand-vicar and coadjutor of the late prelate terminated at his decease, it was for them (the chapter) to take charge of the remains. The archdeacon paid no regard to this remonstrance. The chapter insisted; M. de Lotbinière applied to the intendant, who pronounced for the illegality of the chapter's pretensions. The chapter now refusing to obey the archdeacon as grand-vicar *pro tem.*, its leader and members were summoned to appear before the supreme council, and defend themselves. They denied the competency of any civil tribunal to try them on such a charge; they asserted that the case fell within episcopal jurisdiction only; and intimated in advance, that they would appeal, against any adverse award by the council, to the council of state at Paris. M. Dupuis reminded them, that as in the supreme council were vested functions akin to those of the parliament of Paris (his grand idea), had such a difficulty arisen in France the parliament must needs have first taken up the case; and that, till said supreme court had first dealt with it, no appeal would lie to the council of state. The law, thus solemnly laid down, seems to have been made light of, for tumultuous scenes followed between the contending parties, lay and spiritual. The rebellious members of the chapter, with a crowd at their heels, went to the general hospital, where the deceased had lain and was buried, entered the chapel and called before them the lady directress (*la supérieure*) of the monastery, suspended her from exercising her functions, and put the institution under an interdict.

The superior council, inspired by M. Dupuy, passed a decree (*arrêt*), declaring that the see of Quebec was not really vacant, as M. de Mornay, though absent, was not defunct; and, such being the case, the chapter was rightly inhibited from exercising any interim act whatever. This decree the chapter loftily repelled.—M. de Tonnancourt, a canon, next ascended the cathedral pulpit, on Epiphany day, and read a mandamus protesting against the intervention of the civil power in the matter; an order being given, at the same time, that every parish priest (*curé*) in the province should read a copy of the mandamus after the Sunday sermon (*au prône*).—The intendant, in turn, prepared to prosecute the canon Tonnancourt.

M. de Beauharnais now showed more partisanship, in favour of clerical pretensions, than his predecessor, M. de Frontenac, ever manifested against them. In his place at the council-board, he desired his secretary to read an ordinance interdicting the members from proceeding farther in taking jurisdiction of the quarrel among the clergy; and demanding that any council decrees (*arrêts*) rendered already on the subject, should be revoked. The procurator-general here interposing, was ordered to keep silence by M. de Beauharnais. After the council ordered the governor's secretary to retire, M. Lenoullier, a councillor, acting as procurator-general, took the paper, and read it aloud; he then protested against the insult its tenor and terms conveyed against the council as the supreme court of the colony; and by a formal declaration, justified (*motivée*) in presence of M. de Beauharnais, characterised his gubernatorial pretensions in the case to be as inconsiderate (*téméraire*) as unwonted (*nouvelles*); adding a resolution, that the council would make a complaint to the king against the present infraction of the independence and authority of Canadian tribunals by his Majesty's representative.

M. de Beauharnais, while allowing that the members of council collectively were absolute over every body in the colony, with *one* exception (namely, himself), asserted that he, in turn, was their master in all things. So saying, he left the council chamber in high dudgeon. His next step was to cause his interdict to be read at the head of companies of the colonial forces, regulars and militia; with an order appended, that no decrees of council should be received, unless sanctioned by him. The supreme council replied to this act by a counter-ordinance, of a sensible and spirited character, thus defining the limits of its own jurisdiction and the extent of the legitimate functions of the governor:—" The colonists (*les peuples*) have long known, that those who have authority from the prince to govern them have no right, in any case, to cross their path while striving to obtain legitimate ends; that on occasions where there is a diversity of sentiment among state functionaries respecting things ordained in common, the provisional execution of a measure variously viewed, belongs to the department it regards: therefore, if there be a difference of opinion, as to acts affecting the community, between the governor-general and the intendant, the views of the former are to prevail, supposing the matter in question to be one specially falling within his province as administrative chief—such as the operations of war and the regulation of military discipline: on these subjects, it is competent for him to issue ordinances, without consulting any one, but in no other case whatever. Similarly, the ordinances of the intendant are to have force, provisionally, in matters properly belonging to his office; such as law procedure, police, and finances. The parties, when dissident, (governor, intendant,) to account to the king for their several modes of action, in every case, in order that his Majesty may decide between them. Such is the nature of the government of Canada."

The members of council did not all stand by each other in the struggle against the governor's despotism; some were gained over, others intimidated by him: still the majority held out, and sent to prison those who disobeyed the legal orders they issued. The military, usually the ready instruments of arbitrary power, were called out demonstratively, when the officers poked their sword-

---

* This formal declaration of legal rights, the first and only one distinctly enunciated during the whole time of French domination, was, adds M. Garneau, justified by a regulation (*règlement*) of the year 1684, signed by the king and Colbert. It was followed by others, of similar tenor.—*B*.

points into copies of the council decrees, in contempt of their authors. Those persons arrested by order of council were released by the governor, and caressed at the castle. Learning that some officers murmured at what was going on, the governor sent them to prison. Shortly thereafter, being in Montreal, he transmitted to his lieutenant a sealed warrant (*lettre de cachet*) ordering into exile the two most active members of the council, Messrs. Gaillard and d'Artigny. By this arbitrary act he at once avenged himself, and reduced the council roll below the number required to sanction decrees. The intendant responded by an ordinance, as their president, commanding the members to remain at their post, and enjoining them to disregard the illegal order of the governor.

The secular clergy, whose pretensions the governor had maintained at the outset, sided with him, in return, in his contest with the council. The Recollets went with the chapter; the Jesuits stood neutral.—Parties being thus balanced, a decision at court could alone terminate the difficulty. The result could hardly be doubtful, as the councils of an arbitrary monarch were then directed by a prince of the Church. Cardinal Fleury recalled M. Dupuy, the prime mover in what was doubtless viewed as a parliamentary sedition; and caused an order to be sent to the supreme council to disseise the temporalities of the cathedral chapter, which had been put under provisional sequestration by the law authorities during the contest.—Before the decision of the ministry arrived, the governor forcibly prevented Messrs. Gaillard and D'Artigny from taking their seats at the council-board, and they were not allowed to resume them till the year 1629; long after the other councillors had made humble submission to the authorities.

M. de Beauharnais, however, did not pass uncensured by the minister of marine (Maurepas), under whose jurisdiction he more immediately was. He blamed him for interposing arbitrarily in the process begun against the chapter and clergy. His order for exiling the two councillors was particularly disapproved of, as being an exercise of royal power, which his Majesty would entrust to none of his representatives; and he was enjoined never to repeat such an act.—M. Dupuy, who appears to have acted throughout with all integrity as well as firmness, made no retractions, and was superseded, finally, by M. Hocquart, named royal intendant in 1731.

M. de Mornay, appointed coadjutor of the late bishop M. de St. Vallier, in 1714, was nominated to succeed the latter; but, as we have already mentioned, he had gone to France. He never returned to Canada, yet, retaining his title and authority, he confirmed three grand-vicars, elected by the chapter, who, along with the dean, governed the see in his name. He ranks, nominally, as third bishop of New France.

The cathedral clergy, becoming wanton in their unrestrained powers, treated the inmates of the nunneries with such unmanly harshness, that the Ursulines applied to the supreme council to make the wrongs they endured known to the king. M. Boulard, Coryphæus of the high clericals, threatened the Ursulines with excommunication if they dared to make confession to any priests not chosen by him. And the seven chief sisters (*les discrètes*) of the house actually were debarred from confession and communion for a time, because they owned a partiality for the Jesuit fathers. The overbearing conduct of the canons was disapproved by the court; but which royalty itself was to blame for, through having lately, most injudiciously, pampered ecclesiastical presumption by recognising the rights of church functionaries to ride rough-shod over those of the state.

The episcopal interregnum continued, practically, for a series of years. In 1733, M. Herman Dosquet superseded M. de Mornay, and became, by grace of Clement XII, fourth bishop. He came to Quebec in 1734, returned to France in 1734, and there remained, holding to his episcopal title till 1739, when he gave it up. M. Pourray de l'Auberivière, appointed by Clement XII as his successor, died about the same time as that pontiff. Arriving at Quebec in 1740, while an epidemic was raging, he caught the infection, and died before he could take up his functions. Next year, M. Dubreuil de Pontbriant was nominated to succeed him, by Benedict XIV (Lambertini). In none of the Canadian episcopal appointments or mutations does royal intervention seem to have been permitted or attempted. M. Dubreuil was the sixth and last bishop of Quebec, under the French domination

The system of perpetual curacies, to which the new bishop was opposed, was brought under the notice of count Maurepas, now chief minister of state, in 1742. M. Dubreuil wrote, that if it were thought fit to constitute irremovable parish charges, they ought not to be allowed in benefices where supplementary tithe was accorded; nor yet in parishes annexed to others *quoad sacra*. His lordship recommended, at the same time, that French priests be preferred to Canadian; that "the bishop ought to have power to appoint a vicar for any perpetual curacy, without being required to assign a reason therefor," &c. All things taken into account, he opined that there were only thirteen parishes in his diocese where perpetual curates could be installed, independent of the others where such already officiated.*

Having traced the colony's ecclesiastical affairs thus far, we return to the secular annals of New France, recommencing with the year 1728, when notes of war from the far west resounded throughout the eastern province. They were occasioned by the outbreak of a remnant of the Outagami tribe, supposed to have been rooted out in 1715, but parties of whom, resuming possession of part of the country, were forced to cede it, by M. de Louvigny, in 1717. Become wanderers in the wilderness, they lived a predatory life for some years, and, at the current time, in conjunction with some other western races, infested lake Michigan territory and the routes connecting Louisiana with Canada. M. de Beauharnais, on being advised of the murders and robberies they had lately committed, which had been the means of almost cutting off communication with the Louisianians, swore to exterminate the whole nation. But this oath was more easily taken than kept. Mostly broken savage tribes, the bands of desperate men of the wilds then afoot were not easy to overtake, so as to receive the punishment thus proclaimed to be in store for them.

A force of 450 Canadians, with M. de Ligneris at their head, was collected at Montreal to go in pursuit. The vanguard set out about June 5th. Having ascended the Ottawa in canoes, and crossed lake Nipissing, the party penetrated, by the Rivière des Français, to lake Huron. Here it was joined by 750 savages, and

---

* Documents *penes* M. l'abbé Ferland.

the main body came up. The entire army passed Michilimackinac August 1; and, that day fortnight, reached Chicago. Aug. 15, a body of the Evil Men tribe (*Malhomines*), or Wild Oats (*Folles avoines*), so named because they used a kind of wild rice growing in the savannahs to the south of lake Superior, were found, drawn up in battle array, on the lakeboard, having made common cause with the Outagamis. They were encountered and signally beaten. These were the first and last enemies the army had to deal with. Neither the Outagamis nor their allies were more anywhere to be found, although the Canadians ascended Fox river, following their track, to its sources, and within thirty leagues of the upper Mississippi; burning every horde, hut, and plantation they found in the way. This devastation had the effect, for a time, of allowing the communications, previously stopped, to be reopened.

The decade, 1729-39, was composed of calamitous years for Canada. In 1732, inundations and earthquakes damaged the settlements and affrighted the people. In 1733, small-pox was rife with the colonists, and made fearful ravages among the savages. A dearth also prevailed, in continuation of two years' previous scarcity. During winter 1729-30, many of the inhabitants were fain to use *bourgeons* for bread; or, what they then considered as little better food, potatoes! Many persons died of hunger.* It was in this famine-year (1730) that the Digué du Palais at Quebec, now obliterated to the eye by wharves, was constructed, in order to give useful employment and needful pay to starving people, by forming a river-wall, within which a hundred vessels could winter conveniently.

The year 1731 was signalised by an attempt made to reach the Pacific Ocean overland. About A. D. 1718, this project was mooted, but not carried out. Its realisation was reserved for an enthusiastic explorer, Pierre-Gauthier de Varennes, sieur de la Vérendrye, a gentleman who had trafficked much with the tribes of the west, and gained much information among them of the countries that lay beyond. As M. de Beauharnais was ambitious to give lustre to his administration by a successful expedition

---

* Letter from la mère Sainte-Hélène, in 1737, *penes* M. l'Abbé Ferland.

across the continent, Vérendrye repaired to Quebec to render advice upon the subject. He recommended that the course of the river Assiniboëls should be followed, rather than to cross the Sioux territory, as others had proposed; then to descend such streams as take their rise towards lake Winnipeg: thinking that one of them would infallibly, if followed, lead to the desired goal.

M.Vérendrye having formed a trading copartnery in 1731, with some Montreal merchants, who advanced funds to buy goods for barter, and means of equipment for his journey, set out for lake Superior with Père Messager, a missionary priest. He had received orders to take possession, in the king's name, of all countries he should discover; also to examine them attentively, in order to form an idea what facilities they might possess for establishing a route across them, to connect Canada and Louisiana with the seaboard of the Pacific. To enable him to perform this useful service, no public aid had been accorded to him, if promised; and, as a consequence, he was obliged to linger about the intermediate regions, attending to the interests of himself and partners, till the year 1733. Previously, in 1731, some of his people, starting from Kamanestigoya, a fort constructed, to the north of lake Superior, in 1717, by lieutenant Robertel de Lanoue, passed on to the lake of la Pluie, where they built fort St. Peter; then to the lake des Bois, where they erected fort St. Charles, in 1732; next followed the course of the river Winnipeg, upon a bank of which they raised, in 1734, Fort Maurepas. The adventurers took possession of the country for a double purpose: to fulfil the obligation they owed to their king, and to establish fortified posts useful to themselves for the prosecution of their private traffic. Extending their rounds, they crossed lake Dauphin, and lake des Cignes; they recognised the river des Biches, and ascended to the bifurcation of the river Saskatchaouan or Poskoïac. They constructed fort Dauphin, at the head of lake Manitoba, and fort de la Reine at its foot; also fort Bourbon on the Biches river, at the head of lake Winnipeg; lastly, fort Rouge in the angle formed by the Red and Assiniboëls rivers. They continued afterwards, directed by M. de Vérendrye's brother and sons, to advance westwardly, otherwhiles northwardly, but without attaining to the Ocean they were in quest of.* In one of these explorations, during the year 1736, a son of M. de la Vérendrye, the jesuit Père Anneau, and twenty others, were massacred by the Sioux, in an island of the lake des Bois.

In 1738, the French reached the Mandanes' country; and in 1742, attained to the upper Missouri, ascending its course as far as a river since named the Yellow Stone, which rises at the foot of the Rocky Mountains. At length, the oldest son of M. Vérendrye, and the chevalier his brother, Jan. 1, 1743, found themselves in front of that mountain range reached sixty years afterwards by the famous American travellers, Lewis and Clarke.

The journey thither of the Vérendryes lasted from April 29, 1742, till July 2, 1743; during which time they passed through the horde of the Beaux Hommes, and visited the Pioyas, the nation of the Petits-Renards, the Arc tribes, and the Serpents' nation.

M. de la Vérendrye himself, who had incurred a debt of 40,000 livres, and was no longer able to continue his explorations, repaired meanwhile to Quebec, hoping to obtain a pecuniary grant, but which was delayed, or rather practically denied; for De Maurepas professed to have received reports unfavourable to his character. Beauharnais induced him to remit his commission to M. de Noyelle, for the latter to continue the exploration. Afterwards M. de Beauharnais, and his successor M. de la Galissonnière, overcame the minister's prejudices against M. Vérendrye; and the king, as a cheap compensation, bestowed the order of St. Louis on that unworthily used servant of the state. M. de Maurepas, however, expressed a desire that M. Vérendrye should re-

---

* I have been guided, in thus fixing the sites of the above enumerated forts, to the relation of M. Pierre Margry, an official in the historical section of the ministry of marine and colonies, at Paris. His interesting article appeared in two numbers of the *Moniteur Universel*, official gazette of the French government, dated Sept. 14, and Nov. 1, 1857; his materials were derived from documents reposited in the national archives. We have also been aided, in tracing the route of the explorers, by one of the maps appended to a report by M. Cauchon, one of the Commissioners of Crown Lands, in 1857. [A compiler of that map, Mr. Thomas Devine, Quebec, had himself visited those regions, in 1836, on his return from Hudson's Bay.—*B.*]

sume his journey; and he was about to obey, when he fell ill, and died on the 6th of December, 1749.

This eminent traveller related to Mr. Kalm, a Swedish *savant*, then on a visit to Canada, that he had discovered, in one of the remotest of the countries he reached, at a spot 900 leagues beyond Montreal, some massive pillars each formed of a single block of stone, resting one against the other, or superimposed as are the courses of a wall. He concluded that, thus arranged, the pile must have been formed by human hands. One of the pillars was surmounted by a much smaller block, only one foot high and a few inches across, bearing on two sides graven characters of an unknown language. This stone was sent to Paris. Several Jesuits who saw it in Canada, said to Kalm, that the engraving it bore resembled the Tartaric characters. This opinion, in Kalm's estimation, tended to confirm the hypothesis of an Asiatic immigration to America, and the real origination of a portion at least of the native races found in possession of its two continents and islands.

The sons of Vérendrye claimed the right of continuing the explorations; but the intendant Bigot set their claims aside, by forming an association, composed of himself, the governor (Jonquière), Bréard, comptroller of marine, Le Gardeur de St. Pierre, and captain Lamarque de Marin. This society of professed explorers had chiefly their own trading profits in view, and acted accordingly. Marin was to ascend the Missouri to its source, and thence to follow the course of the first river presenting itself that seemed to flow towards the Pacific. St. Pierre, passing by the fort de la Reine, was to rejoin Marin on the Pacific seaboard in a given latitude. But accumulation of peltry being the grand object, their parties never got further than the Rocky Mountains, at the foot of which they erected Fort Jonquière, in 1752. The chief partners in the speculation, carried on at state cost, divided a large spoil; the governor's share being 300,000 francs.† Thus ended ignobly, a project nobly conceived, but made almost abortive by injustice and selfishness.

---

* Journal of Travels performed in 1742, by chevalier de la Vérendrie, in search of the Western Sea, addressed to the Marquis de Beauharnais.
† M. W. SMITH, *Hist. of Canada*.

An uneasy feeling had pervaded the public mind in Canada for some time regarding the frontier question, which no attempt had latterly been made to settle; and all being left at hazard, both by the French and British authorities, a chance collision between the colonists and the American settlers might, any day, plunge the two nations into war. In 1734, M. de Beauharnais, believing hostilities could not be long averted, wrote a despatch, in cipher, suggesting means to be taken for defence of the colony against invasion; and urging strongly that Quebec should be more strongly fortified. The minister replied that it would be of little use to do so, as Quebec could in no case be made impregnable.* In 1740, when war was imminent, the governor made forts Chambly, St. Frederic, and Niagara, as secure as possible. He laboured, at the same time, to maintain and extend existing alliances between the French and the aborigines. He held long conferences with numbers of their chiefs in 1741; at which he was assured by them, that, irrespective of their partiality for the French, the fear they had of American appropriation of the Indian territories on all sides, would oblige the dispossessed and menaced to adopt the cause of Canada. Certes, the friendship of the Indian population was not to be lightly esteemed at this time, their dispositions and numbers considered; for according to an enumeration made in 1736, among the tribes located between the Abenaquis and Mobile territory inclusive, fifteen thousand warriors could be called into action at short notice.

---

* M. Garneau appends to the above passage in his text, the following statement, which we prefer to give in the form of a note:—" In 1735, Van Rensellaer, lord (*seigneur*) of Albany, foreseeing a resumption of hostilities, visited Canada ostensibly for his own recreation, and secretly informed M. Beauharnais that during the latest war between the Canadians and New-Englanders, M. de Vaudreuil had engaged his savage allies to make no inroads against the New-Yorkers; reminded him that the latter had done the like in respect of Canada, and that they would do so still, if such immunity were reciprocated."—*B.*

BOOK EIGHTH.

CHAPTER I.

COMMERCE, INDUSTRY.

1608–1744.

Canadian trade; evil effects of war upon it.—Its rise and progress: cod fisheries.—Peltry traffic the main branch of the commerce of Canada. From an early date, fur traffic a monopoly.—Rivalry of Canadian and Anglo-American fur-traders.—Policy of governors Hunter and Burnet.—Non-intercourse laws of 1720 and 1727; their evil effects upon French colonial interests.—Various branches of Canadian industry in former times.—Canadian Exports, their nature.—Ginseng, notices of.—Mining and Minerals.—Quebec the great entrepôt.—Manufactures; salt-works.—Posting commenced, in 1745.—Admiralty court; exchange for merchants.—Negro slavery in Canada.—Money of the colony, its nature, and depreciations.

The treaty of Utrecht was followed by some of the most peaceful years Canada had ever known. The American colonists of France and Britain, wearied of an exhausting war, were able to turn their energies to internal improvement.—Despite the financial difficulties of France, which to some extent re-acted on her colonies, Canada was entering upon a steady, if slow, course of progression. Its total population, which was, in 1719, but 22,000, had risen, in 1744, to nearly 50,000 souls; and the value of the exports, which did not exceed 100,000 crowns in 1714, had risen, in 1749, to 2,650,000 francs. (RAYNAL.)

The French were probably first in the field as fishers in American waters. As we have stated in an initiatory chapter, Basque, Breton, and Norman fishermen must have there plied their calling during the earliest years of the 16th century; for one John Dennis, of Honfleur, in 1506 traced a chart of the gulf of St. Lawrence for the guidance of his compatriots. The English, when they first visited that sea region, as industrials, which was not till the year 1517, reported that they found fifty French, Spanish, and Portuguese vessels prosecuting the cod-fishery. In 1536, the French cod-fishery had greatly extended; and, in 1558, there were thirty vessels besides, employed in pursuing the whale. At that date, there were but ten English vessels frequenting the banks of Newfoundland; while there were 100 from Spain, and 50 from Portugal. But in 1615, the relative proportions had greatly altered for at this time they stood thus: English vessels 250, French and Portuguese (together) 400. The English government doubtless fostered their Newfoundland fisheries as a nursery for seamen, [and as yielding an article of ready barter; for supplies of salted fish were not so essential to a protestant as to a catholic population.]

The attention of French adventurers in America was divided, at this time, between the fisheries and the peltry traffic. These pursuits were at first commingled; for the early French fishers of the coasts of Canada and Acadia used to trade with the native seaboard tribes, deriving a double profit therefrom. By degrees, regular relations were formed between the parties; and for the convenience of both, factories were founded on or near the coasts, and these gradually extended to the interior. By and by, opulent merchants obtained from the French government trading monopolies, on condition of sending and establishing colonists. Thus it was, that New France came to be founded.

The first regular patent for a monopoly of the peltry traffic was granted to Captain Chauvin, early in the 17th century. But, for a number of years afterwards, the trade was pursued briskly without regard to Chauvin's license, especially by French fishermen. Several of the chief merchants of France, especially those of La Rochelle, engaging in the peltry traffic, resisted the monopoly which had been thus sanctioned. To prevent further disputes, and regularise the traffic, the Company of the Hundred Partners, with Cardinal Richelieu as its nominal head, was formed in 1637-8. To this association was consigned, *in perpetuity*, as a field for exclusive trade, New France and Florida. The society undertook to colonise the country, to maintain missions, &c.;* on condition of

---

* This arrangement was not found to answer, for any party; and the company gave up to the colonists, in 1645, the peltry monopoly, on condition of being relieved from the charges of the civil list, the support of an armed force, and other governmental burdens.

receiving, 1. a permanent monopoly of the trade in furs, other skins, and leather ; 2. a lease, for 15 years, of the whole colonial trade, by land and sea. But the cod and whale fisheries were still to be free to all ; and a reservation was made in favour of the colonists individually, that they might deal with the natives for peltry, provided it were sold to the company's agents at a fixed price. After an unprosperous existence of 36 years' duration, viz. in 1663, the association of 100 partners, that number then being greatly reduced, became extinct ; and royalty resumed the trust it never should have accorded to any of its subjects.

The trade of the colonists of New France did not long remain free. Untaught by experience of the withering effects of monopoly, the French government, next year (1664) sanctioned the formation of a new association, named the West India Company. The pernicious career of the present band of associators did not endure near so long as the preceding, although in them was vested the exclusive trade for forty years, not merely of all New France, but of the whole Atlantic seaboard of Africa. In America, their privileges were not only as great as those of the defunct company, but Louis XIV promised them a premium of 40 livres for every ton of merchandise they should export from France to her colonies, or *vice versa*. They were also allowed a drawback on dutiable goods, on re-exporting them to a foreign market ; and, to crown all, they were to pay no imposts that others paid, on provisions, munitions of war, or materials for constructing their ships or other vessels.

The discontent of the inhabitants was naturally great at the monstrous concessions thus accorded to their detriment. In a short time, commodities rose to a ransom price. The sovereign council interposed, and issued a tariff, fixing maximum rates : as an inevitable result, no goods were brought to market. This state of things, of course, could not last. In 1666, Colbert caused the monopolists to let go, as their predecessors had been constrained to do before the peltry traffic ; he also freed the colonists from restrictions in their trade with the mother country.*

---

* "This company was to have a right to all mines and minerals, the power of levying and recruiting soldiers in France, building forts, and the right of waging war against the Indians or the neighbouring colo-

The new company, which carried on its trade with more than 100 vessels, and enjoyed the exorbitant privileges we have detailed, did not prosper. In 1674, the year of its extinction, there was a debt accumulated of 3,523,000 livres. The whole capital was but 1,047,000 livres. As part of the company's debt was owing to the war it had to support, as lords of the colony, against the British, Louis XIV, by the advice of Colbert, bought up the Company's shares, discharged its debts, to the amount of the 3,523,000 livres; and revoked all his concessions to it.

When the now abolished company gave up the peltry traffic, it was with the reservation of that branch of it carried on at Tadoussac; also imposing on the trade, otherwise free, for the company's benefit, a subsidy of one fourth on beaver, and one tenth on orignal skins. The latter impost the government had continued, and farmed it to M. Oudiette. It ordained that all beaver-skins should be taken to his factories, and delivered at the fixed rate of four francs ten sous per lb., to be paid, not in money, but commodities; the prices put on which, of course, were virtually left to the paymaster's own discretion. — To M. Oudiette was also farmed the duties in regard to tobacco, which were fixed at 10 per cent.—This arrangement existed in full force, till 1700; at which time the Canadians, finding such exactions insupportable, petitioned the home government to remove or to modify the oppression they thereby endured.

The Oudiette peltry monopoly passed to M. Roddes, who in turn transferred it to M. Piccaud, one of the deputies from the colony; the latter paying 70,000 francs a year, and also undertaking to form an association for carrying it on, in which Canadians might

---

nies. Distinctive armorial bearings were allowed to the association, surmounted by the royal arms of France; and to encourage immigration, all colonists, present and to come, being Catholics, were to have the same rights in France as his Majesty's subjects at home. In addition to the above handsome list of privileges and immunities accorded to this favoured company, its stock or shares were made transferable; and the revenue or profits of them alone could be attached for debts owing by the holders, even to the king himself. His Majesty also agreed to advance one tenth of the whole stock, without interest, for four years, subject to a proportion of all losses which might be incurred by the company during that period." W. H. SMITH.—B.

take one or more 50-livre shares. This society took the name of the Company of Canada; and none but its members could legally participate in the peltry traffic. The seigneurs, with their renters (*censitaires*) were allowed to join in it. The Northern or Hudson's Bay Company, formed some time previously, was merged in this association; which obtained an edict rigidly prohibiting sales of beaver-skins to the New York colonists.

This company, though of a more comprehensive character than the two preceding, yet having the canker-worm of monopoly at its root, had as unprosperous an existence as, and came to a speedier end, than they. In 1706, its debts amounted to 1,812,000 francs. This sum Messrs. Aubert, Nerot, and Guyot agreeing to pay, the Company broke up in their favour.

The colonists, under the new patent, could share in the beaver traffic within the country, but could not export such furs, being bound to deliver them at the patentees' factories.

In the year 1715 appeared two memorials, on the "present state of Canada," by M. Ruette d'Auteuil,* in which the mismanagement of the colonial affairs was very freely, perhaps unprejudicedly, exposed; the writer sparing no maladministrators, not even those in highest place. [The production is interesting to us, from the fit ful glimpses of light it throws upon the inner state of the colony at the time.] Trade with the savages, once considerable, M. d'Auteuil observed, had greatly fallen off. Ship-building, he remarked, was pretty brisk; hemp for cordage, and flax for linen, thread, and tissues were advantageously grown; but he complained that France did not import Canadian timber, while the British drew much of theirs from the American plantations. The Huron copper-mines, he said, were neglected. The monopolist companies he denounced, for not fulfilling obligations solemnly contracted. For instance, they were bound, by contract, to procure an immigration of from 200 to 300 persons yearly; whereas little had been done in this matter at any time, and, since 1663, almost nothing. He now urged that a large immigration was what the colony most wanted. He mentioned that every company's defalcations, in this and other particulars, were ignored by the governors-general, who were always

---

* *Documents de Paris*, series 2.

the creatures or the relatives of the companies' directors. The French intendants, he added, were also compromised in a similar way, or else indifferent; as not meaning to stay in the colony, but only hoping to pass thence, enriched meantime, to higher situations at home. Adverting to the card-money, two million livres of which, he alleged, were in circulation in 1714, he said it was but a moiety of its nominal value; the issues not having been severally commanded by specific royal edicts. He suggested that an inquest for the verification and the regulation of the card-money should be instituted, and that a deputy to represent the inhabitants and defend their interests in this important matter should be received at Paris. Finally, he proposed that the colonial bills of exchange should be duly honoured by the royal treasury.

M. d'Auteuil, to avert administrative abuses, proposed that three state councillors should be appointed to receive complaints from aggrieved colonists; and that the governors-general should be changed at stated periods of three to six years' duration. He added, that both they and the intendants, knowing that their sins of commission or omission were not likely to be reported at court, did just as they liked; and if any of the subordinates of either let out the secrets of mal-administration, they were persecuted; while corrupt and subservient officials were rewarded or promoted.

But, after all, that sturdy exponent of the abuses of colonial administration was thus hewing at the branches, not at the root of the evil tree. The government of the mother country was no less corrupt, to begin with. While money was prodigally lavished on court favourites, the regular allowances made to those who did legitimate state work were miserably stinted, and seldom regularly paid. [Probably the stated salary of the governor-general of New France, at this time, did not exceed £250 a-year; not sixpence of which sum could remain for his own use, if he kept up the following he was expected to maintain. What recourse was there, then, for the needy nobles and gentry who were sent from Old France to *rusticate* as representatives of royalty in New France (which was a great hunting-ground, rather than a province), but to become traffickers in peltry, or exclusive sellers of brandy licenses, or pay themselves by underhand means yet more discreditable ?*]

The Western Company, formed in 1717, succeeded to the monopoly of Aubert & Co., whose lease had expired; and that association, in turn, merged in the Company of the Indies, connected with Law's Mississippi bubble. This company saved from the wreck of that projector's scheme, a trading monopoly, in Louisiana and the Illinois territory, till 1731; in which year these countries re-passed under regal sway, and so remained as long as French domination lasted therein. After fort Oswego was constructed, the peltry traffic of the colonists had a keen competition to contend with, owing to the higher prices given by British traders to the natives. To obviate this, the king was induced to take into his own hands the fortified trading posts founded by the traders at Frontenac (Kingston), Toronto, and Niagara. State funds were, at the same time, misapplied in according bounties to the dealers, to enable them to give more honest prices to the Indians, and prevent them from carrying their produce to the British settlements.†

---

* During De Frontenac's administration, "the home government began to form an opinion that the advanced posts maintained in the colony were of little real advantage, while they were the chief cause of the wars in which it became involved. It was therefore proposed that these stations should be abolished, and that the Indians should be allowed to bring their furs to Montreal. This, however, was opposed by the governor and his council, who being afraid, probably, of losing their own power and patronage, represented that such a measure would have the effect of throwing the Indian allies into the hands of the Five Nations and the British, and of sacrificing the fur-trade. The latter was then a strict monopoly, carried on under licenses granted to old officers and favorites, who sold them to the inland traders. At this time, the average price of beaver-skins, in money, at Montreal, was 2 livres 13 sous, or about 2s. 3d. stering, per pound. The Indians were, at that rate, cheated enormously ; and becoming aware of the fact through occasional intercourse with the British, made incessant complaints: and this, probably, was one great cause of their want of faith in the French." W. H. SMITH: *Canada*, &c., vol. I. p. lviii.—B.

† A miserable complication of purblind expediencies!—At this time, "the amount of trade allowed to each license, usual cost of which being 600 crowns, was merchandise valued at 1000 crowns. To carry on the trade, and to convey returns, the license-holder was bound to employ

It is difficult to form a precise estimation of the annual value of the peltry produce at this or any epoch of Canada's annals. M. d'Auteuil, in the memorials cited above, stated that the annual returns, in 1677, were worth 550,000 francs; and that they had augmented at the time he wrote (1715) to 2 million francs.* Governor Murray, consulting the ill-kept customs registers for 1754 and 1755, found the valuation returns of the former year to give a total of 1,547,885 livres; those of the latter, only 1,265,650 livres. Persons best able to form an approximative estimation of the medium value of the peltry exported from New France during years immediately before and after the Conquest, have rated it at 3,500,000 livres.†

Notwithstanding all disadvantages which French traders had to encounter, from burdens laid upon them, and the restrictions they were subjected to, they had the bulk of the peltry traffic of North America in their hands down to the year 1714; when, by the treaty of Utrecht, they had to relinquish their trade in the Hudson's Bay territory and other regions. Successive governors of New York, meanwhile and afterwards, were incessantly labouring also

---

two canoes, six men in each. The seller of the license had the right of furnishing the goods used in barter, at a price 15 per cent. higher than the market rate. A successful adventure, under such a license, generally gave to the merchants a profit of 400 per cent. on the merchandise, and 600 crowns to each of the canoe-men. The latter were not only entitled to provisions and clothing, but interested in the result of the adventure, by having a legal right to divide the surplus of the returns, after the cost of the license, merchandise, and 400 per cent. profit to the merchant, had been reimbursed." H. W. SMITH: *Canada, Past, Present, and Future,* vol. I, p. lxviii.—B.

* This almost quadrupled value in 38 years' time, if real, tends to disprove what was above asserted, that the trade of the colony with the natives had greatly increased. But perhaps depreciations in the colonial currency may have reduced the greater sum to one million intrinsically. There is also constant doubt in the mind of a transcriber as to equivalents in specie, when "crowns" are mentioned; *i. e.,* whether *gros écus* or *petits écus* are meant.—B.

† A manifest exaggeration! The author, afterwards, vol. II, p. 156, orig. edit., estimates the total value of all the exports of the colony, in the most favourable years, at 3,250,000 livres; the item of peltry figuring for two millions, which is probably quite high enough.—B.

to deprive them of the relations they had established with the western tribes. The price of European merchandise was much higher at Quebec than Boston, and at Montreal than New York. There was a considerable contraband trade maintained between Montreal and Albany; and, by such underhand means, the Canadians received large quantities of woollen tissues and other British imported goods. In one year, Canada received 900 pieces of scarlet cloth for the fur barter, besides muslins, printed calicoes, edging lace (*tavelle*), &c. The company of the Indies (meaning the Canadian monopolists) introduced, for its own account, 1,200 pieces of goods, which were derived from English holders, yet it was strictly forbidden to all other parties to import a single yard! Thus were manufacturers and exporters of France excluded from her greatest colonial dependency.

As we have already seen, Mr. Burnet, when governor of New York (he was afterwards removed to Massachusetts), in 1720 obtained from Assembly a non-intercourse bill to prevent the Canadian traders, during three years, from exchanging their peltry at Albany for European commodities. In 1727, this prohibitory law became permanent. It gave a heavy blow to the Canadian traders, both as buyers and sellers. Linen cloths, which previously fetched at Montreal 15 louis per piece, were sold, soon afterwards, as high as 25 louis.

Fort Oswego, which was erected by Burnet, as we have related elsewhere, was the necessary complement of his non-intercourse policy; a policy ineffectually combated by making the factories of Frontenac, Toronto, and Niagara, royal castles, and according state premiums to quicken traffic, so as to encourage exports from the colony to France, and obtain French goods in return.

In retaliation for the renewed law of 1727, passed by the New York legislature, Louis XIV issued an edict forbidding all commerce with the British colonies, under penalties. Thenceforward, the holders of the French trading-posts had the whole traffic in peltry to themselves: the possesors held them, either by favour, or they bought their privileges, or held them on farm; but in all of these cases, the malign effect upon the public interests was the same. The factories' licences were usually granted for three years; and those who held them, by means fair or foul, strained every nerve to make the most they could out of them during that term. To sell at the most exorbitant rates, and put prices unconscientiously low on the furs offered, was the rule. To beguile the Indians to accept insufficient values in exchange, it was not unusual to ply them with liquor. [It is related that, in 1754, at a western post, on one occasion beaver-skins were bought for four grains of pepper each; and that as much as 800 francs were realized by selling a pound of vermilion, probably dealt out in pinches.]

Peltry was the main article of export from Canada, and hence it is that we have dilated upon that part of its produce. Exports of lumber there seem to have been little or none, till a late date; owing partly, as intimated by M. d'Autcuil in 1715, to the indifference of the home authorities to the abundance and value of Canadian forest produce. "One knows not," says Raynal, "by what fatality such a source of riches was overlooked." The exports of fish from Canada itself were inconsiderable in early times. In 1697, the Sieur de Rêverin formed a factory, and established a fishery at the harbour of Mont Louis, about half way between Quebec and the extremity of the gulf of St. Lawrence, on the southern side. At the commencement the people of the settlement were much disturbed by the English; but their exertions, in both fishing and agriculture, were tolerably successful.* The cod and whale

---

* W. H. SMITH, *Canada, &c.*, vol. I, p. lix.—We never heard of inshore fishings doing much for any country except supplying the people living near the seaboard with a portion of their daily food, and that, not seldom, scantily, or at a dear rate. Bounties to fishermen only serve to make those lazier and more exacting, who were lazy and exacting before. The late prince Talleyrand, who made an extensive and long-continued tour in the United States and Canada when an exile, particularly noted the inertness of the class, upon this continent, and thus delivered himself upon the subject: "The American fisherman has a mind as careless of country as the lumberman. The affections of both, their interests, their strain of life, are things apart from the nation to which they nominally belong. It would be a prejudice for us to think that our American fisherman is a most useful member of society; for he is not a like being with our European industrials of the same name, who, robust in body and alert in mind, make our best sailors. Frequenters of, say two leagues of seaboard, in fine weather, confining their venturings to the range of a mile of it when the weather is uncertain, such is the range within which their venturesomeness is limited. The daily habits of such

fisheries in American waters were almost entirely in European hands; but to the Canadians were left seal and porpoise catching. This industry was plied in the river * and gulf of St. Lawrence, also on the coast of Labrador; tracts of shore in both regions being let on farm for terms of years by the government.†

There were 14 fishing-stations, below Quebec, existing in 1722. In latter years, a tolerable quantity of animal oil and salt fish was exported to France.

Ship-building was never much carried on; although M. de Maurepas, then minister of marine, in 1731 strongly urged on the governor-general to stimulate this branch of industry, promising that if some good merchant-vessels were turned out, a contract would be accorded to the colony for constructing ships of war; perhaps his Majesty would even locate a naval yard at Quebec. Meantime he granted a premium of 500 francs for every vessel gauging 200 tons or over, of colonial build, and sold in France or the Antilles; and 150 francs premium for each barge of 30 to 60 tons, if similarly disposed of. In 1732, ten vessels of 40 to 100 tons were

---

a man are those of an idler, who would not stir at all but for the impulse of his animal appetites. His arm is not the harpoon, but the fishing-line : hence, his contests with prey is not that of manly exertion, but of petty guiles. Fishermen's most laborious action is an occasional pull at an oar or a paddle, which more usually is left dangling at the side of a crazy boat. They have no home, worthy the name, on shore ; there is little sacrifice to make in shifting from one shore to another ; a few cod-fish, more or less, determines their choice of country. When some writers have spoken of the American fisheries as a species of colonial agriculture, they have enounced a delusive plausibility, not a verity in any sense. All the personal virtues, and every patriotic feeling which distinguishes rural colonists, are absent in the chill bosom of American fishermen." *Essai sur les Avantages à retirer des Colonies Nouvelles, &c., par le citoyen* C. M. TALLEYRAND. Paper (one of a series) read at the Institut of France, in 1801-2.—B.

† When the estuary of a great river becomes much frequented by vessels, but especially by *steamers*, the seal bids a long and last adieu to it. We have had occasion to remark this, personally, in our native country. It is doubtless applicable, the observation, more or less, to the shores of the Laurentian lower waters and gulf.—B.

‡ The Esquimaux Bay was farmed in 1749, to a Madame Fournel; and Labrador to M. d'Ailleboust, in 1753.

built in Canada; but the materials were badly chosen, ill seasoned, and the price charged for them higher than those built in the British settlements: in fact, a number of the vessels used in the trade of Canada, were bought of the New Englanders.

[The surplus of provisions for export must have been insignificant, if not null; although it is asserted, that "in good years, 80,000 minots of flour and biscuits" were disposable, after supplying the colony's wants.]

Iron-smelting, on a scale worth notice, was not begun until about 1737; when the foundries, still extant, at Trois Rivières, were brought into activity by a company. Veins of copper, near the shores of lake Superior, were known to the aborigines; even when Cartier visited that region, some of them showed him samples of the ore. In 1738, Louis XIV caused mining to be tried at Chagouamigon by two Germans; but it was soon given up.

An over-famed plant, Ginseng,* discovered in our forests, in 1716, by the Jesuit Lafitan, became a means of enriching the colony, for a time, by its exportation to China. A pound weight of it, worth 2 francs at Quebec, sold at Canton for 25 francs. Its price ultimately rose to 80 francs per pound. One year, there was sent thither, ginseng yielding a return of 500,000 francs. The high price it attained set every body at work to find it. The plant was not in proper condition till August or September; but with purblind avidity, the seekers gathered it as early as May. The fresh plants ought to have been slowly dried in the shade; the gatherers, anxious to get returns, dried them in ovens. They then became worthless in Chinese estimation; and the trade in it ceased almost as suddenly as it began.

Quebec was the entrepôt of Canada. Its merchants and shippers sent out, annually, five or six barques to the seal fisheries; and about as many, laden with flour, biscuit, vegetables, staves, and lumber, to Louisbourg and the Antilles; returning with cargoes of pit-coal, coffee, sugar, rum, and molasses. The trade with

---

* In spite of all that has been written on the supposed virtues of its root, botanists believe the ginseng plant to be nothing more than the *Panax quinquefolium*, found in China and North America, where no such qualities as those ascribed to it by the Chinese are recognized. *Nat. Cycl.*
—B.

France employed about thirty vessels, of good aggregate tonnage. Almost all these vessels belonged to the shippers of La Rochelle, and traded thence.

The author of "Considerations on the State of Canada during the War of 1755,"* estimated the value of the exports at 2½ millions; and that of the imports at 8 millions. The superior amount of the latter was owing, chiefly, to the provisions, munitions of war, &c., supplied during years of hostilities at the cost of the mother country, much of which were wasted, and more embezzled. The imports, for private account, included wines and other liquors, groceries, iron-wares, pottery, articles of clothing and personal adornment, with a multitude of small luxuries.†

Importing to Canada, in those times, was not so gainful as it might at first sight appear; for, although only a part of what was needful, really or pretendedly, for the royal service, was supplied direct from France, the rest was purchased at Quebec or Montreal. Instead of competition by public contract, the charge of supplying what was wanted always fell, by secret confederacy with the higher functionaries, civil and military, into the hands of a furnishing association, known publicly by the too respectable name of the "grand company"; which was found, as if by magic, provided in advance with all that could be asked for; and as the associators bought largely in favorable markets, while they obtained themselves a discount of 15 to 20 per cent., they afterwards, having in most cases bought up all that private dealers could supply, were

---

* Collection of documents, possessed by the Literary and Historical Society of Quebec.

† M. Garneau says, that, "luxury (outward show?) was ever great in Canada, compared with the extent of its riches." And Père Charlevoix, writing of Quebec, in 1720-1, remarks, "Society here, composed mostly of military officers, and noblesse, is extremely agreeable; nowhere is the French language spoken in greater purity. But under a gay exterior is concealed a very general poverty. The residents, while they admit that their English neighbours love to accumulate wealth, console themselves by reflecting that the possessors are quite ignorant how best to enjoy it. They (the Canadians), on the contrary, understand thoroughly the most elegant and agreeable modes of spending money, but at the same time *are greatly at a loss how to obtain it.*"—B.

enabled to re-sell to his Majesty's agents the articles required, at 25 to 80, even 150 per cent. profit.

Manufactures of woven stuffs made but slow progress in New France, the policy of the governments both of France and Britain discountenancing all attempts of their American colonists to fabricate any stuffs or wares for themselves which the mother countries could supply. M. Talon broke through this system to some extent. He stimulated the culture of hemp to supply cordage. And, by him, some parties must have been set at work to make the colony self-dependent for homespun stuffs at least; as, in 1671, he wrote to Colbert, that he had caused drugget, coarse camlet (*bouracan*), bolting-cloth (*etamine*), serge, woollen cloth, and leather, to be manufactured in Canada; adding, "I have, of Canadian make, wherewithal to clothe myself from head to foot." In 1705, Madame de Repentigny span cotton thread, some English prisoners having instructed her; but no extension could be given at that time to any species of manufacture, as prohibition against it then ran very strong. In 1716, however, some relaxation was permitted, by royal order, to give temporary employment to the poor. This permission was immediately turned to account. Looms were set up for weaving woollen and other stuffs in every house, and even in the mansions of the seigneurs. Since that epoch, our rural populations have had abundance of vesture made by themselves, suited for all seasons.

About 1746, in war-time, salt being scarce, M. Perthuis was charged to erect salt-works at Kamouraska; but after having served their turn, they were abandoned. In earlier times, salt was made in Canada, but where or to what extent seems to be unknown.

In 1721, a kind of admiralty tribunal was annexed to the customs department at Quebec. Its judgments were based on the royal ordinance of 1681, and "the Code Michaux." In the same year, an ordinance warranted the opening of a merchant's exchange (*bourse*) at Quebec, and another at Montreal.

In 1721, posting began for the first time. Intendant Bégon granted to M. Lanouiller a monopoly of the posts for twenty years, between Quebec and Montreal. The carriage of letters was to be charged, by a table of fixed rates, according to distance.

In 1689, it was proposed to introduce negroes to the colony.

The French ministry thought the climate unsuitable for such an immigration, and the project was given up. Thus did Canada happily escape the terrible curse of negro slavery.*

As we have already said, Quebec was the Canadian entrepôt; and the merchants' stores were all in the lower town. The usual time of sending freights from France was late in April, or early in May. As soon as they arrived at Quebec, dealers repaired thither to make their purchases. Portions of the goods were put into barges, and sent forthwith towards Trois-Rivières and Montreal, where the chief Quebec houses had agencies. A premium was allowed on payments in peltry. The country people came, twice a

---

* By a stipulation in the treaty of Montreal, the colonists were to be "allowed to retain their slaves," a proof that such human chattels existed; and enslaved blacks were to be found here and there in Canada till the present century. Sir L. H. Lafontaine last year (1859) investigated this matter; and from the published report of his inquiries, it appears that in 1799-1800, "the citizens of Montreal presented requisitions to Parliament, tending to cause the legislature to vindicate the rights of masters over their slaves. The applicants invoked in favour of their demand an ordinance rendered by Jacques Raudot, 9th intendant, dated April 13, 1709, which edict was, they urged, in force when the definitive treaty of peace was signed, and, by consequence, formed part and parcel of the laws, usages, and customs of Canada, recognised by the Act of Quebec. Three bills, on the subject, were introduced, in 1800, 1801, and 1803; but none of them passed. Since that time," says Sir L. H., " no local legislation sanctioned this matter; and, if the act of the Imperial Parliament of 1797 had the effect of abolishing slavery in the British *plantations*, these would of course include Canada." But the act in question, 37 Geo. III, c. 119, did and could have no such effect. It only enacted, that negroes could not be taken in execution as chattles for the debts of their masters, as had previously been the case, in His Majesty's American colonies.

That the " domestic institution," as the Americans call black slavery, was legally recognised in Canada is plain, from an ordinance of intendant Hocquart, dated 1736, regulating the manner of emancipating slaves in Canada. At the conquest, as M. Garneau owns, there were a few slaves in the Province; but adds, that slavery " then increased for an instant, only to disappear for ever." The fact is, that if the British Act of emancipation passed in 1833 [7 W. 4, c. 79] set no slaves free, this was due solely to the accident that they had ceased to be profitable to keep.—*B*.

year, to the towns to supply their wants. For many years, so obstructed or tardy were the communications between Quebec and Montreal, that imported commodities were 50 per cent. dearer at the latter than the former city.

With the exception of wine and brandies, upon which already a duty of ten per cent. was paid, and Brazil tobacco, taxed 5 sous per lb., no other article was dutiable in Canada till 1753; when most other merchandise, imported or exported, was taxed 3 per cent. But exceptions were made, even then, in favour of certain produce, to encourage industry and trade. Restrictions on Canadian commerce, under French domination, chiefly tended to exclude foreign competition.

After 1753, rum (*guildive*) was taxed 34 livres a tun (*barrique*)? wine ten livres, brandy 24 livres a keg (*velt*). Dry goods were variously taxed, probably *ad valorem*.

The customs produced, ordinarily, nearly 300,000 livres a year. No system of bonding existed; which was a great detriment to both importers and buyers, the former having to pay customs and duties on arrival of the commodities.

Coined money was scarce at all times in the colony. The poor expedient of varying its nominal value, of course always failed to keep it in the country, from which it was continually passing, as it produced little, and exported nothing, in early times. In 1670, the Company of the Indies were permitted to coin small silver money to the amount of 100,000 livres. In two years' time, this specie, intended at first for the French Antilles, had currency in all parts of New France, and was rated at 25 per cent. above its intrinsic worth. This heighting did not keep it long in circulation, or it gradually took wing, as other specie had done before, and never returned. The colonial government then began its issues (in 1685) of paper money, to pay the troops and defray other state expenses. This paper (a kind of exchequer-bills, but not paying interest) was preferred for a time to such coin as was then to be had; but the royal revenues in France, (anticipated for several years by the cost of the "glories" of Louis XIV,) and the drafts drawn on the colony not being always duly honoured at the treasury in Paris, the colonial paper-money fell into such discredit that the holders offered to exchange it against half its no-

minal value in specie. As we have already seen, Chevalier de
Vaudreuil made an arrangment with the Regency, by which 3-8ths
of real value instead of 2-4ths (the amount asked) were secured
to the holders of the colonial paper.*

The colonists having suffered this pocket depletion in return for
their confidence in courtly promises-to-pay, parted with no more
of their money's-worth but for specie, which passed from hand to
hand at its value as uncoined bullion; this, of course, was an in-
convenient but not ruinous system. It did not last long, however; for specie gradually becoming scarcer than before, doubtless from the like causes, card-money, abolished in 1717, was again
had recourse to. The cards bore the royal arms of France, and
were signed by the governor-general, the intendant, and the controller. They were of 1, 3, 6, 12, and 24 livres; of 7, 10, and
15 sous; some, as low as 6 deniers (three farthings each).† The
total issue was four million livres, or about £200,000 sterling.
"When this amount," says Raynal, "became insufficient for the
public wants, the intendant was permitted to discharge state obligations with transferable bills, signed by himself only, and without limit as to the quantity. The nominal values of these ranged
between 1 and 100 livres. These circulated in the colony every
year till October came. Then they were converted into bills of
exchange, to be cashed at the treasury in Paris. But the quantity
so accumulated, that, in 1743, the French finances being embarrassed, their redemption had to be deferred. An unfortunate war,
which broke out two years afterwards, greatly added to the amount
of undischarged bills, while it lowered the exchangeable value of all.
Commodities rose to a ransom price for those who could pay only
in currency. As war expenditure had to be maintained in the
colony, the amount of paper issues had become astounding, by the
year 1759, when the finance minister declined to pay any more of
the colonial bills of exchange till their origin and proper value

---

* This was, in commercial parlance, "a composition of 7s. 6d. in the
pound;" a state bankruptcy, in short.—B.

† This is not the smallest French paper-money ever known. The
translator has, among his numismatic *curiosæ*, four 1-*centime pieces card-
money*, received in pontage change for a sou; but such have only a local
circulation.—B.

Vol. II.—G

could be ascertained and tested." Raynal adds, that " the yearly
expenses of the French government, on Canadian account, which
reached 400,000 francs in 1729, and before 1749 never exceeded
1,700,000 livres, knew no bounds after that epoch."

During the latter years of French domination, there was great
confusion in the monetary circulation of Canada. For a time the
card-money was preferred to the intendant's notes, as being most
readily exchangeable; by and by the credit, or rather discredit,
of both, was equal. Generally, purchasers who paid in specie
had a discount of 16 to 20 per cent.: and the discrepancy in the
relative worth of coin and paper would have been greater, but for
the loss of specie when transmitted to a distance, through wrecks,
capture, or other mischances.

[To dilate further* on the commercial relations, internal or external, of a country thus almost destitute of a reliable circulating
medium, would be merely to string empty phrases together. When
nations, or dependencies that they cannot properly maintain, are
sinking into insolvency, with its attendant unbridled corruption of
their administrators, the first are on the brink of a revolution, the
second ready to fall into the hands of a new suzerain. The loss of
New France was the harbinger of successive overturnings in the
mother country, the latest of which we have seen, but the last
of which no man can safely predict.]

---

* Several of the author's speculations on the subject, but none of his
facts, have been suppressed or abbreviated. It is right to add, that for
the above *sommation* of all, he is not answerable.—*B.*

CHAPTER II.

LOUISBOURG.

1744–1748.

Coalitions of European powers for and against the empress Maria-Theresa, which eventuate in a war between France and Britain.—First hostilities in America.—Cape Breton; Louisbourg, and its defensive works.—Expedition of Duvivier to Canso, &c.—Governor Shirley proposes to attack Louisbourg.—His plans disapproved of by the council, but welcomed by the people of New England, and adopted.—Colonel Pepperel and admiral Warren, with land and sea forces, invest the place.—Mutiny in the garrison.—Mr. Vaughan makes a bold and successful night assault, and detroys garrison stores.—Capitulation of Louisbourg; the settlers taken to France.—Project for invading Canada.—The duke d'Anville's expedition, and the work cut out for it to perform.—Of the disasters which attended it from first to last; the duke dies of chagrin, and his successor in command kills himself.—M. de Ramsay menaces Annapolis.—Part of his men attack and defeat colonel Noble and a corps of New-Englanders, at Grand-Pré-aux-Mines.—The American frontiers invaded in many places, and the country ravaged.—Sea-fight near Cape Finisterre, and another at Belle-Isle; the French defeated in both.—Count de la Galissonière appointed interim governor of New France; the previous nominee, M. Jonquière, being a prisoner in England.—Troubles with the Miâmis.—Treaty of Aix-la-Chapelle, and its conditions.—Concluding reflections on the past war.

France and Britain were now on the eve of war,* chiefly for the good pleasure of the German king of the latter, as the chief of a petty continental principality, who set about trimming what was called the "balance of power in Europe." This had been deranged, it appeared, by the part which the French king had taken against the Empress Theresa, when a coalition was formed against her, by Prussia, Bavaria, Saxony, &c. in Germany, with Spain and Sardinia. In January 1745, a treaty of alliance was signed

---

* The editor is responsible for much of this abridged chapter also; having called in other authorities, British and American, as well as M. Garneau's, to illustrate the subject.—*B.*

between the Empress (already at war with the French), the king of Great Britain, the king of Poland, the elector of Saxony, and the United States of Holland, against France.

As on former occasions, the colonial dependencies of the two great nations had perforce to go to war also, whether they understood the points in dispute which led to hostilities between their mother countries or not. There was also a "balance of power" between New France and New England, getting more and more difficult every year satisfactorily to adjust. Canada, however, like the snorting war-horse, seemed to scent the coming hostilities while yet distant; for her administrators had already repaired and munitioned all the frontier posts, especially Fort St. Frederic, and Fort Niagara. The defensive works of Quebec, also, were augmented. Other demonstrations were made, about the same time, by the Canadian Government and its colonists, which showed that a continued state of peace with the British plantations was neither expected nor desired.

After the belligerents were in full tilt in Europe, for the king of Britain and his favourite son* were battling, not with much honour to either, on that eternal fighting-ground, Flanders, there was no appearance, for a time, of either government sending any expedition against the North American dependencies of the other. France had a number of redoubtable European foes to contend with; and parts of the British regular army were wanted, during this and the following year, to repress the second and last Jacobite rebellion. The natural result was, that, during its early stages, the war in America between the two rival races was carried on, almost entirely, without European aid.

In a few months after the declaration of war, the American waters swarmed with French privateers. Several were equipped at Louisbourg, Cape Breton, with amazing dispatch, and made a great number of prizes, before vessels of war could arrive to protect the British colonial shipping. Louisbourg became, in all respects, a kind of hornet's nest in regard of New England, its trade, and fisheries, which it was now determined to dig out if possible.

---

* William Duke of Cumberland, defeated at Fontenoy, May 11, 1745.

Meanwhile, M. Duquesnel, governor of Cape Breton, embarked part of the garrison of Louisbourg with some militia, and made a descent upon the settlement of Canso, in Acadia, which he burnt, and made the garrison and settlers prisoners of war. He then summoned Annapolis, but was deterred from investing it by the arrival of a reinforcement from Massachusetts. Duquesnel returned to Louisbourg, where he died shortly thereafter. Governor Shirley had for some time conceived the project of taking possession of Cape Breton; now rightly regarded as the seaward bulwark of Canada, and a highly important post as a safeguard to the French fisheries and to American trade. The fortifications of Louisbourg, the capital, even in their uncompleted state, had taken 25 years to construct, at a cost, it was reported, of 30 million livres (nearly £1,500,000 sterling). They comprised a stone rampart nearly 40 feet high, with embrazures for 148 cannon, had several bastions, and strong outworks; and on the land side, was a fosse fully four-score feet broad. The garrison, as reported afterwards by the French, was composed of 600 regulars, and 800 armed inhabitants, commanded by M. Duchambois. Upon the same authority we may mention here, that at this time there were not more than 1000 soldiers in garrison, altogether, from the lower St. Lawrence to the eastern shore of lake Erie.

Governor Shirley lost no time in applying for aid to carry out the plan above-mentioned to the British admiralty, and obtained a promise that Sir Peter Warren would be sent out with some ships of war to co-operate with a colonial land-force, if a sufficient amount of support could be raised. Having received this assurance, Shirley proceeded to unfold his conceptions to the members of the general court, first enjoining them to keep the matter secret. After one or more deliberations on the subject, a majority of the court refused to concur in the project, as thinking it both costly and hazardous. The plan got wind, however, and was enthusiastically welcomed by the colonists generally: in a word, " the pressure from without" constrained the council of Massachusetts to give into the views of the governor. In a few weeks an army of 4,000 militia, levied in Massachusetts, New Hampshire, Maine, and Connecticut, were ready for action, under the guidance of a New England merchant, named Pepperel.

About the last day of March, the expedition sailed from Boston, and arrived at Canso on the 5th of April, 1745; when Colonel Pepperel having sent some shallops to ascertain whether the coast was clear of ice, and the report being favourable, the expedition resumed its voyage, and a disembarkation on Cape Breton island was begun at Chapeau Rouge, on the 27th of April. The garrison was, through the promptitude of the invaders, taken completely by surprise. The descent could not have been effected much earlier with safety; for till the end of March, or beginning of April, the ocean in that region is covered with thick fogs, while both the seaboard and the harbours of Cape Breton are choked with thick-ribbed ice.

By this time admiral Warren arrived with a few ships, and more were expected.—His seamen assisted during fourteen days in dragging a siege-train of ordnance, through marshy ground, to the neighbourhood of Louisbourg, which was thought at first to be too strongly defended, on the seaward side, to be confronted by the fleet. Meanwhile, the garrison was in a state of revolt, having demurred to being employed to put the works into a proper state, a duty which had been too long postponed. The men had other grievances besides, being ill paid and otherwise badly treated; but their feelings of military honour being appealed to, they resumed their arms and prepared to defend the place.

During the night of May 13, Mr. Vaughan, son of the lieutenant-governor of New Hampshire, who knew the localities well, having visited the place the year before, landed with 400 men, marched to the north-east part of the bay, and fired some buildings filled with brandy, &c., and naval stores. A party in a neighbouring fort, thinking probably that the incendiaries were the van of a large attacking corps, quitted their post, and took refuge in the town. Next morning, Vaughan was able to surprise a battery, and hold possession of it until the arrival of a reinforcement.

A great mischance for the French now hastened the fall of the place. *La Vigilante*, a ship of 64 guns, with 560 soldiers and supplies for the garrison on board, was captured by admiral Warren. Had this succour reached its destination, it is very doubtful whether Pepperel could have captured the strongest fortress in America, and which was reported to be impregnable.—The next operation was not so favourable to the besiegers; who having tried, with 400 men, to carry a battery on the island of St. John, which protected the entry of the harbour, were driven off, leaving sixty dead, and 116 of their men, wounded or whole, in the hands of the French. But this gleam of success only delayed the certain capture of the place, now that all hope of further succour from without was gone, and its defenders were as discouraged as they were malcontent before. In a word, Duchambon capitulated, and was allowed to march out with the honours of war. In terms of the capitulation, the garrison, and about 2,000 people, the entire population of Louisbourg, were embarked in British transports, and landed at Brest.

Great was the exultation, naturally enough at the success of this expedition thus admirably planned and spiritedly executed. Messrs Shirley and Pepperel were rewarded with baronetcies; and the British parliament voted a sum of money to repay the cost incurred by the colonists in getting up the enterprise.—The discouragement in New France for the loss of Cape Breton, was commensurate with the elation at its capture, in New England and the other Anglo-American provinces. There was really a reasonable cause for alarm in Canada as to what might follow; for Shirley incontinently applied to the British Government for a corps of regulars and a fleet, to conjoin with the provincials in essaying the conquest of New France. The time was not propitious, however, for his aspirations to be attended to. Besides having a continental war on hand, the British metropolis itself had been for a moment put in peril by the Highland army of Prince Charles Edward, and the English people were not recovered from the panic occasioned thereby.*

Unaware of these circumstances, the Canadians were led to

---

* M. Garneau gives an account of an intended invasion, on a large scale, concocted between governor Shirley, Sir Peter Warren, and the Duke of Newcastle, for invading New France in 1745-6. That his blundering Grace, who was far more accustomed to make promises than to keep them, did pledge himself to do something of the sort, without consulting his royal master or any body else, is possible enough; but we may safely assume, that, as nothing came of it, no project of the kind was seriously entertained at the time by the collective ministry of Britain.—B.

believe that the capture of Louisbourg was but the prelude to an immediate attack on Quebec; and the governor-general profited by the apprehensions of the inhabitants of that city to levy rates for strengthening and extending its fortifications; accordingly, an additional tax on liquors was imposed for that purpose.— Other defensive preparations were also entered upon, and M. de Beauharnais called a conference, at Montreal, with 600 savages of various tribes, including some Iroquois: all those promised support in case of war. A body of them, along with a corps of western militia, were sent thereafter to Quebec, as a reinforcement to the garrison.

M. de Beauharnais now wrote to the ministry, to urge the recapture of Cape Breton and the conquest of Acadia, declaring that a corps of 2,500 men would suffice for the latter purpose. He opined that these two colonies ought to be regained, at whatever cost; as, when in French hands, they sentinelled the entry of the Gulf of St. Lawrence; whereas, in British possession, they virtually closed it. He added, "Send me arms and munitions of war; I can trust to the valour of the Canadians and the savages. The preservation of Canada is the great object: if once the enemy master that province, all France may bid a last adieu to the North American continent."

The representations of the governor-general were listened to this time. An expedition, on a respectable scale, was got up, the destination of which was kept secret. A court-appointed nobleman,* of high rank and no experience, was appointed to command the fleet. Seven of these were ships of the line, with three frigates, two fire-ships, &c., and transports having 400 soldiers on board, under the orders of M. Pomeril, major-general (*maréchal de camp*); which were to be joined, on arrival, by 600 Canadians and as many hundreds of savages. The plan of operations to be effected was,—first to re-take and dismantle Louisbourg, capture Annapolis and leave a French garrison in it, then destroy Boston, ravage the whole Atlantic seaboard of the Anglo-American plan-

---

* M. de la Rochefoucauld, duc d'Anville, called "young" by Guérin, was born in the first or second year of the 18th century, and was consequently in the prime of manhood when he died. *Dict. des Dates..—B.*

tations, and harass the British islands in the West Indies. The roads of Chibouctou were appointed to rendezvous in.

All was ready early in May, 1746; but the fleet did not get a fair start till the 22nd of June, on which day it left Rochefort. The time of passage, estimated at six weeks, through the unskilfulness of D'Anville exceeded three months. Scarcely was the fleet in view of port, when a furious tempest arose and scattered its parts. Several vessels took shelter among the Antilles; others in France ;* some transports were lost on the Isle de Sable, and the rest, storm-beaten for ten days, had much ado to reach the place of rendezvous, when a deadly epidemic broke out aboard, which carried off the soldiers and marines by hundreds, even after they were put ashore; the malady also infecting their Abenaquis allies, a third of whom perished. M. de Conflans, with three ships of the line and a frigate, had previously repaired to Chibouctou, by appointment; but finding no fleet there, after cruising for a while he returned to France. At this time, the British admiral Townshend, with a fleet, was stationed at Cape-Breton. Had he been aware of the presence and the condition of the French squadron, the probability was that it would have been annihilated; for, out of 2,400 of its men, 1,100 died at Chibouctou; and out of 200 sick sent to Europe, in hope of their recovery, but one survived the passage!

The French commanders, having learned that a British fleet was so near, held two councils of war, to determine what course

---

* M. Bibaud's account of this ill-starred expedition, and its early experiences, differs, in some important points, from that of M. Garneau; *ex. gr.*—" The fleet was under the orders of M. d'Anville, a sea-officer in whose courage and skill great reliance was placed. There were 11 ships of the line, 30 vessels carrying from 10 to 30 guns each, with transports bearing 3,000 men. This fleet was to be reinforced by four vessels from the Antilles, under M. de Conflans; and it was arranged that the expedition should be joined by the Acadians, with '1,700 Canadians and savages. Hardly had the fleet left the coasts of France, than it was assailed by a tempest, which scattered the vessels; insomuch that but a small number of them, including the admiral's ship, had arrived at Chedabouctou by 12th September." There is no mention here, it will be observed, of the unlikely fact, that any of the vessels were driven back *quite* to France.—*B.*

ought to be pursued; about which great differences of opinion arose. The duke d'Anville, whose haughty spirit broke under the pressure of his ill fortune, died almost suddenly. M. d'Estournelle, upon whom the chief command devolved, and who had proposed to give up the enterprise, committed suicide. It was determined, by a majority of votes, to persevere, and besiege Annapolis; but, being on the way thither, another tempest overtook the war-ships, then reduced to four sail, near Cape-Sable; and it is to be presumed much crippled them, for they finally made the best of their way to France.

Meanwhile, the 600 Canadians already spoken of, who left Quebec in seven vessels, for Acadia, led by M. Ramsay, disembarked at Beaubassin, in the Bay of Fundy. They were heartily welcomed by the Acadians of French race, who all hated their British masters. After awaiting in vain the arrival of the expedition his corps was to reinforce, he was about to return to Quebec, by order of the governor, who then expected that city to be attacked, when an envoy from the duke d'Auville, who had at last arrived, reached him when midway to Quebec, when he forthwith returned, with 400 of his men, and invested Port-Royal (Annapolis), though its garrison was from 600 to 700 strong. One hundred of that number had fallen into his hands, when news reached him of the second dispersion of the French fleet, which induced him to retreat to Beaubassin, intending to take up his winter quarters there.

Governor Shirley, of Massachusetts, upon learning that Ramsay's corps was so near Annapolis, and fearing that the French Acadians would join him in arms, sent to governor Mascarene to take measures to dislodge him. The latter asked for 1,000 men, to effect that end. Five hundred militia, under colonel Noble, were sent, who took up winter quarters at Grand-Pré, in Les Mines, facing Ramsay's quarters, with the bay waters between; intending to move against the Canadians in early spring. But before Noble could take the field, Ramsay sent a body of 300 Canadians and savages, under M. de Villiers, early in February 1747, around the head of the bay, a circuit of sixty leagues of snow and forest, to surprise the New-Englanders in their winter camp. On the morning of February 11, they arrived; and an obstinate battle began, which lasted till 3 p.m. when, Noble being killed, and nearly half of his men killed or wounded, the rest took refuge in a blockhouse, but were soon obliged to surrender on terms.

Beginning with the autumn of 1745, the frontiers of the British plantations themselves were cruelly ravaged in twenty-seven successive raids of the Canadians during three years. Fort Massachusetts, 15 miles above fort St. Frederic, surrendered to M. Rigaud; who, with 700 colonists and savages, devastated the country for fifty miles beyond. M. Corne de St. Luc attacked fort Clinton, and signally defeated an American corps. Saratoga was taken, and its people massacred. Fort Bridgman was taken by De Lery. In a word, the frontier line, from Boston to Albany, being no longer tenable, the inhabitants fled into the interior, and left their lands at the discretion of the enemy.

In Europe, during three years, the war against Britain was not carried on with so much success by the French. Two squadrons equipped, one at Brest, the other at Rochefort, early in 1747, for conveying transports and merchant ships bound for the dependencies of France in America and the East Indies, were, after their junction, encountered by a powerful British fleet, under admirals Anson and Warren, off Cape Finisterre, on the 3rd of May, and a great loss incurred. Six French men-of-war (all that there were present), with four armed Indiamen, were taken; besides other vessels, richly laden with specie, merchandise, and warlike stores.* The marquis de la Jonquière was amongst the prisoners taken by the British on this occasion.

In autumn of the same year (Oct. 14), commodore De l'Etendrière Desherbiers, in command of a convoy of eight men-of-war and two frigates, charged to protect a French merchant fleet on its way to the Antilles, was encountered, when off Belle Isle, by the fleet of Sir Edward Hawke, who had fourteen sail of the line, and five smaller vessels, under his orders. The battle which ensued resulted

---

* M. Garneau says, that "there were led to London 22 waggons loaded with ingots of gold and silver, and other precious effects taken from the fleet, the defeat of which deprived New France of potent succour." The precious metal then taken was freighted to India, (not Canada); the 22-waggon procession, mistakenly adverted to, took place in June 1744, being the rich freight of a Spanish galleon taken by Anson.—B.

in the capture of six of the largest of the French ships. Two others, which escaped, returned to Brest almost wrecks; but the merchant fleet got off clear, which caused Hawke to be severely censured for alleged remissness in duty.

Count de la Galissonière was nominated to fill the place, *ad interim,* of M. de la Jonquière, appointed, in 1746, to succeed M. de Beauharnais as governor-general of New France. In 1748, Francis Bigot, a name already ill-famed in Cape-Breton, and yet to become ignobly notorious in Canada and Louisiana, was appointed fourteenth and fated to become the last Intendant. M. Galissonière arrived at Quebec in September, bringing news of an approaching peace. Previously, even when an intimation had been sent by the British ministry to the American colonists of what was on the tapis, an invasion being expected by the Canadians this year, the rural colonists were ordered to retire inland, and the inhabitants of the Isle d'Orleans directed to quit it, on the imaginary enemies' approach. Simultaneously, a rumour reaching the fort-major of Trois-Rivières that fort St. Frederic was threatened, he marched to the rescue with 1,200 men; but not being wanted there, he made an inroad towards Albany, and met and destroyed an English corps gathered for some purpose or other, not explained, thereabouts.

In 1747, some of the native tribes of the lake country manifested a hostile spirit against the Canadians, who took the alarm on hearing that the Miâmis intended to attack and to massacre the people at Detroit. The commandant, M. de Longueuil, took precautionary measures there, and fort Michilimakinac was strenghtened. The Miâmis, having killed a few colonists, were suitably chastised. Those who abetted them, thence took warning; and security prevailed afterwards in the country.

The negociations, which took place at Aix-la-Chapelle in 1748, were unusually long, but the treaty was at last signed on the 7th of October. The chief parties to it were Great Britain, Holland, and Austria on one side; France and Spain on the other. By it all the preceding great treaties, from that of Westphalia in 1648, to that of Vienna in 1738, were renewed and confirmed. As the French and the British, in terms of its stipulations, mutually gave up whatever territory each had taken, the Anglo-American provincials had the mortification to see Cape-Breton, acquired for the mother country by their independent exertions, pass into the hands of its old masters; leaving their fisheries and outer settlements on the eastern seaboard as unprotected as before. As for the mother country, all that its people gained, in exchange for the lavish expenditure of their resources, and the outpouring of their blood during a generally successful struggle of eight years' duration, was the barren credit of having supported the German sovereignty of Maria-Theresa, and thereby (it was said) "vindicated the rights guaranteed by a pragmatic sanction;" in other words, effected that greatest of all political desiderata, in the estimation of the pedantic publicists of the time, a re-adjustment of "the balance of power in Europe."*

---

* M. Garneau intimates that the French came off second best on the occasion; for "Louis, while he did nothing for France, did everything for her allies." He was not in a condition to make peace, as he vainly boasted, "en roi." His land forces, if not beaten, were greatly reduced; his fleets were almost annihilated. Any kingdom in the crippled condition of France at that time, is lucky if its rulers' loosened hold on the national possessions revert to the *status quo ante bellum*, at the advent of peace.—*B.*

CHAPTER III.

THE FRONTIERS' COMMISSION.

1748-1755.

The peace of Aix-la-Chapelle only a truce.—Britain profits by the ruin of the French war marine to extend the frontiers of her possessions in America.—M. de la Galissonière governor of Canada.—His plans to hinder the neighbouring colonies from aggrandising themselves, adopted by the court.—Pretensions of the British.—Rights of discovery and possession of the French.—The limitary policy of Galissonière expounded and defended.—Emigration of the Acadians; part taken in their regard by that governor.—He causes several forts to be raised in the west; founding of Ogdensburgh (1749).—The Marquis de la Jonquière succeeds as governor ; the French ministry directs him to adopt the policy of his predecessor.—De la Corne and Major Lawrence advance to the Acadian isthmus, and occupy strongholds thereon ; *i.e.*, forts Beausejour, Gaspereaux, Lawrence, Des Mines, &c.—Lord Albemarle complains, at Paris, of French encroachments (1749); reply thereto of M. Puyzieulx.—The French, in turn, complain of British hostile acts on sea.—The Acadians take refuge in St. John's (Prince Edward's) Island ; their miserable condition there.—Foundation of Halifax, N.S. (1749).—A mixed commission, French and British, appointed to settle disputes about the frontier lines ; first conferences, at Paris, on the subject.—Pretensions of the parties stated and debated ; difficulties found to be insurmountable.—Affair of the Ohio ; intrigues of the British among the natives of the regions around that river ; intrigues of the French among those of the Five Nations.—Virginian traffickers arrested, and sent as prisoners to France.—French and British troops sent to the Ohio to fortify themselves in the country.—The governor-general at issue with certain Demoiselles and the Jesuits.—His mortal illness, death and character (1752).—The Marquis Duquesne succeeds him.—Affair of the Ohio continued.—Colonel Washington marches to attack Fort Duquesne.—Death of Jumonville.—Defeat of Washington by M. de Villiers at Fort Necessity (1754).—Plan of the British to invade Canada ; assembly of Anglo-American governors at Albany. —General Braddock sent from Britain with an army to America.— Baron Dieskau arrives at Quebec with four battalions (1755).—Negociations between the French and British governments on the frontier difficulties.—Capture of two French ships of war by admiral Boscawen.—France declares war against Great Britain.

The peace of Aix-la-Chapelle was but a truce, hostilities scarcely ever ceasing in America. The British colonists had noted with great

interest the struggle upon the ocean; they had seen with much
satisfaction the destruction of the last remnants of M. de l'Etendrière's fleet in the battle of Belle Isle. In effect, the French marine, once annihilated, what was to be the inevitable fate of the
possessions of France beyond seas? What was to become of the
beautiful, the vast colonial system of so great a portion of the
New World?

The Anglo-American colonials determined at once to extend their
frontiers to the utmost. A trading association of influential men in
Britain and her dependencies was formed, for occupying the valley of the Ohio. It was not for the first time that the British
coveted the possession of that fertile and delightful country: from
the year 1716, Spotswood, governor of Virginia, had proposed to
purchase parts of that territory from the aborigines, and to establish a traffic therein; but the cabinet of Versailles opposing the
project, it was abandoned.* Contemporaneously, the London
newspapers announced that it was intended to extend, as far as the
St. Lawrence, existing British settlements on the side of Acadia.†
The agitation which was got up in these regards, only confirmed the
French in their fears of some great movement of aggression on the
part of their neighbours. M. de Galissonière, especially, shared
in this sentiment. He was a distinguished marine officer, who,
at a later time, became illustrious by a victory he gained over admiral Byng.‡ He was also active and enlightened as a civilian,
and spent in scientific studies such leisure as his public duties
allowed. He governed Canada only two years; but he gave, during that brief time, a strong impulsion to its administration, and

---

* *Universal History*, vol. xi.
† *Mémoire, &c.*, by M. de Choiseul.
‡ The "victory" was of a negative, not positive character. John
Byng was sent, with ten ships of war, poorly manned, to relieve Minorca,
when beleaguered with a strong land-force, by the French, in 1756.
Falling in with a fleet of far superior strength, a running fight commenced, when Byng, despairing of beating the enemy, drew off his ships,
none of which were taken, or even seriously damaged. Still his supposed remissness in not capturing or destroying the French ships cost
him his life, through an unjust sentence by court martial, executed
March 17, 1757.—*B.*

much good counsel to the French ministry, which, had it been followed, would have preserved our fine country to France. [?]

On arriving at Quebec, M. de Galissonière desired to obtain information regarding the soil, climate, produce, population, trade, and resources of the province. He turned his attention, at the outset, to the Frontier question, which could be no longer safely ignored. He fixed his regards, long and attentively, on the vast expanse of the French colonial possessions; he noted their strong and their weak points; he fathomed the projects of the British, and finished by convincing himself that the Acadian isthmus on the eastern side, and the Alleghanies on the western, were the two chief defences of French America. If the former were lost, the British would break bounds, penetrate to the St. Lawrence, and separate Canada from the sea. If the line of the Alleghany chain were abandoned, they would spread over the lake country, and the Mississippi valley; thus isolate Canada on those sides, induce the savages to renounce their alliances with us, and confine the French to the foot of Lake Ontario. These results he deemed inevitable, having regard to the constant development the British colonies were undergoing. He wrote to the ministry, that the settlements on the Illinois, at first over-prized, had latterly been undervalued; that even although these made no pecuniary returns, they ought not to be abandoned, because they served to prevent the British from penetrating to the interior of New France. "The country once well settled," said he, "we should become redoubtable on the Mississippi side. If in the border war we had 400 or 500 well-armed men among the Illinois, not only should we have been undisquieted, but we should have led into the heart of the enemy's settlements the very tribes which have so often insulted us."

France has been greatly blamed on account of the position she dared to assume in the frontier question; she was even accused by some of her own sons of ambition and unreason (*vivacité*). Voltaire went so far as to say, "such a dispute as that about the frontiers in America of the two colonising races, had it taken place between individuals, would have been settled in a couple of hours by arbitration:" a vain imagination on his part. An arrangement between two great Powers, involving the present possession and the future nationality of territories three or four times larger than

France itself, and now teeming with millions of people, was a difficulty of no such easy solution; yet scarcely did the matter occupy the attention of the cabinet of Versailles at the time, except in the most superficial way.

That of St. James's had thitherto abstained from formalising its pretensions in a precise or definite manner. It now manifested them, so to speak, in a negative form, by contesting the right of the French to establish themselves at Niagara and Crown-Point; objecting, also, to the stay of the latter among the Abenaquis, after the treaty of Utrecht (1713) was signed. Whilst it declared to those savages that the territory between New England and the St. Lawrence was Britain's, it kept silence on the point to the French governors, yet tried to vindicate its pretensions in the sequel.* As for the western frontier, its silence was yet more expressive: for had it not recognized the nullity of its claim therein, by refusing to sanction the formation of an Ohio Company, in 1716? But times were now greatly changed. The treaty of Utrecht gave Acadia to Britain. She now proclaimed that her province extended, on one part, from the river Kennebec to the sea; on the other, from the Bay of Fundy to the St. Lawrence: she maintained that the territory between the Kennebec and Penobscot rivers extended backwards as far as Quebec and to the St. Lawrence, and that said territory always formed a portion of the province. It was finally affirmed that the true frontiers of *Acadie* or Acadia, following its olden limits, were: 1. A right line drawn from the embouchure of the Penobscot to the St. Lawrence. 2. The right bank of that flood and coast of its gulf to the sea, south-westward of Cape Breton. 3. The whole seaboard, from this point to the embouchure of the Penobscot. Her commissioners even declared that the St. Lawrence was the natural and rightful line of demarcation between the possessions of the two races.

---

* A significant circumstance indeed! The Privy Council received, from the Board of Trade and Plantations, in 1713, even before the treaty of Utrecht, a Report, in which it was advanced, "that Cape Breton had always made part of Acadia;" and that "Nova Scotia comprised all Acadia bounded by the rivers Sainte-Croix and St. Lawrence and the sea." Minutes in the British Colonial-office, already cited in this volume.

VOL. II.—H

The region thus reclaimed, outside of the Acadian peninsula, had fully thrice the extent of Nova Scotia, and commanded the estuary of the St. Lawrence; that is, the great waterway of Canada, and the only passage to or from the province, seaward, in winter,— *i. e.* during five months of the year.

The territory which Britain contested, as not being French, beyond the Alleghanies, was likely to be still more precious in coming times. The basin of the Ohio alone, down to its confluence with the Mississippi, is not less than 200 leagues in length. This territory, however, formed but a minor portion of a debateable region, the limits of which had never been, indeed could not be defined: but it still involved an occult right to the possession of the immense countries, laid down in maps, between lakes Ontario, Erie, Huron, and Michigan; the upper Mississippi and the Alleghany regions: countries in which now flourish the states of New York, Pennsylvania, Ohio, Kentucky, Indiana, Illinois; and the lands on either side of Lake Michigan, between Lakes Huron and Michigan, and the Mississippi. Once give up these regions, and French Canada were separated from Louisiana by a long interspace, and completely mutilated. From the walls of Quebec and Montreal, the British flag would have been ever discernible, floating in the breezes on the St. Lawrence. In fine, such sacrifices as were then demanded implied a total abandonment of New France.

In presence of such pretensions to the proprietorship of countries discovered by Frenchmen, forming part and parcel of territory occupied by their descendants during a century and a half, what other duty devolved on M. de la Galissonière than that of asserting his nation's rights? Every movement he directed on the frontiers would have been dictated by the necessities of the situation, even if he had not been convinced of their propriety in the abstract. But that was not all: article 9 of the treaty of 1748 positively stipulated, that "all things should be put on the same footing as they were before the war;" and British hostages were sent to Versailles, to give personal security for the restitution of Louisbourg. Now the French had always occupied the country up to the Acadian isthmus. The construction of fort St. John and the taking possession of Cape Breton immediately posterior to the treaty of Utrecht, were proceedings of public notoriety, indicative of that occupation, the legitimateness of which appeared to be recognized by the very silence of the British ministry on the subject, up to the time when the war which ensued thereafter was terminated; for not till after the year 1748 did the governor of Nova Scotia, colonel Maskereene, attempt to oblige the settlers on the river St. John to swear fidelity to the British king, or appropriate their country.*

After what we have said, it is plain that M. de Galissonière's duty bade him take measures to vindicate French rights, and he obeyed the call. He sent troops forward, and gave orders to repel, by force if needful, the British, should they attempt to quit the peninsula of Nova Scotia and encroach on the continental territory beyond. He also wrote to Maskereene complaining of his conduct to the French settlers on the river St. John; admonishing him likewise to cause the resumed hostilities against the Abenaquis to cease, as they had laid down their arms as soon as they knew of the pacification of 1748. These remonstrances gave rise to a series of pretty sharp letters, written by and to the marquis of La Jonquière and governor Cornwallis; the former being successor of Galissonnière, the latter of Maskereene.

So far the French governors-general stood on the firm ground of national right; but Galissonnière conceived a project which was in no sense justifiable: it was to engage the Franco-Acadians to quit the peninsula in a body, and settle on the northern shores of the bay of Fundy; the ultimate view of the instigator being, to form by their means a living barrier to south-eastern Canada, and collect the people of French race, thereabout dispersed, under closer protection of their country's flag. Such a proceeding, in the actual state of the relations subsisting between France and Britain, was culpable, as its tendency was to induce the subjects of a friendly power to desert; for though the Acadians might rightly refuse, as catholics, to take oaths, or even assume a neutral part, in time of war, between French and British, they were none the less subjects of the king of Great Britain, in terms of the

---

* Memorial of the Duke de Choiseul, prime minister; anonymous *Mémoire sur les Affaires du Canada.*

treaty of Utrecht.* The French ministry, however, adopted the project of La Galissonnière, and set apart a large sum of money to carry it out. The French missionaries in Acadia seconded the polity of their mother country's rulers. Père Germain at Port-Royal (Annapolis), and the abbé de Laloutre, at Beaubassin, made the greatest efforts to engage the Acadians to quit those lands which formed their sole fortune. When the time arrived to leave forever the natal soil, under which their buried dead reposed, great hesitation and bitter regrets were ordinarily manifested by the outgoing French population of Nova Scotia. The emigration began in 1748.

While the governor-general thus laboured to erect a new colonial bulwark, on the south-eastern side, against British intrusion, he was no less busily engaged, on the western lines, in barring against it the entry of the upper Ohio region. The Ohio valley, covered by the grant of the Louisianian letters-patent of the year 1712, had always served as a French passage-way from the Mississippi to Canada. As British traders still persisted to traffic in that territory, the governor-general in 1748, sent M. Céleron de Bienville, with 300 men, to expel them thence once for all, and take formal possession of the country. Bienville set up, in different localities, limitary poles, and buried at their base leaden plates bearing the royal arms; and, as he did so, caused *procès-verbaux* to be drawn up, signed, and read, of every such solemn transaction, in presence of the aborigines; who, by the way, did not see it performed always without murmuring their dissent. That officer also wrote to the governor of Pennsylvania to inform him of what had been done, and asking him to prevent all persons within his jurisdiction from trading, for the future, beyond the Alleghany line; adding that he (Bienville) was commissioned to arrest all such interlopers, and confiscate their goods. Meanwhile Galisonière garrisoned Detroit, reconstructed a fort at Green Bay, formerly dismantled by De Ligneris during his expedition against the Outagamis), ordered a fort to be raised among the Sioux, another (of stone) at Toronto, and a third at la Présentation (Ogdensburgh), on the right bank of the St. Lawrence,

---

* Not to mention a legally prescriptive, if only tacit allegiance, of nearly two-score years' duration.—B.

between Montreal and Frontenac (Kingston), in order to be within reach of the Iroquois, whom he wished to put entirely in the French interest. These savages had sent, late in 1748, a numerous deputation to Canada, to protest anew that they had not ceded their lands, that their independence was intact, and their wish was to live in peace with both French and British.—The condition of the Canadian trained bands (*milice*) had also occupied the attention of the governor. Upon his arrival in the country, he sent the chevalier Péan to review the militiamen of every parish, and to draw up exact muster-rolls of their number. Their total numerical strength at that time might be from 10,000 to 12,000.

While M. de la Galissonière was thus engaged in giving some solidity to the frontier barriers, the marquis de la Jonquière arrived (late in August, 1749) to replace him, in virtue of his commission of 1746. Galissonière communicated to his successor all the knowledge he had himself obtained of the state of the Franco-American possessions; and confided to him every plan and intent he thought befitting for their safety and retention. After returning to France, this now ex-governor of Canada was even thoughtful for the wellbeing of New France. He recommended, among other needful measures for its safety, that the French ministry should send out 10,000 peasants, to people the lake-board and upper valley of the St. Lawrence and the Mississippi. At the close of the year 1750, he sent in a memorial, intimating that if there was a lull in British jealousies as regarded Europe, there was none in their Anglo-American polity. He advised that Canada and Louisiana should be generally fortified; and, above all, that the French should settle down finally in the environs of Fort Frederic (Lake Champlain), and at the posts of Niagara, Detroit, and Illinois.

M. de la Galissonière did not live till the evil days supervened which he anticipated. Charged, in 1756, to transport land-forces to Minorca, for the siege of Port-Mahon, his fleet was met, in returning, by admiral Byng's squadron; when he forced the British, after a brilliant action, to flee before him.*—He did not long survive his victory. Always delicate in bodily constitution, he undertook his last expedition only from an over-sense of duty, and against the advice of his physicians, who foretold that the

---

See ante, p. 111, note.—*B*.

fatigues he must undergo would kill him. Accordingly, October 26, 1756, having halted at Nemours, on his way to Fontainebleau, where Louis XV then was, he died. The king, who had not even conferred upon him the grade of vice-admiral, afterwards alleged (but his assertion may be doubted) that he had called his deceased servant to court, to make him a marshal of France. His loss was much felt in the French royal marine; by the sailors more especially, whose affections he gained by attending to their interests with paternal affection and kind regard.

His administrative and scientific talents even surpassed his genius for active war. The former shone conspicuously in New France; and while he was military commandant at Rochefort, when the commissariat of marine (office for charts, plans, &c.) was organized, he had the direction of that establishment.—Men of science lost a brother by his decease; for he was a devoted student of natural history, being especially attached to those departments of knowledge most contributing to man's well-being. Thus, whatever foreign localities he visited, he endowed with the most useful plants of Old France, and rendered to her, in exchange, whatever was likely to enrich from the New, and other parts abroad.— La Galissonière had a great heart and a beautiful mind, seated in a mean body; for he was both low in stature and deformed in person.*

The plans of Galissonière might have been successfully pursued, had they not seemed to his successor to be too daring. In effect, M. de la Jouquière, probably distrustful of the court, did not think fit to adopt all of them, neglecting more especially those relating to Acadia, from a fear of giving umbrage to Britain; whose commissioners had repaired to Paris, in view of settling the frontier difficulty. His prudence in this regard was stigmatized at Paris, as timidity; and an order sent to him not to abandon a country which France had ever possessed. The chevalier de la Corne, who commanded on the Acadian border, was charged to prepare and fortify a locality on the hither side of the peninsula, for the reception of the expatriated inhabitants of Nova Scotia. At first he chose Chediac, on the Gulf of St. Lawrence; but he after-

---

* *Maritime History of France*, by Léon Guérin.

wards quitted that place because it was too remote, and took up a position at Chipodi, between bays Verte and Chignectou. Governor Cornwallis, pretending that his province comprehended not only the peninsula proper, but its isthmus, the northern shores of the bay of Fundy, and the St. John, sent Major Lawrence, in spring 1750, with 400 soldiers, to expel thence the French and savages; with orders, also, to seize any ships found on their way laden with supplies for the Acadian refugees. At his approach, the male inhabitants of Beaubassin, encouraged by their missionary, set fire to that village, and retired with their wives and children behind the neighbouring river which falls into Chignecton bay. Never did colonists show more devotedness to a father-land. De laCorne came up with his forces, planted the French standard on the right bank of that river, and declared to Lawrence that his orders were to defend the passage, pending the frontiers' negociation then in progress. Thus obstructed, the major returned to Beaubassin; and, upon the smoking ruins of the village, erected a fort (afterwards called Fort Lawrence); he also raised another, at Les Mines. The French, on their side, constructed Fort Beauséjour, on Fundy bay, and that of Gaspareaux on baie Verte, in the Laurentian Gulf; they also fortified their settlements on the river St. John. These things accomplished, the two parties [ostensibly] left all else in abeyance, waiting the result of the Paris conference.

At this time, Lord Albemarle was resident British ambassador at the French court. By orders sent from London, he wrote, in 1750, to the marquis de Puyzieulx, complaining of the encroachments of the French on Acadia. The latter replied, a few days thereafter, that Chipodi and the St. John both were parts of Canada; that France had always possessed them; and, that, as the British had menaced the people there, La Jonquière, without waiting for instructions from the ministry, had felt it to be his duty to send a force for their protection. July 7, his Lordship renewed his remonstrances on the subject. The French, he wrote, had invaded all that part of Nova Scotia lying between the river of Chignectou and that of St. John; that they had burnt Beaubassin, afterwards arming and brigading its inhabitants; finally, that De la Corne and Père de Laloutre had invited the Franco-Acadians to quit their country, partly by means of pro-

mises, partly by causing them to believe that the British meant
to massacre them all. Lord Albemarle further declared that
governor Cornwallis had not formed, and never intended to form,
any settlement beyond the peninsular limits; and demanded, in
conclusion, that the proceedings of La Jonquière in the case should
be disavowed; adding that the troops sent should be withdrawn from
what was really British territory, and the damage done by their
invasions repaired or compensated. Upon these grave accusations
being made, an order was given to write without delay to the
governor of Canada, for a precise account of what had really been
done. "If any of our French people," wrote M. de Rouillé, "have
committed the excesses complained of, they merit punishment;
and the king will make an example of them." In September, a
memorial was sent to Lord Albemarle, replying to the British
complaints, containing a narration of the movements of Lawrence
and those of La Corne respectively, as well as an account of their
interview. In 1751, it became the duty of the cabinet of Versailles to complain in its turn. It represented that British vessels
of war had captured, in the lower Gulf of St. Lawrence, certain
French vessels, among them those carrying provisions to the troops
stationed on the coasts of Fundy bay. The British ministry
making no satisfactory reply to this charge, La Jonquière, in reprisal, caused to be seized in l'Isle Royale (Louisbourg harbour)
three or four British vessels, and confiscated them.

Meanwhile, more than 3,000 Acadians passed into Isle St. John
(Prince Edward's island), and to the seaboard of Fundy Bay.
The failure of the year's crop, and the incidents of war, caused
a famine among the people, which never ceased till Canada was
conquered; but the sufferings therefrom did not prevent their
emigrations, which were quickened by the arrival of 3,800 colonists from Britain, at Chiboucton, to found Halifax, in 1749.
The Acadians, whose place the latter in some measure took up,
directed their wandering steps to Quebec, to Madawaska, to any
place that was pointed out as being likely to receive them, so it
were quite beyond the reach of British domination. This extraordinary flight testified to the despotism and injustice of the
British government, which revenged itself for the desertion of the

fugitives upon those Acadians who still remained in the peninsula, and greatly influenced the dispositions of the war.

So many difficulties had induced the two courts to nominate the commission provided for by the treaty of Aix-la-Chapelle: it was that of France which took the initiative. Her fears had been aroused by the warlike preparations making in Britain; and by the debates in Parliament, regarding a proposal by Mr. Obbs* to foster the fur trade in Hudson's Bay, and for extending the Anglo-American frontiers far into the heart of Canada. The court of Versailles, in June 1749, remitted to that of St. James a memorial, wherein were detailed French rights over the territories in dispute, and proposed that a commission should be appointed to fix amicably the proper limits of the North American colonies of the two nations. The proposal was at once accepted.† The commissioners assembled in Paris: they were, Messrs. Shirley, and Mildmay, on one part; Messrs. de la Galissonière and De Silhouette on the other. Both Shirley and Galissonière had been American governors themselves. Besides attending to the regulation of Acadian limits, the commissioners were charged to settle doubts which had arisen regarding French and British rights over certain Caribbean Islands; namely, St. Lucia, St. Domingo, St. Vincent, and Tobago.

One of the chief conditions stipulated in appointing this commission was, that no innovation should take place in the debateable territories while it was in existence, but all things to remain as they were when it was formed, until its decision on every disputed point should be given.‡ The operations of De la Corne and Major Lawrence, the construction of forts on the Acadian isthmus, were severally recognized for violations of existing treaties by the two courts, while each proclaimed its " sincere desire to preserve

---

* From what region in the political planetary system did Monsieur "Obbs" drop?—We never heard of the rising of this "bright particular star" before. We humbly hint that the story is all a myth, "a weak invention of the enemy."—B.

† Memorial of the Britannic Court, of July 24, 1749.

‡ *Mémoire de M. de Choiseul*, "containing a summary of facts, with corroborative documents, serving as a reply to the Observations sent by the British Ministry to the several European Courts."

peace; and both assured the world of European diplomacy that they had sent orders to their respective colonial governors to stand-at-ease, as it were, and drop all further hostile proceedings for the time.

The commissioners, at great length, brought to view the pretensions of their countrymen. Great Britain reclaimed all the territory situated between the Laurentian Gulf, the Atlantic, and a line drawn from that flood to the Kennebec river, following a parallel due north; while France would not admit of her right even to the whole Acadian peninsula, since a French claim was put in for the whole southern seaboard of the bay of Fundy—all except the town and harbour of Port-Royal (Annapolis), which, it was allowed, were Britain's, because ceded to her specifically by the treaty of Utrecht. A mere glance at a map of the localities suffices to show that the pretensions on each side were the most antagonistic possible. Besides the present Nova Scotia, the countries demanded by the British now form a great part of the American state of Maine, all New Brunswick, besides a large slice of Lower Canada and Cape Breton, with islands adjacent. When the claims on each side were brought under review together, small hope indeed of an accommodation could be entertained. The representatives of the two contending powers enumerated and exhibited the titles by which each party trusted to justify its respective demands. They rummaged the records of Acadia and Canada, from the times of their discovery and settlement till the latest date. Both litigants strove to corroborate their cases by collateral documents tending to prove them, but only citing such so far as the matter they contained served or dis-served each their own or their adversaries' reclamations. This clashing of pretensions lasted, at first continuously, then fitfully, and at last very languidly, during five mortal years; and nothing tangible came of the prolonged conferences but three gross volumes of memorials for text, with documentary appendices attached; the reading through which only perplexed the ministries of both nations, or served to confirm in their minds a belief in the validity of the pretensions of their own several countrymen. Meantime the coming war was not for a moment retarded in its onward course, when once Britain had completed all her preparations for it.

All the while, if the movements which imperilled peace were suspended during the years of conference, encroachments continued in the valley of the Ohio; and while Europe was expecting war to break out on account of the Acadian border difficulty, it was destined to arise first, contrary to the prescience of home politicians, out of the contested limits of Louisiana.

M. de la Jonquière had followed up, in obedience to court instructions, the plan Galissonière had traced for preventing the British from penetrating into the region of the Ohio. Despite all previous warnings and after protestations, the authorities of Pennsylvania and Maryland gave "passes" to their fur-traders to traverse the Alleghanies, and excite the savage nations living beyond against the French; distributing among their tribes arms, ammunition, and presents. Three of these interlopers were arrested in 1750, and sent as prisoners to France. By way of reprisal, the British seized three Frenchmen, and sent them, under arrest, to the southward of the Alleghanies. These acts led to a correspondence between the Canadian and New York authorities, in 1751. Meanwhile, a fermentation existed among the savages of the Ohio country, and the French governor was obliged to send troops thereinto for the purpose of calming it.

While the western barbarians were thus a prey to the hate-inspiritings of the Americans, those of the Five Nations were lending an ear to the advice of the French, who had come nearer to their country since the foundation of the missionary settlement at Fort Presentation, adverted to in a former page of this chapter. The abbé Piquet had a great influence among their tribes. M. de Joncaire, he who founded Fort Niagara, was sent to live among them. The intent of the British, in advancing to the Ohio territory, was to engage the natives to expel the French thence; while the aim of the latter, in approximating to the Iroquois' country, was to induce them to remain neutral if war arose, for they could hardly expect them to take up arms against their ancient allies.

Thus what was passing in Europe and America, between the two peoples, left little hope for a pacific result. Sundry writings were published in London, counselling the ministry to appropriate the Gallo-American dependencies, before the French should be able to re-constitute their royal marine. In 1751, M. de Jonquière began to receive, from France, warlike munitions, with corps of marines and recruits to replace his invalided soldiers. He strengthened the garrison of Detroit, and sent M. Villiers to relieve M. Raymond, then commanding in the lake country, who had sent intelligence that all things were in disorder there, and that the southern tribes of the region were siding with the British.

The governor-general was now touching the term of his career, the last days of which were troubled by pitiful quarrels with the Jesuits. These friars were accused of trafficking at their mission of Sault St. Louis, under the covering name of the Misses Desauniers, and of sending the beaver-skins thereat obtained to Albany for sale. Their example was followed by others; and the resident director of the West India Company had long complained of these misappropriations, which he regarded as done in breach of the Company's privileges. The result was that a royal order was sent to remedy the alleged contravention, and the governor-general shut up the Desauniers' establishment.

It was not long before he felt the vengeance of the Jesuits. They wrote against him to the ministry, accusing him of monopolising the fur traffic of the upper country, and of tyrannizing over the dealers through his secretary, to whom he had transferred the right of signing licenses to supply the savages with strong drinks; finally, he was charged with giving the best public employments to his own connexions and creatures. The aggrieved traffickers, who would not have ventured to prefer such accusations, sustained them when made. The concurring testimony of interested clerics and laics drew upon La Jonquière the animadversions of the ministry. Being called on to reply to the accusations preferred, he affected to ignore them, and made a pompous enumeration instead, of his public services; insinuating that they had been poorly recompensed, and finished by demanding his recal. Before that could arrive, his bodily powers, severely affected by mental irritation, and impaired by age and the fatigues of an over-active career, seemed to give way at once. May 17, 1752, he expired at Quebec; and his remains were laid, shortly thereafter, beside those of De

Frontenac and De Vaudreuil, deceased governors of New France, who, like him, had died in gubernatorial harness.

This ante-penultimate chief of the colony was born, about 1686, in the château of La Jonquière, Languedoc: the family was of Catalonian origin. He served in the War of the Succession, assisted in the reduction of the Cevennes,* and in the defence of Toulon against the Savoyards. He had accompanied Duguay-Trouin to Rio-Janeiro, and fought along with La Bruyère-de-Court against Admiral Matthews, in 1744. France lost in him one of the ablest of her naval officers. He was of an indomitable spirit in action; a precious quality at a time when the war-marine of France was overmatched in physical strength by that of her rival. His person was well formed; but he was low in stature. He had an imposing air; but his mental acquirements, it is said, were not great. He tarnished his reputation by an inordinate love of wealth; and his avarice laid him open at last, after accumulating a large fortune, to attacks which hastened his death. He caused several of his nephews to come to Canada, to enrich themselves under his protection. Not being able to procure an adjutancy for one of them as he wished, (Captain de Bonne-Miselle), he gave him a seigniory and a monopoly of the fur-trade at Sault Sainte-Marie. Although possessed of millions, he denied himself, it may be said, the veriest necessaries of life even in his last moments. [At one time, he wished to introduce printing to the colony, but merely to save repetitive transcriptions in the public offices, and effect a pecuniary saving thereby.]

Baron de Longueil now administered *ad interim*, for the second time, the province, till the arrival of the new governor-general, the Marquis Duquesne de Menneville, in 1752. The latter was a captain in the royal marine, and had been recommended by M. de Galissonière. He was descended from the greater Duquesne, grand-admiral of France under Louis XIV. His instructions were to follow up the policy of his two immediate predecessors. War was now become imminent. The Canadian militia were called out and exercised. Discipline had been slackened in the colonial troops; Duquesne made great efforts to re-establish it. He wrote

---

* That is, he actively persecuted the French Protestants in the south, thrusting them out with fire and sword.—*B.*

to the minister that these corps were badly constituted; that they contained many deserters and bad characters. " Their want of discipline," he observed, was quite astounding; adding, " this arises, from the impunity allowed to their gravest infractions of duty." But the materials were not so bad, after all ; for, in about twenty months, the men became obedient and yet spirited soldiers.

His reforms, however, raised a violent opposition to him, headed by the intendant, Bigot, who was in this, as in many other cases, the evil genius of Canada. " He sent to the minister of marine," recounts M. Dussieux, "the bitterest complaints against the governor. 'The Marquis Duquesne,' he wrote, 'banishes people from the colony, without form of process, or making any inquiry, or consulting the intendant.' Bigot speaks of two mutinous militiamen: the governor kept them in a dungeon for seven months and then banished them. As for them, Bigot adds that being subject to martial law, he says no more; but Duquesne has exiled a colonist from Detroit for having trafficked with the savages against the commandant's orders; Bigot deplores such severity. The militia training is carried too far, he observes: tillage is neglected, the cultivators being always under arms."*

The works at Beauséjour were strengthened ; troops were moved towards the Ohio, whither Bigot wished 2,000 men to be sent and three forts raised, with several magazines for stores; necessary precautions, he said, for assuring to the French the possession of that country.

The troops took the route thither, in 1753, under the orders of M. Péan. The British armed colonials, also, began to move in the same direction. The aborigines, courted by both parties, knew not what side to take; while they were surprised and disquieted, on seeing bodies of soldiers, with artillery and munitions of war, invading their forest solitudes. Fort Presqu'île and Fort Machault were erected, by the French, between lake Erie and the Ohio. It was then that M. Le Gardeur de St. Pierre, who commanded on that border, was warned to retire by the governor of Virginia; who directed, on his part, the colonial troops to move

---

* *Letter* of August 28, 1753, in the Archives of the French Marine; *Le Canada sous la Domination Française.*

towards the Alleghanies. Taking no heed of these notifications of the British, M. de Contrecœur, who was sent to replace St. Pierre, advanced with 500 to 600 men, and caused a small fort to be evacuated which captain Trent had raised on his route. Having reached the banks of the Ohio, he began the construction of Fort Duquesne (Pittsburgh) in 1756. All the chiefs of the French posts in the region had orders to purchase the goodwill of the savages thereof by presents; garrisons were placed in Forts Machault and Presqu'île; transport vessels were built on the lake-board of Erie and Ontario; and the governor of Louisiana was directed to engage the savages within his jurisdiction to join the French on the Ohio.

Amidst these preparations, M. de Contrecœur received intelligence that a large corps of British was advancing against him, led by colonel Washington. He forthwith charged M. de Jumonville to meet the latter, and admonish him to retire from what was French territory. Jumonville set out with an escort of 30 men: his orders were to be on his guard against a surprise, the country being in a state of commotion, and the aborigines looking forward for war; accordingly his night campings were attended by great precaution. May 17, at evening-tide, he had retired into a deep and obscure valley, when some savages, prowling about, discovered his little troop, and informed Washington of its being near to his line of route. The latter marched all night, in order to come unawares upon the French. At daybreak, he attacked them suddenly; Jumonville was killed, along with nine of his men. French reporters of what passed on the occasion, declared that a trumpeter made a sign to the British that he bore a letter addressed to them by his commandant; that the firing had ceased, and it was only after he began to read the missive which he bore, that the firing re-commenced. Washington affirmed, on the contrary, that he was at the head of his column; that at sight of him the French ran to take up arms, and that it was false to say, Jumonville announced himself to be a messenger. It is probable there may be truth in both versions of the story; for the collision being precipitate, great confusion ensued. Washington resumed his march, but tremblingly, from a besetting fear of falling into an ambuscade. The death of Jumonville did not cause the war which ensued, for that was already resolved on, but only hastened it. Washington proceeded on his march; but staid by the way to erect a palisaded fastness which he called Fort Necessity, on a bank of the Monongahela, a river tributary to the Ohio; and there waited for the arrival of more troops, to enable him to attack Fort Duquesne when he was himself assailed.

Contrecœur, upon learning the tragic end of Jumonville, resolved to avenge his death at once. He put 600 Canadians and 100 savages under the orders of the victim's brother, M. de Villiers, who set out directly. Villiers found, on his arrival at the scene of the late skirmish, the corpses of several Frenchmen; and, near by, in a plain, the British drawn up in battle order, and ready to receive the shock. At Villiers' first movement to attack them, they fell back upon some intrenchments which they had formed, and, armed with nine pieces of artillery. Villiers had to combat forces under shelter, while his own were uncovered. The issue of the battle was doubtful for some time; but the Canadians fought with so much ardour, that they silenced the British cannon with their musketry alone; and after a struggle of ten hours' duration, they obliged the enemy to capitulate, to be spared an assault. The discomfited British engaged to return the way they came; but they did not return in like order, for their retrograde march was so precipitate, that they abandoned all, even their flag. Such were the inglorious exploits of the early military career of the conqueror of American Independence. The victors, having razed the fort and broken up its guns, withdrew. War now appeared to be more imminent than ever, although words of peace were still spoken. Villiers' victory was the first act in a great drama of 29 years' duration, in which both Great Britain and France were destined to suffer terrible checks in America.

What was the Frontiers' Commission, in sederunt at Paris, doing all this time? "Whilst all the British colonists," said the Duke de Choiseul, "were getting up a general movement for the invasion of Canada, in conformity to a plan formed in London, their patrons here affected to be solely engaged, concurrently with our commissioners, in finding means to bring about a conciliation." But the duke and other French ministers were not to be duped in this way: they had marked well the British persistence of intrusion as to the Ohio valley; and it was owing to their previous invasions there, accompanied by perceptible agitation among its savage denizens, that the French cabinet, in 1742-3, sent troops to garrison a chain of posts extending from lake Erie to that river; a measure followed up, in 1754, by thrusting Colonel Washington to the further side of the Alleghanies. The British government continued the Commission at Paris, merely to save appearances; at once mystifying the other European courts and lulling the apprehensions of that of France, which, in its state of decrepitude, was ill able to conjure the tempest of war just ready to burst.

The greatest cause for inquietude, at this time, among the ministers of Louis XV, was the state of the royal finances. The treasury was empty; and for some years past the cabinet begrudged the cost of retaining Canada as a French dependency. When the time came of providing for its further defence, this feeling increased; every despatch-ship sent out, bore reprimands to the Intendant for the prodigality of his outlay; while but few soldiers were sent for the defence of the colony, to counterbalance the benumbing effect of such reproaches, although, latterly, the death of Jumonville, and Washington's capitulation, made a great sensation in Europe. Even the French people, excluded from direct participation in politics, and relying blindly on the continuance of peace, began to open their eyes and prepare for war.

Meanwhile, seven colonial governors of as many Anglo-American colonies met in conference at Albany, and signed a treaty of alliance with the Iroquois. They drew up, on the same occasion, a project for a federal union in war-time; the nature of the compact being, that each province, whether attacked itself or not, should furnish its quota, in men or money, or both, so long as hostilities, offensive or defensive, if undertaken for the general interest, should endure. The central government of the meditated confederation was to be headed by a president, nominated by the king, and advised by councillors selected from all the colonial assemblies; said president, in conjunction with the council, to exercise executive powers, including the right of making peace or war with the savage nations, of fortifying settlements, and of levying taxes under royal authority; lastly, of appointing both civil and military functionaries.

This project, however, was rejected by the parties met in conclave for dissimilar reasons: by the colonists, because the plan vested undue power in a president; by the royalists, because it gave too much headway to the popular representatives. But as we have remarked elsewhere, the wars against Canada waged by the British colonies of America tended to make these cling together, and accustomed them, insensibly, to regard a federal government as being that best suited for them. After the rejection of the convention project, it was resolved, in default of a central power, to carry on the impending war jointly with the regular forces sent from Britain, the colonial corps and militia to act as their auxiliaries; meanwhile it was agreed that the several assemblies should vote subsidies and order men to be engaged, armed, and trained. The mother country also put large means at their disposition, and sent out, as her military chief, General Braddock, who had served with distinction, under the Duke of Cumberland, in the wars of continental Europe.

Braddock's Instructions comprised a detailed plan of hostile operations against Canada.* One projected expedition was, to drive the French out of the Ohio valley, and to take possession of it in name of the British crown. Forts St. Frederic and Niagara, those at the foot of lake Erie, and Beauséjour in French Acadia, were to be attacked, simultaneously or successively, according to circumstances. The regular forces assembled in Ireland were embarked on board a squadron, under admiral Keppel, who was directed to aid whatever land-operations were to be undertaken. Arrived in Virginia, Braddock conferred with all the provincial authorities. It was agreed that he should proceed, with the regulars, to capture Fort Duquesne; that governor Shirley should, with the provincial forces, attack Niagara; that another corps, drawn from the northern colonies, and led by colonel Johnson, should assail Fort Frederic; finally, that colonel Monckton, with the Massachusetts militia, should assault Beauséjour and Gaspareaux. The plan being thus settled, the next intent was to take Canada unawares, by a hasty invasion.

---

* Instructions for General Braddock, dated March 25, 1754;—Letters of Colonel Napier, written by command of the Duke of Cumberland, to General Braddock.

Meanwhile, its governor-general received letters from Paris:—
" The dispositions which the British cabinet continue to manifest
for maintaining peace, do not allow us to believe that it can have
authorized the movements so much spoken of upon the Ohio; and
there is yet less appearance that it has sanctioned any hostile
demonstrations on the other frontiers." But France did not
remain long inactive in presence of those preparations; as, for a
long time back, the tone of the English newspapers and parliamentary debates had too plainly expounded the hostile feeling of
Britain. That feeling was all potent in London, and strongly reacted on the government.

In France orders were given to assemble a fleet at Brest, to be
commanded by M. Dubois de la Motte. On board of it were embarked six battalions of veterans, 3000 strong in all*; two of these
were to be landed at Louisbourg, and the others in Canada.
Major-general Baron Dieskau, who had distinguished himself
under Marshal Saxe, was appointed to lead the latter. He had
for his second, the infantry colonel M. de Rostaing, and for aid-
major the chevalier de Montreuil.

M. Duquesne asked to be recalled, and transferred to the marine
service. His departure caused no regret, although he had governed
with great success, and been very heedful of all the colony's wants;
but his haughty bearing made him unpopular. This defect, in an
administrator, is yet more resented in America than in Europe,
because of the greater equality in men's conditions here. Before
leaving, he endeavoured to bind the Iroquois to French interests;
and for that end held a secret conference with some of their chiefs
at Montreal. But these savages always sought to maintain their
independent position between the French and British colonies.
" We could not recognize the native genuineness of Iroquois blood,"
said M. Duquesne, " in recent proceedings at Albany, where, in
presence of seven governors, at a secret council, you betrayed the
cause of the king of France in allowing yourselves to be induced,
by the evil advice of the British, to countenance their intrusions
upon the Beautiful River (Ohio), despite the length of time that
France has been possessed of it. Know you not the difference
there is between the king of France, and the British king? Go,

---
* Official Correspondence.

and examine the forts which our king has erected; you will see that the land beyond their walls is still a hunting-ground. Our forts have been set up, not as a curb upon the tribes, but to be useful for your trade with us. While, no sooner do the British enter upon possession of your lands, than the game deserts them. The forest falls below their blows, the soil is bared, and hardly will you find a bush left upon your own domains to shelter you by night." The governor thus, truly as briefly, characterized the diverse nature of British and French colonizations.

The Marquis de Vaudreuil de Cavagnal, governor of Louisiana, was promoted to the governorship of New France, upon the departure of the Marquis Duquesne, in early summer 1755. The former nobleman was third son of the Marquis de Vaudreuil, governor-general from 1703 till his death in 1725. His descendant was joyously greeted, on his arrival, by the Canadians, who regarded him the more for being a compatriot, and had anxiously solicited the king to appoint him for their chief. Crowds attended his steps in entering upon office; the people remembering in his favour the halcyon times of the father's sway, and trusting that these were to return under the government of the son.

The British fleet, bearing general Braddock and his troops, left port about Jan. 1, 1755, and reached Williamsburgh, Virginia, Feb. 20 ensuing. Admiral Dubois did not leave Brest till late in April; that is, nearly three months after Braddock's departure. He had on board some reinforcements and warlike stores for the king's service in Canada. Here it is needful to note the dates of events; for the British ministry had resolved to intercept the French squadron, and for that purpose despatched admiral Boscawen, April 17.

While these matters were in progress, diplomacy vainly put out its feelers to resume hold of a difficulty which, it was now plain, could only be decided at the cannon's mouth. Jan. 15, the duke de Mirepoix, French ambassador in London, addressed a note to the British Court, proposing that hostilities should be forbidden between the two nations; that all things in the Ohio valley should revert to their state as they were before the last war; that the pretensions of the two crowns regarding that territory should be submitted, in a friendly spirit, to a commission; finally, in order to

allay existing inquietude in France, the British ministers were
solicited by the duke to inform him as to the destination of the
expedition from Ireland, and to explain what were the motives for
sending it abroad.

The reply to this communication bore date January 22. Therein, demand was made that the hold upon the Ohio valley, as
of other territories, should revert, in the first place, to the same
state it was in before the treaty of Utrecht. Now this was setting
up renewed pretensions, and interpreting the terms of the peace
of Aix-la-Chapelle, (1748), by those of the treaty of 1713!
As for the armament which had been equipped and despatched
lately, it was not got up (thus reads the official missive) with any
intent of compromising the general peace, but only for the protection of the British possessions in America.

Mirepoix wrote again (Feb. 6), proposing that the text of the
treaty of 1748 should be adhered to; and as its consequent, that
the British commissioners at Paris should be put in possession, for
further examination, of the evidences of their country's right to
what was now claimed by the cabinet of London.

In the sequel, the French ministry again modified its demand,
and proposed that the people of the two nations should together
evacuate all the territory between the Ohio and the Alleghanies.
This was an acquiescence in the proposal made by the British
cabinet, of date Jan. 22. Louis' ministers had no doubt that the
proffer must needs be accepted; and this the rather because their
envoy had just been assured that the Irish armament had been
equipped solely with the intent of maintaining subordination and
good order in the British colonies. But the British ministry now
advanced new pretensions, as if an accommodation were the last
thing wished for. Accordingly, March 7, a fresh proposal was
made, including the particulars here enumerated:—1. That not
only should the French forts in the region between the Ohio and
the Alleghanies be razed, but all the French settlements between
the rivers Ohio and St. Jerome (Wabash) must be given up. 2.
That the fort at Niagara, and that of St. Frederic (on lake Champlain), should be razed; and that the navigation of lakes Erie,
Ontario, and Champlain should be free to British and French
subjects alike. 3. That France should renounce all further claim,

not only to the entire Acadian peninsula, but also to the isthmus, and a space of 20 leagues of territory beyond the latter, following a line drawn from south to north, and passing from the river Pentagoet to the Gulf of St. Lawrence. 4. That the entire river-board of the St. Lawrence, on the right bank or south-eastern side, should remain unappropriated either by French or British.

These conditions once accepted by the French court, the British cabinet was willing to confide to the commissioners for the two powers the settlement of other conflicting pretensions! Such a proposal was tantamount to a declaration of war; for it involved, if agreed to, the virtual renunciation of Canada, which would have disgraced the crown of France in the eyes of the whole world. Accordingly, it was met by an absolute refusal.* Negociations were prolonged, nevertheless, till the month of July, other devices to reconcile difficulties being proposed and rejected. All the time, both parties loudly proclaimed their sincere wishes for an accommodation; and the British ministry assured the French government, when the latter expressed disquietude as to the destination of Boscawen's fleet, that "certainly the British will not begin the war." The duke of Newcastle, earl Grenville, and Sir T. Robinson said positively to the French ambassador, that no orders had been given to that admiral to assume the offensive. The governor of Canada, who was on board one of the ships of M. de la Motte, was directed by the king not to begin the war, unless certain specified hostile acts were committed by the British.†

Boscawen, who set sail from England April 17, arrived in due time on the Banks of Newfoundland, with 11 men-of-war. The main body of the French fleet, thanks to the fogs of that region, passed towards its destination within cannon-shot of the British;

---

* The minister thus wrote to the governor of Canada :—" Come what may, his Majesty is very resolute in sustaining his rights and holding to his possessions, despite all such unjust and exorbitant pretensions; and much as he values peace, he will purchase it only at the cost of such concessions as may accord at once with his own dignity and the right his (colonial) subjects have to be protected." *Documents de Paris.* The court was sincere, this time, in its protestations.

† *Documents de Paris.*

but two ships, the *Lys* and the *Alcide*, which had for some days accidentally parted convoy, were chased and taken. On board these vessels were several engineer officers and 8 companies of soldiers, the latter being a portion of the 3,000 regulars embarked for America.

M. de Choiseul reported, that M. Hocquart, captain of the *Alcide*, hailed the *Dunkirk*, a 60 gun British ship, and demanded, in English, "Are we at peace or war?" The reply was, "We don't understand you."* Some other words had been interchanged, when the *Dunkirk* poured a broadside from double-shotted guns, and cannon loaded with grape, into the *Alcide*. Immediately, that ship and the *Lys* were surrounded by Boscawen's vessels, and, after having lost many men in resisting the attacks made upon them, forced to surrender. Among the officers killed, was colonel de Rostaing. This action, observes Mr. Haliburton, was the real commencement of the war, although not then formally entered upon. The British government, though not having proclaimed its intended hostilities thus begun, was accused of deception † and piracy, by the neutral powers of Europe. Soon afterwards, 300 merchant-men navigating the seas, reposing on the faith of existing treaties, were waylaid and captured, upon the buccaneering principle, to the irreparable loss of France; which was thus deprived, at one sweeping stroke, of the services of 5,000 or 6,000 sailors.

The news of the capture of the *Lys* and *Alcide* reached London July 15. The duke de Mirepoix forthwith sought an audience of the British ministers; who assured him that the action must have taken place through a misundertanding; adding, that what had happened needed not be a means for breaking up the negociation still pending. The French nation, thitherto taking rank as a leading power in Europe, thus saw itself, through the debility of the government, treated as a kingdom of second or third rate order. Still the court of Versailles, no longer to be hoodwinked, recalled its ambassador, and declared war against Great Britain.

---

* "Nous n'entendons point": which words, given in the duke's *Mémoire*, might also mean, "We can't hear well what you say."—B.

† The author's term is *trahison*.—B.

BOOK NINTH.

CHAPTER I.

THE SEVEN YEARS' WAR.

1755–1756.

Dispositions of mind in Britain and France at the epoch of the Seven Years' war.—France changes her foreign policy in forming an alliance with Austria; which mutation only flattered the self-love of Madame de Pompadour.—Warlike enthusiasm in Great Britain and her colonies; their immense armaments.—Small number of the Canadian forces.—Plan of the first campaign; zeal of the Canadian people.—First operations.—Troops from Boston scour Acadia and capture Fort Beauséjour, &c.; exile and dispersion of the French Acadians.—General Braddock advances towards Fort Duquesne; M. de Beaujeu marches to meet him; battle of the Monongahela; the British defeated, and Braddock killed.—A panic ensues in the American colonies.—The Canadians and savages commit great ravages, and take many prisoners.—British corps formed to attack Niagara and Fort Frederic.—Colonel Johnson encamps at the head of Lake George.—Baron Dieskau attacking him, is defeated and taken prisoner.—General Shirley delays the siege of Niagara.—Results of the campaign of 1755.—Bad harvest in Canada; a dearth ensues.—British preparations for the campaign of 1756.—State of Canada; succour solicited from France.—General Montcalm, sent with a reinforcement of troops, arrives at Quebec in spring, 1756.—Plan of operations.—Disproportion of the forces of the two belligerent parties; invasions projected by the British.

We have said that the French ministry, after learning the capture of the *Lys* and the *Alcide*, recalled its ambassador from London, and declared war against Great Britain. This step, as will be seen presently, was not however taken till after almost a year's delay. The indolent king had great hesitation in resolving to engage in a serious contest at all.

What was the situation of France at this time? The chief ministers of state were,—Count d'Argenson, for the war department; M. Machault, marine and colonies; M. Rouillé, foreign affairs: but Mme. de Pompadour was the real chief of the government. She it was who made and unmade ministries, appointed and cashiered generals, at her sovereign will and pleasure. Twenty-five cabinet ministers were engaged and dismissed (by her) between the years 1756 and 1763. "The state council," says Sismondi, "underwent constant mutations: it had neither unity nor accord, and each member acted independently of the others. As for the nation, it was more occupied with vain ecclesiastical dissensions than the cares of war. The Molinists, backed by the Jesuits, recommenced a persecution of the Jansenists; the parliament interposed, trying to stop it, but was itself assailed, its authority suspended, and a royal chamber (of law) took its place for a time. Amid these troubles in the state, *philosophism* was making progress in French society. Even at court it had its partisans. The king, inimical as he was to innovating ideas, yet had a private printing-press, at which he caused the politico-economical theories of his physician (Quesnel) to be typographed. One of these proposed the doing away with all state imposts but a land-tax. This plan, had it been adopted, would have thrown the burden of supporting the government chiefly on the nobles and churchmen, for they were the chief landholders. But all such proposals began and ended in empty words. Every old-established corporation, spiritual or secular, whose interests would have been seriously affected by this and other proposed changes, and royalty—which had been for a moment cajoled into tolerance, at least, for an exposition of the "new ideas"—shrank timidly from the hazards that might attend their realization. In fine, all was in commotion amongst both moral and political idealists. Public opinions were no longer harmonious; and the government itself, as if ashamed to be guided by olden traditions, moved with a vacillating step in a novel route.

For example: by the fatal treaty of Versailles (1756), France allied herself to Austria, whom she had always combated; and allowed herself to be led into a continental war to sustain Maria-Theresa, who, wishing to retake Silesia from the king of Prussia, adroitly flattered Madame de Pompadour, with whom that empress maintained an epistolary correspondence, in which the courtesan was addressed as a "dear friend." France had now to maintain a war both on land and sea in Europe, although experience had show that a twofold struggle always overtaxed her resources, as Machault tried to make Louis comprehend; but the lady favourite was all for the cause of the empress-queen, while the war minister and the courtiers, heedless of sea-service, longed to glorify themselves by expected victories in land war. The government, thus influenced, and oblivious of the requisites for coping properly with the forces of Britain—which alone had provoked the hostilities now in progress—thus had most of its warlike strength diverted from the quarters where it was most wanted, viz., towards the north of Europe; while it left the defence of New France almost entirely to its own inhabitants.

In Great Britain, there were no signs, as in France, of a revolution looming in the distance. The three kingdoms were never in so prosperous a state at any previous time; the Anglo-American colonies were materially prosperous, their inhabitants united in action, and seemingly satisfied with their mother country. The home government, founded on the broad basis of freedom, habitually yielded to popular inspirations, and, thus observant of national instincts, might safely assure itself, in advance, that success would attend any enterprise undertaken in obedience to the popular will. No preceding war had been so agreeable to the people's taste as that now about to commence. Mr. Fox (afterwards created Lord Holland) was at the head of affairs.* The commons voted a million pounds additional for the war services of the year; an alliance was formed with Prussia; subsidies were accorded to Poland and Bavaria, to bring them into an alliance in order to counterbalance the continental superiority of France, and to secure the possession of Hanover. Within the United Kingdom, the enrolment of seamen for the royal navy was pressed vigorously; and so great was the public fervour, that nearly every city and considerable town in the empire offered premiums to volunteers who would forthwith enlist in the sea or land forces. And in place of the million pounds above mentioned, which the government intended to raise specially by a lottery, £3,800,000 sterling were subscribed at once.†

---

* A mistake of the author. The Duke of Newcastle was then premier; and Mr. Fox lost the leadership of the house of commons in 1754.—*B.*
† SMOLLETT's *History of England.*

Nor was warlike ardour less manifest among the American colonies of Britain, the people in which far outnumbered the inhabitants of New France. Thus, in 1755, Dr. Franklin estimated the provincials at a total of 1,200,000; whilst the whole number of people in Canada, Cape-Breton, Louisiana, &c., was under 80,000 souls. The disproportion was as great in the relative commerce of the two dependencies, and consequently in their pecuniary resources severally. The American exports, in the year 1753, were valued at £1,486,000 sterling; imports, £983,000.* About the same date, the exports of Canada did not exceed £100,000 in value; while its imports might extend to £400,000; but most of the latter were for government account, and did not pass through the ordinary channels of trade. It was no marvel, therefore, that the British provincials should urge the mother country to carry on the war with vigour for their behoof. Franklin, as astute a politician as clever in science, was their principal mouth-piece. He who, 25 years thereafter, repaired to Paris, to arouse the public feeling of France and entire Europe against Britain; the same who came to Canada to revolutionize it in 1776, was, in 1754, the greatest promoter of the coming invasion of the French possessions in North America. "There needs never be permanent repose expected for our thirteen colonies," urged he, "so long as the French are masters of Canada."†

The disproportion between the military forces of the French and British, brigaded in America at this time, continued so long as the war lasted. But, by a sage foresight, France manifesting her accustomed superiority in the art of war, took up a defensive line far from the centre of Canada, and thus obliged the enemy to divide his strength. The narrow isthmus of Acadia, the wild and unexplored valley of the Ohio, the mountain gorge of lake George; such were the far-removed positions she chose for the operations of her soldiers—these became fields of battle, wide apart, where she kept in check for five years, without being dislodged, her numerous foes, and made them suffer sanguinary defeats, unparalleled thitherto in America. They blame wrongly, therefore, those who

---

* *Encyclopédie méthodique*; American Annals.
† Barbé-Marbois.

censure the defensive system adopted by or for our people during the Seven Years' War.

The regulars maintained in Canada, ordinarily about 1000 in all, were, in 1755, augmented to a total of 2,800 men, by the arrival of four battalions of infantry, under General Baron Dieskau. The militia was armed, and the governor continued to place large detachments on the frontier posts; insomuch that there was soon ready for action, in garrison and field, an army 7,000 strong, besides 800 men employed as escorts. These forces, however, were still very insufficient to make head against those of the enemy, who had already 15,000 soldiers equipped, of whom 3,000 were draughted to attack Beauséjour; 2,200 directed on Fort Duquesne; 1,500 against Niagara; and from 5,000 to 6,000 against Fort St. Frederic: these being four distinct attacks, which the British willed to make simultaneously.

If the secret influences at work on the public mind in France paralyzed the energies of the nation and crippled the martial action of the government; if a faulty organization, political and social, caused the philosophic and enlightened classes in the mother country to become sceptical and indifferent as to the good or evil chances of the coming struggle; the heart of Canada, at least, was still sound; and its inhabitants, chiefly cultivators or fur traders, were still imbued with the confident spirit of the French in early times, and had all the military ardour needed to make them vigorous soldiers. Deprived, by the nature of their government, of all share in its direction, and being few in number, they paid little attention to public affairs except when their homesteads were menaced by aliens; and as that was now the case, they took up arms with a firm determination to combat for the interests of the mother country, none the less bravely for the neglect which theirs had met at her hands. Not for one moment did their self-reliance give way, from first to last; and although their perfect devotedness has not always been appreciated by some historians of France, irrefragable proofs of it are given in the official papers, still extant, embodying the whole "form and pressure of the (latter) times" of French domination.

  · The seasons for warlike operations having arrived, the respective forces of the two belligerents entered their several fields of action. M. de Vaudreuil, uncertain of the enemy's projects, but in obedience to orders from France, sent a corps to attack the important fort of Oswego. General Dieskau, with 4,000 men and 12 guns, was charged with this enterprise, the success of which was considered certain. Two thousand troops had already set out from Montreal for that purpose, and had reached Frontenac (Kingston), when news of Johnson's army having appeared on Lake George, caused a portion of the Oswego expeditionary force to be recalled. Johnson's orders were, to act against Fort Frederic. The meditated attack on Oswego was now deferred; and Dieskau despatched, contrary to his own wish, to put a stop to the further advance of the British on the lower lakes. Sept. 1st, he took post, at the head of Lake Champlain, with 1,500 Canadians, 700 regulars, and 800 armed savages,—in all, 3,000 combatants; a sufficient force to keep Johnson in check. Meanwhile, the transmission of soldiers to Lake Ontario still continued; and a battalion took the route of Niagara, with orders to take post there, after making the ruins of its fort defensible: here was a palisaded house, surrounded with a fosse. Another battalion encamped under the walls of Frontenac. In autumn, the security of three important positions —St. Frederic, Niagara, and Frontenac—thus seemed to be properly cared for.

In the valley of the Ohio, Fort Duquesne, a very faulty construction, but commanded by M. de Contrecœur, a brave and skilful officer, had a garrison of 200 men only; but he had within reach a certain number of Canadian foresters and savages, whom he could call in aid. The other fortified posts, widely scattered in remote localities, had each a garrison equally scanty in number. But intervening thickets and distance were their chief protection.

On the Acadian side, forts Beauséjour and Gaspareaux had for commanders, the former, M. de Vergor, a favourite of Intendant Bigot; the latter, M. de Villeray. These officers had barely 125 soldiers at their disposal; but if attacked, they could reckon upon the aid of the Acadians settled around them, or who were roving in their vicinity: as if these poor people, whom the British regarded as subjects of king George, had been free to act!

Of the four enterprises which Britain projected against Canada, that first attempted was on the side of Acadia. The troops selected for this duty were Massachusetts men, and about 2,000 strong. They were led by Colonel Winslow, a prominent man in that colony. His force, embarked in 41 vessels, left Boston, May 20, and arrived at Chignectou June 1, where they landed, and were joined by 300 regulars. They marched at once, followed by an artillery train, against Beauséjour; but were stopped, for a short time, on the banks of the river Messuaguash, by a few French, who had raised a blockhouse there, with cannon mounted. This post was defended for about an hour; the garrison then set fire to the building, and retired. The British continued to advance, sweeping before them a small corps of armed Acadians, whom M. de Verger had charged to defend a height at some distance from his own post.

The garrison of Beauséjour consisted of 100 soldiers and 300 Acadians. No part of the works was bomb-proof. The besiegers completed their first trench June 12, and in four days, after a feeble resistance, Vergor capitulated. The garrison retired with the honours of war: the regulars were sent to Louisbourg; and the Acadians, by stipulation, were left unmolested. Fort Gaspareaux, after a short defence by a score of soldiers and a few inhabitants, surrendered on like conditions. Beauséjour was re-named Fort Cumberland, and Major Scott left in command of it. This officer disarmed the people in and about the place; and they refusing to take an oath of fidelity to the British crown, he retained as prisoners all of them he could lay hands on, in pursuance of orders from governor Hobson, who had succeeded to Cornwallis as chief of the Nova Scotian government.

After these conquests, the victors sent three war-ships to the river St. John, to capture a small fort which the French had lately erected there and which M. de Boishébert commanded; but his garrison being very weak, that officer set fire to the fort, and directed his small force to form a junction with the Acadians located at the upper end of the bay of Fundy. Having armed the latter, he, by their aid, beat the British in several combats; but could not prevent them, in the sequel, from burning out the people, who at first took refuge in the woods, and afterwards emigrated to Cape Breton, to the Isle St. John (Prince Edward's), to Miramichi, to Chaleurs Bay, and to Quebec; those unfortunates, whithersoever they went, presenting a living example of perfect devotedness and complete destitution.

Such was the success of the enemy in the beginning of the campaign. Although it was more nominal than real, seeing that the British could advance no farther on the Acadian side, they being restrained by armed bands, it caused great discontent at Paris, especially when its terrible results to the unhappy Acadians, all worthy of a better fate, became known. The king wrote an autograph letter to M. de Vaudreuil to summon a council of war, himself to preside, and call before it Messrs. Vergor and Villeray and their officers, to answer for their alleged dereliction of duty. Their trial took place, the year following, in the castle of St. Louis, when all of them were acquitted by a unanimous vote. The evacuation of Acadia by most of its inhabitants of French race, left those remaining, designated as *neutres*, at the mercy of the British. The latter, however, although they continued to reside in their native land, were still Frenchmen in their hearts. Of the total number of Acadians (between 15 and 18 thousand) living in the peninsula when the emigration began, there now remained only about 7,000, all of the more opulent class; forming a community whose gentle manners furnished the colouring for an attractive picture of the race, painted by Raynal:—

"They were a simple and good race, a people who abhorred bloodshed, and entirely followed agricultural pursuits. They had settled in low grounds, liable to be flooded, but which they protected by raising dykes and mounds about the lands they tilled. Upon these reclaimed marshes they grew crops of wheat, rye, barley, oats, and maize; with abundance of apples, which were brought largely into use for diet.

"Immense meadows were covered with their numerous herds and

---

* Royal letter, dated Feb. 20, 1756. The papers of the process are reposited in the Library of the Literary and Historical Society of Quebec. —"The chief consideration," said Montcalm, "in favour of the capitulator at Fort Beauséjour was this, that the beleaguered Acadians constrained Vergor to accept terms which would save them from being hanged, they having taken an oath of allegiance to Britain, and being found in arms against the British forces. As for Gaspareaux, merely a wide space staked about, with a garrison 20 strong only, it was not a place fitted to sustain a siege at all." *Lettre au Ministre, en* 1757.

flocks. They had as many as 60,000 head of horned cattle at one time. Most of the families had horses, but the tillage was done with oxen. The dwellings, almost all wooden, were commodious withal, and furnished as well as those of European cultivators in easy circumstances. Much poultry was raised, of every kind; which served to vary the abundant and wholesome fare served at all tables. Cider and beer were the usual beverages of the country. The spirits drunk were distilled from sugar.

" Home-grown and home-spun flax, hemp, and wool, were the materials of the stuffs they wore for ordinary clothing; the same materials being woven into blankets and sheets. The few who wanted finer tissues, had to procure them from Annapolis and Louisbourg. These two towns took, in exchange for those and other luxuries they supplied, grain, cattle, and peltry.

" The neutral French-Acadians had nothing else to offer to their neighbours. Barter among themselves was very limited, for every family had within itself all the necessaries needful for its own subsistence and comfort. Paper-money, so much in use in British America, was unknown to them. The small amount of money which came into the colony was in the form of specie, a medium not imparting that activity to pecuniary circulation which is the life of a trading community.

" The manners of this people were extremely simple. There never was a law-case, civil or criminal, among them, of sufficient importance to be judged in the court at Annapolis. The rare differences which arose between individual colonists were always settled amicably by the arbitration of the elders. The religious pastors drew up all family papers, and attested wills. The remuneration of the clergy for their services, spiritual and secular, was the voluntary contribution of a 27th part of the crops and other produce. The returns from the lands were abundant enough to allow the hands which grew them to bestow generously. Destitution was unknown; beggary was forestalled by giving in advance. And as succour was proffered without ostentation on one part, it was accepted without any sense of humiliation on the other. French Acadia formed a universal brotherhood, every member in which was as ready to donate as others might be to accept that which was thought to belong of right to all mankind.

"This state of harmony was not disturbed by those licentious sexual attachments (*liaisons de galanterie*) which so often banish peace from families. Such immunity from vice was much owing, doubtless, to the fact, that celibacy among the adult population was unusual. When a youth arrived at the age of puberty, a house was built for his separate use; fields were cleared around it, and the interior stored with a year's provision, to enable the new household to wait the returns of the coming harvest. The female he took to wife, brought farming stock for a dowry. The additional family grew and prospered, as all the rest had done before. Who is there whose heart was not touched in witnessing the innocence of manners, the tranquil lives, of those happy communities! Who would not have breathed a wish that such prosperity as theirs should endure for ever?"

Vain aspirations all! The hostilities of the year 1744 began the misfortunes of these good people; the Seven Years' War brought about their total ruin. For a long time previously, British agents treated them with the greatest rigour; the tribunals, by flagrant violations of the law, by systematic denials of justice, had become, for the people, objects of terror and hatred. The pettiest jack-in-office became a despot for them. "If you fail to supply my men with fuel," said a certain Captain Murray, "I will demolish your houses and make firewood of them." "If you don't take the oath of fidelity," added Governor Hobson, "I will batter your villages with my cannon." Nothing could tempt the honourable minds of Acadians to take an oath of fealty to aliens, repugnant to their consciences; an oath which, it was and is the opinion of many, Britain had no right to exact. "The Acadians," says Mr. Haliburton, "were not British subjects, for they had not sworn fidelity: therefore they were not liable to be treated as rebels; neither ought they to have been considered as prisoners of war, or rightly be transportable to France, since, during half a century, they had been left in possession of their lands on the simple condition of remaining neutral." But numerous adventurers, greedy incomers, looked upon their fair farms with covetous eyes. Smouldering cupidity soon burst into flame. "Reasons of state polity" were soon called in, to justify the total expulsion of the Acadians from Nova Scotia. Although the far greater number of them had done no act which could be construed into a breach of neutrality, yet, in the horrible catastrophe preparing for them, the innocent and the guilty were to be involved in a common perdition. Not one exception was made. Their fate was decided in a secret council, headed by governor Lawrence, at which assisted admirals Boscawen and Mostyn, whose fleets were then cruising along the Acadian coasts. It was resolved to remove, and to scatter among the British colonies, the whole remanent Gallo-Acadian population. This was effected by gathering the people simultaneously, in so many troops, at different points of the country. Proclamations, drawn up with perfidious skill, ordered them to assemble in the principal villages, under the most rigorous penalties. Four hundred and eighteen heads of families, putting their trust in British honour, met together, on the 5th day of September, at three o'clock in the afternoon, in the church of Grandpré. Thither came Colonel Winslow, with great parade, and, after showing the governor's warrant for what he was about to do, he said they had been called together to hear the decision the king had come to respecting their fate. He then said he had a painful duty to fulfil; but that his Majesty's orders were imperative, and must be obeyed. These were, that "the lands, farming stock, and whole moveables of the Acadians, except their bed and table linen and their plate, were confiscated to the crown. Further, that the persons of said Acadians should be transported from the province of Nova Scotia." No reason was assigned for this decision.

A body of soldiers, hitherto kept in the background, now started from their hiding-place, and surrounded the church. The people, thus entrapped, could make no resistance. The soldiers then collected the women and children outside. More than a thousand persons were thus made prisoners at Grand-Pré alone. Some few Acadians having escaped into the woods, the country was devastated to prevent their finding means of subsistence therein. In Les Mines, some hundreds of houses, twelve mills and a church, were burnt. Those of the race who manifested British predilections were no better treated than the rest. Thus the aged notary Le Blanc, who had done Britain great service, died at Philadelphia destitute and broken-hearted, while in search of his sons, scattered about the colonies of his oppressors. Permission was given to all, before embarking, (and this was the sole grace accorded to any), to pay a visit, by tens, to their families, and, for the last time, to look upon those fields, those valleys, those hills, lately so smiling and so tranquil in their view; amongst which they were born, to which they had now to bid an eternal farewell.

The 10th [of September?] was the day fixed for the embarkation. A calm resignation had succeeded to their first feeling of despair. But, when the hour of leaving arrived; when the time was fully come that they must perforce live apart from each other amidst an alien people, of novel manners, customs, language, and religion, their courage gave way, and they were overwhelmed with sadness. By a violation of sworn faith, and an unparalleled refinement of barbarity, families were broken up, and the members of them dispersed among diverse transports. Before embarking, the prisoners were ranged six abreast; the young men in front. The latter refused to move, reclaiming the execution of the promise made to them that they should accompany their relatives; but a body of soldiers were called, who drove them on with fixed bayonets. The road from Grand-Pré chapel to the river Gaspareaux, was a mile long; it was lined on both sides with women and children, who, on bended knees, and in tears, encouraged their husbands, sons, fathers, pouring upon them parting blessings. The sad procession passed on slowly, praying and singing hymns. The heads of families walked after the young men.

At length the train reached the sea-shore, when the males were consigned, in troops, to this vessel and that; the women and children were stowed away pell-mell in other vessels, without the least attention being paid to their wants, or any regard had for their convenience. Governments have sometimes been severe, even cruel, during times when vengeance waked and mercy slept— as when revolutions, civil or religious, were in progress; but we can find no instance, in modern history, of so heavy a chastisement being inflicted on an entire people of inoffensive character, with so much coolness and barbarity united, as that which the Acadians now received at British hands.

The details we have given above, more especially depict what passed in one locality; but the like might apply to all other instances of the forced expatriation carried out elsewhere at the same time.

The transports, freighted with victims, set sail for the Anglo-American colonies. They discharged their living cargoes, at intervals, along the whole seaboard, from Boston to Carolina, destitute of means of subsistence and without any protection. During many days after that which witnessed the departure of the Acadians from their homesteads, unsheltered cattle wandered about the desolated farms, and dogs, now masterless, made the nights dreary with piteous howlings.

Most of the British colonists—to their honour be it said—received the homeless Acadians with such kindness, as intimated a tacit reproach to the home government for its inexorable rigour. M. Benezet, for one, who was a descendant of a banished huguenot family, received those of them who went to Philadelphia as if they had been his own kin.

Some of the exiles took shelter in Louisiana; others went to French Guiana: and certain Frenchmen, banished themselves to Sinnamari, found there, in 1798, an Acadian family whose members received them hospitably; saying, "You are welcome! Our ancestors were expelled from their country, even as you are now. They taught us to succour the unfortunate. So come into our cabin, and let us have the pleasure of rendering you such consolation therein as we have to bestow."

The Acadians, in the sequel, founded a canton in Louisiana, and gave to it the ever-dear name of *Acadie*. Louis XV, touched by their patriotic fidelity, made overtures, but in vain, through his ministers to those of Britain, to be allowed to send vessels thither for transferring the inhabitants to France. Mr. Grenville hastened to reply, "Our Navigation Act stands in the way; French vessels may not take cargoes in a British colony:" as if that law could not, for once, be made to conform to the dictates of humanity! Nevertheless, some of the Acadians did reach France; their descendants now inhabit two flourishing communes wherein the peaceful habitudes and rustic peculiarities of their race are still recognizable, among the verdant oases which dot the moorlands (*les landes de Bordeaux*) of Gascony.

Britain reaped no benefit from her harsh polity in Nova Scotia, eventuating in the expatriation of the Açadians. On the contrary, the Canadians, noting the treatment their compatriots had just received at her hands, became more determined to resist to the last the alien domination intended to be forced upon them.

While steel and flame were doing their desolating work on the fair face of what was once Acadia, General Braddock was busied in preparing to thrust the French out of the Ohio valley; that is, to realize the second part of the general plan of invasion. Will's Creek, beside the Alleghanies, was the place of rendezvous for the colonial auxiliaries, who were to come in aid of the regulars, to effect that enterprise. When all his force was assembled, Braddock set out, cheered on by the population, with a small army, but including an enormous train of artillery, baggage waggons, &c., occupying four miles of a course, obstructed by forest, river, and mountain. While this cumbrous mass was stumbling on slowly, much time elapsed, and Braddock began to be impatient, fearing that Fort Duquesne, which, he knew, was but scantily manned, might receive succour, and be hard to take. He divided his forces; and, leaving Colonel Dunbar with 1,000 men and most of the artillery, baggage, &c., put himself at the head of 1,200 others, including his most active and best disciplined soldiers. Early morning, July 9, he crossed the river Monongahela, at a spot about 15 miles distant from Fort Duquesne, and in great haste marched along its southern side in the direction of a prize which, in idea, was already his own. George Washington attended him, as a colonel of his staff. " He was often heard to remark in after life, that he had never seen a finer sight than that presented by the passage of the British troops, on this memorable forenoon, towards the French post. Every soldier was in his best trim; the men were ranged in the most perfect order, forming a steadily advancing column; the sun shone brightly on their well-polished arms, the river flowed on peacefully at their right side; on the left, the nearer trees of the huge forest wilderness shaded them in solemn stateliness. Officers and men alike marched onward buoyantly, in full assurance of overcoming the foe." *

About noon, this proud array re-crossed the river, at a ford about ten miles from Fort Duquesne, and debouched on a plain, about half-a-mile in breadth, with a riverward margin but a few

---

* GUIZOT: "Life, Correspondence, and Writings of Washington."

feet above the water-level. At the extremity of this plain the ground took the form, for some space, of a gentle acclivity, and was abruptly terminated by the sudden uprising of lofty hills. The route, from the ford to the fort, lay along the plain and slope, traversed a height, and was prolonged through a woody country, of rugged surface. Colonel Gage led the van, composed of 300 regulars; another corps, of 200 men, followed; behind was the main body, headed by Braddock; the artillery, &c., closed the march.

M. de Contrecœur commanded at Fort Duquesne. One of his scouts informed him, July 8, that the British were but six leagues off. He resolved to attack them on the way, and proceeded himself to mark a place of ambuscade. Next day, 253 Canadians and 600 savages, led by M. de Beaujeu, left the fort, about 8 A. M., to take post in the ravines and thickets bordering the road along which the British were about to pass. This troop was in act of descending the slope bordering the plain above noted, just as Colonel Gage began to ascend it. The two masses soon met in mid-career, and before the French were able to reach the ground they had been directed to take up. There was now nothing for it, but for each party to try its strength in driving its adversaries off the line of road. The British, taken by surprise, had to sustain a hot fire, galled by which their ranks gave way somewhat, and Gage was fain to fall back upon the main body of Braddock's forces. The path being thus cleared, the French were enabled to complete the operation planned beforehand, and mostly ensconced themselves in every covert of brushwood and behind each rock which could be turned to sheltering account; while the mounted Canadians took post on the river, as if it were only they who meant to dispute the passage, whereas the foot soldiers and savages, posted at intervals, right and left, formed a half-circle, the horns of which curved outwards so as to enclose the approaching enemy.

The British van, its ranks re-formed, and closely supported by the main body, were advancing confidently, when a semi-concentric fire, from unseen gun-muzzles, was opened upon them, seemingly from every side, under which they first staggered, were then brought to a halt, and finally threw their ranks into confusion.

Braddock, however, by great exertion restoring order, they opened fire on as many of their foes as they could see; and the artillery coming up, began to play upon the French central corps. One of the first cannon-balls shot killed M. de Beaujeu. M. Dumas, second in command, placed himself at the head of the French not under cover, and, well sustained by M. de Ligneris and other officers, dashed forward on the British. A desperate struggle ensued. The savages, who had been scared by the cannonade, observing that the Canadians did not flinch under it, with yells resumed the sheltering-places they had left. The British long put a good face upon the matter, and even made a forward movement, the men being impelled onward by their officers, sword in hand; but, fairly confounded by the murderous fire kept up, and which ever thinned their ranks the more they further advanced, the whole body of regulars fell into hopeless disorder. So perplexed were some fusileers, that, firing at random, they killed several of their officers and some of their own comrades. The colonial militia alone seemed to preserve their presence of mind on the occasion; but even they were in the end borne backward by the panic-stricken regulars. Meanwhile Braddock did his best to reform his men, and lead them back to the charge, but all in vain. The balls flew round him like hail; two horses he rode were killed; he mounted a third, but only to receive a mortal wound, for most of the French and savages, firing under shelter, were able to single out, at their leisure, all whom they chose to hit. After a three hours' struggle, the British column gave way entirely, abandoning the cannon. The Canadians now advanced hatchet in hand, and the savages quitting their lurking-places simultaneously, both fell upon the rear of the retreating British and Americans, and made frightful havoc; those whose swiftness of foot did not exceed that of their pursuers, were cut down or drowned in the Monongahela, in a fruitless attempt to gain the opposite banks.* M. Dumas, knowing that Colonel Dunbar's corps was still intact, and would serve as a rallying body for such fugitives as had gained the advance, pursued them no longer; and called a halt the rather, as the savages had betaken themselves to pilla-

---

* M. POUCNOT: "Memoirs on the late War in North America."

ging, and it would have been a hard matter to get them off their prey.

The carnage thus concluded had scarcely an example in the annals of modern war.* Nearly 800 out of the 1200 men led to battle by Braddock were killed or wounded. Out of 86 officers, 26 were slain, and 37 hurt; for they made heroic attempts to rally and inspirit their baffled men.† Washington excepted, all the mounted officers received wounds, mortal or other. The luckless general was carried to Fort Necessity, where he died July 13, and was buried at the roadside, near that paltry post. He was a brave and experienced officer, but an arrogant man; contemning his enemy, despising alike militia and savages; yet had he the mortification to see his regulars madly flee, while the Virginians stood firmly and fought bravely to the last.

The beaten soldiers, when they reached those of Dunbar, infected them also with their own panic; and in an instant, the corps broke up. The cannon were spiked, the ammunition destroyed, and most of the baggage burnt; by whose direction no one knew. There was no semblance of order had, till the fugitive rout attained Fort Cumberland, in the Alleghanies.‡ Washington wrote thence: "We have been beaten, shamefully beaten, by a handful of French, who only expected to obstruct our advance. Shortly before the action, we thought our forces were equal to all the enemies' in Canada; we have been most unexpectedly defeated, and now all is lost."

The French gained a great booty. The baggage of the vanquished, their provisions, 15 cannon, many small arms and much munitions of war, the military chest, Braddock's papers—in fine, all became fair spoil for the victors. These documents unveiled the projects of the British ministry, and served to justify the indignant sentiments expressed against its polity in a memorial addressed, by the Duke de Choiseul, to the different European courts. There were taken, after the battle, from amidst the dismounted and broken vehicles left on the field, from 400 to 500 horses, including those which had been killed or hurt.

---

* Mr. JARED SPARKS: *Life of Washington.*
† The author adds, "Several officers killed themselves in despair:" a doubtful assertion.—B.
‡ Life, Correspondence, &c., of Washington.

The victory cost the French only about 40 men. M. de Beaujeu was much regretted by the Canadians, his compatriots, and by the Indian tribes, who held him in great respect.

Thus ended the combat of Monongahela, one of the most memorable battles known to American history. The beaten bands took up their quarters in Philadelphia. The news of their discomfiture spread universal consternation throughout the whole of British America. The back settlements of Pennsylvania, Maryland, and Virginia, were abandoned forthwith. Even the colonists near the seaboard began to be doubtful of their future security The clergy, from their pulpits, had to admonish their flocks to view their position more calmly.

The victory gained by the French assured them the possession of the Ohio valley for the time, as Washington's defeat at Fort Necessity prevented the British from obtaining the mastery there the year before.

While the operations we have just detailed were progressing beyond the southern limits of Canada, the British forces charged to reduce Forts Niagara and St. Frederic assembled at Albany. They set out thence, to the amount of 5,000 to 6,000 men, under the orders of General Lyman; Colonel Johnson followed, with the artillery, boats, provisions, and battering train. Having reached the portage between the Hudson and Lake George, Lyman began to erect Fort Edward, to serve as a base for the double line of operations intended.

Meanwhile Johnson continued his march, to the right, and attained the head of Lake George; and Lyman made great exertions, on his part, to put as much means of embarkation afloat as possible, hoping to secure the important pass of Carillon (Ticonderoga) before the French could make it impregnable. But instead of being the attacking party, the British soon found themselves assailed at their head-quarters on the lake.

We have mentioned, on a preceding page, the inquietude felt by M. de Vaudreuil at the presence of Johnson on Lake George; and we narrated, at the same time, that the governor-general deferred the meditated attack on Oswego, to make head against the British at Lake George. In consequence, Baron Dieskau, then in command of 3,000 men at Fort Frederic, was informed,

Sept. 1, that Johnson was coming to assault the place. He learned, too, that the works of Fort Edward were not complete, and might easily be carried; while in that locality Johnson's magazines were situated. Dieskau resolved to attack the British at once, with a moiety of his force; leaving the other half at Carillon, to fall back upon, in case he were repulsed.

The corps he set out with was composed of 220 regulars, 680 Canadians under M. de Repentigny, and 600 savages, led by M. de St. Pierre. On the way, he was told that 900 Anglo-Americans were intrenched under the walls of the place; but this intimation he heeded not; for, like Braddock, he held militiamen very cheap. M. de Vaudreuil's instructions were positive, too, that he should undertake no enterprise with a divided force;* both the Canadians and savages blamed him for leaving the half of his strength at Carillon: but the baron was consumed with a desire to eclipse the success, gained with small means, in the Ohio country. Already jealousies were arising between the French-born and native soldiers of the colony, which, being fomented by their respective officers, were sure to increase.† Fearing that a large number of men would impede his march, and lessen the chances of striking a sudden blow successfully, he neglected the wary counsels proffered to him, and thus tempted the evil fate of the expedition.

At once to hide his advance and avoid contact with Johnson's corps, Dieskau embarked his men on Lake Champlain, which having ascended to South-bay, he landed them at a point fully 20 miles distant from Fort Edward. Sept. 7, in the evening, he bivouacked on the Hudson, within three miles of Fort Edward. His intention was, to attack the place at daybreak next morning but his savages, malcontent at the small number of soldiers they were conjoined to, declared they would not fight at all: assigning for a pretext that Fort Edward was situated within the British territory, as it lay on the banks of the Hudson. They added, that they would not object, on the other hand, to attack Johnson's camp, because that had been pitched on French ground. The Canadians, seeing the savages were resolute in maintaining their resolve,

---

* Instructions of M. de Vaudreuil: *official correspondence.*
† Letter of M. de Lotbinière to the minister, dated Oct. 28, 1755.

backed it with an advice to the Baron to take them at their second word. The general unwillingly yielded to both; and, next morning, instead of assaulting Fort Edward, his troops were directed, in three columns—the regulars in the centre—towards the mountains previously behind them; the design being to fall suddenly upon Johnson's corps, 2,500 strong, then distant about 15 miles.

Johnson, on his part, after learning that Fort Edward was to be attacked by the French, had detached Colonel Williams that very morning, with 1200 men and 200 savages, to lay an ambuscade for the invaders, on their expected return from Fort Edward. Dieskau, when within four miles of Johnson's camp, was informed by a prisoner there taken, of this detachment being on the way, and sure to be met with shortly. He halted his central column, and directed the two others—namely, the Canadians (who laid aside their haversacks to lighten themselves for action) and the savages—to post themselves, the former on the right, the latter on the left, but 300 paces in advance, with orders to lie squat on the ground amid the woods, and not to turn round on the approaching enemies' flank till musketry was heard from the centre. In this position Dieskau waited for the British, who were thus about to fall into a trap similar to that they meant to set for the French; but the savages, on the left wing of the latter, showed themselves before the concerted time, and put the former on their guard. Dieskau, seeing his ambuscade thus unmasked, at once pushed on his regulars and the Canadians, before the British corps could get out of marching order and form for action. The savages, too, rushing forward, fell with fury upon the British, if only to avenge the death of their leader, M. de St. Pierre, who was killed at the outset by one of Williams' men : the latter they hacked to pieces with their tomahawks. The colonel himself was also slain, along with Hendrick, a famous Indian chief. The struggle was short, bloody, and decisive, ending in a victory for the French over the British vanguard. A second corps which came up was as quickly disposed of, and whatever troops were behind took to flight. Dieskau was preparing to follow up his success, hoping to be able to enter, pell-mell with the fugitives, Johnson's lines; but this was not to be done with such half-disciplined combatants as he led. A part of the Canadians and savages were attending to the wounded; others were disposed for rest, after the fatigues of the contest, and the severe toil of a march through a rugged and steep country. In a word, a moiety of the savages and Canadians, satisfied with the success already gained, would proceed no further for the time.* The general, nevertheless, hopeful that his example would be imitated, continued to advance with his regulars and as many others as chose to follow him, and arrived in front of Johnson's intrenched camp, with scarcely a moiety of his entire force, about 11 o'clock, A. M.

The entrenchments which the French now had to encounter and the British to defend, were situated near the margin of Lake George, on an eminence afterwards the site of Fort George, and barricaded with bateaux, dismounted carts, felled trees, &c. mounted with artillery, and were further isolated by two wide brooks and marshy grounds. The first objects discerned by the French on their arrival, were the cannon muzzles directed towards them. When within about 200 paces of the place, Dieskau suspended the march of his troops to form them into attacking columns; this halt, short as it was, gave time to the British to prepare for what was coming, and to put their defences in order.

The attack was made with great vigour. Dieskau's regulars, after delivering a well-maintained platoon fire, dashed forward with fixed bayonets, hoping to penetrate the barricade; but they were fain to retire repulsed from the works, so hot and heavy was the fire of musketry and grape directed against them point-blank. Their broken ranks, having been re-formed, again they returned to the charge, and continued their bootless efforts from noon till 2 P. M. The Canadians and savages, who had followed Dieskau or afterwards rejoined his force, noting the inutility of these attempts, took possession, scatteredly, of a wood on the left, while others occupied a height on the left, whence they poured a plunging fire into the entrenchments, at a distance from them of only 12 or 15 paces,† and kept it up till the close of the day. The French general,

---

* Letter from the Chevalier de Montreuil to the minister, dated Oct. 10, 1755.

† The regulars marched, as near as I could tell, six deep in close order, and reached about 20 rods in length. The Canadians and Indians

with his regulars on one side, and the Canadians on the other, led on a final assault, sword in hand; which had no more success than the preceding attacks. The assaulters having attained the foot of the defences, were still unable to force them; and while they were brought to a stand-still, the British marksmen were able, at their ease, to pick out all those they chose to victimize. At this crisis, Dieskau, while turning round towards the Canadians, and ordering them to advance, received three shots almost at the same instant of time. M. de Montreuil, though he had an arm crippled by a ball, aided the general to retire under a tree, and then called two Canadians to remove him out of shot-range. One of them was killed on arriving, and his body fell on the general's legs; the other was wounded. Without losing his presence of mind, Dieskau desired Montreuil to repair to the left wing and quicken the attack on that side, which had become slack; and declined any farther aid to help him out of danger; saying, " The natural couch he occupied was as fit for him to die upon, as any bed that could be sent him." He demanded his telescope and riding-coat, and enjoined his domestics and those Canadians nearest to him to retire.* At this instant, a portion of the Canadians and savages gave way, and the chevalier de Montreuil vainly sought to rally the baffled regulars, now reduced to 100 in number; while almost every one of their officers had been killed or wounded.

The affair had lasted five hours, when the French drew off, without being molested in their retreat; the British being cowed by the fiery valour of their assailants, and, with a few exceptions, keeping safely ensconced within their lines. One of the individuals who did overpass them, on seeing Dieskau seated helpless at the treefoot, pointed his piece at 15 paces' distance, and fired a ball through the lower part of the general's body. The fellow having safely accomplished this *heroic* feat, claimed the object of it as his pri-

---

at the left having come on helter-skelter, the woods being full of them, running with undaunted courage downhill upon us, expecting to make us flee, as they had before done at the ———, and just now did to our men."—Extract of a letter from the American Colonel, Pomeroy, dated Sept. 10, 1755.

* Relation of the Campaign of 1755.—Letter from Baron Dieskau to M. de Montreuil, dated Bath, Jan. 26, 1758.

soner. He was a Canadian deserter, who had been residing, during a dozen years, in New-York.

Meanwhile, De Montreuil succeeded in rallying a part of the troops, within 500 paces of the intrenchments, and infused an orderly spirit among them. By this time, all the French corps was broken up, and parts of it gathered into bands. One of these still remained on the morning's scene of action, another was in full retreat; De Montreuil, with a third party, took the road leading to the Grand-Marais, bearing along about 100 wounded men; lastly, the Canadians and savages, still master of the eminence mentioned above, on the British right flank, and not cognizant of what had passed out of their view, still kept up their fusillade on the works.

The enemy, after the beleaguerers retreated, certainly were in error not to follow up their success by issuing from their lines, and seeking out those French who were scattered over the neighbourhood. De Montreuil, in two days, reached the Grand-Marais with his men, but all foot-sore, and famished, the Canadians not having regained the provision sacks they had laid aside in action. Another column, in the like plight, arrived at the Grand-Marais before De Montreuil. By degrees other parties came up, and the collective body embarked on the lake and descended it to Carillon (Ticonderoga).

The loss of the French, in Dieskau's expedition, was smaller than might have been expected. It amounted however to 310 regulars, and every fourth man of those Canadians and savages who assailed the British entrenchments; including, among the killed, wounded, or missing 13 officers, 9 of whom were Canadians.* The British loss, on the other hand, reckoning that sustained in the first contest, was relatively greater. Colonel Titcombe was killed on the field; colonel Johnson, and Major Nichols, were wounded in the entrenchments. Their successful defenders admitted, afterwards, that the British were 2,200 strong, and yet that to their works and their artillery were they indebted

---

* Letter of M. Dorell to the minister, dated Oct. 20, 1755. Letter of Baron Dieskau.

for safety; while their assailants had not a single piece of ordnance.*

When Baron Dieskau was led into the British lines, Johnson, with refined humanity which did him honour, caused his prisoner to be taken to his own tent, and ordered that the hurts the general had received should be examined before his own (Johnson's) wound was attended to. In other respects, the unceasing kindnesses he showed to Dieskau while under his charge were ever gratefully remembered by its object. The latter was detained in England till the war ended, when he returned to France. After intermediate years of suffering from his wounds, he died of their effects, in 1767, at Surenne, near Paris.

Like Braddock, this general owed his discomfiture to an absurd reliance on European discipline, and to neglecting the advices of the governor-general and Canadian officers as to the best mode of warring in America. A misplaced persistence, based on imperfect local inquiries, added to an under-estimation of the colonial forces, induced him to attack, with veteran regulars indeed, but exhausted even by their successes, entrenched enemies double in number to his own men. He thereby sacrificed the flower of his army; and caused the Canadians to lose the confidence they thitherto had in European generalship. The minister was advertised, in consequence, that "the colonists would not march to do battle, with so much confidence, under French leaders, as when led by their own officers."

The repulse of the French served to raise the spirit of the British colonists, depressed as it had been by the bloody defeat of Braddock; but the effects of our temporary check were not so great, in their favour, as they expected. At first, their exaltation at it was excessive, for it was trumpeted as a splendid victory; the plain fact being, that their soldiers had been able to hold their own and no more, against a spirited assault, with inferior numbers and no artillery, on formidable field-works. Newspaper writers,

---

* "Our artillery played briskly on our front the whole time, and the breast-work secured our men."—" They (the French) made a bold attack and maintained it bravely; our cannon and breast-work saved us."— " We were effective about 2,200 at the time of the engagement."—*Documents de Londres.*

none the less, strove with each other who should most exalt the talents and courage of Johnson; the house of commons voted £5,000 to him, and George II created him a baronet.

The Anglo-Americans, believing that the way to Montreal was thenceforward open, and finding Sir William to be in no hurry to advance in that direction, began to murmur at his tardiness for not following up the late victory; all thinking that he should at least have come down upon fort Frederic. The authorities even sent an order to him to march thither, if only to show regard for the general wish; but this he declined to do, and continued to strengthen his position. He was then accused of a want of enterprise, of indulging an indolent feeling of contentment with laurels already gained, and an imputed dread of tarnishing them by running dangerous hazards in his country's service. Johnson, piqued at these insinuations, wrote to his superiors that his troops were destitute of all proper necessaries for taking the field; that, furthermore, they had not recovered from the terror of French heroism, and that it was the last desire in their hearts to tempt fate by encountering the ever-terrible Canadians.* After this exposition, most of the army was disbanded,† and only 600 men retained to guard Fort Edward and the lake encampment; to which the name of Fort William Henry was given, after it had been transformed into a permanent fastness.

The news of Dieskau's defeat, which so rejoiced the British colonists, caused great inquietude in Canada. The governor-general knowing how important it was to keep hold of the upper end of lake Champlain, charged M. de Lotbinière to erect a wooden fort at Carillon (Ticonderoga). He ordered the troops to take post there meantime, so as to be ready to oppose the enemy if he should descend by the Whitehall road, or by lake George; and to cover the position of St. Frederic (Crown-Point), the key of both lakes. In a few weeks, however, tranquillizing accounts of the enemies' inaction and real intents arrived. Besides the disbandment of most of Johnson's army, as above noted, news came that a draft of

---

* MINOT; *Continuation of the History of Massachusetts' Bay.*

† And not too soon either, if the above account of its unmilitary *moral* be truthful, but which we rather doubt.—*B.*

1,500 men from that region had been made, for the siege of fort Niagara, just then undertaken by general Shirley; but the latter, it was ascertained, not being able to complete his preparations in time for that enterprise, had turned landward, leaving colonel Mercer to guard Oswego, and erect new works around that place. It appeared also, that the discomfiture of Braddock had discouraged the enemies' soldiers, great numbers of whom deserted; likewise that the Five Nations were opposed to the war, which ruined their fur traffic; finally, that the arrival of succours at Frontenac (Kingston) and Niagara, had quite deadened the enemy's hope of capturing these important posts.

Thus the three principal enterprises meditated by the British, against forts Duquesne, St. Frederic, and Niagara, all failed, and had to be postponed for the current year at least; results which exceeded the highest previous hopes indulged by the Canadians. Their forces maintained every position they held when the year's campaign began, fort Beauséjour excepted; the loss of which little subtracted from the military strength of the frontier on that side, for M. de Beauséjour, its guardian, was still master of the open country.

The checks the enemy had to endure, on the other hand, proved most disastrous for their back settlements. The Anglo-American forces having been defeated or forced to retreat, unopposed bands of Canadians and savages had a rare time of it, spent in devastating the nearer British colonies, from Nova Scotia to Virginia. More than a thousand people were massacred or dragged off as prisoners by these redoubtable warriors; who came down upon the helpless, like to an overwhelming torrent, leaving nothing but ruin behind them. The former terror-stricken colonists, to avoid being butchered, left their houses in despair, and sought an asylum in the seaboard countries. The people everywhere were astounded at this fearful result of a hopeful campaign. "Four armies were got on foot," said Minot, an American historian, "to resist French encroachments; our coasts were guarded by the fleet of the brave and vigilant Boscawen; we waited only for the signal to be given, to go up and possess New France. How bitter our present disappointment! We have had some success in Acadia, 'tis true; but Braddock was defeated; while Niagara and Crown Point are still French fortresses. The while that barbarians, uncurbed, ravage our lands, and slay their on-dwellers, our seats of government are distracted by factions, and the provincial finances are exhausted."—The cost of the abortive preparations against fort Frederic, to New England alone, was £80,000; yet the British provinces found themselves subjected, at the year's end, to the worst evils of a war, the wageing of which was entirely due to the ambitious aspirations of their inhabitants.

The French troops were cantoned, for the winter, near Montreal. Public security in Canada itself had been little troubled; but if most things therein looked calm for the time, its future, to the prescient eye, appeared sombre enough. Dearth was in the land, and absolute famine imminent. The year's harvest in Quebec had failed, while extraordinary supplies were wanted to subsist the troops, the armed savages, and the destitute Acadian exiles. The poor in the towns began to perish of want. This afflicting state of things, however, was but a prelude to greater sufferings the people had to endure, the natural accompaniments of this long and cruel war.

Already announcements were made in England, that the next campaign would be undertaken with a great increase of the British forces. In Canada, a counter-resolve was formed, to put the colony, without a moment's delay, in a fit state, not only to defend itself, but to carry the war into its enemies' territories, on every tempting occasion. The governor-general and the intendant, meanwhile, demanded of the French ministry reinforcements of soldiers, also supplies of provisions and of munitions of war. In their applications for succour, they contrasted the relative material strength of the French and British American colonies. The chief military officers in the colony corresponded with the court in a similar strain. Some of them had apprehensions of evil results, which they cared not to hide. "The situation of the colony," wrote M. de Doreil, war-commissary, " is every way critical; abundant succours, promptly forwarded, are now indispensable. I venture to declare, that if this be not done, our chances in the coming year are of the most perilous character."

A universal wish expressed in such missives, was that a generalissimo, of tried bravery and proper military experience, should be sent out to replace Baron Dieskau; and along with such a one, some engineers (there being none as yet) and artillery officers "We ought to have in the field next year," urged the intendant, "several corps for the campaign of the spring, and 1,600 or 1,700 land troops: now, 1,000 or 1,200 colonists will not suffice; portions of the latter must be retained for garrison service in the towns, others are wanted to guard the outposts. Hence it is that Canadians compose the bulk of these armies (of ours), not to mention that 1,000 to 1,200 are always employed in escorting. The Canadians, being thus engaged in military services, do not till the grounds already cleared, much less set about clearing new. What is to become of the colony! it will soon be in want of all necessaries, supplies of grain especially. Till now, care was taken not to levy men till after seed-time; but this could not be done since we have had winter expeditions to provide for, and our forces for next year's campaign must be afoot by early April. Add to all, that the Canadians are sensibly diminishing in number; many have died of fatigue and disease: while the savages are to be relied on," added the intendant, " only so long as we can hold our own, and minister to their needs." Such and so grave was the officially declared situation of New France at the close of 1755.

The second year of hostilities between the men of French and British races in America was now closing, yet their respective governments had not formally proclaimed war as existing, and diplomacy between them was still at work. December 21, 1755, M. Rouillé de Jouy, foreign minister, Paris, addressed a note to Mr. Fox, in which he demanded signal reparation for the insults the flag of France had lately received; adding, that a refusal to make such amends would be regarded as evidencing the fixed intent of the British ministry to break up the peace of Europe. The tone of that note, however, testified the weakness of the French court's polity. "It is not the fault of our king," wrote the minister, " that the differences concerning America have not been settled before now by conciliatory means; and this averment His Majesty is able to demonstrate, in face of the whole world, by authentic proofs. The king, ever animated by a sincere desire to preserve the general peace, and be on terms of amity with his Britannic Majesty, has negociated with perfect good faith and unbroken confidence, on all the subjects in debate between them. The like assurances, on the other part, which were enounced and renewed unceasingly both orally and in writing, would not, in fact, allow the king to admit a doubt into his mind of the pacific intents of the court of St. James's. But it is not possible to reconcile such verbal assurances with the hostile instructions drawn up in November 1754, for the guidance of general Braddock, in America; or with those of April 1755, to admiral Boscawen.......... His (Most Christian) Majesty, therefore, in duty to his subjects and himself, now addresses his Britannic Majesty, and demands that entire and prompt restitution be made of all those French vessels, both ships of war and merchantmen, which have been captured by the British navy, along with their several crews, marines, &c., and all their equipments respectively. The king would much prefer to have had accorded to him, out of a sense of equity in the mind of his Britannic Majesty, that satisfaction which is now demanded as of right."

The British minister replied to M. Rouillé, Jan. 13, 1756, in civil but positive terms, that such satisfaction as was demanded could not be given so long as the chain of French armed posts to the north-west of the Alleghanies existed; that his royal master, in none of the hostile orders given to his officers, had done more than retaliate upon those of France their acts of war committed in time of peace; that his Majesty had done only what was due to his own honour, or in defence of the rights and possessions of the British crown; finally, that he had not gone an inch beyond what was just, or in fact unavoidable."

After all that had now taken place, viewed in connection with long and inimical debates in the British parliament, no further good understanding between the two nations was possible to exist, and Louis XV had perforce to arouse himself for open war against Great Britain. Dunkirk was fortified; all the British subjects in France were ordered to leave; every British vessel then in French port was seized; large fleets were equipped; and the shores of Britain were menaced with invasion. King George solicited aid, too, from Holland and Hanover.* But that threat

---

* The king needed not Dutch aid; and the resources of Hanover were more completely at his disposition, by far, than those of Britain.—*B*.

masked another design, soon to be manifested to the British people in the defeat of admiral Byng and the capture of Minorca.

In Europe, as in America, was heard a universal din of arms. May 17, the British declaration of war was proclaimed; June 16, that of France was promulgated. These manifestoes, solemn in form, were supererogatory in nature; for war was virtually begun, years before they were drawn up.

The French ministry resolved on sending to Canada two new battalions, and young soldiers to recruit the old already therein. They also sent a supply of provisions, and 1,300,000 livres in specie. This money, strange as the fact may seem, did much harm to the colony; for, as we have already remarked, when treating of Canadian trade, it caused a reduction in existing paper-money values of 25 per cent.

The king selected the Marquis de Montcalm, promoting him to a major-generalship (*qu'il fit maréchal de camp*), as Dieskau's successor. This officer had seen much service. He was born, in 1712, in the château of Candiac, near Nismes, and descended of one of the greatest families in Rouergue. He had campaigned in Italy and Germany; and signalized himself in the battle of Placentia, also at the siege of Assiette; having received five wounds in these two actions. He had likewise gained distinction, under Marshal de Belleisle, in the famous retreat from Prague. But he possessed all the defects of French generals of his time; he was at once full of vivacity and heedlessness, timid in his strategic movements, and audacious in battle to a degree inconsistent with prudence. Of his complete personal courageousness no one could have any doubt.

General Montcalm embarked for Canada along with two battalions, comprising 1,000 men, and 400 recruits. The vessel in which he was reached Quebec about mid-May, 1756; the others, later in that month and early in June. They bore, also, a quantity of provisions (anxiously expected) and munitions of war. These reinforcements, added to 1,600 soldiers of two battalions sent the previous year, along with the colonial troops, composed a body of 4,000 regulars; this was nearly the whole French force sent to Canada while the war lasted.

With M. de Montcalm also came several officers: among them

was M. de Levis, chevalier (afterwards duke) de Lévis, and finally a marshal, but at that time brigadier-general only,—a distinguished officer; one "well skilled, of a high military spirit, and prompt to decide in action." M. Montcalm, in characterizing him, said he was "indefatigable, courageous, and of a good school in war." There came, too, M. de Bougainville, then Montcalm's aide-de-camp and captain of dragoons; but who was destined to become one of the most illustrious of French navigators; for, "while attending to his military duties, he still found time for scientific studies."* Other officers who now arrived were M. de Bourlamaque, M. de Montreuil, &c.

Montcalm, shortly after landing, proceeded to Montreal, to hold a conference with M. de Vaudreuil, who had gone thither to be nearer to the seat of war. After a close view of the country's situation and resources, it was arranged between these its chief men, that two principal camps should be formed : one at Carillon (Ticonderoga), the other at Frontenac (Kingston), in order to be within observation of forts Edward and Oswego; at which places the British had begun to assemble, in order to advance upon lakes Champlain and Ontario. One battalion (de Béarn) was despatched to Niagara, where a few men had been left in autumn 1755; and M. Pouchot, an officer of infantry but a good engineer also, was directed to fortify the post there. Two battalions were sent to Frontenac, with orders to strengthen themselves there, and to maintain a communication with 1,000 Canadians and savages disseminated thence towards Niagara. M. de Bourlamaque was charged with the chief command on that frontier. At Carillon, by the end of July, 3,000 men, a moiety being regulars, were assembled, under the orders of M. de Levis.

For the protection of the Gaspé fisheries 120 men were assigned; and M. de Boishébert was left in charge of the Acadian frontier, with a corps of Canadians and savages. In the West, M. Dumas relieved M. de Contrecœur, at fort Duquesne ; and M. de Bellestre replaced M. Demery at Detroit. These chiefs had for lieutenants Messrs. de Repentigny, de Langlade, Hébert,

---

* *Le Canada sous la Domination Française,* by M. Dussieux, professor of history at the Imperial School of St.-Cyr, corresponding member of the Historical Committees. 1855.

Beaubassin, &c. On this frontier 3,500 Canadians and savages were in arms, from lake Erie to New Orleans, following the line of the Ohio, Illinois, and Mississippi valleys. The whole military force at this time on foot for the defence of New France, from Cape Breton to the Illinois, did not exceed 12,000 combatants at the very most; and large deductions had to be allowed for, even from that small amount, during the spring and fall, when many of the militiamen were absent on furlough, to enable them to attend to country labour in seed-time and harvest.

At Louisbourg, a stronghold of capital importance, there was a garrison of 1,100 troops; and even that considerable number was too small. This deficiency was felt at court, and 600 more men were embarked for Cape Breton, in a frigate named the *Arc-en-Ciel;* but they were fated never to reach their destination, as that vessel was captured by a British privateer when near Louisbourg.

Such were the preparations of the French for the campaign in America of the year 1756. Those of the British were far more considerable as to the means to be employed. The plan of invasion, on their part, remained unchanged. The home government sent liberal supplies of men and money, hoping to wash out in the enemies' blood the stain caused by the defeat of Braddock; also to avenge the loss of Minorca; two events which had produced a great sensation in Europe. America, as the chief field of military operations, almost absorbed the attention of British statesmen. The earl of Loudon, a veteran officer, first was appointed governor of Virginia, and then generalissimo of the British armies in North America. General Abercromby also was sent thither with two new regiments. The house of commons voted £115,000 to aid the colonials to levy and arm their militia. The different provincial governors met at New York, and resolved to raise 10,000 men, to take Fort Frederic and obtain the mastery of lake Champlain; 6,000 more, were to besiege Niagara, and bar the Ohio valley against the French; 3,000 besides, to capture Fort Duquesne; lastly, 2,000 additional soldiers were to make a hostile demonstration against Quebec, by way of the Chaudière, and keep that central district of Canada in a state of alarm. These colonial corps, with flying bands on the frontiers and regulars not included, made up a force themselves of 25,000 men—fully double the collective military strength of New France. But despite all this array, and a numerous navy, with war-ships stationed at every point of the coasts, we shall soon see that the Anglo-American campaigning of 1756 was yet more inglorious than that of the two preceding years.

CHAPTER II.

CAPTURE OF OSWEGO AND FORT WILLIAM-HENRY.

1756-1757.

Alliances with the savages; the Iroquois affect a neutrality.—Military preparations.—Canadian bands afoot the whole winter of 1755-6. —Fort Bull razed, and an enemy's convoy of 400 bateaux dispersed. —Disaccord begun between the governor-general and Montcalm.— Siege of Oswego; The garrison capitulates; booty gained by the victors; The savages kill many of the prisoners; the works of the place razed; joy at its fall in Canada.—The British suspend all further operations in the field for the year; the savages ravage their provinces.—The Canadians capture Grenville.—Dearth in Canada; an arrival of famished Acadians, to make matters still worse.—Aid demanded from France.—Rapid increase of colonial expenditure.—Montcalm proposes to attack Acadia, rather than forts Edward and William Henry.—Pitt obtains ministerial power in Britain.—Renewed efforts made by the British government and people, in view of achieving American ascendancy in 1757.—Abortive enterprise against Louisbourg.—Canadian bands afoot again during the winter of 1757-8; exploits of M. Rigaud.—Succours arrive from France; the alliance of the savages secured.—Siege and capture of Fort William Henry;— massacre of many of the prisoners taken, by the savages; the works of the place razed.—The dearth in Canada becomes a famine; the troops murmur at the privations they endure.—Disagreements become notorious among the colonial chiefs.—Varying fortunes of the French forces in Europe, Asia, &c.—The British raise an army 50,000 strong, for their American campaign of 1758.

During the succeeding winter, M. de Vaudreuil turned his best attention to the important business of maintaining alliances with the savage nations, and especially the Iroquois tribes, the chiefs of which expressed their willingness to take a neutral stand between the French and British while the war lasted, if the integrity of their territory were respected. He received with great parade a numerous embassy sent by these people; and he assured them that his great desire was to be on good terms with them. They returned home, after protesting that they would not take part against the French. It was partly in view of conciliating the Iroquois, always jealous of intrusion upon their wild domains, that Fort Oswego was dismantled after being taken.

The season for warlike operations was now near; but the enemy, who had learnt to be cautious, were not so forward to enter the field as hitherto. The levying of a suitable force had also been found difficult. There was a hitch, too, as to precedence between the officers, in the British regulars and the colonial leaders respectively. According to established routine in the enemy's army, the latter were bound to conform to the directions of the former This arrangement had lately given great umbrage to the Americans, and they now refused to conform to it; so that lord Loudon was fain to give way, and ordain that the old equality should prevail. In other respects, the mixed military organization remained intact. Among the defenders of Canada, similar pretensions were set up, and the like jealousies for a time were excited- but wise counsels prevailing in the colony, the evil was nipped in the bud; M. de Vaudreuil, the friend and protector of the Canadians, repelling all attempts to subordinate the colonial officers to those in the French regular army.

The prolonged inaction of the British in spring-time this year gave the governor-general and his subalterns an opportunity for resuming the project, lately laid aside, of attempting the capture of Oswego; a British outpost, the existence of which had always been regarded as a standing menace by the French. During previous months of winter, armed parties had been kept on foot to destroy the petty posts maintained by the British between Albany and Oswego, cut the communications between them, and discourage the garrison of that lake fort. Thus, in March, a force of 300 men captured a considerable magazine, called Fort Bull, between Schenectady and Oswego; destroying there a great quantity of warlike stores, the loss of which greatly retarded the after movements of the enemy. Fort Bull was a block-house, girt about with palisades, and equipped with loop-holes; but formed in such strange sort, that the latter served as a protection to assailants, who could fire under cover at the defenders within, and whose persons were completely exposed. The palisades having been cleared with hatchets, the fort was taken by assault, and the whole garrison put to the sword.

M. de Vaudreuil sent, early in spring, M. de Villiers with 900 men as a corps of observation, to the vicinity of Oswego to disquiet the British there; with the enemy he had several preliminary skirmishes. July 3, he attacked a convoy of 300 to 400 bateaux, which were returning after provisioning the fort, dispersed them, killed several of the people on board, scalped others, and took prisoner many more.*

This success obtained, the investment of the place was determined on, and the troops received orders to march thither at once. It was then the public began to perceive that a coolness existed between the two chiefs, military and civil, of the colony. At first they were mutually agreeable to each other, but by degrees an estrangement took place. A natural dissimilarity of character, and the evil inspirations of certain parties interested in setting them at variance, confirmed their personal dislike. For a time, the intimate friends of both alone perceived an aversion, which was destined to seriously affect the public well-being; but it was not slow to become manifest to every observer.

Montcalm, through a fatal presentiment, never had faith in a happy issue to the war, as his letters too plainly prove; thence arose in him an apathy of mind, which would have allowed him to neglect every occasion of aggressive hostilities, but for the impulsiveness of M. de Vaudreuil; who, whether from conviction, whether through policy, never appeared to despair; he both conceiving and causing to be executed some of the most glorious enterprises that have illustrated the military annals of France. Such headway, however, did the mistrustfulness of Montcalm make in the

---

* Letter of M. de Montcalm to the minister, dated July 20, 1756. He wrote that the success would have been greater, had the savages not attacked too soon. Letter of M. de Vaudreuil, of August 30. Most of the American historians ignore this enterprise. Smollett reports that the British were led by colonel Bradstreet; that they completely beat their opponents after a three hours' fight, and took 70 prisoners; but Sismondi, speaking of Smollett, observes that he took for granted, generally, the averments of British newspaper writers, which merit little attention: an observation equally applicable to those of America.

army, that the governor-general wrote, in a letter he addressed to the court after the capture of Oswego,—" Had I been deterred by all the idle discourses which took place on this subject, I must needs have renounced an enterprise which was destined to disarrange completely all the plans of the British generals." In fact, Montcalm only half approved of it, and had great doubts of its success; thus expressing himself in one despatch : " The object which is in view by my passage to Frontenac, appears to me possible enough, in a military sense, if all the details be well combined; but I shall set out to effect it, without being assured or convinced." Moreover, Montcalm was scared by the natural obstacles of the locality in the way of successful campaigning. " There are no routes other than rivers full of rapids and cataracts, or lakes to navigate so storm-vexed, as to be often impassable by bateaux."

Fort Oswego, erected by the British on the south-eastern shore of Lake Ontario, for the protection of their commerce and the settlements they had formed between the Hudson and that inland sea, acquired in time of war a double importance from its situation. It served, on one side, to curb the Iroquois; and endangered, on the other, the line of communication between the lower and upper extremities of Canada; because the British could, operating from this stand-point, readily attack fort Frontenac, and hold mastery of Lake Ontario. It was important, therefore, to expel them thence, and confine their forces to the valley of the Hudson. This was what the French government saw was needful to do, and which M. de Vaudreuil determined should be done.

The latter had so well arranged all preliminaries, that the army unawares, in a manner, fell upon the enemy; who, kept in check meantime by our detachments, were not able to make extended reconnaissances. He had assembled 3,000 men at Carillon (Ticonderoga), and Montcalm had gone thither very ostentatiously, in view of attracting and confining British attention to that point. While they supposed that this general, whom they much redoubted, was still at Lake Champlain, he returned suddenly to Montreal; and three days thereafter (July 21), he resumed his journey to put himself at the head of the expeditionary force, which was assembled at Frontenac, by the management of M. de Bourlamaque. A camp of observation had been formed by M. de Villiers, at Niaouré, 15 leagues from Oswego, under the command of M. Rigaud de Vaudreuil, brother of the governor-general, with orders first to protect the disembarkation of the army, and next to form its advanced guard. In order to forestal any obstacles on the part of the Iroquois, and to obtain hostages for their neutrality at least, a number of their chiefs had been detained at Montreal and others at Niagara. Two barks, one carrying 17 guns, another 12, were set to cruise before Oswego; and a line of wood-rangers were posted between that place and Albany, to intercept any messages that the British might attempt to interchange.

General Montcalm arrived at Frontenac July 29. On the 4th of August two battalions and four cannon, the first instalment, were embarked, and reached Niaouré in three days. The second division arrived there Aug. 8; it was composed of a battalion of regulars and a Canadian corps, with fully 80 bateaux, laden with artillery, baggage, and provisions. The troops, when united, formed a body 3,100 strong, including 1,350 regulars, 1,500 Canadians and colonial soldiers, with 250 savages.* To conceal the operation, the army moved to its destination in the night-time only; the men ensconcing themselves in the woods near the shore by day, thickly overlaying their bateaux with leaves. By stages of this kind they reached, undiscovered, Aug. 10, a sheltering cove, about a mile distant from their goal; and, next day, the advanced guard began the investment of Ontario.

The defensive works of the place consisted of two fortlets, and Fort Oswego proper, the ramparts of which were mounted with 18 cannon and 15 howitzers. One fortlet, named "Ontario," recently erected, stood on a plateau, within a fork formed by Lake Ontario and the Oswego river; the other fortlet, called Fort George, was situated on a height 600 yards from Oswego Fort, which also it commanded by its position. Fort George was a staked entrenchment of earth, with a few cannon mounted. These three works, collectively, had a garrison of 1,600 or 1,700 men, of Shirley's, Pepperell's, and Schuyler's regiments; designations which the Louisbourg expedition had made popular. Colonel Mercer was the head commandant at Oswego.

* The American authors say 5,000. We give the official figures.

The French having fixed their camp at the disembarking cove, passed two days (Aug. 11–12) in forming a road across a woody morass intermediate to Fort Ontario. Colonel Bourlamaque was charged with the conduct of the siege. A trench was soon opened to within 200 yards of Fort Ontario, and mounted with six cannon, despite a heavy fire of artillery, and brisk musketry, well kept up by the besieged, under the personal orders of colonel Mercer. The latter, finding his ammunition exhausted, spiked the cannon, and drew off his men; the French forthwith entering on possession of the work.

Mercer then sent 370 men to maintain the communication between Fort George, where Schuyler commanded, and Fort Oswego, where he resumed his own place; but at daybreak, Aug. 14, M. Rigaud de Vaudreuil crossed the river, by swimming, with a corps of Canadians and savages, drove away the British, and taking up a position between the two uncaptured forts, greatly intimidated the defenders of both. A battery of nine cannon was now promptly constructed on the escarpment of the river, facing Fort Oswego, and began to pour a plunging fire into that main work, which furnished no cover to its defenders' bodies anywhere above their knees. It soon became plain, that the place was untenable. Early in the morning, colonel Mercer was killed; a few hours thereafter, the besieged, discouraged by the rapidity of the siege-works, the bold passage of the river, which cut off their means of retreat, and the death of their commander, offered to capitulate. During this time, a corps 2,000 strong, under general Webb, was posted at a small distance; and Montcalm, who fully expected an attempt by Webb to relieve the place, had made preparations to give him a warm reception. Mercer had written to Webb, before daylight, describing his critical situation, and asking for succour; but scarcely had the missive left the precincts of the fort, when the messenger who bore it was stopped, and the document delivered to Montcalm; its contents determined him to press the siege all the more earnestly. Webb, then at Wood's Creek, was informed that Oswego was now in French hands, upon which he retreated with great precipitation.

The capitulation was signed at 11 A. M. Colonel Littlehales, who replaced Mercer, and his garrison 1,780 strong, with about

100 women and children, were taken prisoner. There fell into the captors' hands seven armed vessels, carrying each from 8 to 18 guns, 200 batteaux, 107 cannon; 14 mortars, 730 muskets, abundant stores of all kinds, 5 stand of colours, and the garrison chest, containing 18,000 francs. This handsome conquest was gained with small loss incurred by the French. The besieged, on the other hand, lost about 150 men, killed or wounded, including several soldiers who were fleeing to the woods when the capitulation was in progress, and got cut down by pursuing savages.

These barbarians, who expected to pillage the place, finding that no assault was made, and their hopes of obtaining fair booty thus baulked, fell upon the isolated prisoners, whom they despoiled and massacred. They also forced the garrison infirmary, and scalped a number of its inmates. A hundred persons were victimized by them. At the first intimation of these sanguinary disorders, General Montcalm took energetic measures to put a stop to them; but they were only partially successful, though he had to make promises of giving rich presents to the savages to call them off their human prey. "This will cost the king some eight or ten thousand livres," he wrote to the minister afterwards; "but the gift will assure to us more than ever the affection of the savage natives; and any amount of money would I have sacrificed, rather than that there should be a stain on French honour, resulting from this business."

All the fortifications at Oswego were razed, by order of the governor-general, in presence of the Iroquois chiefs, who were well pleased to see forts demolished that had been erected upon their territory, and which had always been an eyesore to them. This act was a wise one in another respect: the French had no soldiers to spare for garrisoning a place hard to keep, having the waters of Lake Ontario almost at its feet.

The time for gathering the year's crop being now come, many of the Canadians had leave to repair to their homesteads. The bulk of the army embarked with the prisoners for Canada, where Montcalm's victory spread universal joy, and was recognized by public rejoicings. *Te Deum* was solemnly chaunted in all the towns' churches, while the walls of some were properly decorated with the flags taken, as being suited to excite the patriotic zeal of the people. The corresponding extent of the mortification of the British at the loss of Oswego, served to prove how great was its importance in their eyes. In truth it had the most paralyzing effect upon their further operations for the year. General Abercromby accused colonel Schuyler of not giving him a proper account of the weak state of the works. General Winslow now received orders not to march on Carillon, but to entrench himself so as to command the routes of Lake Champlain and Oswego. General Webb took post, with 400 men, on the portage at the head of Lake George; while Sir Wm. Johnson, with 1,000 militiamen, occupied German Flats, on the Hudson. The expedition by way of the Chaudière was given up, or rather dwindled into a marauding raid; that against Fort Duquesne was postponed indefinitely. The movements necessary to canton the British forces, were all that ensued before the year ended.

The reduction of Oswego, projected by M. de Vaudreuil and effected by M. de Montcalm, did the greatest honour to both of these men; but the success attending the enterprise did not become a means for a reconcilement of their differences. Montcalm still appeared to be malcontent and morose, and it seemed as if he even regretted the victory gained, because it belied his evil forecastings. He wrote to Paris: "Never before did 3,000 men, with a scanty artillery, besiege 1,800, there being 2000 other enemies within call, as in the late affair; the party attacked having a superior marine, also, on lake Ontario. The success gained has been contrary to all expectation. The conduct I followed in this affair, and the dispositions I made, were so much out of the ordinary way of doing things, that the audacity we manifested would be counted for rashness in Europe. Therefore, monseigneur, I beg of you, as a favour, to assure his Majesty that if he should accord to me what I most wish for, employment in regular campaigning, I shall be guided by very different principles." He complained too, during the autumn, of several petty disagreeablenesses inflicted on him by the governor; asserting that both he and M. de Lévis usually received official letters and genera orders from him, drawn up in purposely equivocal terms, so that, if an evil effect ensued, the blame of it should fall on them. He gave his opinion, also, that the Canadian soldiers had neither discipline nor subordination, &c. The praises which the governor accorded the latter in his despatches, had aroused, it seems, the jealousy of the regulars; and general Montcalm, whose aspirations perhaps were for filling the highest post in the colony, led him to play the part of chief censor, to the ministry, of the existing administration of Canadian affairs.

As we have said above, the British suspended all further warlike projects for the year; and no hostile operations took place anywhere on the frontiers for the time, except a few skirmishings at Lake George. The French forces withdrew to the interior, and took up winter quarters; leaving a few hundred men in garrison at Carillon and Fort Frederic, under Messrs. de Lusignan and de Gaspé.

In the Ohio valley, nothing important took place; but the savages still continued their devastating raids in Pennsylvania, Maryland, and Virginia. More than 60 square leagues of country were deserted again, at this time, by the inhabitants, who fled across the Blue Mountains for safety; leaving their homesteads, farming stock, and crops, at the disposal of those barbarians. The American militias, decked out and tattooed as the men were, Indian fashion, could not stay for an instant the desolating course of the invaders. For a while, the town of Winchester was thought to be in peril. Colonel Washington, who commanded on that frontier, wrote mournfully to the governor of Virginia on the deplorable state of the country; adding, " I declare solemnly I would willingly offer my body as a sacrifice to our barbarous foes, if that would induce them to spare our people."

M. Dumas, in August, captured Fort Grenville, distant only 20 leagues from Philadelphia. Some time before, Washington with 300 to 400 men, took by surprisal a large village of the Wolf tribe (*Loups*), called Astigué, the inhabitants of which took to flight; but being met by M. de Rocquetaillade and some Canadians, they together turned against the pursuers, whom they routed and dispersed in the woods.

Everywhere, therefore, the French were in the ascendant; to their greater honour, as, with 6,000 men, they had beaten or paralyzed the efforts of more than 12,000 enemies, assembled between the river Hudson and Lake Ontario. They also took the strongest of the British fortified posts, as a separate enterprise. To recompense the courage and zeal of the troops, Louis XV promoted several officers, conferring on some the prized knightly order of St. Louis.

Yet amidst so many military successes, the colony itself was in a critical state. The most clamant of its ills was a scarcity of food, a foe yet more hard to encounter than any other. The destitution prevailing among the humbler people at this time and afterwards, caused the most resolute spirit to quail. Small-pox, too, broke out, and extended its ravages to the friendly savage tribes. The Abenaquis especially, so brave of themselves and long true to France and catholicity, had already been almost exterminated by that destroyer of mankind; and the few survivors sought protection from the Anglo-Americans, their nearest neighbours.

The harvest of the year, like some others before and after, was a comparative failure; insomuch that, but for the husbanding of stores of provisions taken at Oswego, it is doubtful whether the French posts at Frontenac, Niagara, and on the Ohio could have been victualled. Within the colony, the intendant was obliged to furnish grain from the king's stores to bakers in towns, for bread to be dealt out by them, in small portions, to the famishing people; who literally snatched it from the hands of the distributors.* Meanwhile provision transports, sent to Miramichi, returned with a living freight of Acadians, craving more food, and offering to die with arms in their hands for king and country in recompense for a subsistence. Their presence, of course, only made matters worse; there were already more combatants than food could be had for. Horse flesh was given to these unfortunates to eat. Part of their number died of small-pox; but bands of them finally settled in certain lordships of Montreal and Trois-Rivières, where they founded the parishes of Acadia, St. Jacques, Nicolet, and Bécancour; the rest led a miserable life for a time in the towns and rural cantons, and the ultimate survivors became absorbed in the general population of Canada.

Letters from Canada now poured into France, representing the

* In May 1757, the people of Quebec, previously put under short allowance of bread, were reduced to a supply of four ounces a day per head.

critical situation of the colony, and soliciting prompt succour. The governor-general, generals,and staff officers,with the intendant, all concurred in one request, that the home government would come to the rescue, reduced to extremity as the colony was, by over powerful enemies without, by impending famine within. The success of the coming campaign, it was said, would entirely depend upon the amount of aid accorded by the mother country, especially the quantity of provisions furnished; this was the capital point. As for the reinforcement of men needful, M. de Vaudreuil suggested that 2,000 might suffice, provided that Britain did not send many more soldiers to America than she had already done. At the time this application was made, the regulars in Canada, &c., did not exceed 2,400 in all.

Yet these moderate demands were considered exorbitant, in France. Her government, having adopted a fatuous polity, was wasting the national resources in German and Italian campaigns, for interests not French; leaving empty coffers to those ministers who would have inclined to send wherewithal to secure the continued possession of Canada as a dependency of France. The ministers, collectively, aware of what ought to be done in the case, yet consenting to gratify Madame de Pompadour (the contemner of New France), disputed every item of the demands made on behalf of Canada. It was observed, at the same time, that, in ordinary years, the colony cost the mother country from 1,000,000 to 1,200,000 livres per annum; and that, since the war began, the amount of expenditure had risen gradually to 8 millions a year; that, since 1756, the colonial exchequer was indebted to the royal treasury, through supplementary calls upon it, 14 million livres; nearly a moiety of which sum was represented by colonial exchequer-bills falling due next year. Intendant Bigot wrote that the army stores were quite exhausted at the close of 1756; that the expenditure occasioned by maintaining the posts on the Ohio would reach from 2 to 3 millions; and that the colonial budget, for the year 1757, would absorb 7 millions at the least. This demand in advance, made the ministry apprehensive that a far greater amount than even this enormous sum would be required. Ignorant home politicians, along with the favorites of the king who participated in his debaucheries, or persons who profited by court prodigality, called out in concert, that Canada, being a forest wilderness or icy region, cost far more than it was worth. If Old France, astounded at the profuse expenditure in the New, doubted the probity of her agents, or distrusted the carefulness of the royal representatives there, she ought at once to have demanded their dismissal or recal; but she ought never to have been oblivious of the fact, that the possession or renunciation of Canada was a question deeply affecting maritime potency and national greatness.

When the time came for despatching the yearly supplies to Quebec, the French ministry, while enjoining the expectant functionaries in Canada to exercise the severest economy, still refused to accede to the added demands made for provisions and munitions of war. It was after the supplies for 1757 came to hand, that the provisioning of the army, which up to that time had been entrusted to state functionaries, who made all purchases, began to be effected by contract; conformably to recommendations made by Bigot when in France in 1755. Cadet, a rich butcher of Quebec, partner and secret agent of Bigot, became the army contractor of all the armed posts for nine years. This system, adopted in France for the prevention of abuses, became a means of aggravating peculation, to an enormous extent, in her greatest transatlantic dependency.

Yet it seemed as if the evils already existent, in this regard, could scarcely admit of any increase, by what change soever. For a length of time previously, there existed a secret association among most of the public agents commissioned to make state purchases, and Bigot was its chief member. This fraudful society probably had its confederates in France.

Bigot, who played an odious part during this notorious epoch of our history, owed his place and influence only to the circumstance of being a near relative of M. de Puysieulx (minister of state), and Marshal d'Estrées. Personally, he was of an amiable disposition, and Montcalm liked the man though he censured the functionary. He was low in stature, well but slightly formed; his visage was by no means handsome, and disfigured by pimples. He was addicted to gambling, fond of display, and given to gallantry. He was haughty, repulsive, and of difficult access for those who pleased him not; but acted very judiciously in all affairs where undue personal interests were not in question; and was very laconic in his responses.

This official forestalled, in the king's name, all the grain and cattle within his reach, at low prices; and then caused them to be re-sold, by the secret association, at exorbitant rates. Thus, in the article of bread and meat, what cost the confederates 3 sous and 6 sous a pound, was charged to the public from 20 to 30 sous, and from 40 to 60 sous, respectively! It is on record, that he reduced the people of Quebec to 2 ounces of bread each *per diem*, in order to raise the price of necessaries; thus creating dearth in the midst of abundance.

The " Society "—such being the current name of this *thieves' committee*—was composed of, 1. Cadet, commissary-general, mentioned above. He was of previous good repute, but ignorant and greedy; led into peculation by others' example, he robbed the king up till the year 1757, and afterwards both king and people. Cadet soon became as tricksy and hard-hearted as his associates; but was at last duped by them, and re-passed to France less rich than was supposed. 2. Varin, commissary-intendant at Montreal. 3. De Péan, a man of enormous wealth and prodigal expenditure. 4. Chevalier le Mercier, who came from France a private recruit, in 1740; he taught in a school afterwards at Beauport, then became a cadet, and finally artillery commandant of Canada: it was said, that he had great influence with the governor. 5. De Coprin and Morin, two mercantile clerks, who came to Canada poor, and quitted it with huge fortunes. 6. De Bréard, marine controller. 7. D'Estèbe, head store-keeper; he settled at Bordeaux with a fortune valued at 700,000 to 800,000 francs. 8. Perraut, first a peasant at Deschambault, then an innkeeper, next purveyor and governor's secretary, finally a major-general of militia. Lastly, one Penissault, and a number of others, more or less interested in the company.*

The operations of this Society were as fatal to us as those of the common enemy; for to the full extent that public interests declined, those of the association became flourishing; its coffers

---

* *Historical Portraits*, drawn from the extracts made by M. Ferland; MSS. in the French archives.

getting filled as rapidly as those of the state were becoming empty.

Meanwhile, general Montcalm advised the ministry to throw aside the project formed by M. de Vaudreuil, to capture Forts Edward and William-Henry next campaign—two enterprises, the second of which he judged to be difficult, the first inexecutable; and rather to make a diversion on the side of Acadia, with a squadron, a corps of French regulars, and 2,500 Canadians. This bold proposal was not relished; possibly because it seemed to be both uncertain of success and utility, or else dangerous; for, as M. de Lotbinière observed, it would not be proper to divide the colony's forces, already so few in number, and send a portion of them so far away, at a time when its heart was about to be struck at.

In the reply sent to Montcalm, the ministers enjoined him to do his utmost to bring the minds of the soldiery and inhabitants into accord; admonishing him also, that it was equally important to treat the savages considerately, and to compliment them on the bravery they were so proud of possessing. The complaints sent to Paris of the arbitrary conduct of the French military, whose arrogant spirit, too, was often manifested in their own letters, were, doubtless, the cause and justification of these wise injunctions being imposed on Montcalm and his officers. As for M. de Vaudreuil's double project, no ministerial decision was come to at that time.

While France was occupied, so far, in taking measures for the defence of her North American dependencies, Britain, ashamed of recent defeats in the Old and New Worlds, meditated avenging herself signally on her enemy in the campaign about to open. The ministry, in order to re-attract public confidence, took to its bosom Mr. Pitt, afterwards famous as Lord Chatham, and Mr. Legge, two [?] of the most illustrious statesmen of England.* It was now resolved to wage war with great vigour. Squadrons and a numerous land-force were destined to act in America; and, in order to prevent the French colonies from receiving that food

---

* The descendants, if there be any surviving, of the red-tapeist Legge, who for a while became a cabinet *warming-pan*, will doubtless be proud of M. Garneau's coupling his "illustrious" name with that of the greatest statesman of the age. "How WE apples *do* swim together!"—B.

which was their most urgent want, the British parliament passed a law to prohibit the exportation of provisions from any port of the British possessions.

A rumour spread about in France, that a project had been formed in London to attack Louisbourg, or Canada, by sea. Pitt desired to obtain, at whatever cost, supremacy in the New World ; and it was affirmed he had said, that 10,000 additional men, at least, would be needful therefor; but if this number were not sufficient, he would triple it to gain his ends (the reporters of Pitt's alleged words added). Notwithstanding these rumours, the French ministry departed not from their first intention, of sending to the menaced provinces only a small corps of soldiers; and vainly did Marshal de Belleisle represent the danger thence likely to arise, in a memorial submitted to the council of state. "Several months since," wrote he, "I insisted that we ought to despatch to America, independently of the recruits wanted to complete the colonial troops, and replace casualties in our French regiments there, the four regiments of M. Fischer......He has under his orders a body of distinguished officers, almost all men of birth, most of whom care not to return to Europe, neither do their soldiers; and such a corps, so minded, would become a living bulwark, now and for the future, wherever stationed for the defence of the colonies......I think it impossible for me to insist too strongly in the matter. Perhaps repentance for not taking such a step will come when too late. I own that the expense of transporting the corps will be great; but I think that it were better to have some fewer ships of the line afloat, and to appropriate their cost to means of preservation for the colonies."

We know not what influence such a reinforcement as the Marshal urged the ministry to send, would have had on the result of the operations of 1759; but it is sad to think, that the fate of Canada may have depended on the granting or not granting the pitiful sum needed to defray the cost of sending 4,000 disposable men to America ! All that the ministry did, in addition to what we have already noted, was to despatch a squadron to take station at Cape-Breton, with orders to the commandant to send some of his vessels to cruise in the lower St. Lawrence.

As for Canada, it could only remain on the defensive and wait events; but its defenders were ready to take advantage of every favourable circumstance which should arise, and never for a moment did they cease to observe the movements of its enemies.

In pursuance of the new and more vigorous system adopted in Britain, Lord Loudon assembled at Boston, in January 1757, the governors of the northern colonies, Nova Scotia included, to concert a plan for the year's campaigning. The project of separately attacking, followed in 1755 and 1756, was abandoned, and it was resolved not to divide the general forces, but direct them on one point simultaneously. Louisbourg, which was the most salient seaward point of the French possessions, would of course attract the first notice of British invaders; accordingly, the general opinion of the conference now was, that hostile operations should begin with an assault on that sentinel of the St. Lawrence. Each colony was ordained to furnish its quota of soldiers for the projected expedition; and in consequence, soon thereafter levies were made in the different provinces, and other needful warlike preparations commenced with spirit. Lest the real destination of the armament (which for the time was concealed) should become known, an embargo was laid on all vessels then in port, and the envoys who had been sent from Louisbourg to Boston were prevented from returning home. The custody of the frontiers was confided to the militias. Still Washington commanded on the side of the Alleghanies. From two to three thousand soldiers were left in garrison at Fort William-Henry, and at the head of Lake George. In July, the British forces in the field numbered 25,000 men, 3-5ths of whom were regular troops; besides numerous militiamen, ready to march at the first signal.

Lord Loudon set sail from New York June 20, for Louisbourg, with 6,000 regulars, embarked in 90 ships. July 9, reaching Halifax, his convoy was joined by Admiral Holbourn's fleet, on board which were 5,000 more soldiers, all veterans. While still in port, news came that admiral Dubois de la Motte had arrived at Louisbourg from Brest; that he had now 17 ships of the line and 3 frigates under his orders; and that the town had a garrison of 6,000 French regulars, 3000 militiamen, and 1,200 savages. Hearing this, Loudon held a council of war, at which it was unanimously agreed that the attempt to take Louisbourg had no chance of being successful, and ought to be abandoned. In consequence, the troops were sent back to New York; while Holbourn, with 15 ships, 4 frigates, and a fire-ship, stood toward Louisbourg to reconnoitre. Nearing the place, he was recognised; and the French admiral was preparing to meet him, when he turned helm, and sailed back to Halifax. He returned towards Louisbourg, in September, leaving there four ships more than before. La Motte, now the weaker party, declined battle, in turn, pursuant to orders he had received, not to risk against odds a finer fleet than France had been able to equip any time since the year 1703. Shortly thereafter, a fearful tempest assailed the British fleet, and brought it to the brink of perdition. The *Tilbury*, a 60-gun ship, was cast ashore and half of her crew drowned; 11 vessels were dismasted, and obliged to throw their ordnance into the sea. The other ships reached sundry ports of Britain, in a dismantled state.

Notwithstanding the dearth prevailing in Canada, hostilities never ceased during the winter of 1757-8, which was unusually rigorous. In January, a British detachment, sent from Fort William-Henry, was fallen upon near Carillon (Ticonderoga), and destroyed. February following, General Montcalm thought of sending 850 of his men to take the British by surprise and endeavour to capture Fort William-Henry by a sudden escalade. The governor approved of the project, but thought fit to increase the attacking force to 1,500; namely 450 regulars, 800 Canadians, and 300 savages. He gave the command of the enterprise to M. Rigaud (his own brother), to the great disappointment of the regular officers and M. de Montcalm, who had pitched on M. de Bourlamaque for its leader.

This expedition set out February 23. The corps traversed lakes Champlain and George, and made 60 leagues of way, on snowshoes, with their provisions in sledges, and passing the nights on bearskins laid on the snow sheltered by a piece of canvas. March 18, they reached the vicinity of the fort; which, having reconnoitred, M. Rigaud judged it too strong to be carried by a sudden assault. He confined his hostilities to destroying all the outworks and exposed constructions; this he executed, despite the fire of the British, during the four nights of March 18—22. Four armed brigantines, each of 10-14 guns, 350 bateaux, all the mills, external stores, and palisaded dwellings, were burnt. The garrison, shut in as it were by fire, for nearly 100 hours, sought not to interrupt the devastations of the assailants, who left undestroyed only the main building of the fort. Some of the latter, on their retreat, experienced a singular affection of the eyes, involving temporary privation of sight, from the continued glare of the snow; similarly to the ophthalmia experienced by many of the French when crossing the sandy region of Egypt under Napoleon Bonaparte. But in the former case, two days after reaching headquarters, the stricken men's sight returned.*

So many victories, and especially the capture of Oswego, bound the savages firmly to their alliances with the French. The Iroquois confederation, despite the efforts of the British, sent a second great embassy to Montreal, to renew friendly protestations. It was received in presence of envoys from the Nipissings, Algonquins, Poutouatamis, and Ottawas. Such demonstrations were of some import, for they made men easy as to the security of the frontiers; but which, we may observe casually, had been little disturbed since the war began.

The succours solicited from France, and which the governor-general's renewed demands fixed at 5,000 men, the British forces being so numerous,—did not arrive in Canada till late in the season, and then only to a small amount. By mid-July nearly, only six hundred soldiers and scanty provisions had arrived.* During the whole summer, only about 1,500 men in all disembarked at Quebec. Such delays were fatal to military enterprise. After detaching 400 men to the relief of fort Duquesne, which was in peril, troops were sent, as soon as the season allowed, to line the frontier of lake Champlain. M. de Bourlamaque had 2,000 under him at Carillon. A battalion was located at St. John's; a second, at Chambly; two more garrisoned Quebec and Montreal. Many Canadians, lately under arms, were engaged for the time in field labour. Matters being in this state, news of the departure of Lord Loudon for Louisbourg caused the heads of the colony to profit

---

* The affected French soldiers in Egypt were not so lucky. The cases referred to were very numerous, and many never recovered their sight. Baron LARREY: *Military Surgery*.—B.

by the absence of the bulk of the enemy's forces to attack fort William-Henry, the site of which brought the British within a short day's march from Carillon—also giving them the command of lake George, and enabling them to fall upon us unexpectedly at any time. To rid us effectually of neighbours so dangerous, it was necessary to thrust them back to the Hudson; and, as the work was urgent, it was begun without waiting the arrival of the succour, in men and provisions, expected from France.

On call made by the governor-general, the Canadians found both soldiers and wherewithal to feed them; for they comprehended the utility of the enterprise in hand. They left in their homesteads the chief provisions they had laid up, for family use in their absence; and were content to subsist on maize and vegetables. "They had neither flour nor bacon to use," wrote M. de Vaudreuil to the court: "they denied themselves ordinary food, with equal zeal and generosity, for their king's sake." Warlike preparations for the enterprise were made quietly as well as promptly; and all the artillery was forwarded to Carillon by the end of July. At short notice the whole attacking force assembled, consisting of 3,000 regulars, fully 3,000 Canadians, and 1,600 to 1,800 savages, of thirty-two different tribes; in all, 7,600 men. The preliminary success of the bands who scoured the enemy's country augured well for our success. Lieutenant Marin took prisoner several of the British, and scalped others, even up to the walls of fort Edward. Rigaud, with 400 men, encountered colonel Parker on lake George, which he was descending, with 350 to 400 Americans, in 22 barges, sent to reconnoitre. Rigaud sank all the barges but two, killed or drowned 160 of the men, and took prisoner 165 others. After these happy preludes, Montcalm gave the word to advance.

The vanguard started July 30; it was led by M. de Lévis, and was composed of some grenadiers, three Canadian brigades, and 600 savages—total 2,800. It took the land route, on the eastern margin of lake George, in order to protect the landing of the main corps, with the artillery and siege material.

August 2, in the evening, Montcalm landed with his troops in a small bay, a league distant from fort William Henry; the battering train arrived next day. De Lévis was despatched towards fort Edward, to reconnoitre and intercept the enemy's supplies; the army, meanwhile, marching in three columns, advanced through the intervening highlands, to the scene of action. The garrison, erewhile only 1,500 strong, had been reinforced, the night before, and now numbered 2,700. The French troops defiled behind the fort, and, while investing it, as well as an entrenched camp under the walls, and too strong to be carried by assault, they stationed their left at the lake, near the site of Caldwell, where the artillery was to be landed; with their right on the heights towards fort Edward. Skirmishers were thrown out on that side, and echeloned along the route beyond, in order to give timely notice in case general Webb should be on the way to relieve the place, he having a corps of 4,000 men, between five and six leagues off.

Colonel Bourlamaque directed the siege operations; colonel Monroe commanded the besieged.

The first trench was opened 4th August, about 8 p.m., 700 yards distant, amidst an opposing fire of bombs and balls, which did not slacken, except during a few short intervals, while the siege lasted. Next day (August 5), on report made that Webb was on the way with 2,000 men, De Lévis was sent with a detachment to meet him; and Montcalm was about to follow, with a large force, in support, when a letter was brought to him, which had been found on the person of an enemy's courier, killed by the way. This letter informed Monroe that, considering the state of fort Edward, the writer opined that it would be imprudent either to leave it or to send any relief whatever to him (Monroe). It advised the latter, that the French were 13,000 in number, that they had much artillery; and that these (discouraging) particulars were set down for his consideration, so that he might try at obtaining good terms of surrender, in case he (Monroe) could not hold out till the arrival of succour, which had been demanded from Albany. Webb's exaggeration of the French strength hastened the reduction of the place. August 6, at day-break, a battery on the left, of 8 cannon and a mortar, was unmasked and opened fire. It was briskly answered by the besieged. Next day, another battery disclosed itself. Montcalm now suspended firing, and sent his aide-de-camp, Bougainville, with Webb's letter to Monroe. The latter declared, notwithstanding, that he would defend the fort to the last. At

9 A.M., the cannonade recommenced, amid the yells of the savages, who screamed with joy as the shot told upon the defences of the fort. Towards night-fall, 500 of the besieged made a sortie, in order to cut their way to fort Edward; but M. de Villiers barred the way with a free company and the savages. After a struggle, he drove the enemy back, killing 50, and taking others prisoner.

A third battery opened fire, August 8; before it was finished, and about noontide on that day, the glitter of arms was observed on the crest of a hill near by. Presently troops were seen forming in battle order; all which seemed to excite great interest in the entrenched camp below the fort. The call to arms was beaten by the besiegers' drummers; but, after a few musket-shots were wasted, the soldiers on high re-entered the woods, and were seen no more.

On the morning of the 9th of August, a flag of truce was displayed, in sign of a desire to capitulate. The following conference was short; it was agreed that the troops of the fort, and those in camp, numbering 2,372 in all, should march out with the honours of war, and return to their own country, with their arms, baggage, and one field-piece, conditioned, however, that they were not to serve against any of our people, or any of our savages allies, during the existing war; also it was stipulated, that all French prisoners of war then in the British colonies should be sent to Carillon within four months. It was owing to a deficiency of provisions that the garrison were not to be retained.

There were found in the place 43 pieces of artillery, 35,835 lbs. of gunpowder, with balls, &c., in proportion, and provisions enough to subsist our army for six weeks; while, on the lake, were 29 small vessels, which were all given up.—The loss of the French was 54 men; that of the enemy about 200.

The capitulation was accompanied, like that of Oswego, by an event ever regrettable, but which it was almost impossible to prevent, on account of the independent ways of the savages. The British, moreover (*du reste*), were in part themselves to blame for what happened, through having neglected to spill their liquors, as M. de Bougainville, by Montcalm's orders, prayed they would do, to prevent the savages from getting drunk upon entering the place.

The men in garrison were to retire to fort Edward. De Lévis caused them to set out next morning, escorted by a detachment of regulars, and accompanied by all the interpreters of the Indian warriors. They had not gone much more than a mile on the way, when the savages, malcontent at the terms of capitulation, which baulked their hopes of spoil here as at Oswego, excited by drink, and urged by the Abenaquis (who owed a grudge to the British), took to the intermediate woods, whence they fell unawares upon the prisoners, killed some, stripped great numbers, and led back all the rest. The escort did its utmost to restrain the barbarians, and several of the soldiers in it were killed or wounded, while trying to snatch victims from their hands. As soon as Montcalm learned what was passing, he hastened, with all his officers, to put a stop to it; and succeeded in saving most of the prisoners whom the savages had brought back, causing them to take shelter in the fort. Nearly 600 of the enemy's soldiers, dispersed in the woods, reached, by degrees, fort Edward; but naked, unarmed, and spent with hunger and fatigue. The savages took 200 to Montreal, for whom the governor paid a heavy ransom; 500 re-entered fort William Henry, as mentioned above. Montcalm re-clothed those who had been stripped, and sent them on, with a strong escort, after expressing regret at what had taken place.—These unfortunate disorders left strong resentments in the hearts of the British. But the prisoners themselves rendered this justice to their French conquerors, that they used all their efforts to limit the evils done; and owned that they succeeded in preventing greater.*

The fort having been razed, and the enemy's camp obliterated, Aug. 16 our army re-embarked, in 250 barges, for Carillon. But for the necessity of sending the savages back to their hordes, and allowing the Canadians to secure their crops, Montcalm would have been able to disquiet fort Edward at least. The Americans so fully expected his arrival there, that all their militias—infantry, cavalry, and artillery—had been put in requisition, everywhere in Massa-

---

* The atrocities succeeding the surrender of William Henry are but half narrated in the above account, and those which are recounted are glossed over very neatly. Not a word is said of the massacre, within the fort, and in its precincts, of women and children; or of the Aceldama of gore and ashes which the French and their savages transformed the place into. "Oh they were fiends!" to use the words of SHELLEY, in another case.—B.

chusetts; and the colonists westward of the river Connecticut had orders to demolish their wheeled vehicles and shut up their cattle. "It is inconceivable," said Hutchinson, "how four or five thousand enemies should cause such a panic!" The provincials' apprehensions, however, were not quite unreasonable, for the instructions of M. de Vaudreuil bore, that after taking William Henry, Montcalm was to attack fort Edward; but the fear of subsistence failing the troops, the needful absence of the Canadians, and the strength of the place itself, with the probability of its being succoured besides, had induced the general to give up the attempt prescribed to him; but this exercise of his own discretion by Montcalm, caused great differences between him and the governor-general. In other respects, the difficulty of finding food for the army being ever present, and dearth always increasing in Canada, the most welcome trophy resulting from its latest conquest was the mass of food, including 3,000 *quarts* of flour, and much bacon, brought in triumph to Carillon; a booty this, which was prized at Montreal and Quebec as worth a great victory.

This campaign over, our army retired within the Canadian lines; and, in autumn, took up its winter-quarters in the interior.

The year's harvest entirely failed. In several parishes, hardly enough grain was reaped to provide seed for the next crop. Cereals, which promised well as they grew, gave small returns or none, owing to the flooding summer rains. It was feared that the country would have no bread at all by the coming month of January. For precaution against the worst, 200 *quarts* of flour were kept in reserve, to supply the wants of the sick in hospital till the month of May. In the religious houses, the daily portion was reduced to $\frac{1}{2}$ lb. each person; and it was proposed to supply to each of the towns' people 1 lb. of beef or horse-flesh, or cod-fish, along with the *quarteron* of bread allowed, but which was judged insufficient of itself. The intendant bought up 12 to 15,000 horses for the shambles. Stored subsistence failing, the troops were quartered upon the people in rural districts, as these were thought to be best provided in a time of general dearth. Only a few soldiers were kept in the towns, to do garrison duty. At the close of September, De Lévis, having reduced the soldiers' rations, was told that they murmured thereat. Forthwith he assembled the grenadiers, and

reprimanded them severely for insubordination. He reminded
them that the king sent them to Canada not only to fight, but also
to endure all unavoidable privations imposed on them; that they
were to consider the colony as a city besieged, and cut off from
supplies; that it was for the grenadiers to give a good example of
submission; finally, that any mutinous sign would be punished with
severity. Murmurings thereafter ceased for a time. In December, the daily rations were further reduced, and the troops being
proffered horse-flesh for beef, refused to take it. M. de Levis assembled and harangued them again. He ordered them to conform
to circumstances; and added that if, after the distribution, they had
any representations to make to him, he would listen to them willingly. Having taken their rations, they justified their complaints
with soldierly frankness; and said in conclusion, that horse-flesh
was not nourishing; that every deficiency of supply fell upon them;
that the civilians denied themselves nothing, and that the dearth,
said to be universal, was not even so general as people pretended.

M. de Lévis replied, in order, to all the grievances expressed. He
assured them they were ill informed of the colony's real state; for
a long time, he said, the Quebec people had tasted no bread; adding
that the officers in Quebec and Montreal had not then a *quarteron* [1]
per diem each. He adverted to the Acadians, whose sole food was
horse-flesh and cod-fish; and reminded the veterans present, that
the troops had eaten horse-flesh at the siege of Prague. This discourse seemed to have a good effect, for the mutineers returned to
barrack, and remonstrated no more. It turned out afterwards,
that insubordination among the regulars had been excited by some
of the inhabitants and malcontent colonial soldiers.

Early in April, the daily ration for the Quebec people was reduced again, and fixed at two ounces of bread daily, with eight
ounces of bacon or cod-fish. Men began to fall down in the streets
with hunger. More than 300 Acadians died from privation, at
this time.

While the country was thus a prey to a famine which seemed
to aggravate every incertitude as to the future, Montcalm complained bitterly that various persons sought to depreciate his merit
and lower him in the public regard; that De Vaudreuil, in particular, set himself to lessen the credit due to the regular troops

and their general in achieving the late successes. Every victory gained seemed, in fact, to increase the discontent of Montcalm. An ill-satisfied ambition kept his mind ever open to all the sinister influences of others' malevolence.

Meanwhile, the ministers at Paris were constrained to attempt solacing the evils suffered by Canada. They knew that the British cabinet had ordered, during the winter, an increase of Canada's military force in a larger proportion than during the two preceding years. But the weakness of the French government allowed it not to organize sufficient succour, to secure success either present or future. The colonial expenditure for 1757 had far exceeded the sum allotted to meet expected wants, and the bills of exchange drawn on the royal exchequer had risen to 12,340,000 francs. Private correspondence with France continued to signalize financial abuses and great dilapidations. Bigot stood out prominently among the culpable functionaries denounced. The difficulties of the time, the evils of war, even famine; but, more than all, the distance from home supervision, enabled him to multiply his opportunities of robbing with impunity. Having full power to gratify his most exorbitant desires, he satisfied them without any stint. The letters of Montcalm (whose eyes began to open), those of De Lévis, Bougainville, Montreuil, Doreil, Pontleroy—all abounded in accusations against Bigot. Doreil, writing in cipher to the minister of war, Oct. 22, 1757, said, " I blame not the commissary-general alone; there are many things to be said as to others, but I hold my peace. It grieves me to see so interesting a colony, and the troops who defend it, exposed, through the cupidity of certain persons, to perish from hunger and destitution. M. de Montcalm will perhaps enter into this matter at large; I leave to him the ungrateful task. Nothing escapes his attention, or can lessen his zeal for the public well-being. But what can he do, any more than I, (in the way of prevention)? why, only make remonstrances which delinquents are always ready to parry; or it may be, we are not even listened to!

Three days afterwards, Doreil adverting to the prevailing famine, and to an epidemic which the last-arrived troops brought with them, thus referred to the doings of the intendant: " The remedies to be applied to public ills ought to be potent and prompt.— For myself, I long only for the blessed time when, by royal permission, I shall return to France, and witness no more, an idle spectator, the monstrosities which daily challenge my attention...... M. de Moras, minister of marine, knows not the true cause of our situation. It belongs neither to M. de Montcalm nor to me to attempt informing him. We abstain, the rather because any representations we should make would probably never reach him.*

Montcalm, writing under date Nov. 4, observed that the commissary had bought much brandy and wine, but little flour; why? "because there accrued more profit to him from strong liquors...... but," he added, "let us cover this matter with a thick veil; to raise it would compromise some of the highest folks in this land. ......I conclude, from what was said to me at Paris, before I left, by M. de Gournay (minister of commerce), he is informed of all that I must not write......". Montcalm complained, afterwards, of defaultings in military engineering works: "How many abuses M. de Pontleroy will have to reform in his department! but in what branch are reforms *not* wanted?"

The European birth and home nomination of defalcating agents, who always manifest far more hardihood in a colony than in the mother country, the favouring prejudices of the minister, with the hurries attending warlike enterprises, did not allow of a searching investigation being then made; and all that was done in the matter at head-quarters was, to recommend economy in every outlay!

The colonists had earnestly applied to their king to send them provisions. The new minister, M. de Moras, despatched 16,000 quintals (cwts.) of flour, irrespective of the supply demanded by Cadet, which amounted to 66,000 quintals. An order was transmitted, also, to draw supplies from the Ohio, from the Illinois country, and Louisiana. The victualling vessels left France in early spring, but most of them were captured by British ships of war or by privateers. Those that escaped arrived very late at Quebec, the earliest of them not till late in May. This tardiness greatly inquieted M. de Vaudreuil, who, fearing procrastinations, sent three ships in succession to France, the first as soon as the season allowed, to solicit prompt succours. By mid-June,

---

* Because one of the underlings of the ministry, at Versailles, named La Porte, connived with Bigot.

no more than one frigate and 20 transports had arrived, bringing 12,000 *quarts* of flour in all.

As to reinforcements of soldiers, none were to be hoped for; as it was not found possible to get any passed to Canada. Despite the good-will of some ministers, Marshal de Belleisle, in charge of the war department, could obtain but a few indifferent recruits, to complete the companies in battalions to 40 men each; and, even of such recruits only from 300 to 400 came during the whole year. France experienced great vicissitudes in the campaigns of 1757 : alternately beating and beaten in Europe, she was victorious in America, and unfortunate in India. Her councils were guided by the capricious impulses of Madame de Pompadour, who, from day to day, employed or dismissed generals and ministers without regard to their merits or capabilities. The attempts made to obtain mastery on land and sea had exhausted France's military forces, and undid their harmonious unity: so there was nothing for it now but to look on, and see Britain double the forces she had on foot in America when the war began; while Canada possessed, May 1, 1758, only eight battalions of regulars, 8,781 strong, including recruits levied in the country: add thereto the colonial regulars, (numbering 2,000 men in the preceding year and not increased since), there resulted a properly disciplined force of not quite 6,000, to defend 500 leagues of frontier. It was plain, that the Canadians must needs form the bulk of an army capable of opposing, with any chance of success, the overwhelming numbers of the enemy.

Moreover, the checks the British received in America, compensated by their victories in the East, did but excite them to make greater efforts than ever to crush, by force of numbers alone, the defenders of Canada. This was all the more easy, as Britain's finances were in a flourishing state, and her superiority at sea no longer contested. The capture of Oswego and of William Henry, by ensuring French supremacy on lake Ontario and lake George, made the situation of the enemy on the American continent less favourable, after four years of struggle, than it had been any time since 1752. But the ardour of Mr. Pitt now inspiring the British cabinet, it was bent on solving the question of British or French mastery in North-eastern America. Doubtless, unprescient of the great events of 1755, he willed that his country should be sole dominatrix there; and accordingly he planned such enterprises as must necessarily ensure the fall of the Franco-American establishments in every part of the continent and its adjuncts. The British forces, both for land and sea service, were rapidly augmented; Lord Loudon was invalided, and General Abercromby appointed Anglo-American generalissimo; while his army was reinforced by 12,000 additional regulars, sent out under General Amherst. All the colonial governments were enjoined to raise as many regular soldiers as their respective populations would allow of; and in a short time Abercromby found himself at the head of a properly disciplined force 50,000 strong, including 22,000 British regulars; yet exclusive of 30,000 enrolled militia-men, who, if all called out, would thus have made the collective force of Britain in America 80,000 combatants.

The accumulation of such a host of armed men, thought to be needful to conquer Canada, implied a proud homage to the prowess and patriotic spirit of her defenders, French and colonial; for the armies embodied against them, or about to be, exceeded in numbers the population of our province at that time, including all its men, women, and children.

With such a signal disparity of numerical strength, then, did the respective belligerents open the campaign of 1758.

CHAPTER III.

BATTLE OF CARILLON (TICONDEROGA).

1758.

Canada, left to her own means of defence, determines to fight to the last. Plan of the British campaign: proposed simultaneous attacks on Louisbourg, Carillon, and Fort Duquesne.—Capture of Louisbourg, after a memorable siege, and invasion of the island of St. John (Prince Edward's); the victors ravage the settlements of Gaspé and Mont-Louis.—Defensive measures in Canada.—General Abercromby advances, with 16,000 men, on Carillon, defended by scarcely 3,500 French. BATTLE OF CARILLON, fought July 8: defeat and precipitate retreat of Abercromby.—Colonel Bradstreet captures and destroys Fort Frontenac.—General Forbes advances against Fort Duquesne. —Defeat of Major Grant.—The French burn Fort Duquesne, and retreat.—Vicissitudes of the war in different parts of the world.— Ministerial changes in France.—Dissidences between Montcalm and the governor.—The French ministry takes Bigot to task.—Intrigues for superseding M. de Vaudreuil.—The ministry accept the self-proposed recal of Montcalm; the king opposes it.—Conciliatory despatches sent to the rival chiefs, with knightly orders, &c. for them, and promotions of their subalterns; but accompanied by no soldiers or other substantial succours.—Defection of the French Indians, who at Easton adopt the British side.—The British decide to advance upon Quebec, with three armies, to rendezvous under its walls.—Amount of Canadian force in hand to resist this triple invasion.

The persevering efforts of Great Britain to appropriate Canada, so often defeated, made it probable that she would now try, once for all, to gain her ends; and at the same time wipe out her past disgraces, by crushing, at one blow, the small opposing force likely to be ranged against her overwhelming armed hosts. France, hopeless probably of finally preserving her finest dependency, made almost no further attempt to retain it by force of arms; still its native defenders, all but abandoned by their mother country, none the less girded up their loins to face the storm of invasion about to assail them. "We shall fight," wrote Montcalm to the minister; "and we shall bury ourselves, if need be, under the ruins of the colony." Others said, "All our most alert and valid males must march and fight; let the civic officers, the priests, the women, with persons of tender or advanced age, do the small labour—the wives of all functionaries, civil and military, setting an example to the rest." Such was the stern resolution formed, by every class alike, to defend their common country to the last.

The British, on their part, with forces fully capable of much subdivision, determined to attack, concurrently, Louisbourg, Carillon, and Fort Duquesne. The capture of Montreal was to be the appendix to that of Carillon. A large fleet and 14,000 of a land force were assigned to assault the first-named place; from 16 to 18 thousand men were ordered to invade Canada by way of lake George; and 9,000 others marched into the Ohio country to expel the French thence. Only an imperfect notion was formed, in Quebec, of the numbers which were about to conjoin in a leaguer of that city; but the temporary safety of both capital and colony were entirely due to the coming victory of Carillon, where, as at Cressy, the victors repulsed an army five times more numerous than their own.

During spring this year, the French troops, after some delay from want of provisions, marched to resume their positions on the frontiers, with orders to throw out parties to harass the enemy, cause him to divide his forces, and ascertain his hostile designs. Near Carillon 3,000 of our soldiers rendezvoused; and as many assumed positions on the banks of lake Ontario and at Niagara. These measures taken, the soldiery stood to their arms; while the colonists scattered in the furrows of their ploughed fields the few handfuls of seed-corn they had been able to redeem from the reserved stores which gaunt famine had broken into and nearly devoured.

Simultaneously, the British broke bounds; and it was upon Louisbourg that their first blows fell.—Admiral Boscawen sailed thither from Halifax, (N. S.) May 28, with 24 ships of the line, 18 frigates, and many transports, having troops on board and a large siege train. June 2, the expedition reached Louisbourg. Here were, in garrison, 2,100 regulars and 600 militiamen; with 5 men of war and 5 frigates, moored in the harbour, to aid in defending the place against a combined force of 30,000 British soldiers and sailors. M. Drucourt, who had succeeded to the Comte de Raymond as governor, resolved to make a stout defence, and not give in, even should no relief come, so long as the works were at all tenable by the small number of their defenders.

The fortifications, indeed, had become everywhere ruinous, for want of reparation. The *revêtements** and most of the curtains† had entirely crumbled away, and there was but one casemate‡ and a magazine that were bomb-proof. The chief strength of the place lay in the difficulty of an enemy's disembarking to attack it, and in the facility with which the harbour entry could be barred against him. What remained undilapidated of the original works of defence, being formed of friable stone, as above noted, joined with bad mortar too, the probability was, that it could not long withstand the shock of heavy projectiles; the governor, consequently, prepared rather to oppose the enemy's disembarkation, than await his approach behind such ruins. Therefore it was, that he carefully fortified all the weak points of the coast in the environs of the town as far as to Gabarus bay, distant 1½ mile and near to where the British fleet anchored. Cormorant cove, being the most accessible part of that line of coast, he bordered with a solid parapet, pierced for cannon and swivel-guns (*pierriers*) of heavy calibre. In front of this entrenchment he formed a breastwork of felled trees (*abattis*); so closely set that it would have been difficult to find a passage through it, even when unmanned; though it presented an appearance, to the deceived eye, of an expanse of unbroken natural verdure. (RAYNAL.)—A series of interchained barges was ranged from Cape Noir to Cape Blanc, and batteries were erected upon them, commanding all points where a landing was practicable.

In presence of such obstacles, that operation became both difficult and dangerous; yet as the British could have no certainty of the concealed strength of resistance at Cormorant cove, it was precisely there that they touched ground on the 8th day of June. To perplex the attention of the French, they prolonged the line

---

* Linings of stone, brick, &c.
† Walls between bastions.
‡ A subterranean chamber with a vaulted roof, used as a guard-house to defend the curtains, fosses, &c.—*B.*

of their vessels, so as to threaten the whole seaboard, feigning to disembark at Laurembec and other points of it; but suddenly most of the British attacking corps, formed in three divisions, landed at the cove, while General Wolfe with 100 men, at a spot a little beyond, scaled a rock judged thitherto inaccessible, and kept possession of it, despite all attempts of the armed townsmen and savages, who tried to dislodge the enemy's soldiers.

The governor, after leaving only 300 men in garrison, was present here with the rest. The works at Cormorant cove were thus manned by 2,000 soldiers and some savages. The British, who saw not yet the trap that had been set for them, continued their landing. Louisbourg would have been saved if, the disembarkation once completed, they had advanced inland, in full confidence of having no formidable obstacles to encounter; for then they must have quailed under the hail-storm of cannon-shot and musket-balls which the French, under secure covert, would assuredly have poured upon them. It is not likely that one of them, in such a case, would have escaped death by bullets, or in the waves; for the sea at that time was in a very troubled state, and an orderly re-embarkation they would have found difficult, or rather impossible. But French impetuosity, says Raynal, caused a well-laid scheme to miscarry. Hardly had the British landed their vanguard, and their vessels, nearing the shore, were about to disgorge the main body, than a brisk fire of musketry reaching those already on shore, and assailants hitherto concealed in the abattis coming numerously into view to take part in the fray, the danger of advancing further became apparent to the dullest of the British officers. Preparing to retrace their steps, they saw no other means to descend than by way of the rock where Wolfe had posted a detachment. That general, then engaged in re-embarking the troops and getting off the barges, forthwith ordered one of his officers to the perilous spot.

It was Major Scott who went thither with his company. The shallop he was in having sunk the instant after he put foot on land, he alone held to the rock with his hands; and he now found only ten soldiers alive, out of the hundred lately posted on it. With this small number, however, he contrived to gain the heights. Thanks to a covert of brushwood, he stood his ground heroically against a party of French and savages seven times more numerous than his own. The British troops, braving at once the raging sea, and the firing from the French batteries promptly directed on the contested rock, succeeded in securing the only point suitable for their disembarkation on this side. The position of the French, on the other hand, thenceforth became untenable. Fairly outflanked, one of their batteries was soon carried. At that instant, it was rumoured that General Whitemore had disembarked at Cape Blanc, and was about to pass between the 2,000 French soldiers at the cove and the town; into which the latter were forthwith recalled by the governor, after leaving 200 men killed, or captured. The fall of Louisbourg was now only a question of time; but as a prolonged defence might become a means for delaying, perhaps preventing, a direct attack on Canada, the commandant refused to let the five men-of-war in the port put to sea.*

The British operated briskly. June 12, General Wolfe, with 3,000 men, garrisoned the Pharo battery, the Royal battery, and other deserted works. The Pharo battery was important, as it commanded the port, the town fortifications, and a battery on the island facing the place. The siege of the latter forthwith commenced. It was courageously defended. Seven thousand men at the most, including disembarked sailors, and a regiment which came in aid by sea during the siege, fought against a quadruple force during two months, with admirable courage and patience.

The besiegers, favoured by the broken ground, advanced their lines to within 600 yards of the town walls. The besieged made several sorties, but could not much interrupt the operations actively carried on by the British. June 19, the Pharo battery, seated on a height scarcely attainable by the garrison's fire, began to play on the town. The cannonade, on both parts, was heavy; but the French were obliged to bring the men-of-war 600 yards nearer to the town, to escape the enemy's shot; which began to tell, also, upon the town-wall facing the Pharo. Three new batteries were erected, in succession; and a mound (*épaulement*) 450 yards long, was raised by the enemy, to facilitate their approaches, upon another site which commanded the place. June 29, the be-

* Letter from M. Drucourt to the minister, dated Sept. 23, 1758.

sieged, fearing lest the British fleet should enter the harbour, sank four vessels at the narrowest part of its entry. July 1, two more were sunk, in the same view, their masts standing above water. The fire from all the ramparts, meantime, was constant, and several sorties were made. The governor's wife, Madame de Drucourt, immortalized herself by her heroism during the siege. To encourage the soldiers, she often passed and re-passed along the ramparts amid the cannonading, fired several great guns herself, rewarding the most alert artillerymen. She also dressed the hurts of the wounded, kept up their courage by her kind words, and, in short, endeared herself to the men no less by a masculine courage than by exercising the gentler virtues more becoming her sex.

Meanwhile, the walls ceased not to crumble everywhere under the enemy's projectiles: yet, determined as was the attack, no less persistent was the spirit of defence. The breaches made in the works were constantly repaired, as far as possible. July 21, a shell set fire to a French 74-gun ship in the harbour; its powder-magazine blew up, and the fire spread to two more vessels, which also were consumed. Only two French men-of-war remained afloat; and to save these, it was needful to steer them clear, not only of the enemy's cannon-range, but that of the burning ships; for the guns of the latter being shotted, they were going off at every instant. Present salvage, however, proved to be no final gain, but the contrary; for, ere the siege ended, they were captured by the enemy, who entered the harbour during a dark night, cut out one, and burnt the other.

This last blow determined the French to give in. It showed that the port was quite assailable and all but defenceless seaward; while it was a scene of wreck within. The land works, also, were become untenable, for every battery on the ramparts was disorganized; scarcely a dozen cannon remained undismounted, and many practicable breaches existed in the line of defence, which the weakened garrison could not now repair, a third of its numbers being killed or wounded. As, from hour to hour, a general assault was apprehended by the townspeople, they adjured the governor to capitulate. He reluctantly yielded, and had to accept the terms granted by the foe, July 26, 1758.—Thus did Louisbourg, or rather its ruins, with the whole island of Cape Breton, pass into

British hands: the surrender of the isle of St. Jean (Prince Edward's) being also promised by the governor. He and his garrison, reduced to 500 soldiers and sailors, remained prisoners of war; while the townspeople, it was ruled, were to be transported bodily to France.

This conquest, which cost the besiegers only 400 men, killed and wounded together, greatly rejoiced Great Britain and her American colonies. Sent to London, trophies of the victory gained were paraded from Kensington palace to St. Paul's cathedral; and thanksgivings were celebrated in all the churches, with the greater ostentation as an offset was needful to make the people forget the discomfiture of Carillon, the unwelcome news of which had only then reached Britain.—Yet, after all, Louisbourg was but a paltry fastness (*une misérable bicoque.**)

After this exploit, the British fleet set out to take possession of isle St. Jean, and to destroy the settlements of Gaspé and Mont-Louis, established in the Laurentian gulf by the Acadians and poor fishermen, all of whom the enemy bore away. The expedition afterwards made an attempt on Miramichi, and finally retired about mid-October. Simultaneously, others of the British erected petty forts, as if to secure a foothold, on the northern margin of the bay of Fundy. The fall of Louisbourg and the loss of Cape Breton left Canada without a seaward defence, and cleared a free passage to Quebec for the enemy to enter in at.

While General Amherst and Admiral Boscawen were gathering laurels in Cape Breton, and on the adjoining seaboard, General Abercromby, ensconced (*tapi*) at the end of Lake George, was chewing, in silence and inactivity, the bitter cud of shame for the stinging defeat he had experienced just before.

This general had reserved for himself the command of the

---

* "Louisbourg is a little place, and has but one casemate in it, hardly big enough to hold the women. Our artillery made havoc among them (the garrison) and soon opened the rampart: in two days more, we should certainly have carried it. If this force had been properly managed, there was an end of the French colony in North America in one campaign; for we have, exclusive of seamen and mariners, near forty thousand men in arms."—*Letter from General Wolfe*, to his uncle Major Wolfe, *dated 27th of July*, 1758.

troops which were to act in the Champlain lake region, theirs being the chief operation in the tripartite campaign, as planned at head-quarters. His army was composed of 7,000 regulars and 9,000 provincials, besides from 400 to 500 savages, led by Colonel Johnson; the collective force being cantoned near Lake George. When all was ready for an advance towards Montreal, the road to which Abercromby undertook to clear of every obstacle set in his way, the first thing to be done was to force the French defensive line. M. de Vaudreuil doubted not that Carillon (Ticonderoga) would be attacked, after General Amherst departed for Louisbourg; but, as he had as yet received no provisions from France, he thought the best means of defending the central frontier would be to make a diversion. Therefore it was, that he persisted in a plan he had formed, to throw a strong corps on the southern lake-board of Ontario, force the Iroquois to renounce the British alliance, prevent a refoundation of Oswego, make an irruption on Schenectady, and constrain the enemy to quite abandon the Champlain region. Such a demonstration, both in its political and military complexion, was of a very ticklish character: still Lévis, with 800 regulars and 2,200 Canadians and western savages, prepared to realise it; but, just as he was about to proceed, word came from M. de Boulamaque, commandant on the Champlain frontier, that Abercromby, then at Fort Edward, was about to come down upon him with a large army. The original order to De Lévis was now countermanded; and General Montcalm, after some wrangling with Vaudreuil regarding his instructions, set out from Montreal, June 24, with M. de Pontlevoy, chief engineer, to take charge of the troops at Carillon, where he arrived on the 30th. He there found 3,000 men assembled. Montcalm seemed surprised on finding that the British were already in act of descending Lake George: although, ever since spring-time, he had himself directed [Vaudreuil's?] attention to Fort Edward, and pressed [him?] to send troops to Bourlamaque in any event. He now, without delay, sent word of what was passing to the governor-general, who hastened the march of the troops, already then on their way for his relief, under De Lévis: whose corps was composed of 400 regulars, 1,600 Canadians, and a few savages. The militias, too, were ordered to come up as soon as possible; but only a few reached the scene of action, even by forced marches, till the pressing need for them no longer existed.

July 1, Montcalm made a movement in advance, *echeloning* * his troops from Fort Carillon to the foot of Lake George, to curb the enemy, and obstruct their landing.

July 5, the British embarked, at the lake head, in 900 barges and 130 bateaux, while on numerous rafts cannon were mounted, constituting so many floating batteries. "The sky was serene," says Mr. Dwight, "and the weather superb: our flotilla sped its way in measured time, in accord with inspiriting martial music. The standards' folds floated gaily in the sunshine; and joyous anticipations of a coming triumph beamed in every eye. The firmament above, the earth below, and all things around us, formed together a glorious spectacle. The sun, since his course in the heavens began, rarely ever lighted up a scene of greater beauty or grandeur."

The British van, 6000 strong, led by Lord Howe, reached the lake foot, early on the 6th, and landed at Camp Brûlé. As it approached, Bourlamaque fell back on La Chute, where Montcalm was posted; after waiting, but in vain, the return of M. de Trépézée, whom he had sent on a reconnaissance, to Mont Pelée, with 300 men. The latter, at sight of the enemy, meant to rejoin Bourlamaque, but lost his way in the woods; thereby, through the delay ensuing, just as he reached the spot whence he had set out his corps was surrounded by the enemy, and two-thirds of the men were killed, or drowned in attempted flight. The rest, who formed his rear-guard and had taken another route, arrived safely at La Chute, whither Trépézée and another officer were borne mortally wounded. It was also in this fortuitous skirmish that Lord Howe lost his life. He was a young man, but an officer of much promise, whose death was greatly mourned over by his compatriots.

The amount of the enemy's force, and his intents, were now alike discernible. Montcalm broke up his camp at La Chute; while, supported by the colonial regulars and 400 to 500 Cana-

---

* *Echelon*, Fr., is a stepping-bar or round in a ladder; hence the military term *échelonner*, dispose parties of soldiers *en échelon* (ladder-fashion); *i. e.* range them in detachments on a line, with interspaces at rminate intervals.—*B.*

dians, just come up, he defiled towards the heights of Carillon, where he proposed to do battle; for it had been determined that, whatever might be the disparity in the numbers of the two armies, the entry to Canada should not be given up without a struggle. Montcalm at first elected to make his stand at Fort St. Frederic (Crown-Point); but M. de Lotbinière, who knew the country well, counselled him to prefer the heights of Carillon: the enemy, he said, could not pass that way, if it were (judiciously) occupied; and it would be easy to strengthen the pass by entrenching, under the cannon of the fort; whereas, he observed, the works needful to cover St. Frederic would take two months to execute: not to mention that, Carillon once cleared, the enemy could safely descend Lake Champlain, leaving the former stronghold unassailed, in his rear. Montcalm, feeling the cogency of this reasoning, halted the troops as soon as they reached Carillon in their retrograde march; then he gave them orders to take up a position in advance of the fort, and there entrench themselves, as proposed.

The heights of Carillon are situated within a triangle formed by the discharge of the superflux waters of Lake George, named La Chute river, and Lake Champlain, into which they here flow. Some bluffs (*buttes*), which are not lofty, and rise highest at the summit of the triangle, terminate, by an easy slope, towards the lake; but present a steep frontage (*escarpement*) to the river, the latter having a strand alongside it about 50 yards broad. At the extremity of the triangle, on the edge of the frontage aforesaid, was a small redoubt, the fire from which radiated on the river and lake; enfilading, too, the sloping ground along the course of the stream. This redoubt was connected, by a parapet, with Fort Carillon (the ruins of which may still be seen). The fort, which could contain 300 to 400 men, lay in the lap of the triangle, and commanded the centre and right side of the plateau, as well as the plain below, in the direction of Lake Champlain and the river St. Frederic. The enemy in our front bivouacked during the night of July 6–7. The glare of their numerous fires indicated that they were in great number near the portage. The French entrenchments, of zigzag outline, were begun in the evening of the 6th, and carried on most actively on the 7th. They began at the fort, followed for some length the crest of the heights, in the direction of La Chute river, and then turned to the right, in order to traverse the triangle at its base, following the sinuosities of a gorge, of little depth, running across the plateau; and, finally, descended to the hollow (*bas-fond*), which extends to the lake. The lines of entrenchment might have about 600 yards of development, and a height of five feet: they were formed of felled trees, placed each on others; and all disposed in such sort, that the larger branches, stripped of their leaves and pointed, turned outwards and formed a rude kind of chevaux-de-frise. Each battalion as it arrived, first taking the place it was to occupy in action, constructed its parts of the defences intended to cover all. Every man worked with ardour at his separate task. The Canadians, who did not obtain hatchets till noon on the 6th, began their assigned portion of the abattis, in the hollow towards Lake Champlain, and finished it just as the advancing British came into view. As the intermediate country between the troops and the enemy was thickly wooded, Montcalm had caused the nearer parts of it to be cleared, so that the latter should be the sooner seen, and have no covert when within gun-range.

Meanwhile, Abercromby was completing the disembarkation of his army. Some prisoners he took misinformed him that the French had entrenched themselves merely to gain time, expecting the arrival of 3000 additional men, under De Lévis, said to be on the way. The *wily* Abercromby determined to fall on at once, before the (imaginary) succour could come up. An engineer, sent by Abercromby to reconnoitre, returned and reported that the French works were incomplete; upon which, he (boldly) put his army in motion. The vanguard, led by colonel Bradstreet, did not halt till it came within a short mile of the French entrenchments, late on 7th July. Here the enemy's advanced corps passed the night; the line of adversaries on each side of the narrow interspace making ready for next day's action.

The British army, deducting a few hundred men left at La Chute (probably for guarding the boats at the foot of the lake), consisted of 15,000 prime soldiers, under experienced officers—all full of confidence in their superior numbers proving irresistible; while the French forces were only 3,600 strong, including 450 Canadians and marines; there being no armed savages present. Montcalm put fort Carillon in charge of 300 men ; the rest lined the entrenchments, three men deep. Order was given to each battalion to keep in reserve a grenadier company and a piquet of soldiers, to take post behind, and repair, on occasion, to any overpressed part of the line. De Lévis, who arrived just that morning (the 8th), commanded the right wing; under him were the Canadians and their chief, M. de Raymond ; Bourlamaque commanded the left wing, Montcalm the centre. Such was the French order of battle.

About half-past 12 noon, the outposts re-entered the abattis, after skirmishing with those of the British. A cannon-shot, fired from the fort, gave the signal to the men within to stand to their arms, and be ready to open fire.

Abercromby divided his army into four columns, the heads of which were ordered to attack simultaneously. The grenadier companies, posted in front of all, had directions to force the entrenchments at the bayonets' point, but not to fire till they had fairly cleared the barricade. At the same time, an allotted number of gun-barges were to fall down La Chute river, and menace the French right flank. By one o'clock P. M. the British columns were moving onward; they were intermingled with light troops and savages. The latter, as they advanced under tree-covert, kept up a galling fire on the French. The enemy's four columns, leaving the uncleared woods behind, descended into the gorge in front of our entrenchments, advancing upon them with great boldness and in admirable order; two of the four columns being directed against the French left wing, one against the centre, and the fourth against the right, following the sinuosities in the slope of the hollow where the Canadians were posted. The firing was commenced by the marksmen (*tirailleurs*) of the column opposed to the French right wing, and extended gradually from that point to the French left, the column facing which, composed of highlanders and grenadiers, tried to penetrate the barrier on M. de Lévis' side. That officer, discerning the danger, ordered the Canadians to make a sortie and assail the flank of this column. The manœuvre succeeded; for the Canadians' fire, and that of the two battalions on the sloping ground or hillock (*coteau*), forced this column to incline towards the next, in order to avoid a cross flanking-fire. The four columns, obliged to converge a little in advancing, either to protect their flanks or the better to attain select points of attack, became massed in debouching near the heights. At that instant, 30 bargos appeared on La Chute, sent to inquiet the French flank. A few shots from the fort, which sank two of them, and an assault upon the others, from the banks, by a few men, caused their crews to retreat.

Montcalm had given an order that the enemies should be allowed to come un resisted within 20 paces of the entrenchments, and it was punctually obeyed. Arrived at the marked line, the musketry which assailed their compact masses told so promptly and terribly, that they were first staggered, and then fell into disorder. Forced to fall back an instant, the broken forward ranks were re-formed, and returned to the attack; but forgetting their consign (not to fire, themselves, till they had surmounted the barricade with fixed bayonets), they began to exchange shots, at a great disadvantage, with the ensconced French. The firing on both sides, along the whole line, became very hot, and was long continued; but, after the greatest efforts, the surviving assailants were obliged to give way a second time, leaving the ground behind them strewed with dead. Once again, however, they rallied at a little distance, re-formed their columns, and, after a few moments' halt, threw themselves anew upon the entrenchments, despite the hottest opposing fire imaginable.

Our generalissimo exposed himself as much as the meanest of his soldiers. From his station in the centre, he hastened towards every point where there was most danger, giving orders and bringing up succour. Finally, the British, after unexampled efforts, were again repulsed.

Astonished more than ever at so obstinate a resistance, Abercromby, who thought nothing would withstand his forces, could not yet believe that they would ultimately fail before enemies so much inferior in numbers; he thought, that, let his adversaries' courage be ever so great, they would at last renounce a contest which, the more violent and prolonged it were, would end all the more fatally for them. He resolved, therefore, to continue his assaults with added energy till he should achieve a triumph. Accordingly, between 1 and 5 o'clock P. M. (four hours! he ordered up his troops six times, to be as often driven back, each succeeding time with increasing loss. The fire kept up against them by the French was so hot and close, that part of the fragile ramparts which protected the assailed ignited more than once.

The enemies' columns, not succeeding in their first attacks made simultaneously but independently against the whole French line, now conjoined their strengths, and in a solid body tried to force, sometimes the centre of the French, at other times their right, and again their left wing—all in vain. But it was the right of the French works that was longest and most obstinately assailed; in that quarter, the combat was most sanguinary. The British grenadiers and highlanders there persevered in the attack for three hours, without flinching or breaking rank. The highlanders above all, under Lord John Murray, covered themselves with glory. They formed the head of the troops confronting the Canadians, their light and picturesque costume distinguishing them from all other soldiers amid the flames and smoke. This corps lost the half of its men, and 25 of its officers were killed or severely wounded.*
At length this mode of attack failed, as the preceding had done, owing to the cool intrepidity of our troops; who, as they fought, shouted *Vive le roi!* and cried "Our general for ever!" During the different charges of the enemy, the Canadians made several sorties, turned their flanks, and took a number of them prisoner.

At half-past five, Abercromby, losing hopes of success for a moment, withdrew his columns into the woods beyond, to allow the men to recover their breath; yet he resolved to make one last attempt before quite giving up his enterprise. An hour having elapsed, his army returned to the charge, and with its massed strength once again assaulted the whole French line. This final attack failed even as the others. Thus fairly baffled, the British had perforce to retreat, leaving the French masters of the field; the rear of the former being protected by a swarm of riflemen, who skirmished with the Canadians sent in pursuit till night-fall.

By this time, the French were exhausted with fatigue, but in-

---

* Scarcely any of the wounded highlanders ever recovered, even those sent home as invalids; their sores cankered, owing to the broken glass, ragged bits of metal, &c. used by the Canadians, instead of *honest* shot.
—B.

toxicated with joy. General Montcalm, accompanied by chevalier de Lévis, and the staff-officers, passed along the ranks and thanked the victors, in the king's name, for their good conduct during this glorious day, one of the most memorable in the annals of French valour. Scarcely believing, however, that the present retreat of the British army would be definitive, and fully expecting that they would renew the combat next day, he issued orders to prepare for their reception as before. The troops therefore had to pass the night in their position; they cleaned their arms, and when daylight dawned next morning, set to work to complete and add to the entrenchments; constructing two batteries, one to the right with four cannon mounted, and another on the left, with six. After a pause of some hours and no enemy appearing, Montcalm sent out some detachments to reconnoitre, one of which, pushing on beyond La Chute, destroyed an intrenchment which the British had formed there, but abandoned. Next day (July 10), De Lévis advanced to the foot of Lake George with his grenadiers, volunteers, and Canadians; and there found many evidences of the precipitation of Abercromby's retreat. During the night following the battle, he continued his retreat, without stopping, to the lake; and this retrograde movement must have become a veritable flight. His soldiers left by the way their field implements (*outils*), portions of the baggage, and many wounded men (who were all picked up by De Lévis); their general having re-embarked his remaining troops by the first morning light, after throwing all his provisions, &c. into the lake.

Such was the battle of Carillon, wherein 3,600 men struggled successfully, for six hours, against 15,000 picked soldiers. The victory gained on this memorable day (July 8, 1757) greatly raised the reputation of Montcalm, whom good fortune attended ever since he came to America, making him the idol of the soldiers. In his army but 377 men were killed or wounded, including 38 officers. Amongst those hurt was M. de Bourlamaque, who was severely wounded in the shoulder; M. de Bougainville, who had just been promoted to the grade of assistant quarter-master (*aide-maréchal de logis*), was wounded likewise. De Lévis' clothes and hat were ball-pierced in several places. The British owned to a loss of 2,000 killed or wounded, including 126 officers; but the contemporary French accounts estimated the British loss at from 4 to 5 thousand.

"Montcalm," said M. Dussieux, "stopped invasion by his brilliant victory of Carillon; certes, that was a deed to be proud of. But Montcalm spoke modestly of what he had done: 'The only credit I can lay claim to,' wrote he next day to M. de Vaudreuil, ' is the glory accruing to me of commanding troops so valorous... The success of the affair is due to the incredible bravery manifested both by officers and soldiers.'"

" During the evening of the battle-day, the fortunate and illustrious general wrote, upon the battle-field itself, this simple and touching letter to his friend M. de Doreil: 'The army, the too small army of the king, has just beaten his enemies. What a day for [the honour of] France! Had I had two hundred savages to serve for the van of a detachment of a thousand chosen troops, led by De Lévis, not many of the fleeing enemies would have escaped. Ah! such troops as ours, my dear Doreil—I never saw their match."

Abercromby made his way to the head of Lake George in hot haste. Arrived there, he entrenched himself in the camp which he occupied before his short campaign ; ordering general Amherst, from Louisbourg, to join him without delay. The latter, who re-landed at Boston Sept. 13, took the road for Albany with 4,500 men. But the season was then too far advanced to make any new attempt for the current year—supposing always that Abercromby had inclinations that way ; and renewed invasion of Canada had to be adjourned till a more propitious time. Furthermore, the Carillon pass would have been more hard to force on a second attempt than at the first; because the entrenchments there, which were then barricaded with felled trees, now consisted of regular embankments flanked by redoubts armed with artillery. Bands of Canadians, and savages, also scoured the country far and near, and held in check the whole British army. They attacked its detachments even under the walls of Fort Edward; near to which, M. de St. Luc captured a convoy of 150 waggons.

Nevertheless, the great numerical superiority of our enemies made their losses of men little felt, for the recruits they constantly received more than compensated such deductions; whereas the very successes of the French diminished the chances of their ultimately prevailing in so unequal a struggle as they had to maintain.

Abercromby, having learned that his descent on Carillon was the cause why De Lévis had been called away from Fort Frontenac (Kingston), and that the place was nearly abandoned, sent colonel Bradstreet, with 3,000 men, bearing 11 guns and mortars, to surprise that important post, which was the entrepot of the French marine on Lake Ontario. That officer reached his destination Aug. 25, having left the British camp secretly, and descended the Oswego river to the lake. The fort contained only 70 men, but their commander, M. de Noyan, did not surrender it till the enemies' bombs made it untenable. The victors captured many cannon, quantities of small arms, loads of provisions, and nine newly armed barks,—part of the trophies brought from Oswego. After loading his barges to the water's edge, Bradstreet released his prisoners on parole, burnt the fort, also seven of the barks, and returned to his own country; where, soon afterwards, he re-established Fort Bull.

This expedition did honour to the American colonel, and for a moment inquieted the colonial authorities, for it seemed to put in peril our superiority in the lake country, as that partly depended on the flotilla, laid up in ordinary at Frontenac. The mastery of Lake Ontario appeared to be so important, that M. de Vaudreuil, on learning that Bradstreet had made his descent at Frontenac, caused the *générale* (call to arms) to be beat, and ordered the town-major of Montreal, M. Duplessis, to gather all the savages he could, and recal 1,500 Canadians from field labour; then to lead them forward, by forced marches, to relieve the garrison of Frontenac. That officer, however, upon reaching Fort Présentation (Ogdensburgh), was informed that Frontenac was already taken; upon which he halted, and waited the arrival of further orders. He was then directed to detach 600 of his men for Niagara, in order to strengthen the post there. M. de Vaudreuil also sent for general Montcalm to Montreal, to deliberate upon what was to be done, now that Louisbourg had fallen, and Frontenac was ruined. It was resolved by the two chiefs that the latter should be refounded; and that Niagara should be re-taken were it to fall into the enemy's hands temporarily, as was then feared, being but weakly garrisoned; while Oswego was to be attacked, if the British thought fit to re-fortify that place. De Lévis was named commandant of the great lake frontier; and M. de Pontleroy, chief engineer, appointed to restore the defensive works of Frontenac; but this labour was not to be performed till the year following, the season being too far spent.

If their superiority in numbers assured to the British the advantages of a campaign in the Gulf of St. Lawrence, the same cause produced a like result in the Ohio valley, where the successes of the French were insufficient to compensate their numerical weakness. General Forbes directed the enemy's operations on this frontier. His army, composed of regular troops, under colonel Bouquet; and of militiamen, under colonel Washington, assembled 6,000 strong at Raystown, 30 leagues from Fort Duquesne, which they were to attack. An unpleasant recollection of Braddock's defeat induced the enemy to approach that fort by a new route, across the highlands. In mid-September, the British troops were still at Loyal-Hanning, where they raised a fort, 45 miles distant from the French post. Before setting out himself, Forbes sent a detachment, 1,000 strong, under Major Grant, to reconnoitre; and this corps reached undiscovered a spot within a short mile of Fort Duquesne. Grant's intent was to attack, during the night, those savages who usually camped round the place; but the fires lighted before their huts, the common indicators of their presence, had been let burn out before he arrived, and he was obliged, before doing any thing further, to retire at break of day to the crest of a neighbouring hill, where his presence surprised the French. M. de Ligneris, successor of M. Dumas, at once assembled 700 to 800 men, who, led by M. Aubry, ascending to the position of the British, attacked and drove them into the plain. The savages, who had retired beyond the river, so as not to be come on unawares, retraced their steps, and, seeing the enemies' repulse, joined the Canadians. The British, attacked again, were completely routed and dispersed; they lost 300 men, killed or wounded, and more than 100 were taken prisoner, including 20 officers and Grant himself. Those who fled rejoined Forbes at Loyal-Hanning, whence he had not stirred. It was now November, and the season's snows began to fall; it was therefore decided, in a council of war, that further aggressive operations should be postponed till next year; but, before a retrograde movement was made by the British, some prisoners they took unfortunately disclosed the weak condition of the French. The allied savages had left for their own villages, and the auxiliary corps from Detroit and the Illinois, sent in aid, through a misunderstanding that the enemies were already on their homeward route, had retired; in fine, scarcely 500 men were then in garrison at Fort Duquesne. Forbes now changed his mind: leaving behind him his tents and heaviest baggage, he advanced, by forced marches, towards the place with all his troops and light artillery. M. de Ligneris, not able to face so superior a force, and hopeless of succour, embarked his artillery in bateaux, burnt the fort, and retired with his men to Fort Machault, near lake Erie. Forbes took possession of the relinquished ruins of a place, which had been such an eyesore to the British. The latter, willing to compliment their great minister, gave the name of Pittsburg to the heap of ashes found in a locality, now the site of a rich and flourishing city.

Everywhere the season for repose was come, and the forces of the belligerents, on all the frontiers, entered into cantonments. Upon Lake George, the British armies, after receiving reinforcements which mutual inaction rendered useless, took up their winter-quarters; that of Abercromby, before retiring, burnt the defensive erections and obliterated the trenches formed at the head of Lake George.

The balance of material advantage in the campaign of 1758, the fifth since hostilities began, inclined to the British side in America: for they became masters, in autumn, of Louisbourg and Isle St. Jean; they burnt the Gaspé settlements, and gained a foothold on the north coast of Fundy Bay; they razed Fort Frontenac and forced the French to leave that place, as well as Fort Duquesne: but so far as military glory was concerned, the French rose superior. Everywhere they had to contend against far greater numbers than their own; at Louisbourg, disparity was as 1 to 4; at Carillon nearly 1 to 5! Never did our race fight with more devotedness or greater intrepidity. If its chiefs committed some faults, it cannot be said that those faults caused the evil consummation becoming inevitable, the responsibility of which must be laid at the door of their sybaritic sovereign. Canada, left a prey to famine and the sword, could not for ever maintain a contest against a maritime Power, mistress of those seas across which new armies were ever passing to reinforce Canada's enemies, far too powerful before.

In other regions of the globe, France's fortunes were better that year. In the East, her fleets captured Gondelour, and burnt there ten British frigates; they also took fort David and Divicoté on the Coromandel coast. After a check at Raga, the French conquered the naboby of Arcate. In Europe, France achieved successes and sustained some reverses; upon the whole, her position there was made no worse. A few victories counterbalanced some defeats in Germany; and the duke d'Aiguillon annihilated at St. Cast the rear-guard of a British force, which for some time menaced the French coasts. So many efforts, however, to sustain a war over land and sea in every part of the world, ended by emptying the royal treasury. Pitt, aware of this, strove with redoubled energy to destroy or paralyse the forces of France in the New World.

Financial embarrassments, added to gloomy prospects, now caused a new change in the French ministry. "For some time before," says M. Guérin, "successive ministers flitted across the political scene like so many shadows; this was true of the marine as of all other departments, under the semblance of a government which France possessed during that sad epoch of our history. Hardly had a newly inducted state functionary begun to acquire the routine duties of his place, than he was forced to renounce it before effecting any thing. Only a little month after Péraine de Mauras succeeded to Machault in the bureau of marine and colonies, he had to make way for De Massiac, who in turn, after a few weeks' possession, was displaced in favour of Nicolas-René Berryer, a personage not less hurtful than Jérôme Pontchartrain had been before. Berryer had been lieutenant of police; and, as such, a chief purveyor of lodgers for the Bastille, in which capacity he earned the favour of Pompadour: among the Paris commonalty, atrocious acts were laid to his charge, and he ran some risk of falling a victim to the popular fury therefor. To this contemned, detested, and above all incompetent man, did the ruling demirep consign the department of marine; now had our British enemies tried their utmost to deal a brain-blow to French interests, they could not have succeeded better than did the court favourite by this odious appointment." Marshal de Belle-Isle succeeded M. de Paulmy as war minister; and the duke de Choiseul replaced cardinal de Bernis, as minister of foreign affairs. These changes foreshadowed an ascendancy for the war party at court. Still, military interests fared no better for the change; and disasters to the French arms continued increasingly, as we shall have too much occasion to see. To Canada, the new ministry was even less favourable than the old; none of its members took thought for the necessities of the colony, or cared to stir up others to send out the succours which had been so urgently solicited.

Meanwhile the paucity of soldiers and scarcity of victuals in the colony, became increasing as well as abiding evils. A portion of the cultivators having been diverted from their proper work in compliance with the exigencies of war, many farms lay fallow; consequently, supplementary supplies of food were needful. Large imports had taken place in previous years, larger were wanted now. On the other hand, hostilities, hotly maintained on the ocean, made transmission by sea hazardous, and imports uncertain; thence it became indispensable to order matters so, that the greatest number of rural labourers, which could by any possibility be spared at intervals, should have allowance to quit the army, during seed-time and harvest: thus war and agriculture became each other's bane, and both were now advancing on the road to ruin.

As early as the month of October, the governor-general and the intendant wrote to the minister, to inform him that the British meant to besiege Quebec in the ensuing year with large forces; adding, that if Canada received no succour, attacked as it would be on all sides, its people must needs succumb; that there were only 10,000 disposable men in arms to confront hosts of foes, as 4,000 troops (all there were besides) were wanted for transports, the garrisoning of Niagara, Frontenac, Présentation, &c. "We cannot count for much the inhabitants," it was observed: "they are wearied out by continual marchings; yet it is to them we trust, as scouts for the army.* Their lands are but half cultivated; their

* " Ce sont eux qui font les découvertes pour l'armée :" the above is a true if free interpretation of the foregoing words, if we mistake not.—B.

dwellings are falling to ruin; they are ever campaigning, far away from wives and children, who mostly have not bread to eat.......... There will be no tillage this year, for want of husbandmen." It was stated also by the authorities, that a distribution to the poorer classes, of bullock or horse flesh, at reduced prices, would have to take place. And, going into details, as to the amount of food considered to be indispensable, 35 ships of 300 to 400 tons each, it was intimated, would be wanted to bear it across the ocean.

All the private correspondence of the time evidences the truthfulness of the official picture thus drawn of the colony's deplorable state. The breaches of trust and robberies habitually committed by the intendant and his confederates, progressed concurrently with the failing ability of the country to bear them. M. de Bougainville repaired to Paris, in view of urging upon the court the necessity there was for making an effort to avert the utter ruin of the colony, become imminent; and M. de Doreil, who was to follow, was directed to sustain Bougainville's representations. Pressing as these were, they fell dead-born from the remonstrants' lips.

In their impotence to succour the noble dependency of France she was about to lose, the king's ministers, as if to justify themselves, took to addressing reproaches to the intendant, regarding the excessive expenditure of the Canadian government. For some months, they had been advertised of what was going on; for as early as August preceding, M. Doreil, emboldened by Montcalm, who honoured him with his friendship, thus wrote to the minister respecting a peccant functionary in the commissariat : " Péan has made so rapid a fortune (in eight years), that he is reputed to have netted two millions............Canada is Britain's own, next year ....We are here like men moribund, whose last agony is near, although warded off for a short while by medical means."......
......" You may look upon him (Péan) as one of the primal originators of the mal-administration and approaching loss of this unfortunate country. I told you just now, that he is two millions in pocket; could we trust to public report, the sum that he has netted is nearer to four than two.........."

A communication written in cipher, dated December 1758, transmitted to Paris, informed its recipient that all financial matters were in Bigot's hands; that he was uncontrolled in their management, acted under no direction, and was subject to no supervision; further, that while his only care was to enrich himself, he played the part of an official despot. Partly to stifle animadversion, partly from weakness, it was added, he allowed his accomplices to share in the public spoils. Among the most important of the latter, was one not named, but plainly indicated as "the minister's right hand" (*l'œil même du ministre*): this was M. de la Porte, a court functionary at Versailles.

Bigot really monopolized the whole trade of the colony, inner and outer, by the help of Péan, Le Mercier, and others, who furnished provisions, implements, fuel, everything the government had need of; and the party habitually diverted the means of transport, provided for public use, to private purposes. "Bigot," we read in one letter, "ordered from France all that Canada was likely to want, not for account of the king, but to be entered in name of the 'great society;' which association sold stores for state use at whatever price the directors chose to put upon them." Bigot was also accused of falsifying the public accounts in his own peculiar way (*à sa façon*), changing the titles of items of outlay, enhancing the amounts of articles delivered, &c. At length, Montcalm decided to indite (April 12, 1759) certain incriminating facts which he had previously declared (Nov. 4, 1757) "he could not bring himself to write." In a long ciphered despatch, addressed to marshal de Belle-Isle, then war minister, he began by imparting his own inquietudes regarding the destiny of Canada; repeating that food and money were both wanting to the colony, and that the spirit of its people was depressed. "I have no faith whatever," added he, "either in M. de Vaudreuil or M. Bigot. The former is not fit to plan a military enterprise; he has no activity, he gives his confidence to pretenders (*empiriques*). As for Bigot, his only aim is to enrich himself, his adherents and toadies (*complaisants*) ....Greediness has infected every one—officers, storekeepers, clerks—those who intermediate with the Ohio posts, and the savage tribes in the west, &c............and all realise astonishing fortunes; one officer, who entered as a private soldier 20 years ago, has netted 700,000 livres............False accounts are exposed to no test; if the savages had but a quarter of what is charged to the king on their account, he might have every nation of them at his command, even those now in British pay. ....All this corruptness exerts a malign influence on the conduct of the war. M. de Vaudreuil, for whom one man is as good as another, would as lief entrust a great military operation to his brother, or to any other colonial officer, as to M. de Lévis............The choice is sure to fall on some one who has a finger in the family pie (*le choix regarde ceux qui partage le gâteau*): accordingly, M. Bourlamaque was not put in command at fort Duquesne, nor M. Senezergues, as I proposed. Had either been sent, the king would have been all the better served. But what abuses may not be expected to arise out of such a system! under which the smallest cadet, with a sergeant and one cannoneer, manning some petty outpost, shall return from it with certificates for 20,000 or 30,000 livres, as vouchers for the (pretended) value of articles furnished to the savages............It would seem, really, that every one is in hot haste to realize a fortune before the colony is quite lost to France: several perhaps wish for the ruin to be total, so that all recorded evidences of their speculations may be covered by its wrecks."—Recurring to the facts notified in the anonymous letter of December, Montcalm wrote concerning the fur trade, on merchandize for savages' use, transports, &c. *ex. gr.*: "Immense forestallings are going on of all sorts of articles, which are re-sold at 150 per cent. advance of prices, for the benefit of Bigot and his adherents.......I have often spoken, in respectful terms, about their prodigal expenditure, to Messrs. de Vaudreuil and Bigot, but each throws the blame of it on the other."

In a letter written the same day (April 12, 1759) to M. le Normand, intendant for the colonies, Montcalm signalized the huge frauds of the colonial engineers charged with the direction of military works; their dishonest contracts were also attested and denounced by M. de Pontleroy, royal engineer, whose own hands were unsoiled. A chief peculator in this department was Le Mercier, a creature of Vaudreuil and Bigot; the king he grossly defrauded in all purchases made of ordnance equipments, such as portable forges, ammunition and baggage carts, siege implements, &c.

M. de Vaudreuil, an honest but weak man, had been encircled, seduced, and mystified (*étouffé*), by Bigot and Co. to such an extent as to be entirely at their disposal; his ignoble subjection to them embroiling him with Montcalm, Lévis, Bougainville, Doreil,

Pontleroy—in fine, with every honest man who could and would have set him right. So hoodwinked was he content to be, that in a letter to the minister of marine, dated Oct. 15, 1759, he formally defended the system of the intendant! and on the strength of the certificate of good conduct thus signed in favour of Bigot, that worthy continued his depredations, without feigning any further sense of shame.*

All these complaints, all those accusations, disquieted the ministers, without stimulating them to remedy the abuses denounced, or to supply needful succours to prosecute the existing war. But it was thought decent to *say* something, at least. Berryer, therefore, wrote to the intendant (Jan. 19, 1759), that the exorbitant wealth of his (Bigot's) subalterns, exposed their superior's administration of the colonial finances to labour under general suspicion. In a letter, dated Aug. 29, the same minister being previously advised that the colonial drafts (*lettres de change*) for the current year had risen from 31 to 33 millions, testified still greater discontent, reproaching Bigot for outlays sometimes made without royal sanction, often without any necessity, and always without any regard to economy. Thus did he terminate his strictures on this occasion: "You are directly accused of hampering the free provisioning of the colony; for your commissary-general buys up all commodities, and sells them again at his own price. You have yourself, sir, bought at second and third hand, what you ought to have obtained at once, for the king's service, at a cheaper rate; you have enriched persons, your connexions, whose interest you alone studied in your purchases, or in other ways; you live in splendour, and indulge in high gambling,† in a time of general privation...... I desire you to reflect seriously on the manner in which you have till now performed the administrative duties which were laid upon you. It is of more consequence to you that this be done, than perhaps you are aware of."

This despatch, which menaced to lay bare the secret doings of

---

* The above details are borrowed from the admirable (*beau*) work of M. Dussieux, intituled, *Canada sous la Domination Française*.

† Bigot played to an amount sufficient to astonish the most hardened of our present gamblers. During the carnival of 1758, he lost over 200,000 livres.

the intendant, seemed to affect him little, but in reality he felt self-humiliated and apprehensive of consequences; for he was now made sensible that he was a fallen man in the estimation of his patrons at court. A second despatch re-produced the foregoing reproaches; with super added threats, of a more pointed and explicit character than those indicated by the first.

Misfortunes and obstacles sour men's tempers, and end by engendering evil passions in the noblest hearts. Discords between de Vaudreuil and Montcalm assumed a graver character than ever before, after the battle of Carillon.

The latter, and his partisans, accused the former of having exposed the army to the risk of utter destruction, by dispersing it about lake Ontario and at the foot of lake George, by not calling the Canadians and armed savages to be ready to act at every point liable to be endangered. After the battle of Carillon, Montcalm wrote to the minister that the governor's acts had exposed him, without proper means of defence, to the enemy's blows; but since victory had repaired this fault, there was no more to be said on that head. He now declared, however, that to th eregulars was due the whole credit of the triumph—an ungenerous observation, which serves to show the jealous animus which we have adverted to more than once. Then, after soliciting the rewards merited by soldiers so valorous, he added: "As for me, I ask for no other guerdon than my recal from the king. My health is failing, my purse is getting thin; by the year's end, I shall owe 10,000 crowns to the colonial treasurer. Worse than all, what between the unpleasantness and contrarieties I have to endure, along with my impotence to do good or to prevent evil from being done—all things, in short, impel me to supplicate earnestly that his Majesty would let me return to France, for that is the only royal grace I covet." M. Doreil, who chose to express his friend's sentiments still more explicitly, criticized long before, as we have seen, but now with greater asperity, all the acts of the colonial administration. After the late victory, more especially, he put no curb upon his strictures: "The negligence, the ignorance, the tardiness, and the obstinacy of the governor, have well-nigh caused the loss of the colony....... Inaptitude, intriguing, lying, and cupidity conjoined, will doubtless consummate its perdition." And as public report attributed to the Canadians a great part of the successes obtained during the war, and as the king might overrate their devotedness, from what he had been told, M. Doreil informed the minister that Montcalm assured him in a confidential letter, that the Canadians and colonial regulars present at Carillon made but a poor figure; whereas Montcalm said quite the contrary in his official despatch sent to Paris. After sending several letters written in the above strain, Doreil thinking he had disposed the ministry for what was coming, in the last of them (which was more violent than all the rest) he advised them to supersede Vaudreuil, and put Montcalm in his place: "Whether the war continue or not," urged he, "if Canada is to be retained by France, and its government based on a solid foundation, let his Majesty confide the direction of it to the general. He possesses political science, no less than military merit. Fitted to give counsel as well as to carry it out, he is indefatigable, a lover of justice, scrupulously disinterested, perspicacious, active, and has ever in view public well-being; in a word, he is at once a virtuous and accomplished man............while, even were M. de Vaudreuil his equal in such regards, he can never rid himself of the original demerit of being a born Canadian."

All those intrigues, the particulars of which were publicly whispered, at length came to the governor's knowledge. In advance of the expected change, the French officers and soldiers began to carp at, and next to stigmatize unreservedly, the conduct of De Vaudreuil, attributing to him all the privations they endured. He thought it was full time to put a term to such a state of things, which might eventuate badly for every one; but while protesting against what was going on, he laid himself open to the charge of defending himself no less passionately than others had attacked him. Thus, in a letter full of recriminations which he addressed to the ministers, he demanded the recal of Montcalm, under the pretext that the general had not the qualities in him needful for directing a Canadian war; intimating, at the same time, that much gentleness and patience were indispensable for leading Canadians and savages, and he asserted that Montcalm possessed neither of these qualities. He wound up all by indicating chevalier de Lévis as a fit person to succeed M. de Montcalm as leader of the troops.

Montcalm, on his part, wrote to the minister, that "it was hard upon him to be always exposed to the necessity of justifying himself." The day afterwards, he sent an intimation to De Vaudreuil, that he thought they were both in the wrong, and a change ought to take place in their way of dealing with each other. Montcalm also sent to him M. de Bougainville as his intermediator. A better understanding appeared to follow between them, but unfortunately lasted not long. Bougainville, when rendering an account of his mission to the minister, assigned as the origin of the differences, various " misapprehensions (*tracasseries*), in the minds of both chiefs, raised by subalterns interested in creating mutual distrust;" adding, that ." intriguers who had perhaps a pecuniary interest to serve, and had reasons arising out of their peculations to discredit the severe judgment of their conduct by a scrutinizing and honest reporter, would doubtless endeavour to embroil the dissentient parties more yet."

These unfortunate differences the ministers knew not how to deal with ; a note, however, was drawn up and submitted to the council of state, to recal Montcalm, in obedience to his own expressed wish, but with the title of lieutenant-general ; De Lévis to be his successor, with the grade of major-general. The king, on due reflection made, did not approve of this arrangement, and the matter remained in abeyance. It was thought dangerous, perhaps, on the one hand, to recal a successful and popular general ; and on the other, hazardous to supersede a viceroy who had obtained from the Canadians such sacrifices of their means and lives without a murmur, as only the most devoted subjects would submit to. The system of having two chief functionaries in one colony, almost equal in power, was faulty in itself. It would have been better, at the outset, to have nominated a governor-general capable of ruling the state as well as leading the army; instead of which, the minister had written to Montcalm, on his appointment, that he was to be subordinate in all things to M. de Vaudreuil : while, in addressing the latter, he wrote that M. de Montcalm was to command the land forces, but that he was to do so under his (Vaudreuil's) orders, to which he was to conform in every way.

At length, conciliatory missives were drawn up for the two chiefs, one addressed to Montcalm, the other to Vaudreuil, by the ministry in the king's name, strongly recommending union and concord between them. In spring, M. de Bougainville arrived in Quebec, his hands full of recompenses. Vaudreuil received the grand cross of the order of St. Louis; for M. de Montcalm there was promotion to a lieutenant-generalship, for M. de Levis the grade of major-general.* Bourlamaque and Sennezergues were appointed brigadiers. Bougainville was made a colonel, and a knight of St. Louis; Dumas, aid-major general, and inspector of the colonial regulars. Badges of honour and promotion were also awarded to several officers of inferior note to the foregoing. These recompenses, and still more the pressing instances of the ministers, brought the rival chiefs into closer personal connexion, but with feelings as much estranged mutually as ever.

Meanwhile the war minister gave small hopes of any considerable succour being sent; it was therefore in vain that Montcalm informed him—no unexpected stroke of good fortune intervening, such as a great and successful demonstration by sea against the British colonies, or some enormous blunder to be committed by the enemy's leaders—that Canada would certainly be conquered in the campaign of 1760, if not in that of 1759; for the British, he observed, had 60,000 men ready to take the field, whereas the French (in Canada) had but 10,000, or at most 11,000. The minister wrote in reply, that reinforcements must not be expected; adding, that, "not only would additional troops be a means of aggravating the evils of the dearth which has too long afflicted the colony, but the chances are great that, if sent thither, they would be captured by the British on their way to you; and as the king cannot pretend to send forces in any equal proportion to those which the British can oppose to ours, the only result of our increasing the latter would be, that the cabinet of London would augment theirs in an over-proportion, so as to maintain the superiority which Britain has acquired in that part of your continent."† Accordingly, 600 recruits, two frigates, and 12 to 15 merchant vessels, chiefly Bigot's, and bearing cargoes for him—these were all the succours which reached Quebec before the enemy's fleet came up. Although this virtually released the Canadians from the

* These are the nearest English equivalents to *maréchal de camp* and *major-général.*—B.

† Letter, of date Feb. 19, 1759.

fealty they owed to France, since she recognized the absolute superiority of the British in America, not one of them yet spoke of surrender ; they had still blood to shed and sacrifices that they could make for their fatherland ; and if some despairing words did arise, they proceeded from the French regulars rather than from the Canadian ranks.

The British Government well knew Canada's distress, and prepared to profit by it. The parliament freely granted all the supplies wanted, of men, money, and ships, to ensure the realization of the great enterprise the ministry had undertaken. If British advantages already gained were not brilliant, they were solid and important; the roads to Quebec, to Niagara, and into western Canada lay open ; and the native tribes of the latter region were gained over. The savage nations of the west, foreseeing the coming fall of French domination in America, and willing to secure favour in time, had formed in October preceding an alliance at Easton,† where attended Sir Wm. Johnson,† along with several governors and a number of leading colonials. Thus was breaking up daily that admirable system of alliances, formed by Champlain, and organized by Talon and Frontenac. The Treaty of Easton, says Smollett, paved the way for the military operations projected against Canada, and effected in 1759.

The British persisted in their plan for invading our country simultaneously, at the centre and by its two longitudinal extremities. The immensity of their forces always necessitated a subdivision of them ; for, in a mass, its parts would have encumbered each other, and some become useless. Louisbourg having fallen, Quebec was the second fastness which had to be attacked by sea. Beneath the walls of the capital the three invading armies were to meet, and overpower that last bulwark of France by their very weight. General Amherst, who had been formally thanked by parliament, as well as Admiral Boscawen, for reducing Louisbourg, was sent to supersede Abercromby, the defeated of Carillon. A corps, 10,000 strong, was assigned to General Wolfe, a young officer who

---

* About 90 miles from Philadelphia.—*B.*

† A slight mistake : the worthy baronet did not attend on the above occasion.—*B.*

had gained distinction at Louisbourg. While he should ascend the
St. Lawrence, and invest Quebec, 12,000 men, under Amherst
himself, was to make a renewed attempt (the third) to force a
passage by lake Champlain, descend the rivers Richelieu and St.
Lawrence, and join his forces to Wolfe's at Quebec. Next, General Prideaux, with a third corps, of regulars, provincials, and
thousands of savages led by Sir W. Johnson, was charged to take
Fort Niagara, descend lake Ontario, &c. towards Quebec, capturing
Montreal by the way, and equally join his forces to those which
would already have arrived at the capital of Canada. Lastly, a
fourth but smaller corps, under Colonel Stanwix, was to scour the
country, reduce French fortlets wherever found, and clear the
lake-board of Ontario from every enemy to Britain. The collective
forces of the enemy which thus took the field this year, exceeded
30,000 men; they were accompanied by parks of artillery, and provided with all warlike requisites for sieges, &c. In addition to this
land armament, there was sent from Britain, to aid the operations of
her army, a fleet of 20 ships of the line, 10 frigates, and 18 smaller
war vessels, under Admirals Saunders, Durell, and Holmes, with
many transports for conveying Wolfe's division, from Louisbourg
to Quebec; the whole expedition by sea, it being arranged, should
rendezvous in the St. Lawrence, and cover the siege of that city by
land. If we reckon the number of sailors and marines thus employed at 18,000, and make an allowance for troops left to guard
the British-American provinces, it will be found that the estimation of the enemy's strength, made by Montcalm, was not far wide
of the mark. To conquer Canada, the invaders were obliged to
embody three times more men than it contained soldiers and
colonists fit to bear arms :* this fact attests the fear which its
warriors, so few in number, had inspired in their enemy's hearts.

In view of preparing to oppose such hosts, an inquest was made in
winter 1758-9, to ascertain the number of valid males in the colony,
between the ages of 16 and 60: when this was found to be rather

---

* The Anglo-American journals estimated the British land-force at
60,000 men. "Britain has actually more troops afoot in this continent
than Canada numbers inhabitants, including men, women, and children.
How is it possible to make head against such an armed multitude ?"—
Letter of M. Doreil to the minister.

more than 15,000 in all. The regular force afoot scarcely exdeeded 5,000.* At all times, it is well known, the Canadians were trained to the use of arms. May 20, the governor-general sent a circular to all the captains of militia, ordering them to have their companies ready to take the field at the first signal, each man provided with six days' provisions. In April preceding, the people were informed that the storm of war was about to burst, and the bishop ordained prayers to be offered up in all the churches. The parishioners went thither in crowds on these occasions, in such sort as they had been used to when entering on a campaign.

Early in spring, Captain Pouchot set out for Niagara with 300 men, regulars and Canadians, to repair and defend the fort there, if attacked; but were it not so, he was charged to succour the posts near the Ohio, also to attack enemies in the field, on tempting occasions. Some war-barks were built, during winter, at Fort Presentation (Ogdensburgh). M. de Corbière ascended beyond, to refound Frontenac (Kingston), in order to resume the mastery of Lake Ontario. Other craft were built at the foot of Lake Champlain, to protect the communications of Forts St. Frederic and Carillon; and, whatever might befal these, to defend Fort St. John's (on the Richelieu). As soon as the season permitted, about 2,600 men took posts at intervals, on that frontier, from Chambly (below St. John's) to the foot of Lake George. This force was under the orders of brig.-general Bourlamaque, who was charged to strengthen the position of Carillon. But the additional works needed there were not completed when news brought by Colonel

---

* Government of Quebec—
  (Official enumeration returns). 7,511 men and youths.
  Three Rivers................ 1,313 " "
  Montreal................... 6,405 " "
      Total......15,229 " "

‡ The number of regularly trained soldiers was—
Eight battalions of the line.............. 3,200 men.
Two ditto of colonial regulars....... 1,500 "
Recruits (just arrived from France)....... 600 "
     Total...... 5,300 "

Bougainville (from France), made it probable that Quebec was about to be assailed. An order, therefore, was sent to Bourlamaque, enjoining him, should the enemy come down in force, to destroy all the defences at both the above forts, and retreat to the Isle-aux-Noix (just below the embouchure of Lake Champlain). The chevalier de la Corne, charged to keep the field at the foot of Lake Ontario with 12,000 men, was also, if needs must, to retire to the St. Lawrence rapids below la Présentation and there make a stand. These precautions having been taken, the rest of the troops were ordered to remain in readiness in their respective quarters; while the governor-general, and Generals Montcalm and De Lévis, assembled at Montreal, waiting the first movements of the enemy, to ascertain from these, in what direction it would be proper to send the disposable forces; as the superiority of the British in numbers made them masters of the situation for the time.

Montcalm, however, soon chafed at this state of enforced inaction. He thought, too, that the dispositions (by Vaudreuil) for the defence of Quebec had been tardily made—which was true enough; but France ought to have had the capital properly fortified long before. We have already particularized what was done in that matter. In vain had M. Galissonière, as well as so many others, enlarged upon the necessity of fortifying Quebec. He demonstrated, too, the necessity there was for preserving Canada itself, in behoof of the French royal navy and the trade of the mother country; and he observed that, if the colony was costly to her, the numerous strongholds which bristled with arms along the European frontiers, cost far more to maintain in defensive order. Vainly did he reason thus, again and again, with the king's ministers: a fatal repugnance ever prevented them from taking action in the case. In 1759, it was too late to repair the error. Our chief city's outer line of defence (*mur d'enceinte*) was incapable of sustaining a siege. Montcalm, after extending his observation over all its most assailable parts, did not venture to decide, as yet, upon what should be done—and this the rather as the British forces were to act simultaneously at points removed each from the other: he therefore stood ready till some one of their armies should take the initiative, when he would know satisfactorily how he had best oppose them all.

BOOK TENTH.

CHAPTER I.

VICTORY OF MONTMORENCI AND FIRST BATTLE OF ABRAHAM.—SURRENDER OF QUEBEC.

1759.

Invasion of Canada.—Defensive means adopted.—The French army entrenches itself at Beauport, &c., below Quebec.—The British troops land on the Isle d'Orléans.—Proclamation addressed by General Wolfe to the Canadians.—That General, judging an attack on the French camp to be too hazardous, determines to bombard the city and ravage its environs.—The former set on fire.—Attack on the French lines at Montmorenci.—Wolfe being repulsed, returns dispirited to his camp, and falls ill.—He vainly attempts to put himself into communication with General Amherst at Lake Champlain.—His officers advise that he should take possession, by surprise, of the Heights of Abraham, and thus force the French to quit camp.—General Montcalm sends troops to guard the left bank of the St. Lawrence, above Quebec, up to the river Jacques-Cartier.—A great number of the Canadians, thinking all danger passed, quit the army to attend to field labour.—On the Lake Champlain frontier, M. de Bourlamaque blows up forts Carillon and St. Frederic, and retreats to the Isle-aux-Noix, followed by General Amherst with 12,000 men.—The British generals Prideaux and Johnson, operating towards Lake Erie, take Fort Niagara and force the French to retire to la Présentation, below Lake Ontario.—The British scale the Heights of Abraham, Sept. 13.—First drawn battle; defeat of the French and death of Montcalm: capitulation of Quebec.—General de Lévis takes command of the army, and intends to offer battle instantly; but learning the surrender of the capital, retires to Jacques-Cartier and entrenches his troops.—The British army, enclosed in Quebec, prepares to winter there.—Proper succours asked in vain from France, for re-capturing the city.

While M. de Vaudreuil and the generals were at Montreal, they received despatches from France, which determined Montcalm to leave for Quebec, where he arrived May 22; followed soon afterwards by the governor-general and M. de Lévis. The ships had brought a confirmation of the report that a British fleet was on its way to the capital, which therefore became the first point to be defended. May 22, an express brought word of some enemy's ships having reached Le Bic. " Coming events " thus " casting their shadows before," there was no time to lose, and all was now activity to realize means for a stout defence of the capital. In order to obstruct the enemy's approach, river-buoys and all other indicators for safely navigating the flood were removed ; while fire-floats were prepared for igniting the enemy's ships as soon as they should reach the port. The garrison stores and government archives were removed to Three-Rivers, and the army magazines fixed at Montreal : only necessaries for one month were reserved at Quebec, to supply the daily wants of the troops and inhabitants. A portion of the little grain remaining in the upper country was purchased with money advanced by army officers. Finally, goods were bought to give as presents to those savage tribes about Niagara and Detroit, which either remained true to the French, or whose people disowned their alliances with the British. The gifts thus awarded would at least, it was hoped, secure their neutrality.

These preliminaries arranged, the chiefs turned their attention to organizing the army, and to strengthening Quebec; the loss of the latter, it was likely, would eventuate in that of all Canada. But as for the city defences, they were judged to be anything but impregnable, and especially weak on the landward side; where the rampart, which was unprovided with parapet, embrasures, and cannon, was but six or seven feet in height, and protected outwardly neither by fossé nor glacis: it was therefore decided unanimously, that the city should be put under cover of an entrenched camp, to be occupied by the bulk of the army.

Quebec is built, as has been said before, at the extremity of a promontory. To the east and the south the St. Lawrence, here about a mile wide, rolls its deep waters; to the north is the fine valley of the St. Charles river, which, at its embouchure, along with the greater stream forms a basin three or four miles in extent. The St. Charles' lower bed is entirely covered at high tide; but at full ebb, it is fordable. The promontory on which Quebec stands, being very steep towards the St. Lawrence, with an elevation ranging between 160 and 300 feet, was considered inaccessible, especially on the city side.* The weakest points towards the port were protected by palisades and walls; and the communications between low-town and high-town were cut, and defended by artillery. It was thought that batteries erected on the quays of the lower-town and on the scarp of the upper, would together bar all passage against an enemy, whether ascending from the lower, or descending by the upper flood. If this were so, all that was further wanted, in regard of the city's safety, was to close up the entry of the St. Charles river, and thence fortify its left strand, &c, (*la Canardière*), along with the northern shore of the St. Lawrence, from Beauport to the embouchure of the Montmorenci; said fortifying line to be continued inland for some distance along the right bank of the latter stream, which, descending from the Laurentian highlands, crosses the highway along the left side of the flood it falls into just below.

The entry of the St. Charles, at a point facing the Porte du Palais, was boomed with masts chained together, kept in place by anchors, and protected in front by five barges, each mounted with a cannon. Behind this first barricade three merchant-vessels were sunk, having a platform laid across them, and a battery superimposed, armed with heavy ordnance, the gun-range of which radiated over the whole expanse of the bay. There was besides, at the near end of the Beauport and Charlesbourg roads, a bridge of boats, traversing the St. Charles, defended at each extremity by a hornwork. The right bank of the same river, from the pontoons over it to the Porte au Palais, was bordered with entrenchments, having artillery mounted to defend the entry of the suburb of St. Roch, and prevent the enemy from gaining by surprise the heights of Quebec.—The army now changed position; it passed from the right bank (of the lower St. Charles), whereon it was first entrenched (on the city side), to the left bank of the St. Lawrence; following a line beginning at the bridge of boats just mentioned, and continued to the embouchure of the Montmorenci, with a short

---

* "There is no reason to believe'—thus was the order of battle worded (June 10)—"that the enemy will think of passing in front of the city and landing at the Anse des Mères; and, so long as the frigates remain to us, we have nothing to apprehend on that side."

prolongation inland, as aforesaid. This line was covered by entrenchments, which followed the sinuosities of the ground, and were flanked by redoubts, with cannon mounted at every point where an enemy could land easily. In the centre of the line, at the issue of the Beauport stream, was moored a floating battery of 12 guns.

The flotilla still remaining, consisting of two frigates, the barges, and fire-ships, were put in charge of Captain Vauquelin. Sentinels were posted at intervals, on the margin of the flood, from Quebec to as far above it as the Anse du Foulon (" Wolfe's Cove "), where a steep path (*rampe*) was formed to communicate with the Plains of Abraham, on the plateau above. A small redoubt, with cannon mounted, guarded that passage.—Such were the preparations made for defending Quebec and its environs.

According to the plan adopted (always supposing the St. Lawrence were barred in front of Quebec, and the Beauport army too solidly entrenched to have its lines forced), there was no chance for the invaders but to land on the right bank of the flood, proceed a certain distance upward, cross to the opposite (left) shore, make a short detour inlaid and re-descend. By the semeans, the French army might have been assailed in its rear, if either the Charlesbourg or Bourg-Royal road were followed. But this operation would have been difficult, and doubtless was so considered (by the British), because an enemy's retreat would have been impossible in case of a repulse.

The French army was strengthening daily, by the arrival of militia-men from all parts of the country. In rural homesteads, there remained behind only aged men, women and children. Every male fit to bear arms presented himself at Quebec, at Carillon, at lake Ontario, at Niagara, or at a post on lake Erie, or, in fine, at some point or other, even if as distant as that portion of the Ohio valley still possessed by the French.

In the arrangement of the field forces, Montcalm's right wing, composed of the militias of Quebec and Trois-Rivières districts, 4,380 strong, under Messrs. de St.-Ours and de Bonne, occupied La Canardière (facing the city) ; the centre, composed of 2,000 reguars, under brigadier Sennezergues, guarded the space between the lower St. Charles and Beauport church ; the left, composed of the militia of Montreal district, numbering 3,450 men, under Messrs.

Prud'homme and d'Herbin, extended from said church to the river Montmorenci. General de Lévis commanded the whole left, Colonel de Bougainville the entire right, of the general position; while M. de Montcalm, taking charge of the centre, there established his head-quarters. A corps in reserve, composed of 1,400 colonial soldiers, 350 horsemen and 450 savages, under M. de Boishébert (an officer just returned from Acadia), took up a position behind the centre of the army, on the heights of Beauport. If to these forces we add the sailors and 650 others in Quebec garrison (the latter being armed citizens), under M. de Ramesay, there is a resulting total of 13,000 combatants. "We had not reckoned," said an ocular witness, "on realizing so large a force, because so great a number of Canadians was not expected to be present: those only being called on who were most able to bear the fatigues of war; but there was so great an emulation among the people, that we saw arrive in camp even octogenarians and lads of 12 to 13 years of age. Never were subjects of any king more worthy of his favour, whether regard be had to their constancy in toil, or to their patience in sufferings which have really been extreme in this country. In the army itself, every heavy burden was laid upon them."

In the position we have described, then, the approaching enemy was to be confronted. The governor-general and the civil administrators quitted the city meantime, and repaired to Beauport; the chief families left for country places, taking with them their most precious effects.

Meanwhile the first arrived British ships anchored at le Bic (the inaction of which caused surprise) formed only the van squadron, under Admiral Durell, despatched from Louisbourg, to intercept and take vessels that might be sent from France. A powerful armament, under Admiral Saunders, sailed from England in February, to take on board, at Louisbourg, Wolfe's corps and transport the men to Quebec. But Saunders, finding the shores of Cape Breton clogged with ice, repaired to Halifax till the obstruction should clear itself. When Louisbourg harbour became accessible, Wolfe * there embarked with 8 regiments of the line, 2

* Wolfe did not take ship at Louisbourg, but at Portsmouth; having returned to England immediately after the capture of the former place —B.

battalions of Royal American fusileers, 3 companies of Louisbourg grenadiers, three companies of rangers, an engineer corps, 1,000 royal marines; in all nearly 11,000 men.*

General Wolfe was a young officer full of talent, who was consumed with a desire to distinguish himself by brilliant feats of arms. The duke of Bedford had given him a considerable place on the Irish staff, but he renounced it for more active employment: thus taking his chance of obtaining promotion through his services in war. "Fortune has always favored our family," he wrote; "and even upon me she has bestowed a few of her smiles: to her in future do I devote myself." His conduct at the siege of Louisbourg attracted public attention, and caused him to be chosen to command the expedition to attack Quebec; it was a charge which demanded activity, daring, and prudence combined. Lieutenants were assigned † to him, of a like temper: these were brigadiers Monkton, Townshend, and Murray,—all three in the flower of manhood, leaders who had studied the art of war, and gained experience in action. Wolfe was son of an invalid general, who had served with distinction. The three brigadiers were of noble blood, and Townshend was heir-presumptive to a peerage. All four generals were in full hopes of success. "If General Montcalm," cried Wolfe, "be capable of frustrating our efforts once more, this year, he may pass for a clever officer indeed; or the colony has more resources than we know of; or else our own generals will turn out to be even worse than usual."

The British combined fleet, consisting of 20 ships of the line, with 20 frigates and smaller war-vessels, followed by many transports, ascended the St. Lawrence, and safely reached the Isle

---

* The orders for payment of the troops prove, that there were at least 10,000 men; including officers, and exclusive of royal marines. [If the " ordonnances de paiement " prove this, they prove something more : namely, that the *Bigots* were not all in one camp; and that there must have been falsifiers of regimental accounts among the British paymasters ; they making charges for many more than they could justify by correct muster-rolls.— B.]

† They were not *given* to him, as M. Garneau supposes : he was allowed to make his own selection of every officer of rank in his detachment; for such his corps was, rather than an "army," its amount being nearly a third less than that stated above.—*B*.

d'Orléans, June 25. Everybody was surprised at the enemy's luck, in thus escaping the dangers of the upward passage; but it has transpired in our own time, that a captain of a French frigate, named Denis de Vitré, taken prisoner during the war, piloted the ships to Quebec; a piece of treason for which he was rewarded by a commission in the British service. In a short time, there were 30,000 armed enemies, soldiers and sailors together, ranged in front of the city. The land-force disembarked on the Isle d'Orléans, which was quitted by all its people the night before, and took up a position at its upper end, facing Quebec and Beauport. The fleet rendezvoused under cover of the island, and its commandant reconnoitred the basin and outer port; James Cook, who immortalized himself in after years, as a navigator, was employed to take the soundings. It is worthy of remark, that two of the greatest of those commanders who ever circumnavigated the globe, Cook and Bougainville, were then in adverse presence, under the walls of Quebec.

During these proceedings, the French had prepared their incendiary machines. June 28, the night being dark and the wind favouring, seven fire-ships, each of 300 to 400 tons burden, were launched against the British shipping, then lying at anchor near the Isle d'Orléans; but the matches having been lighted too soon, the enemy, startled at their flaming approach, sent out boats to intercept them; and the crews taking them in tow, led them to the shore, where they soon burnt out harmlessly. A month afterwards, some fire-rafts were let down, with an equally bootless result: in fact, such devices, to which the vulgar once ascribed the most destructive effects, are ordinarily harmless enough, if the party against whom they are directed be on the alert to avoid them.

General Wolfe, who on his arrival addressed a long proclamation to the Canadian people, after carefully examining the situation of Quebec and that of its covering army, found the difficulties in his way to be greater than he at first supposed : on one side of him was a city founded on a rock, seemingly inaccessible; on the other a numerous army strongly entrenched, blocking up its land approaches. Wolfe's hesitations were interpreted by Montcalm as a tacit acknowledgment of the redoubtable nature of his own works, and confirmed him in the intention of standing firm to his post at Beauport. Until he should find some vulnerable point to attack his adversary with effect, Wolfe resolved to bombard the city and ravage the country, in hopes of obliging the Canadians to remove from the environs, if only to put their families and goods in places of greater security.

A portion of the British army crossed to Pointe-Lévy June 30, and took up quarters facing the French left, after dislodging a corps of Canadians and savages who were sent across as a party of observation. This movement of the enemy was what Montcalm feared the most but could not prevent, from the nature of the localities. Not daring to risk a larger detachment for the service, he ordered M. Dumas with 1,400 to 1,500 men to surprise and destroy the batteries and other works General Monkton procceded to erect on that side. Dumas crossed the flood to the falls of the Chaudière (upper right bank of the St. Lawrence) in the night of July 12-13, and marched downward in two columns; but in the darkness, one column shot ahead of the other while passing a wood, and that behind suddenly perceiving troops before them (its own van) mistook them for enemies and fired upon them. The latter in turn, under a like misapprehension, returned the fire; and fearing their retreat would be cut off by the imagined enemy, retreated in disorder. Their panic being shared by the men in the column behind, these running as fast as those, they all arrived together at the shore early enough to be able to re-cross the flood before six o'clock in the morning, July 13. This skirmish was called the "Scholars' battle" (*coup des écoliers*), because some boys from the city schools, who formed part of the detachment, were the first causers of the mistake.

During the same night, the batteries at Pointe-Lévy opened fire on the city. It was now seen that the besiegers would not hesitate to resort to any extreme measure of hostility, and that the harshest laws of war they would most rigorously execute; for a useless bombardment could not advance their enterprise a single step. But such a measure, in America, was only the following up of a system of devastations which, in Europe, would have called down upon its author the animadversion of the public (*les peuples*). The earliest projectiles which fell upon Quebec, every house in which became a butt for the enemies' gunners, caused an instant exodus of the citizens, who took refuge first in the suburbs and next in the country. The gunpowder in store was removed, and a portion of the sappers and miners set apart as a corps of firemen. In a month's time, the cathedral and the best houses were consumed. The Lower Town (*basse-ville*) was entirely burnt, during the night of Aug. 8–9; while the finest and richest portion of upper Quebec became a mere heap of ruins, and numbers of its chief citizens, opulent erewhile, were thus reduced to indigence. Not a few of the inhabitants, too, were killed outright. The cannon on the ramparts became useless: but this was of the less consequence as the distance across the flood was too great for their shot to tell upon the British batteries, which were besides undistinguishable to the naked eye, masked as they were by forest and brushwood.

After destroying the city, General Wolfe fell upon the country parishes. He burnt all the dwellings, and cut all the fruit-trees, from Montmorenci Falls to Cape Torment (30 miles below Quebec), on the left bank of the St. Lawrence. He did the same at Malbaie (90 miles), and at the bay of St. Paul (60); also throughout the Isle d'Orléans, which is 20 miles long. The parishes on the right bank of the flood, from Berthier (24 miles) to the Rivière-du-Loup (80 miles), a range of twenty-three leagues, were ravaged and burnt in their turn; as well as those of Pointe-Lévy, St. Nicholas, Sainte-Croix (33), &c. Wolfe chose the night-time for committing those ravages, which he perpetrated on both sides of the St. Lawrence, wherever he could obtain a footing: he carried off (*enlevait*) the women and children, [?] the victual and cattle. As the season advanced, this war of brigands extended itself; for Wolfe indulged in it to avenge himself for the checks he received, as well as to terrify the inhabitants. A detachment of 300 men, under Captain Montgomery, having been sent to St. Joachim, where some of the people stood on their defence, committed there the greatest cruelties. The prisoners taken were coolly and most barbarously slaughtered.* M. de Portneuf, curate of the place, who

---

* " There were several of the army killed and wounded, and a few prisoners taken, all of whom the barbarous Captain Montgomery, who commanded us, ordered to be butchered in a most inhuman and cruel manner." Manuscript Journal relating to the Operations before Quebec

struck by his parishioners, in view of ministering to their spiritual needs,* was attacked and hewn to pieces with sabres. From the Beauport camp were seen, simultaneously, the flames rising from Beaupré, and from the Isle of Orléans, also from sundry parts on the right bank of the flood.

These devastations, in which more than 1,400 houses were consumed in the rural districts,† did not tend to bring the war to a nearer conclusion; for still the French stirred not one foot. After so much delay and so many ravagings, Wolfe, seeing no other alternative, resolved to attack the position of Montcalm, on its left flank. In order to this, he caused the bulk of his army to be taken across the north channel of the Isle d'Orléans to l'Ange-Gardien, while he sought means of fording the river Montmorency above the falls; a ford there was, but Montcalm had been precautionary enough to raise a redoubt to prevent an enemy's passage. Frustrated on this side, Wolfe turned his attention elsewhere. Profiting by a favourable wind, he set sail, July 18, with four war-vessels and two transports, braving the fire poured upon them, and passed safely above Quebec, by keeping near the shore on the Pointe-Lévy side; but after examining the left bank of the

---

in 1759, kept by Colonel Malcolm Frazer, Lieutenant of the 78th or Frazer's Highlanders. [The captain here slandered, was the gallant and humane General Richard Montgomery, who afterwards fell in an heroic attempt, as an American leader, to take Quebec by a midnight assault.—*B.*]

* This soldier of the "church militant" (in a literal sense), was slain fighting bravely with arms, not the cross, in hand.—*B.*

† "We burned and destroyed upwards of 1,400 fine farm-houses, for we, during the siege, were masters of a great part of their country; so that 'tis thought it will take them many a century to recover damage." Journal of the Expedition up the river St. Lawrence, &c., published in *the New York Mercury of 31st December* 1759. Nevertheless a contemporary writer, speaking of the conduct of M. de Contades and Marshal Richelieu in Germany, as contrasted with Wolfe's in Canada, adds: "But, said the late General Wolfe, Britons breathe higher sentiments of humanity, and listen to the merciful dictates of the christian religion; which was verified in the brave soldiers whom he led on to conquest, by their shewing more of the true christian spirit than the subjects of His Most Christian Majesty can pretend to."—[Mark the *naïveté* of all this, mockingly adds M. Garneau.—*B.*]

flood, he found that any attempt at landing his forces between the city and Cape Rouge would be a perilous operation: he thought fit, therefore, to send up a detachment to Pointe-aux-Trembles to take prisoners; and prepared to assail the French entrenchments in front. He did not venture to disembark above Cape Rouge river, we know not why; for if he had landed his men there, he would have outflanked Montcalm, and forced him to quit his position. An attack either on the right or the centre of the French presenting too many dangers to Wolfe, he resolved to assail them on their extreme left, facing the St. Lawrence, and along the right bank of the lower Montmorenci river. Such were his next dispositions.

As the left bank of the Montmorenci, just beyond its embouchure, is higher than the right, Wolfe strengthened the batteries he already had there, the gun-range of which enfiladed, above that river, the French entrenchments. The number of his cannon and pieces for shelling, was raised to sixty. He caused sink, on the rocks level with the flood below, two transports, placing on each when in position, 14 guns. One vessel lay to the right the other to the left of a small redoubt which the French had erected on the strand, at the foot of the road to Courville, in order to defend, not only the entry of that road, which led to heights occupied by the French reserve, but also the ford of the Montmorency below the falls. Cannon-shots from the transports crossed each other in the direction of the redoubt. It became needful, therefore, to silence the fire of the latter, and cover the march of the assailants on this accessible point of our line; therefore the *Centurion*, a 60 gun-ship, was sent afterwards to anchor opposite the Falls, and as near as might be to the shore, to protect the ford which the British forlorn hope was to cross, as soon as the attacking force should descend from their camp of l'Ange-Gardien. Thus 118 pieces of ordnance were about to play upon Montcalm's left wing.*

Towards noon, July 31, all this artillery began to play; and,

---

* Thirty at least of these *bouches à feu* must be deducted from M. Garneau's figures of summation; for it is not likely, that, while the starboard side of the *Centurion* was pouring broadsides on the enemy, her larboard guns were battering the opposite (Orleans) shore, occupied as it then was by the British under Major Hardy !—B.

at the same time, Wolfe formed his columns of attack. More than 1,500 barges were in motion in the basin of Quebec. A part of Monkton's brigade, and 1,200 grenadiers, embarked at Pointe-Lévi, with intent to re-land between the site of the *Centurion* and the sunken transports. The second column, composed of Townshend's and Murray's brigades, descended the heights of l'Ange-Gardien, in order to take the ford and join their forces to the first column at the foot of the Courville road, which was ordered to be ready posted, and only waiting for the signal to advance against the adjoining French entrenchments. These two columns numbered 6,000 men. A third corps, of 2,000 soldiers, charged to ascend the left bank of the Montmorenci, was to pass that river at a ford about a league above the Falls, but which was guarded (as already intimated) by a detachment, under M. de Repentigny. At 1 P.M. the three British columns were on foot to execute the concerted plan of attack, which would have been found far too complicated for troops less disciplined than Wolfe's.

Montcalm, for some time doubtful about the point the enemy would assail, had sent orders along his whole line, for the men to be ready everywhere to oppose the British wherever they came forward. As soon as the latter neared their destination, De Lévis sent 500 men to succour Repentigny (at the upper ford), also a small detachment to espy the manœuvres of the British when about to cross the lower ford; while he sent to Montcalm for some battalions of regulars, to sustain himself in case of need. The General came up, at 2 P.M. to examine the posture of matters at the left. He proceeded along the lines, approved of the dispositions of De Lévis, gave fresh orders, and returned to the centre, in order to be in a position to observe all that should pass. Three battalions and some Canadians, from Trois-Rivières, came in opportunely to reinforce the French left. The greatest part of these troops took post, as a reserve, on the highway, and the rest were directed on the ford defended by M. de Repentigny. The latter had been already hotly attacked by a British column, but he forced it to give way, after some loss of men. The retreat of this corps permitted that sent to succour Repentigny, to hasten back to the arena of the chief attack.

Meanwhile, the barges bearing the Pointe-Lévi column, led by

VOL. II—Q

Wolfe in person, after making several evolutions, meant to deceive the French as to the real place for landing, was directed towards the sunken transports. The tide was now ebbing; thus part of the barges were grounded on a ridge of rock and gravelly matter, which stopped their progress and caused some disorder; but at last all obstacles were surmounted and 1,200 grenadiers, supported by other soldiers, landed on the St. Lawrence strand. They were to advance in four divisions; and Monkton's brigade, which was to embark later, had orders to follow, and, as soon as landed, to sustain them. From some misunderstanding, these orders were not punctually executed. The enemy formed in columns, indeed; but Monkton's men did not arrive to time. Still the van moved, music playing, up to the Courville road redoubt, which the French at once evacuated. The enemy's grenadiers took possession of it, and prepared to assail the entrenchments beyond, which were within musket-shot distance. Wolfe's batteries had been pouring, ever since mid-day, on the Canadians who defended this part of the line, a shower of bombs and bullets, which they sustained without flinching. Having re-formed, the British advanced, with fixed bayonets, to attack the entrenchments; their showy costume contrasting strangely with that of their adversaries, wrapped as these were in light capotes and girt round the loins. The Canadians, who compensated their deficient discipline only by their native courage and the great accuracy of their aim, waited patiently till the enemies were a few yards distant from their line, meaning to fire at them point-blank. The proper time come, they discharged their pieces so rapidly and with such destructive effect,* that the two British columns, despite all their officers' endeavours, were broken and took flight. They sought shelter at first, against their foes' fire, behind the redoubt; but not being allowed to re-form ranks, they continued to retreat to the main body of their army, which had deployed a little further back. At this critical time, a violent thunder-storm supervened, which hid the view of the combatants, on both sides, from each other, while the reverberations of succes-

---

* "Their (men of) small-arms, in the trenches, lay cool till they were sure of their mark; they then poured their shot like showers of hail, which caused our brave grenadiers to fall very fast." *Journal of a British officer.*

sive peals rose far above the din of battle. When the rain-mist cleared off, the Canadians beheld the British re-embarking with their wounded, after setting fire to the sunken transports. Their army finally drew off, as it had advanced, some corps in the barges, others marched landward, after re-crossing the Montmorenci ford. The fire of their numerous cannon, however, continued till night set in: and it was estimated that the British discharged 3,000 cannon-balls during the day and evening; while the French had only a dozen pieces of cannon in action, but these were very serviceable in harassing the disembarking British. The loss of the French, which was due almost entirely to artillery fire, was inconsiderable if we remember that they were for more than six hours exposed to it. The enemy lost about 500 men, killed and wounded, including many officers.

The victory gained at Montmorenci was due chiefly to the judicious dispositions made by De Lévis, who with fewer troops in hand than Wolfe, contrived to unite a greater number than he did at every point of attack. Supposing the British grenadiers had surmounted the entrenchments, it is very doubtful whether they would have prevailed, even had they been sustained by the rest of their army. The ground, from the strand to the Beauport road, rises into slopes broken by ravines, amongst which meanders the Courville road; the locality, therefore, was favourable to our marksmen. Besides, the regulars in reserve were close behind, ever ready to succour the militiamen.

General Wolfe returned to his camp, in great chagrin at the check he had just received. Imagination depicted to his apprehensive mind's eye the unfavorable impression this defeat would make in Britain; and he figured to himself the malevolent jibes which would be cast at him for undertaking a task which he had proved himself to be incompetent to perform! He saw vanish, in a moment, all his proud illusions of glory; and Fortune, in whom he had trusted so much as we have seen, seemed about to abandon him at the very outset of his career as a commander-in-chief. It seemed as if his military perceptions had lost somewhat of their usual lucidity, when, after losing all hope of forcing the camp of his adversary, he afterwards sent Murray, with 1,200 men, to destroy the French flotilla at Trois-Rivières, and to open a communication with General Amherst at Lake Champlain. Murray set out with 300 barges, but did not go far up the country. Repulsed twice at Pointe-aux-Trembles by Bougainville, who with 1,000 men followed his movements, he landed at Sainte-Croix, which place he burnt, as has been already noticed. Thence departing, he fell upon Deschambault, where he pillaged the French officers' baggage. [!] He then retired precipitately, without fulfilling his mission. His incursion, nevertheless, much disquieted Montcalm at first; for he set out incognito for the Jacques-Cartier, as fearing lest the British might take possession of its lower course, gain à firm foothold there, and cut off his communications with western Canada; but learning that the latter were in full retreat when he arrived at Pointe-aux-Trembles, Montcalm retraced his steps.

After this new repulse, a malady, the germ of which was present in the bodily frame of Wolfe long before, now suddenly developed itself and brought him almost to death's-door. As soon as he convalesced, he addressed a long despatch to Secretary Pitt, recounting the obstacles against which he had to struggle, and expressing the bitterness of his regret at the failure of all his past endeavours. This letter (if it did little else) expressed the noble devotedness to his country's weal which inspired the soul of the illustrious warrior; and thus the British people were more affected at the sorrow of the youthful captain than at the checks his soldiers had received.*

The spirit of Wolfe, no less than his bodily powers, sank before a situation which left him "only a choice of difficulties;" thus he expressed himself. Calling those lieutenants in aid, whose character and talents we have spoken of, he invited them to declare

---

* A sentimental assumption, hazarded from an imperfect knowledge of facts. The despatch in question, written sixteen days before the capitulation of Quebec, came to hand only two days before Townshend's despatch, relating that event; and was published only with the latter. It would never have seen the light for years, in all probability, but for the success following it which its writer had almost ceased to hope for; while its dark shading, by contrast, gracefully toned the vividness of the details given by others of the events of the hero's closing career, and of the supreme hour in which all of him that could die sank upon that earth which thenceforward became consecrated ground to every true Briton.
—B.

what might be their opinions as to the best plan to follow for attacking Montcalm with any chance of success; intimating his own belief also, which was, that another attack should be made on the left wing of the Beauport camp. He was also clear for devastating the country as much as it was possible to do, without prejudicing the principal operation of the campaign.*

Generals Monkton, Townshend, and Murray replied, Aug. 20, that a second attack on the Beauport camp would be a hazardous enterprise; that, in their opinion, the surest means to strike a decisive blow would be, to land upon the right side of the St. Lawrence, pass along its banks for some way, cross to those opposite and operate above rather than below Quebec. "If we can maintain a new position on that side," wrote the generals, "we shall force Montcalm to fight wherever we choose; we shall then be not only situated between him and his magazines, but also between his camp and the forces opposed to Amherst. If he offer us battle, and he should lose the day, then Quebec, probably all Canada, would fall into our hands—a result far greater than any that could accrue from a victory at Beauport: and again, if he cross the river St. Charles with forces enough to confront us in the position we have supposed, the Beauport camp, thereby weakened, might be all the more easily attacked." The naval forces of the British giving them mastery on the flood, enabled Wolfe to transport his troops to all accessible places. The plan of the three generals was approbated by their chief, and the necessary orders were given to execute it without delay. The idea of assailing Quebec on its harbour side had been given up before, as it would have been worse than rash to attempt such a thing.

After decision taken, the British decamped from the Montmorency, taking their artillery, &c., to Pointe Lévy, Sept. 3.—Montcalm was reproached, by some, for not disquieting them in their retreat; but this would have been difficult, not to say dangerous, considering the nature of the localities. The bombardment of the city and the ravagings of the country were the only successful enterprises, as yet, of the enemy; enterprises in them-

---

* It would be but right to call upon the author for his proofs of these suggestions, especially the latter, having been made by Wolfe.—*B*.

selves a species of terrible homage rendered to the indomitableness of the defenders of Canada.

Montcalm, noting that the enemy was about to operate on parts above Quebec, now paid more attention to guarding the left bank of the flood; but this he did only after being solicited to do so by the governor-general and some of his officers. He persisted ever in the belief, that the Anse-des-Mères, the Fuller's (Wolfe's) Cove, and that of Samos, were inaccessible or very sufficiently guarded. " None but God," he observed in a letter written to Vaudreuil, July 29, " knows how to effect the impossible. You know, Sir, the force of the army. If you wish for a strong garrison in the city, you have but to give the word, and the thing will be done; but, in that case, you must give up the position you now occupy; I yield, in advance, to your opinion in the matter, for I can neither divine nor be answerable for events which may follow in a case so uncertain (*matière si obscure*). Every night, you incur as many risks as you are exposed to in the present. According to M. de Lévis,' the enemy musters as strong at the Falls as usual; and it is certain that he has set 800 men at work to make fascines to fortify his camp. You have, besides the (armed) inhabitants, 500 men in garrison in the city, 1,500 men on the batteries, and 100 armed labourers. Vigilant patrolling is all that is wanted in addition; for we need not suppose that our enemies have wings to enable them, in one night, to cross the flood, disembark, ascend broken-up steep-ways (*rampes rompues*) and resort to escalade; an operation all the more unlikely to take place, as the assailants would have to bring ladders."*

Nevertheless, Montcalm was persuaded to change his opinion.

---

* Montcalm wrote once again to Vaudreuil : "In so far as you have fears about the Anse-des-Mères, send thither to pass the night, till further orders, from 100 to 200 of those which Montresson has at the port till daytime to-morrow; and join to him 50 from Trois-Rivières who are unfatigued; or send thither St. Martin with 100 Trois-Rivières men. I swear to you that 100 men (properly) posted, will stop an army, give time to us to wait daylight, and then come up from the right (of our position in the field). At the slightest nocturnal alarm, I shall march to your relief with (the regiments of) Guyenne and Béarn, which encamp in line to-morrow. Show lights to-night in canoes; and if the darkness be great, light up fires."

He gave to Bougainville, who was in command on that side, 1,000 men, part regulars and militia; among whom were five companies of grenadiers, and the cavalry: he also reinforced the guard-houses, placed on the line between the city and Cape Rouge. Becoming more apprehensive, our commanders soon found these augmentations too small, upon seeing the line of British armed vessels extended from Sillery to Pointe-aux-Trembles. Fearing for the safety of the provision stores, they sent more reinforcements to Bougainville. Already nearly all the savages of the army had joined his detachment, so that the latter had now 3,000 men, posted between Sillery and Pointe-aux-Trembles: they were the flower of the troops. He was once more admonished to watch all the enemy's movements, which for several days menaced simultaneously the Beauport camp, the city, and the magazines of the army.

Meanwhile, matters looked favourable in the direction of Quebec; but the news from lakes Champlain and Ontario were less encouraging. Bourlamaque, who commanded on the Champlain frontier, had under his orders 1,500 soldiers and 800 Canadians. His instructions ran, that he was to fall back, should the enemy confront him with superior forces. General Amherst operated, on this side, with an imposing army; but remembrances of the sanguinary defeat of his countrymen at Carillon warned him to act prudently. After assembling his troops at Albany, Amherst set out thence June 6, and encamped under shelter of Fort Edward, he ordering each regiment to cover itself with a blockhouse (*blochaus*);* so much did he dread being surprised by our people. June 21, he moved to the head of Lake George, where his chief engineer, Colonel Montresson, traced the plan of Fort George, on a height at some distance from the lake, and from the site of Fort William Henry. Amherst embarked on the lake, July 21, with 12,000 men, including 5,700 regulars, with 54 pieces of ordnance. When his van reached the lake-foot, it had some skirmishings with Bourlamaque's outposts, which retiring, the British in two days more reached Carillon. Here Bourlamaque made a show of taking his stand, in order to gain time

---

* A *conte*, doubtless, this part of the story, founded on a Yankee jibe, and not undeserved by the British Fabius.—*B.*

for an orderly retreat to St. Frederic, leaving 400 men in Fort Carillon, but who left it on the 26th, after blowing up a portion of the walls. This important position was thus gained, at the cost of about 60 men, by the British.

Bourlamaque, fearing to be outflanked by the enemy, blew up Fort St. Frederic, and retired to the Isle-aux-Noix. Forthwith (Aug. 4), Amherst, with most of his army, took post at the site of St. Frederic, and began to erect a new fort, named Crown-Point, intended to check the irruption of Canadian bands. Concurrently, for obtaining the mastery of Lake Champlain, he gave orders to construct some new vessels and to upraise the barks which the French sank before evacuating Carillon. These cares absorbed his whole attention till the month of October!

Bourlamaque, on his side, expecting every moment to be attacked in the isle, employed all the means in his power to put obstacles in the enemy's way, by barring the double outlet of the lake, and fortifying the island between. But here, as at Quebec, the frontier was considered as lost by the French, had Amherst acted with any vigour.

Intelligence sent to our people from Lake Ontario and Niagara was still worse. M. Pouchot, who set out for the latter place in autumn previous, but had not been then able to get beyond La Présentation, received orders to resume his march early in spring, so as to arrive in due time to relieve M. de Massan. He left Montreal accordingly, late in March, with about 300 soldiers and Canadians, tarried at La Présentation till two corvettes of 10 guns each were got ready, and reached Niagara April 30. He forthwith began to repair the fort, the walls of which were in ruin and the fossés all but filled up. Charged to cause the Ohio posts to be evacuated if they should be attacked, and hearing no news from that quarter, he sent a reinforcement, with supplies, to Machault, where M. Ligneris commanded. His design was, to destroy the British forts of Pittsburgh and Loyal-Hanna, if opportunities occurred. The greatest agitation then prevailed among the Ohio and Lake tribes, because some of them still obstinately clung to the French side, though treaties had been concluded (in name of all) with the British. The successes of the latter were about to settle these difficulties in their favour, to the disquiet of many of the savages, whose future fate they thought likely to be injuriously affected thereby. The commandant of Niagara had many interviews with their envoys, but no important results attended them. The Five Nations clung more closely than ever to the British; insomuch that Pouchot could obtain from no Iroquois any precise account of the movements of enemies whom he thought still distant, when, July 6, they suddenly arrived in the vicinity of his post.

In accordance with the plan of campaigning adopted by Britain, one of her armies was to lay siege to Niagara. Brigadier-general Prideaux, charged with this service, left Schenectady, May 20, with five battalions of infantry, a park of artillery, and a large corps of savages led by Sir W. Johnson. He left Colonel Haldimand at Oswego, with directions to build a fort there, and himself embarked on Lake Ontario, July 1; disembarking, six miles distant from Niagara, without the French being informed of his approach.

Fort Niagara, being erected on a point of land, was easily invested. Pouchot had just finished its ramparts; but the batteries of the bastions, which were à barbette,* were not yet completed. He formed them of barrels, filled with earth. He strengthened with blindages † a large house, towards the lake, for an hospital; and covered by other works his powder-magazines. His garrison was not quite 500 strong.‡

As soon as Pouchot was certain of the enemy's presence, he sent a courier with messages, to Chabert at the Portage fort, to Ligneris at Fort Machault, and to the several commandants of Detroit, Presqu'île, Venango, and Le Bœuf, to fall back on Niagara with all their men and savages. Thus was abandoned a vast extent of territory, in one of the finest regions of the world. Chabert burnt his fort, and reached Niagara July 10. The night of that day, the British began a parallel 600 yards from the walls. July 13-22 they unmasked, in succession, several batteries,

---

* A barbe, or barbet, is a platform without an epaulement: "à barbette," barbe-fashioned.—B.

† Blindes are felled trees, interlaced with each other, to form a covering for a trench.—B.

‡ Pouchot: Mémoires sur la dernière Guerre de l'Amérique Septentrionale. 1771.

mounted with cannon and mortars, and attained to the outer wall of the place. The death of General Prideaux, killed by the bursting of a mortar, did not slacken the siege operations, which Sir W. Johnson took charge of provisionally, and quickened to the utmost. Despite a hot fire kept up by the besieged the bastions were at length ruined, and the batteries on them quite swept away. The French were now fain to form others with packages of peltry, and to wad their cannon with pieces of blanket and shirt-strips. Still the enemy's firing increased in violence, and the defences were crumbling to pieces everywhere. A practicable breach existed, and there was but one man left for every ten feet of space there was to defend. During 17 days nobody had gone to rest, and many men were helplessly wounded. While Pouchot despaired of succour arriving from the evacuated French posts, July 23 he received letters, from D'Aubry of Detroit and from De Ligneris, which informed him that there were on the way, to aid him, 300 French from Illinois, 300 others, and 1000 savages: Unfortunately the enemy knew all that passed in the fort, through the treachery of the couriers of D'Aubry and De Ligneris, who had even had with the savage allies of the British an interview, at which Johnson attended. The latter, informed by them of the approach of the French, resolved to lay an ambuscade to intercept them. He hid most of his own troops behind a rampart of felled trees, on the left side of the road leading from the Falls to the Fort of Niagara. The French, who had left 150 men at the foot of lake Erie in charge of the boats, were coming on unsuspectingly, 450 in number, with 1,000 savages, when they perceived the British. Seeing the Iroquois in the latter's company, the French savages refused to advance, under a pretext that they were at peace with the first-named. Though thus abandoned by their chief force, Aubry and Ligneris still proceeded on their way, thinking that the few savages they saw were isolated men, till they reached a narrow pathway, when they discovered greater numbers beyond. They prepared to range their men in battle order, but neither time nor space would allow of this. At the first shock, indeed, they forced the British, who came from behind the fence (*abattis*) to attack them, to flee precipitately; and they were about to charge them in turn behind their covert, when they were assailed in front and rear by 2,000 men. The tail of their column, unable to resist, gave way and left its head exposed to the enemy's whole fire, which crushed it entirely. Some 50 men only were left upright, who tried to retreat and fight both; but they were charged with the bayonet and mostly laid prostrate. The remaining French were hotly pursued. The savages who had refused to fight were equally exposed to the fury of the enemy, and many of them fell under the blows of the latter in the woods. Almost all the French officers were killed, wounded, or taken. Aubry, Ligneris, and other chiefs who were wounded, fell into British power. Those who escaped the massacre, joined M. de Rocheblave, and with his detachment retreated towards Detroit and other western lake posts.

After this disaster, Johnson transmitted a list of his chief prisoners' names to M. Pouchot, who, doubting its accuracy, sent an officer to ascertain the facts, who reported that all were true. Then the garrison, reduced by a third in numbers, and worn out, accepted the honourable terms proposed by Johnson; who was anxious to possess himself of the fort before the arrival of General Gage, then on his way to take the chief command as Prideaux' successor.

Niagara was one of the most considerable strongholds in Canada, and the most important of the lake posts through its situation. Its fall separated the upper lakes from the lower province, and the French found themselves thereby thrust back, on one side, to Detroit; on the other, towards the St. Lawrence rapids above Montreal, for time had not permitted Fort Frontenac to be refounded. Lake Ontario, therefore, now belonged to the British; whose progress much embarrassed M. de Vaudreuil. In such a critical state of things, it was needful to run some risks to amend it if possible: he resolved to send M. de Lévis to make an armed tour of inspection of the upper province, to ascertain and report as to what were needful to be done, in order to retard the marches of the enemy towards the St. Lawrence and on Lake Champlain. He had under him 800 men, including 100 regulars draughted from the Beauport army, to reinforce the troops under M. de la Corne, who commanded above Lake St. François. M. de Lévis set out Aug. 9, from Quebec, and left at Montreal, in passing, 400 men to aid in reaping the crops, or until certain news were received of the advance of the British. He encouraged, at the same time, the priests, the women, the *religieux* and *religieuses* to take part in harvesting duties, as upon the returns of the season greatly depended the salvation of the colony. De Lévis made a reconnaissance as far as Frontenac; he examined every thing, indicated all the parts necessary to defend or to fortify, from Lake Ontario to Montreal; and ordered M. de la Corne to dispute possession of the ground foot to foot with the British, who were then 6,000 strong on that line. He afterwards visited Lake Champlain, and approved of all that Bourlamaque had done on that side.

De Lévis returned finally to Montreal Sept. 11. On the 15th of that month, at 6, A. M. an express arrived with a letter from the governor-general, communicating the sad result of the battle of Abraham and the death of Montcalm. The courier sent had orders to press the chevalier to descend promptly to head-quarters, and take charge of the army. [To the operations of which, meanwhile, we now recall the reader's attention.]

While M. de Bougainville was espying the movements of the British before Quebec, they were making sundry feints to hide their meditated designs. During the 7th, 8th, and 9th days of September, a dozen of their vessels ascended the St. Lawrence, and cast anchor at Cape Rouge. They had troops on board, and detachments of these were sent ashore at different points, to divide the attention of the French. A moiety of the soldiers were landed on the right bank of the flood, while their officers closely examined the opposite shore, from Quebec to Cape Rouge, trying to discover the pathway (*chemin*) at the Fuller's Cove ascending to the plains of Abraham. About the same time, two French soldiers deserted, and informed General Wolfe that a convoy of provisions was to pass before Quebec during the night 12–13 Sept. ensuing.

Ever since the British were masters of the flood above the capital, the provisioning of the army by water conveyance had become almost impossible. It was needful, therefore, to transport supplies by land, from the magazines at Batiscan and Trois-Rivières; and as there remained in the country parts only aged men, women, and children, it was yet by their weak bodies that the transport service had to be performed. Thus were conveyed, on 271 carts, from Batiscan to head-quarters, on a line 18 leagues long, 700 *quarts* of bacon and meal, yielding subsistence enough for 12–15 days; but the difficulties attending this mode of transit were great; many of the carts employed in it got broken; the women and children engaged becoming disgusted with the heavy work, it could not be expected they would long endure it; and the men, who had leave to secure the crops only, could not forego that pressing duty. In this strait, the great water-way was once again employed, hazardous as it might be to use it, to enable a supply to reach its destination quickly : thus it was that the convoy we have spoken of, happened to be expedited. Unfortunately, the two deserters communicated the watch-word (*consigne*) that the crews of the provision barges were to give to the sentinels on shore while gliding down the flood: and to complete the chapter of cross accidents, in the evening of Sept. 12, Montcalm, without forewarning the governor-general, drew off the battalion he had consented to send two days previous, to the heights above Quebec. General Wolfe determined to profit by those fortuitous circumstances by landing his army at the Fuller's Cove (*Anse du Foulon*) and striving to carry the adjoining heights. The better to conceal his intent, he directed that several of his war-vessels should make threatening demonstrations in front of the Beauport camp, as if a descent were there intended, while the other vessels remaining at Cape Rouge neared St. Augustin to attract the attention of Bougainville in that quarter. These orders given, all his thoughts were turned to disembarking his army safely.

September 13, about 1 A.M., the hour being one of great darkness, a portion of the British troops, who had been embarked the evening before, took the flood in flat-bottomed barges, which were borne down silently on the ebbing tide, to the Fuller's Cove. Officers who spoke French had been selected to respond to the sentinels' challenge (*Qui vive?*), with "Hush! this is the convoy of provisions," (*Ne faites pas de bruit, ce sont les vivres*) : and in the obscurity prevailing at the moment, the barges were allowed to pass on ! The ships of admiral Holmes followed, with the rest of the troops on board, at 45 minutes' interval. Arrived at the goal, the British vanguard landed, without resistance, between the post of St. Michel and that of the Foulon. The light infantry, headed by Wolfe, as soon as they set foot on the bank, forced the guard-house at the foot of the steep pathway leading to the superincumbent cliff, then scaled an escarpment, partially clothed with trees and brushwood; and, having reached the table-land above, they surprised and dispersed, after exchanging a few musket-shots, the men on guard, whose commander was taken prisoner in his bed.* During this time the landing-boats returned to the vessels, and brought away the remainder of the troops, who were in charge of General Townshend. In fine, as day broke, the British army was seen ranged in battalia, on the Plains of Abraham.†

M. de Montcalm received intelligence of the unexpected disembarkation at six o'clock in the morning; but he could not (at first) put faith in it. Then he imagined it must be some isolated detachment (of no account) which had landed; and, carried away by his usual vivacity, he set out with a portion only of his troops, without making known his arrangements to the governor-general.‡

At this time, the Beauport army was reduced to about 6,000

---

* This officer was the inept Vergor, who, three years before, surrendered the fort of Beauséjour to the British. Called before a court martial to answer for that act, he had been acquitted, thanks to the intendant's intrigues. He was a captain of the colonial regulars. It was to this favourite, all-worthy of the patron, that Bigot wrote upon occasion of his once setting out for France, whence it would have been well that he had never returned : "Profit to the full, my dear Vergor, by your place: let it be ' cut-and-come-again' (*taillez, rognez !*) you have every facility to do so; you will be all the sooner able to rejoin me in France, and buy an estate in my neighbourhood."

† After the battle, the British officers told the French officers that they did not expect to succeed; that Wolfe had adventured the disembarkation above Quebec in order merely to have it acknowledged that he had fairly tried an (impracticable) enterprise (recommended to him by others); but that he intended to sacrifice only his forlorn hope (*avantgarde*) of 200 men. Only for the post being surprised, Quebec and Canada had been saved. [A hundred years ago, it seems a *canard*, could be hatched, though the present name for that creature was as yet uninvented]—B.

‡ We do not see how he *could* have done so, considering the incertitudes that then possessed his mind as to the British movements.—B.

combatants, as different corps had been draughted from it; when strongest, it numbered 13,000, but 800 had gone with M. de Lévis; Bougainville had 3,000 under him (all prime soldiers), besides the cavalry; the garrison of Quebec, 700 to 800 strong, took no part in the battle; finally, a great many Canadians were absent, harvesting; while the aged and young (volunteers), thinking all danger was past, had returned home, so that our army was reduced by a moiety. General Montcalm took with him 4,500 men,* leaving the rest in camp. Those troops defiled by the bridge of boats across the St. Charles river, entered Quebec by the Porte-au-Palais, on the north, traversed the city, left it by Portes St. Jean and St. Louis, to the westward, on the side of the Plains of Abraham; and arrived at 8 A.M., in sight of the enemy. Montcalm saw, not without surprise, the whole British army ranged in battle order, and ready for his reception. Through a fatal precipitateness he resolved to attack at once (*brusquer l'attaque*), despite all the contrary advices that were given him; in disregard of the opinion of his aid-major-general, chevalier de Montreuil, who represented to him that he was in no fit condition to attack enemies so numerous; finally, in the face of a positive order from the governor-general, who wrote to him to stand on the defensive till all the forces could be got together, intimating, at the same time, that he was himself on the way with the troops that had been left in guard of the camp. But the General, fearing that the British might entrench on the plain, and so make their position impregnable, gave orders for instant battle. The British were in number two to one; there were more than 8,000 of them present under arms.† But Montcalm liked to brave evil chances; haply, fortune might again justify his hardihood (*couronner son audace*), as she had done at Carillon !

He ranged his troops, in battalia, on one line only, three men deep; his right rested on the road of Sainte-Foy, his left on that of Saint-Louis, without any corps in reserve. The regulars, whose grenadiers were with M. de Bougainville, occupied the centre of that line; the militia of Quebec and part of the armed Montrealers form-

---

* Official correspondence.
† On the 24th December, the ten British regiments still numbered 8,204 rank and file, exclusive of officers.

ed the right wing; the militia of Trois-Rivières and others of the Montrealers formed the left wing. Platoons of colonial soldiers (*troupes de la marine*) and savages were distributed about the two wings. Montcalm, without giving time to his men to recover breath (after their hurried march), ordered them to advance against the enemy. They obeyed so precipitately, that their ranks became disordered, some battalions getting out of line, so as to make the British believe that those most advanced were the heads of attacking columns. This was more especially the case at the French centre.

The British army was ranged squarely, fronting the Buttes-à-Neveu, which eminences hid the city from view; the right supported on the wood of Samos, and on a petty height at the edge of the escarpment of the St. Lawrence; on the left was the Borgia mansion. One of the sides of the square faced the Buttes; another the Sainte-Foy road, along which it was ranged; and a third faced the wood of Sillery. Wolfe had begun to construct, along the Sainte-Foy road, a line of petty earthen redoubts, which were prolonged semi-circularly behind. Six regiments, the Louisburg grenadiers, and two pieces of cannon, made up the side of the square facing the city. Three heavy (*gros*) regiments, arranged *en potence*, were disposed on (*garnissaient*) the two other sides. The Scots Highlanders formed a part therein, with two pieces of cannon.* That corps was the 78th regiment, of itself 1,500 to 1,600 strong. Another regiment, in eight divisions, was placed as a reserve in the centre of the lines.

The action was begun by the Canadian marksmen (*tirailleurs*) and the savages; they kept up a very lively fire along the British line, which bore it unflinchingly, but not without suffering from its effects. Wolfe, convinced that retreat would be impossible were he beaten, passed along the ranks of the army, animating his men to fight well. He caused them to put two balls in each of their pieces, and not to pull trigger till their enemies were within 20 paces

* The British would naturally be very thankful had they had the two additional cannon thus liberally *imagined* for their use, but which certainly never came into play if they existed at all; for, wrote Townshend to Pitt, (*London Gazette*): "They (the French) brought up two small pieces of artillery against us, and we had been able to bring up but one gun," &c.—B.

of the muskets' muzzles. The French, who had never formed in proper order (*consistance*) opened a platoon fire irregularly; and, as to some battalions, at too great a distance, consequently with little effect. Still their front ranks boldly advanced upon the enemy's; but, when within 40 paces of the latter, they were assailed with so deadly a discharge, that, owing to their previous disorder, it was impossible to direct their movements, and in a few instants, they fell into a marvellous (*étrange*) confusion. Wolfe chose this moment to attack in his turn; and, though already wounded in the wrist, he led his grenadiers on to charge the French, but had not advanced many steps, when he was struck a second time, the ball entering his breast. He was carried to the rear; and his troops, few of whom knew of his hurts, till after the battle, continued their charge. They set out in hot pursuit of the fleeing French; a part of whom, not having bayonets, gave way in little time, despite the efforts of Montcalm and his chief officers. One person near to Wolfe called out, "They flee!" "Who?" demanded the dying general, his features momentarily lighting up. "The French," was the reply. "What! already?" he rejoined; "then I die content," the hero said, and expired.

Almost about the same time, colonel Carleton received a wound in the head; while general Monkton, struck by a ball, had to quit the field: therefore upon general Townshend, third in command, devolved the chief leading of the British.

The victors now pressed the fugitive French everywhere with bayonet chargings and onslaughts with the broadsword (*sabre*). Little resistance was made, except by the skirmishers. Messrs. Senezergues and De St. Ours, both brigadier-generals, were mortally wounded and fell into the enemy's hands. General Montcalm, who had already received two wounds, yet made every effort to rally his troops and to regularize their retreat; but, arrived at a spot between Porte St. Louis and the Buttes-à-Neveu, a bullet transpierced his reins, and he fell, mortally wounded, under his horse. He was carried by a party of grenadiers to the city, into which a part of the French were now retreating; while others, the greater number, were pressing towards the bridge of boats on the river St. Charles. The governor-general arrived from Beauport just as the defeated troops were breaking up. He rallied 1,000 Canadians, between

VOL. II.—R

Portes Saint-Jean and Saint-Louis, put himself at their head, and stopped for some time the enemy's advance by a very brisk fire, which saved the fugitives.* The rout was complete only as to the regulars; the Canadians fought ever, even in retreating, under covert of the brushwood which grew about them, thus forcing several British corps to give way, and yielded, at last, only to superior numbers. Of the Scots Highlanders who had gone in pursuit, 300 were attacked by them on the hill of Sainte-Geneviève, and obliged to fall back, till they were extricated by two regiments sent to their assistance.

Colonel Bougainville, who was at Cape Rouge, did not receive, till eight o'clock A.M., an order to march towards the Plains of Abraham. As soon as he received it, he set out with a moiety of his troops, which had been posted, at intervals, all the way to Pointe-aux-Trembles. Not being able to get up in time to take part in the action, and seeing that the day was lost, he withdrew his men. The British did not think fit to take advantage of the confusion their adversaries were in, to penetrate Quebec, or to possess themselves of the camp of Beauport; in consequence, the troops who took shelter in the city were able afterwards to return to their entrenchments.

Such was the conclusion of the first battle of Abraham, which mainly decided the question, who should be masters of a country as vast as a half of all Europe. The loss of the French, on this fatal day, was considerable; it amounted to nearly 1,000 men, including 250 who were made prisoners, as well as most of their wounded. Three general officers died of their wounds. The loss of the British reached very nearly 700 men; among whom were their chief general and some of the principal subalterns.†

---

* Despatches of M. de Vaudreuil and other officers to the minister.

† The respective losses are here somewhat magnified for one side, and considerably *minified*, we conceive, as to the other. A week after the battle, when full time had elapsed for collecting and testing the returns of British casualties, we find them thus reported officially in the London Gazette:—" *Killed, in the battle of the* 13*th*, 1 general, 1 captain, 6 lieutenants, 1 ensign, 3 sergeants, 45 rank-and-file, (total, 57). *Wounded*, 1 general, 4 staff officers, 12 captains, 26 lieutenants, 10 ensigns, 25 sergeants, 4 drummers, 506 rank-and-file, (total, 588). *Missing*, 3 rank-

Montcalm acknowledged, when too late, the fault he had committed. He might have waited the arrival of Bougainville, called forth, from city and camp the troops left to guard them, and, with all his forces combined, led an attack on the enemy in front and rear: as, in fact, Wolfe seems to have apprehended would be done, from his having ranged his army in normal order. Or he might have entrenched his army on the Buttes-à-Neveu; and, as the season was well advanced, waited for the British within his lines, which would have caused them to fight at a disadvantage, the season pressing them to act promptly.* Besides these primary faults, he committed another, almost as grave, by ranging his army on one line, without giving time for bringing up the field artillery there was in the city, so as to counterbalance the inferiority of his troops in numbers and discipline. He is reproached, also, his army being partly of militiamen, for choosing to fight in battle order. It is said that " he ought to have waited the enemy's approach, and profited by the nature of the ground to place the Canadians, by platoons, among the tufts of brushwood which were near; for, in such a situation, they surpassed in address as marksmen all other troops whatever."

Whatever the general's faults may have been, his death would seem to have sufficiently expiated them; and in presence of his tomb among us, we wish to be mindful only of his valour and his triumphs. His contemporaries, French-born and Canadians alike, deplored his death as a public loss. He had acquired an ascendancy over the minds of both, as much by his energy, as by his skill in turning their courage to account. None but he was supposed to be capable of risking a battle (against odds), with a certainty of gaining it. The people seemed to ignore the fact, that there remained among them a general who was superior to him in many respects, namely chevalier de Lévis; and

---

and-file. ARTILLERY,—*Killed*, 1 gunner. *Wounded*, 1 engineer, 1 bombardier, 1 gunner, 5 matrosses, (total, 9; collective total, 657)." General Townshend computed the loss of the French at 1,500; it could not be much, if any, less.—*B.*

* This is true, in respect of the fleet: the land forces were not under any such constraint. The whole army could have remained, if properly cared for: and perhaps the conquest might have been sooner completed, had it done so.—*B.*

who was destined, some months later, to wipe away the stain of the defeat they had just suffered.—Meanwhile, Montcalm, after receiving all the sacraments of the Church with much piety and devotion, drew his last breath during the morning of September 14th, in the castle of St. Louis; and was interred, late the same day, by flambeau-light, in the chapel of the Ursuline sisterhood, the several chief officials, &c. left in Qecbec being present. His grave was a trench along the wall edifice, formed by the ploughing of a bomb-shell.

The deceased was of low stature, and small bodily proportions, but had a handsome visage, and remarkably bright eyes. An Indian chief, surprised that the man who had effected such prodigies should be so small-bodied, exclaimed, when he first saw him, "Ah, how little thou art! But I discern, in the glances of thine eye, the height of the oak and the vivacity of the eagle."

Endowed with an ardent imagination,* he shone more by dint of a well-furnished memory, than by profundity in the art of war! he was brave, but not enterprising; he neglected the discipline of his troops, and initiated no important warlike undertaking. He inclined not to attack Oswego (for instance); he was constrained to do so, it may be said, by the reproaches addressed to him for his timidity, by M. Rigaud—a man of limited capacity, but an officer full of courage and hardihood, accustomed to woodland war. Montcalm would have renounced the siege of Fort William-Henry, but for the chevalier de Lévis; and before Quebec, not daring to flatter himself with the hope of (successfully) resisting general Wolfe, he spoke of abandoning the place to the enemy, upon the retention of which that of Canada itself mainly depended. His disputes with the governor-general, of whom he was jealous, and whose opinions he affected to disdain, also led to deplorable results. The popularity he found means to acquire among soldiers and people, made him perilously independent of the head of the colony. He was never weary of decrying De Vaudreuil among his own intimates; characterizing him as incapable, irresolute, and faithless: while, by an artifice too often successful, he sought to exalt

---

* Portrait of Montcalm, by Moreau de St. Méry, in an *Eloge* of the Chevalier de Lévis.

own reputation by debasing that of his official superior. In some Notes attributed to M. de Bourlamaque, reposited in the French war-office, it is indited that the precipitation with which Montcalm acted on the plains of Abraham arose from his jealousies : De Vaudreuil it was, who gave the direction to wait till all the forces were assembled—that was enough, observes the writer, to determine the general to run counter to what was suggested, already disposed to envy the share his private soldiers had in a glory common to both. His ambition was, that his single name should outshine all others; and this passion of his not a little impelled him to cause those enterprises to miscarry, the honour attending which he could not monopolize. The germs of jealousy quickly fructified, and occasioned misunderstandings between the different corps, which, aggravated by a divided authority in the command, caused distrust and censurings to mount from grade to grade up to the highest places, where they occasioned ravages, the results of which inevitably became disastrous." *

Montcalm had a natural taste for literary studies, and attained an extensive knowledge of languages and the *belles-lettres*. He retained his love of general science amid the occupations of war. He liked to live luxuriously, but was unselfish (*désintéressé*). At the time his decease, he owed to the colonial treasury (as we have seen) 10,000 crowns; a sum which he had borrowed to maintain his proper rank, and to succour some of his officers, during the dearth that prevailed in Canada. His (inordinate) ambition, and the ill-concealed desire he cherished to supplant M. de Vaudreuil, were in great part the causes of that disunion between them to which might be attributed principally the calamity which befel the colony in his defeat.

During the evening of the battle day, the governor-general held a council of war, at which most of the officers present expressed an opinion that the army should retire beyond the river Jacques-

---

* Not being sure whether the meaning of the above citation, so loose in construction, has been fully brought out, the original words are here transcribed : " De ce germe de jalousie naquit bientôt entre les différents corps une mésintelligence à laquelle le partage de l'autorité dans le commandement prépara les voix pour remonter de grade en grade jusqu'aux chefs, où elle produisit les ravages dont les suites devaient être si funestes."—*B.*

Cartier, in order to provide means for retreat, and to secure communication between the army and its magazines. De Vaudreuil, Bigot, and Bougainville alone were of a contrary sentiment : they were for once more trying the chances of war. The sentiments of the majority however, ultimately prevailed. Montcalm, who was consulted also, replied that there were three courses, which might be followed : to attack the enemy, to retire as aforesaid, or to capitulate for the whole colony.—After a kind of agreement for the present was come to, De Vaudreuil detached 120 soldiers to reinforce the garrison of Quebec, which was before composed of citizens and mariners only; yet who, during the battle, kept up a brisk cannonade against the batteries of Pointe-Lévis. He next wrote to M. de Ramesay not to resist till the enemy should be ready to carry the place by assault, but to hang out the white flag as soon as provisions failed him. The army, meanwhile fearing every moment that its supplies would be cut off, began its retreat, as soon as night set in; and for want of carriages, abandoned part of its baggage, artillery, and munitions of war. The van defiled, in silent march, through Jeune Lorette, Ancienne Lorette, traversed St. Augustin, and reached Pointe-aux-Trembles on the evening of the 14th. In order that the British should be unapprised of this evil movement, the tents of Beauport were left standing; while M. Bougainville, who led the rear-guard, took post at St. Augustin. That retreat was every way fatal. It left Quebec (all but) destitute of soldiers and subsistence ; it weakened the army itself, because the militiamen of the nearer parts of the country would not leave their families foodless behind them, or go they knew not whither themselves. Accordingly, desertions became rife; husbandmen quitted their standards and returned to their homesteads, while many other parties took to marauding. Next day (15th), the bulk of the army reached the Jacques-Cartier river, while the rear-guard attained Pointe-aux-Trembles. In this position it was agreed to wait the arrival of De Lévis, who was coming by express from Montreal, as has been already narrated.

On the 17th, he arrived at head-quarters accordingly. Before leaving, he despatched orders to the commandants on the western frontiers to forward, without delay, to the beaten army all their spare ordnance, warlike munitions, implements and provisions.

In his first conference with De Vaudreuil, he represented the absolute necessity there was for suspending the retreat, and returning to the field of action, if only to put a stop to the melting away of the forces, and to restore order in their ranks; finally, he urged that an attempt should be made to retake Quebec, at all hazards: adding that the British were not numerous enough to invest the place, or prevent the French from re-entering it. He said that the woodlands about Cape Rouge, Sainte-Foy, and St. Michel ought to be turned to account as a covert for reaching the enemy unperceived; that thus, finding himself between two fires, he would be impotent to besiege Quebec and attack the French army concurrently; that, even if the latter were defeated, its retreat would still be open towards the height of Cape Rouge, a strong detachment being left behind in the hollows about the flood, for facilitating the withdrawal of the garrison, after burning the city. The marquis approved of all; and despatched an express to M. de Ramesay, to inform him that the army was about to come to his relief. The return march, however, was delayed till next day for want of provisions. As it was known that the garrison was equally destitute, each ration of bread being reduced to 4oz. (*un quarteron*), M. Rochebeaucourt was charged to load 100 horses with biscuit, and seek admission to the city. On the 18th, the main army bivouacked at Pointe-aux-Trembles; and Bougainville, with the van, bivouacked also, at Cape-Rouge river.

General de Lévis took command of the army at a time when affairs were indeed in a desperate state; but he was one of those men whose talents and energy are best brought out in such a crisis. He was born in the castle of Ajac (Languedoc), and a scion of one of the oldest houses of French nobility. Entering the army early, he soon became distinguished for his activity and bravery. In Canada, he manifested a sober and reflective mind, was attentive to his duties, and severe as a disciplinarian; the latter a rare qualification in French commanders of the time. " He was endowed by nature," said M. Moreau de St. Mâri,* " with that happy instinct which enabled him to see all things in their true light. Montcalm was discreet enough to consult him on important occa-

---

* *Eloge du Chevalier de Lévis.*

sions. Responses frankly expressed, but which were ever justified by the event, established perfect confidence between the twain."

Next day (19th) De Lévis marched towards Lorette, and Bougainville towards the river St. Charles, where the latter was informed of the surrender of the city, although its commandant had received a positive order to break off the negociations begun with the enemy, and promised to do so. The same news reached De Lévis while at St. Augustin: at which he could not restrain his indignation, and he gave way to it in the bitterest terms too. The evil was remediless, however.

The abandonment of the Beauport camp had quite depressed the spirit of the people of Quebec. The city militia officers, mostly traders, met at the house of M. Daine, lieutenant of police and mayor of Quebec,* where a requisition was drawn up adjuring M. de Ramesay to capitulate.† That officer, interpreting too freely De Vaudreuil's direction not to abide an assault, was weak enough ‡ to consent to the citizens' request.

The reduction of Quebec was a natural result of the inconsiderate words (of discouragement and distrust) Montcalm had scattered among the troops. One only among the officers in garrison, M. de Fidmont,§ a young man whose name merits remem-

---

* At this turn of affairs, the title *maire* again is heard, after long disappearing from public view. A great crisis was needed to cause that name to surge up, effaced as it had been by the superior and more suitable appellation of "lieutenant of police."

† "*Mémoire du Sieur de Ramesay*, knight of St. Louis, (commandant) of Quebec, respecting the reduction of that city, and the Capitulation of Sept. 18, 1757 (*sic*); presented to the Ministry (*la cour*) after his return to France."—This family was unfortunate. M. de Ramesay was son of De Ramesay, who had been governor of Trois-Rivières ten years, and of Montreal twenty years. His three brothers died in the service. The eldest was killed at the battle of Rio-Janeiro; the second was massacred by the Cherokees; the third, a captain, perished by the shipwreck of *Le Chameau*. [De Ramesay was doubtless of Scots descent; possibly, also, a near relative of the Jacobitic author of *Les Voyages de Cyrus*; the latter being an intimate friend, also the chosen biographer and literary imitator of the great and good François de la Motte Fénelon, Archbishop of Cambrai.]—*B*.

‡ Human enough, rational enough—we should rather say.—*B*.

§ Yet, in our French text, the proper name of the individual so signalized is misprinted Piedmont!—*B*.

brance, expressed his opinion, in the council of war, that the place should be defended to the last extremity. Though the city was short of provision, and its works might be carried by a sudden onset (*coup de main*), an assault was not imminent; and it was known that De Lévis was coming to the rescue.

In fact, the British were not even dreaming of taking Quebec except in due form. Immediately after the battle, they finished the redoubts they had previously begun around their camp, and commenced some batteries on the Buttes-à-Neveu, facing the rampart, which would have commanded its whole length, meaning to breach it. Two days more were wanted to finish those works; which were to be mounted with 60 cannon and 58 mortars: when, lo! the operation was suspended by the unexpected display of a white flag by the besieged. At sight of a column of marching troops, and some British men-of-war sailing up, the men in garrison imagined they were to be attacked simultaneously on the land side and from the harbour; and, a mercantile spirit being in the ascendant, a hasty capitulation was drawn up, all the articles in which were acceded to by General Townshend except the first, which bore that the garrison was to march out with the honours of war, and, with eight cannon, be allowed to join the French army at Jacques-Cartier river: this was modified so that the troops in garrison should be sent to France. Next day, Sept. 18, the city was given up to the British, [who were obliged to supply food for the people and 400 to 500 wounded then in hospital, none of whom had tasted anything for 24 hours before. In terms of the capitulation, the inhabitants preserved their privileges, their goods, and the free exercise of their religion till a national peace should take place.] Thus did weak counsels, prevailing in a conference of subaltern officers, render irreparable a check which might have been remedied.

Despite the loss of their capital, [which the Canadians attributed to treason!] "these brave people," says Sismondi, "as French in heart as if they had lived among the French, did not despair!" Though Quebec was destroyed by bombs; though the shores of Beaupré, the Isle of Orléans, and 36 leagues of cultivated country (containing 19 parishes), lying on the right bank of the flood, had been burnt; notwithstanding the inhabitants had lost their vestments their furniture, their agricultural instruments, almost all their horses, and the whole of their farming stock; although, on returning to their lands, they, their wives and children, were obliged to take up with such shelter as was fit only for savages; though a great many of the inhabitants of Quebec and people of the country, for want of food, were necessitated to emigrate to the districts of Trois-Rivières and Montreal: despite all this, the Canadians spoke not of surrendering; they demanded, rather, to be led again to battle: theirs was the Vendean indomitableness, theirs the unconquerable determination of the provincials of olden France from whom many of our Canadians descend, whose bravery, inflexibility (*caractère*) and boundless devotedness Napoleon appreciated so highly.

After the reduction of the capital, General de Lévis saw nothing better, for the moment, than to fortify his position on the Jacques-Cartier, about 27 miles distant from Quebec; accordingly, he retired thither, leaving detachments at different points by the way. He began to erect a fort on the right bank of that river, which protected the locality, and made the passage of the stream easy to defend. There the army remained till campaigning time was over for the season. M. de Vaudreuil shifted the seat of his government to Montreal, whither also he retired himself. The rural Canadians returned to their homesteads during the last days of October. Shortly afterwards, the troops left all parts of the frontier to take up their winter-quarters in the jurisdiction of Montreal and in that of Trois-Rivières. Only a few detachments remained at the outposts, the reduced circumscription of which showed too plainly to France, at the close of 1759, the little that still remained to her of the immense territories which she was once so proud of possessing. Three hundred men were put in charge of Fort de Lévis, situated in an island, a little below Présentation, at the head of St. Lawrence rapids; 400 men, under De Lusignan, were ordered to hold the Isle-aux-Noix, at Lake Champlain, where Amherst had made no headway: this corps was to be supported by 300 men, stationed at St. John's. Finally, 600 men were left at Jacques-Cartier, under M. Dumas, major-general of the colonial regulars.

After having thus made arrangements for the season, De Lévis rejoined De Vaudreuil at Montreal, Nov. 14; and both wrote despatches to Paris, by the hands of M. le Mercier, commandant of the artillery, informing the king of the situation of Canada, and indicating what succours were most needed. This officer embarked at Montreal in a vessel which descended the flood, passed Quebec unperceived by the enemy, and reached France in safety.

After the capitulation of Quebec, the British troops encamped around the city, till quarters could be found for them inside the walls. Their commanders thought no more of following up their success for the current season. It was resolved to rebuild or repair, without delay, 500 houses, and to garrison the entire army till the succeeding spring: all except the three companies of Louisbourg grenadiers, and five companies of the Royal American rangers; these were re-embarked some aboard the fleet, which set sail for Britain, some went to other British colonies. General Murray was nominated governor of Quebec. His garrison, after the departure of the troops above-mentioned, was (Dec. 24) still composed of 8,000 regulars (not reckoning officers), the artillerymen, and the remaining rangers, the latter together comprising several hundred combatants.* There were drawn from the stores afloat, before the fleet left, sufficient provisions, ammunition, &c. to supply the wants of the garrison and army for one year.—The city streets were cleared, and the redoubts raised on the plain obliterated; but others were erected, facing the rampart, on the summit of cliffs

---

* M. Smith, in his History of Canada, says 5,000; although the authors whom he followed textually, Knox and Mante, say "more than 7,000 men." The archives of the provincial secretary at Quebec contain a register of the orders for payment of Murray's troops, the data in which ought to be sure means for settling this question in future. These orders testify the exact number of men and non-commissioned officers in each regiment according to the returns, Dec. 24, 1759:

	Men.		Men.
47th regiment	680	2nd battalion of Fusileers..	871
35th "	876	3rd " " ..	930
43rd "	693	28th regiment	623
58th "	653	48th "	882
78th " (Scots Highlanders) ..	1377	15th "	619
		Total........	8,204

(*falaises*) bordering the St. Lawrence; lastly, the existing city rampart was strengthened, and mounted with artillery fit to defend the place.

Such was the finish of the campaign of 1759 in Canada. The French found themselves cut off from the sea, and shut up between Quebec, the region of Lake Champlain, and that of Lake Ontario. Our remaining soldiers were few in number, and those few poorly paid, ill fed, and short of ammunition. The two British armies which invaded Canada by land and sea were then but 70 leagues distant from each other; both would assuredly concentrate their forces, along with added reinforcements, in the heart of the province, during the ensuing spring. General Amherst, who advanced to Fort Frederic, had, however, got little further forward. He left strong garrisons at Crown-Point and Carillon, the ruinous parts of which he repaired, and called the place "Ticonderoga:" he left the country himself to winter in New York, the better to communicate with the mother country and attend to the supervision of her seaboard colonies of North America.

As to Detroit, and the upper posts, they were still, indeed, in French power; but owing to the loss of Frontenac, the people in them had no further succour to expect from any quarter but Louisiana, whose people became thenceforward their only sustaining allies, and the south-western territories a place of refuge for the upper lake garrisons when the time for retiring thither should arrive.

CHAPTER II.

SECOND BATTLE OF ABRAHAM AND LAST VICTORY OF THE FRENCH.

CESSION OF CANADA TO BRITAIN AND OF LOUISIANA TO SPAIN.

1760–1763.

Diverse impressions which the capture of Quebec causes in Britain and France.—The ministers of Louis XV leave Canada to its fate.—The British organize three armies to finish the conquest they have begun; measures taken in the colony to resist this triple invasion; respective French and British forces.—General de Lévis marches towards Quebec.—Second battle of Abraham : complete defeat of the British army, which shuts itself up in the city ; the French lay siege to it, in expectation that the succour they demanded will come from France.— Common belief in the colony that, of the antagonistic armies in Canada, the one first to be reinforced will have the mastery of Canada.— Arrival of a British relieving fleet.—De Lévis raises the siege of Quebec and begins his retreat towards Montreal ; deficiency of provisions forces him to disband the militia and disperse his regulars.—State of the frontiers towards Lakes Champlain and Ontario.—The enemy sets out to attack Montreal.—General Murray leaves Quebec with 4,000 men ; brigadier Haviland, with a corps nearly as numerous, descends Lake Champlain, and General Amherst sets out from Lake Ontario with 11,000 soldiers and savages ; the French fall back and rendezvous at Montreal 3500 strong.—Impossibility of longer useful resistance becoming manifest, a general capitulation follows.—Triumphal demonstrations thereat in Britain.—Trial and condemnation of Canadian dilapidators at Paris.—Situation of the Canadians ; immense losses they sustained through the depreciated state paper-money.—Continuation of the war in other parts of the world.—Peace of 1763, by which Canada is ceded to Britain, and Louisiana to Spain.—State of France at the time of this too famous treaty, as depicted by Sismondi.

After the defeats sustained by Britain during four years in Canada, news of the capture of Quebec, a city so renowned in the New World, filled the whole three kingdoms with joy. London and other cities and chief towns sent congratulatory addresses to the king, filled with praises of his government; which Pitt, of course, knew were directed to his own address, as the prime mover of the polity of Britain. The parliament ordered a statue to be erected in Westminster Abbey, commemorative of the death and merits of General Wolfe; it also decreed that public thanks should be rendered to each of the chief British sea and land officers who had taken part in the expedition to Quebec; while the king ordered that grateful acknowledgements to Heaven should be offered up to the Lord of Hosts throughout the whole British empire.

In France, where the people, excluded from the government, could exercise no influence on the polity of the men in power, for a long time past all hopes were given up of being able to preserve those beautiful countries for whose defence so much blood had been shed, and so much heroism had been manifested: their loss was but one calamity the more of a long series, which precipitated, if they did not solely cause, the perdition of the olden monarchy before the century ended. The loss of the colony of French America, and the death of Montcalm, without surprising any one, yet' made a painful impression on the public mind. In the court of Louis, its frequenters enervated by orgies, no one dreamed of succouring the ancient warriors of the broken French cohorts who still survived; nor to sustain those transmarine subjects who were ready to combat, if no longer for victory, at least for vindicating the national honour to the last.

"Entire Europe also," said Raynal, "believed that the reduction of Quebec had finished the grand international quarrel in North America. No one imagined that a mere handful of French, debtitute of all things, whom evil fortune had almost deprived of hope itself, would dare to brave the approaches of an inevitable destiny." The height to which their courage could rise was not yet known,— nor their devotedness, nor the glorious battles they had fought, nor could divine others they were yet willing to fight in these remote countries, where, neglected by the rest of the world, they prodigally shed their blood for their country. It was forgotten that the war was one of races; that the defenders of Canada would lay down their arms only when they should be hemmed in, crushed, by masses of enemies; and, until then, they would hope on, hope ever.

The Canadians, who believed that the home government was

going, or at least meant, to make great efforts to save them from the
fate with which the British menaced them, were deceived in their
expectation. M. le Mercier, when he arrived in Paris, found the
Marshal de Belle-Isle at the point of death. After he expired,
the Duke de Choiseul, already minister of foreign affairs, took
charge of the war department. Le Mercier, like other officers
once in garrison at Quebec, gave to the minister all needful information as to the wants and desperate plight of Canada. The
despatches he produced solicited succours of every kind: provisions,
munitions of war, and recruits. They advised the court of the
project formed to retake the capital ; and answered for its success,
if the aid now asked should arrive before reinforcements came from
Britain. Unfortunately this demand was made at a time when,
owing to prolonged deficiencies in the finances, the treasury was
not able to meet the most pressing calls made upon it. The administrators of the royal exchequer, constantly changed, could
find no remedy for ever-increasing evils. Each new functionary
brought forward his plan of reform, but indeed, got displaced before
he could take the first steps for realizing it; and did any financier propose to tax the privileged orders as well as the people, he
was repelled scornfully, and dismissed. The absence of patriotism in the higher classes of society made the evil incurable, and
exposed the nation to every kind of misfortunes; but it especially
involved the loss of that great military reputation which still
constituted the strength and glory (from recollections of the past)
of those sensual and degenerate nobles who now refused to make
any sacrifice for the commonweal. Had a unanimous and general effort been made, matters might have been easily put on a
good footing; since, at a later time (1784), when the annual expenditure of the state was 610 millions, and its revenue nearly 585
millions,—although the nobles, landed gentry, and clergy, possessors
of the greatest part of the French territory, were still exempted
from taxation,—yet, even then, M. Necker * said that the yearly

---

* *De l'Administration des Finances de la France.* The interest of the
public debt was then 207 millions of francs, or about the same as that
of the British national debt at the same date (1784). At present the
debt of Britain is double or triple of France. [The British debt was once

deficit might be more than filled up, if those privileged and wealthy classes would submit to be taxed, and help to develop the resources of the kingdom. But the selfishness of the great was destined to ruin the state.

M. de Silhouette, who had succeeded to M. de Boulogne in the finance department, fell before the opposition got up against his project of a territorial impost which would have reached all the owners of real estate; and he was replaced by M. Bertin, a financier of mediocrity, but more conformable in his views to courtly and aristocratic sentiments. The latter could neither, however, bring the finances into order, nor find means to supply the most pressing daily wants of the public service. The bills of exchange drawn in Canada upon the royal exchequer he could not honour; a circumstance as pernicious to the colony as the loss of a battle. In this contingency, it is easy to conceive how little inspiring the bold resolve of re-taking Quebec would be found at Versailles, where the courtiers regarded the possession of Canada rather as a loss than a gain to the kingdom. In such a state of things, all the government could find means to do, was to send 400 men and three or four vessels, loaded with provisions and warlike stores, convoyed by a frigate; the captain of which thinking fit to occupy precious time by the way, in picking up some 13 or 14 sail of British vessels as prizes, was obliged himself, ultimately, to run his ship into the bay of Chaleurs to seek shelter from pursuing enemies; where his frigate was burnt, with all her convoy, by Captain Byron, then cruising in the Gulf of St. Lawrence. Byron, who had a numerous fleet, also destroyed a cluster of cabins on shore, which some Acadian refugees and poor fishermen had erected under the protection of two petty batteries built on a rock, which miserable place they dignified with the name of "New Rochelle."

While sending to Canada those succours, nearly useless because insufficient, the ministers addressed despatches to the colonial

about twice that contracted in the name of France, but has been considerably diminished in our own day, and is not increasing. The French debt has been largely augmented during recent years, and is constantly augmenting. The chances of ability or willingness to continue paying interest in the two countries severally, are, probably, as ten to one in avour of the British stockholder.—B.]

chiefs, which did not come to hand till next June, recommending them to dispute possession of the colony with the British, foot to foot; and to sustain the honour of the French arms to the utmost: as if people who were being crushed under the weight of owerpowering numbers of adversaries, wanted words of encouragement alone, instead of the substantial aid that was denied to them!

The British government, spurred on and sustained by the powerful voice of the nation, conducted itself very differently. It obtained from Parliament all the subsidies asked for, to carry on the war with vigour. Numerous squadrons covered the seas of Europe, the Indian Ocean, and the Atlantic. It was resolved to bar the sea-way between Canada and France, and to employ for this purpose such an amount of force, as to deprive the latter of the least chance of being able to send succour so as to re-establish her supremacy in America; and it was a result of this determination that the latest convoy was sent for our relief; but which never reached its destination, as above noted.

Behind those rampart lines, which covered America and separated Canada from France, Britain now organized, as in the year preceding, three armies, to finish the colonial abasement of a power which she never ceased combatting ever since she planted a rival flag on the continent, and over whom Britain's great superiority in numbers were about to give her the victory. All the Anglo-American provinces continued to manifest their accustomed zeal for realizing a conquest they had so long and ardently desired. Their different legislatures voted supplies of money and men with so much the greater eagerness, as fruition of their wishes seemed to be near. The three armies were to conjoin beside Montreal, and capture that last city which held out.

The garrison in Quebec was to be reinforced early in the campaigning season, so as to be strong enough to ascend the Laurentian valley. Brigadier Haviland had orders to assemble his troops on Lake Champlain, force a passage at the Isle-aux-Noix and St. John's, and march towards the point indicated; finally, General Amherst was to assemble a numerous army at Oswego, descend the St. Lawrence, capture every post by the way, and join his to the two other corps before Montreal. The French knew of all their enemies' preparations; De Vaudreuil and De Lévis thought only of getting the start of the British by a sudden attack of Quebec, in order to extend their hands towards the expected succours from France; and which, should they arrive before British aid came, might, with the resources in hand, have saved the colony.

It was resolved, at first, to assail Quebec during winter, but it was found necessary to wait till the spring-time. This delay gave time to reorganize our army, collect provisions, and prepare the boats needed to descend the flood when the seasonal ice broke up. Despite the most earnest efforts, De Lévis could not procure enough of siege requisites. He was short of heavy ordnance, and had but a scanty store of gunpowder. Still he did not despair of succeeding, either by a surprise, or through the help of expected succours.

To prevent the enemy from divining his intents, but above all to keep up the courage of the Canadians and harass the British garrison, he kept up petty hostilities against the latter all the winter through.

General Murray, on his part, neglected nothing to put himself in a state to repel all hostile attempts till the following campaign. He was well provided with artillery and stores of every kind, and under him were the finest soldiers Britain could produce. No sooner was he established in the city, than he addressed a proclamation to the Canadians, representing to them the inutility of a longer resistance, as it would expose them to all the evils result from an opposition becoming objectless. Eleven neighbouring parishes, evacuated by the French, gave in, and took the oath of fealty to king George. Their houses had been burnt, and the women and children, who had taken refuge in the woods, were forced to leave them, to escape death from cold and destitution. The inhabitants of Miramichi, Richiboucto, and other places about the Gulf of St. Lawrence, impelled by like misery, had submitted already to Colonel Frye, British commandant of Fort Cumberland at Chignectou.

General Murray, meanwhile, pushed his outposts as far as Lorette and Sainte-Foye, two or three leagues from Quebec; and a war of skirmishings continued, despite the season's rigour. The garrison, throughout the winter, was busily employed in such petty expeditions, fetching firewood from Cape Rouge, and working at the city defences, which, after incredible labour, were made fit to sustain a siege; the ramparts were completed and mounted with mortars and heavy cannon; the redoubts too, already mentioned, eight in number, were now finished. The soldiers executed these works, notwithstanding maladies which broke out among them, between Dec. 24 (1759), and April 24 (1760), and proved fatal to nearly 500 of them.

On their side, the French were exhausted by the fatigues attending petty war, but still more from dearth of provisions. De Lévis, who had cantoned most of his troops in different parishes of the governments of Trois-Rivières and Montreal, now began his preparations for an enterprise he meditated; "an obstinate defence," as he expressed it, in a memorial to Vaudreuil, "which could not fail to be advantageous to the state, by cutting out employment for its enemies in America, as well as be honourable to the arms of France."

To re-animate the courage of the people, and induce them to make new efforts and submit to fresh sacrifices, the solemn voice of the Church was called in aid: a voice sure to find an echo in the heart of a population profoundly religious. The bishop, M. Dubreil de Pontbriant, who had taken refuge in Montreal,* issued a pastoral letter (*mandement*) in which he said, "You are not to forget, in your prayers, those who have died in defence of their country; the names of the illustrious Montcalm and so many respectable officers, with those of the (slain) soldiers and militiamen must be kept in memory.... You will pray for the repose of their souls." They are very grave, very touching, such mortuary words, to which religion adds a character of sublimity! This call for the prayers of the faithful, in favour of the brave who died in de-

---

* Why the good bishop should thus be spoken of as a refugee; we cannot say; yet the words in the author's text convey an insinuation that he was driven out of Quebec, in violation of article 6 of the capitulation, granting "free exercise of the roman religion, safeguards to all religions (cloistered) persons as well as the bishop;" the latter "being invited to come and exercise freely and with decency the functions of his office whenever he shall think proper."—*B.*

fending their religion, their laws, and their homesteads,—at a time when a call to arm was issued,—revived the national spirit, and redoubled the warlike energies of the Canadians. As for the regular soldiers, if a passion for military distinction alone inspired *them*, they had now a fair opportunity of acquiring it.

After great efforts, De Vaudreuil succeeded in collecting as much provision as would subsist the army for some time when the scattered parts of it should re-unite. In April it was ready to begin the campaign, though the winter's ice had not yet cleared away.

The regulars, especially their grenadier companies, had been recruited from the two colonial battalions; with the latter, they numbered 3,600 men. Those militia forces called on to take part in the expedition numbered a little more than 3,000, including 370 savages. The collective army, wherein the Canadian element thus predominated, still did not comprise quite 7,000 combatants in all. Such was the whole armed force which could be raised to march against Quebec, for the inhabitants of the lower districts who had not submitted to the enemy could not join the little army till after the investment of the place; while those of the valid male inhabitants directed to remain at Montreal and Trois-Rivières, were wanted there to lay the year's seed in the ground, and to defend the frontiers on the side of Lakes Champlain and Ontario.*

Without waiting for the navigation seaward to be quite open, De Lévis sent orders (April 16 and 17) to the troops to quit winter-quarters and march direct to Quebec, some by land, others by water. The fields were then covered with snow, and the banks of the St. Lawrence still clogged with unloosened ice, while its current was encumbered with floating ice, which moved with the flux and reflux of the tide. De Lévis issued a general order to the army, in

---

* Extracts from the instructions of the governor-general to the chevalier de Lévis: "We have, after much exertion, collected all the (material) resources of the colony, supplies of provisions and warlike stores alike; both are in limited or rather insufficient quantity, therefore let every means be employed that zeal can suggest to supply deficiencies. —Our forces consist of nearly 3,500 troops, 3,000 militiamen of the governments of Montreal and Trois-Rivières, with 400 savages of different nations."

which he appealed to its sense of honour for making a signal reparation of the loss sustained on the 13th of September previous; and reminded the soldiers, that the foes they had to face again were such as they had conquered at Oswego, Fort George (William Henry?), and Carillon. The troops, for whom these were glorious remembrances, set out on the 20th. Those who descended the flood itself were on board two frigates, which served as a convoy for the smaller vessels, loaded with the artillery, provisions, and siege materials. But as the floating ice became more obstructive the farther the flotilla proceeded, the troops were landed at Pointe-aux-Trembles. Only part of the artillery reached the Foulon (Wolfe's Cove). The whole of April 25 was spent in assembling the army at Pointe-aux-Trembles; and the vanguard, under Bourlamaque, took the road next day.

The occasion was pressing; for De Lévis wished to fall unawares upon the enemy. Having found it impossible to cross Cape Rouge river at its outlet, because the banks, which are high and steep on the Quebec side, were guarded by the enemy he resolved to traverse the stream at Lorette, two leagues higher up, and pass over the marshes of La Suède, in order to reach the heights of Sainte-Foye.

Bourlamaque restored the bridge over the river, which the British had broken down at his approach, and deprived them of the post they occupied at Lorette. De Lévis, who arrived just then, perceiving they had neglected to destroy a wooden causeway which had been laid across part of the marshes of La Suède, caused the head of it to be occupied by the savages. His vanguard reaching those marshes at night-fall, he pursued his way over them, despite a thunder-storm, then raging, and took possession of some houses on the further side: he was now separated from the enemy only by a wood, about a mile in breadth. At daybreak, April 26, the French van cleared this wood, and confronted the British, whose position De Lévis proceeded to reconnoitre, while the rest of his troops, who had marched all night—their path indicated, it may be said, by lightning flashes—crossed the swamps and drew up on the further side.

Our army, however, was not able to advance rapidly or secretly enough to be able to reach Quebec unobserved. Although a rumour was designedly spread abroad all the winter, that the French were about to come down upon Quebec with an army 12 to 15 thousand strong—the intent being that, when the threat were realized, at a later time, Murray should be less on his guard through previous false alerts—still that general, having always been in doubt on the subject, stood prepared for whatever might occur. During April, menacing rumours assuming a more tangible shape, he judged it would be proper to rid himself of the city population, which would have become burdensome to him in case he were besieged; and he gave notice to the people, on the 21st April, that they must leave the place by the 24th. When the day came, the garrison soldiers, used as they were to all war's horrors, could not without pity see the wretched townsmen, with their wives and children, driven forth of the city walls, to seek shelter they knew not where, in a devastated country bared of all subsistence. Murray also caused the Cape Rouge bridges to be destroyed, as already narrated; and sent troops to observe the movements of the French, if they came up. Those were the soldiers ranged before ours on the heights of Sainte-Foye; they numbered from 2,500 to 3,000, and had some field-pieces: their lines extended from Sainte-Foye church to the left bank of the road of La Suède, by which the French were ascending in order to debouch on the plateau.

The wood whence the French were issuing was 400 yards distant from the enemy's front: now as the forest soil was marshy, the French could debouch only upon the highway. The space between the wood and the British was not wide enough to allow De Lévis to form his men and lead them on without disadvantage. His situation thus became difficult, for the hill of Sainte-Geneviève and the river St. Charles, alike barred his way, if he elected to march on Quebec either by the road of St. Ambroise or that of Charlesbourg; and the enemy might reach the above eminence before the French, having only the cord of the arc to pass along : he therefore resolved to attain the Sainte-Foye road by a flanking march.— Nightfall come, he ordered his troops to defile, on the right, along the skirts of the wood, till they would have got beyond the British front, and then turn round their left flank. This manœuvre, if successful, gave him both a good position, and a chance for cutting off the corps of observation posted at the Red River outlet to the

St. Lawrence; but the stormy weather, and the difficulty of countermarching at that season, with wearied men, prevented the operation being essayed with due celerity. Next day Murray, who hastened to the imperilled spot, had leisure to extricate his troops with the loss only of their baggage, &c. Becoming pressed in his own retreat, he took shelter in the church of Sainte-Foye, which he fired as he left it; and he was finally able to resume his march to Quebec, leaving De Lévis master of a field of battle which he would have had much difficulty to conquer.*

The French horsemen dogged Murray's retrograde steps, and skirmished with his rear-guard as far as Dumont Mill, within a mile and a half of the city ramparts. Murray posted a strong guard within the mill, with orders to hold it (if attacked) till night. The French troops took lodging in the houses between the church and the mill. The rain fell, meanwhile, in torrents, and the weather was frightful.

During the night the British left the mill, fell back on the Buttes-à-Neveu, and began to entrench themselves there. When day broke, De Lévis took possession of the mill, and the whole plain of Abraham as far as the flood, in order to cover the Anse-du-Foulon (Wolfe's Cove), whither the French vessels (laden with provisions, artillery, and baggage) which had not effected their discharge at St. Augustin, had received orders to repair. While this was effecting on the 28th, our army was to take repose, so as to be ready next day to assail the British at the Buttes, and drive them into the city.

No sooner, however, was Murray within the walls, than he determined to make a sortie with all his troops; intending, either to give battle if an occasion presented, or else to fortify himself at the Buttes-à-Neveu, should De Lévis' force appear to be too considerable to resist in open field; for the report of a French cannoneer (who fell in while disembarking, was floated down the flood, and rescued by some British soldiers on guard) left no further doubt in his mind that the force so long spoken of had now arrived. He left the city in the morning of April 28, at the head of his

---

* *Sic in orig.*; the reflection superadded, like many others elsewhere not being over-intelligibly expressed.—*B.*

whole garrison,* the regulars in which, not including officers, alone numbered 7714 combatants.† Excepting some hundred sick

---

* "The 28th day of April, about 8 o'clock in the morning, the whole garrison, exclusive of the guards.... marched out of town with 20 pieces of field artillery."—*Fraser Manuscript.*

† Referring to regimental orders for liquidating arrears of pay up till April 24, or within four days of that of the second battle of Abraham, we have the following direction for paying the 78th or Highland regiment then in garrison:

"By the Honble. James Murray, Esq.,
Governor of Quebec, &c.

"You are hereby required and directed, out of such moneys as shall come to your hands for the subsistence of His Majesty's forces under my command, to pay or cause to be paid to Lieut. James Henderson, Dy. Paymaster of His Majesty's 78th Regt. of Foot or his assigns, the sum of two thousand one hundred and sixty-three pounds nineteen shillings and sixpence sterling; being for subsistence of said Regiment between the 24th day of February and the 24th day of April 1760, both days inclusive, as per account annexed: and for so doing this, with the acquittance of the said Lieut. James Henderson or his assigns, shall be to you a sufficient warrant and discharge.

"Given under my hand, at Quebec, this 27th day of November 1760.
(Signed,) "JAS. MURRAY.
(Countersigned,) "H. T. CRAMAHÉ.
"To Robert Porter, Esq.,
Dy. Paymaster General."

56 Sergeants	@ 1s. *p. diem*	....	£2	16	0
56 Corporals	@ 8d.	"	1	17	4
28 Drummers	@ 8d.	"	2	18	8
1195 Privates	@ 6d.	"	29	17	6
1335	Total for one day	....	35	9	6

Total for 60 days £2,163 19 6
(Signed,) "JAS. HENDERSON,
Lt. and Dy. Paymaster 78th Regiment."

[We firmly believe that Murray's strength scarcely exceeded a moiety of that assigned to him in the text; to which M. G. appends, by way of proof, returns of the strength of one regiment. As we intimated before, there may have been *Bigots* (even *Varins*) in the British as well as the French camp. Thus, on examining Lieut. Henderson's figures, we find that he charges for 61 days' pay, instead of 60; thus pocketing, inadvertently or not, £35 9s. 6d.; the precise excess over £2,128 10s. 0d., the proper total. But, in any case, the document, either on or off the face of it, does not justify the author's hardy assumptions.—*B.*]

in hospital, Murray left in the place only soldiers enough to mount guard and, with a force from 6,000 to 7,000 strong, advanced, in two columns, with 22 cannon.

De Lévis, who rode out, with his staff officers, far in advance of his men to reconnoitre the position of the British on the Buttes-à-Neveu, no sooner perceived this forward movement than he sent orders to his main army to quicken its march towards the plains of Abraham. Murray, seeing only the French van as yet, resolved to attack it before the soldiers could take breath after their march; but he had to deal with an adversary of mark, and cool temperament withal. The former ranged his troops in advance of the Buttes, his right resting on the hill (*coteau*) of Sainte-Geneviève, and his left touching the cliff (*falaise*) bordering the St. Lawrence: his entire line extended about 6 furlongs. Four regiments, under Colonel Burton, formed his right, placed astraddle (*à cheval*) on the road of Sainte-Foye. Four regiments, and the Scots Highlanders, under Colonel Fraser, forming the left, were similarly ranged on the road of St. Louis. Two battalions were kept as a reserve; and besides these last, the right flank of the British army was covered by a corps of light infantry under Major Dalling; the left flank by Captain Huzzen's company of Rangers and 100 volunteers, led by Capt. Macdonald. All being arranged in the form described, General Murray gave orders to advance.

The French van, composed of six companies of grenadiers, set in battle order, part on the right, in a redoubt erected by the British, the year preceding, to the eastward of the Anse-du-Foulon; part on the left, in Dumont mill, the miller's house, the tannery, and other buildings close by, on the road to Sainte-Foye. The rest of the army, on learning what was toward, hastened its march, the men closing ranks as they came near; but the three brigades were hardly formed, when the British began the attack vigorously.

Murray felt the importance of getting hold of Dumont mill, which covered the passage (*issue*) by which the French were debouching, and he assailed it with superior numbers. He hoped that, by overpowering the grenadiers who defended it, he should be able to fall afterwards upon the centre of the force still on its way, push them far off the line of operation, and cut off the French right wing, hemmed in, as it were, on the road of St. Louis.

Lévis, to prevent this design, withdrew his right to the entry of the wood which was in its rear, and caused the grenadiers to evacuate the mill, and fall back, in order to lessen the distance for the arriving brigades. At this turn, Bourlamaque was severely wounded by a cannon-shot, which also killed his horse. His soldiers, left without orders, seeing the grenadiers hotly engaged and overmatched, simultaneously flew to their support, and formed in line just as the enemies bore down on this point in mass with all their artillery; their field-pieces and howitzers, loaded with ball and grape, playing upon the space occupied by this wing, which staggered under so deadly a fire. The French grenadiers advanced quick step, re-took the mill after an obstinate struggle, and kept it. These brave soldiers, commanded by Captain Aiguebelles, almost all perished this day. While those events were passing on the left, De Lévis caused the soldiers to re-capture the redoubt they had evacuated in order to fall back. The Canadians of the Queen's brigade, who occupied that petty redoubt and the pine wood on the margin of the cape, regained their ground and soon charged in turn, supported by M. de St. Luc and some savages. The combat was not less hot on this line than at the left. All the troops were now in action, and the fire was heavy on both parts. Militiamen were seen to crouch on the ground to load their pieces, rise up after the cannon-shot passed over them, and dash forward to shoot the British gunners. Those of Montreal fought with great courage, especially the battalion led by the brave Colonel Rhéaume, who was killed. This brigade posted in the centre, and commanded by M. de Repentigny, itself arrested on open ground (*rase campagne*) the British centre, when advancing at quick step, and with the advantage of high ground. It also repulsed several charges, and slackened, by its firmness and rapid firing, the enemy when pressing the grenadiers of the left; thereby facilitating their after march onward: in fine, this was the only brigade that maintained its ground during the whole time the obstinate struggle lasted.

By this time, the attack, which gave the British the mastery, for a moment, over the positions occupied by the French van when the fight began, was everywhere repulsed, and our people in re-possession of all the ground they temporarily lost; thus Murray's offensive movement by the road of Sainte-Foye had failed, and that check enabled the French to attack him in their turn.

De Lévis, observing that the British general had over-weakened his left to strengthen his right, resolved to profit by it. He ordered his troops to charge the enemy's left wing with the bayonet, and to thrust the British off the St. Louis road on to that of Sainte-Foye. By this manœuvre, he took in flank the whole of Murray's army, drove the corps headlong off the height of Sainte-Geneviève, and cut off the enemy from the line of retreat to the city. Colonel Poulardier dashed forward at the head of the Royal Roussillon brigade, attacked the British impetuously, transpierced their whole mass, and put them to flight. At the same time their light troops gave way, and the fugitives, throwing themselves in front and in rear of the enemy's centre, caused his fire to be suspended. De Lévis profited by this disorder to cause his own left to charge the British right wing, which the former completely routed.

Then the whole French army advanced in pursuit of the beaten foe; but as his flight was rapid, the short distance they had to run did not allow of throwing them towards the river St. Charles. De Lévis, nevertheless, might have been able to effect this object but for an order ill delivered by an officer, whom he charged to call upon the Queen's brigade to sustain the charge of the Royal Roussillon brigade at the right; and who, instead of causing it to execute the prescribed movement, thus made it take place behind the left wing.

The enemy left in the victors' hands their whole artillery, ammunition, and the intrenching tools they brought with them, besides a portion of the wounded. Their loss was considerable; nearly a fourth of their soldiers being killed or wounded. Had the French been less fatigued than they were, and assailed the city without allowing the enemy time to recover themselves, it would probably have fallen again under the domination of its former masters, says Knox; for such was the confusion, that the

British neglected to re-man the ramparts; the sentinels were absent from their posts when the fugitives sought shelter in the lower-town; even the city gates stood open for some time. But it was impossible to exact further service from the conquerors. They had to oppose to the fire of the enemy's 22 cannon that of only three small pieces, which they painfully dragged across the marsh of La Suède. They, too, experienced great loss, having been obliged to form rank and remain long immovable under the enemies' fire. A brigadier, six colonels or majors (*chefs de bataillon*) and 97 other officers, with a savage chief, were killed or wounded.

The numbers of the two contending armies were nearly co-equal, for De Lévis left several detachments to protect his artillery, barges, and the bridge of Jacques-Cartier river, in order to assure himself a way of retreat, in case he were worsted. The cavalry took no part in the action.

The savages, who were nearly all in the wood behind during the fight, spread over the vacated battle-field, when the French were pursuing the enemy, and felled many of the wounded British, whose scalps were afterwards found upon the neighbouring bushes. As soon as De Lévis was apprised of this massacre, he took vigorous measures for putting a stop to it.—Within a comparatively narrow space, nearly 2,500 men had been struck by bullets; the patches of snow and icy puddles on the ground were reddened with the bloodshed that the frozen ground refused to absorb; and the wounded survivors of the battle and of the butchery of the savages were immersed in pools of gore and filth, ankle-deep.

The transport of the wounded, which took up much time, formed the concluding act of the sanguinary drama performed this day. The wounded were borne to the General Hospital, the distance to which was much increased by the deviations from the straight way to it that had to be made. "It wants another kind of pen than mine," wrote a *religieuse* from the house of suffering, " to depict the horrors we have had to see and hear, during the 24 hours that the transit hither lasted, the cries of the dying and the lamentations of those interested in their fate. A strength more than human is needful at such a time, to save those engaged in tending such sufferers from sinking under their task.

" After having dressed more than 500 patients, placed on beds obtained from the king's magazines, there still remained others unprovided with resting-places. Our granges and cattle-sheds were full of them...... We had in our infirmaries 72 officers, of whom 33 died. Amputations of legs and arms were going on everywhere. To add to our affliction, linen for dressing ran out, and we were fain to have recourse to our sheets and chemises......

"It was not with us now as after the first battle, when we could have recourse, for aid, to the *hospitalières* of Quebec... the British having taken possession of their house, as well as those of the Ursulines and private dwellings, for the reception of their wounded, who were even in greater number than ours. There were brought to us 20 British officers, whom their own people had not time to carry away, and whom we had to take charge of..."

After the action, which lasted three hours, the French took post on the Buttes-à-Neveu, and established their camp on the same plains where they had just so gloriously avenged our defeat thereupon in the preceding year.

Next day, the labours of the siege began. It was decided to crown with a parallel the heights fronting the three upper bastions of the city, and that thereon batteries should be erected, in expectancy of the arrival of ammunition and heavy ordnance which had been demanded from France. M. de Pontleroy had charge of the siege; four batteries were established on the Butts, besides a fifth, placed on the left bank of the river St. Charles, to take the rampart in reverse. The four first mentioned cost much labour to construct, because, working on the living rock in order to form the epaulements, it was necessary to fetch the earth from a great distance, in sacks. The besiegers could not open fire till the 11th of May; but the distance of the city walls, and the feebleness of the battering pieces, gave small expectation of their making a breach, if the facing (*revêtements*) were at all solid. Besides, the fire of the besiegers was so much superior.

By shutting himself in Quebec, Murray meant to make a stiff resistance till the arrival of succours from Britain, whither he had hastily despatched a vessel with information of the presence of the French. He addressed these words to his troops: "If the issue of the action of the 28th April has not been favourable to the arms of his Britannic Majesty, our affairs are not so discouraging as to deprive us of all hope. I know by experience the bravery of the soldiers under my command, and I am sure that they will strain every nerve to regain what has been lost. A fleet is expected, and reinforcements are already on the way. I ask the officers and soldiers to bear their fatigues with patience; and I beg that they will expose themselves with a good heart to all perils: it is a duty they owe their king and country, as well as to themselves."

He caused his people to work without ceasing at the city fortifications on the landward side: new embrazures were opened in the ramparts, behind which his army encamped; the parapet which covered the men was strengthened by an embankment formed of fascines and earth; and on these works 104 cannon were mounted, most of them of heavy calibre, taken from the batteries on the port side, which were of little utility there. The projectiles thrown from the line of defence, told upon the environs of the French camp and places two miles beyond. The besiegers had as yet only 15 pieces to attack with; the greater number of which, all being of small calibre too, became unserviceable in a short time; while, for want of ammunition, only 20 shots apiece were fired from any of them, during every 24 hours. All that the French could do was to protect their lines, and wait for succour from Europe. But the time running on, every day increased doubts as to the expected aid. On their side, the besieged, despite their ramparts and great guns, felt not assured of safety till a fleet should arrive from Britain. Thus, in both camps, the belief was mutual, that the city would finally belong to the nation whose standard should first unfurl in the port. "Matters with us had arrived at such a pass (adds Knox), that if a French fleet had entered the gulf before ours, the place would have fallen again into the hands of its original masters." Accordingly every man, besieger or besieged, directed his regards towards the lower St. Lawrence, to see whose nation's flag would be first to come in sight. The military power of the two nations, severally present in this distant region, were now in equipoise; and that which bore the sceptre of the ocean would, by laying it in the balance, incline the beam to its own side, and the vast territory of New France become its glorious prize.

On the 9th of May, a frigate entered the port. "Such were the hopes and fears of the soldiery," says the British historian, "that we remained long in suspense, not daring to look fixedly in the fateful quarter; but soon were we convinced that the stranger was from Britain. Not but that some among us, willing to seem wiser than their neighbours, sought to cloud our joy by obstinately maintaining a contrary opinion; till all doubts were set at rest by the frigate's saluting the city with 21 guns, and by her men launching a boat and making for the shore. "No tongue can express," he continues, "the intensity of pleasure which pervaded the minds of the whole garrison at this time. Officers and soldiers both mounted the ramparts facing the French camp, and during an hour hurra'd continuously, throwing their hats up in air! The city, the enemy's camp, the port, and the neighbouring country for several miles around, resounded with our acclamations and the booming of our cannon; for the soldiers, in the delirium of their joy, did not tire of salute-firing for a long time. In a word, it is impossible to give a proper notion of the exultation of the time, to those who have not suffered the extremities of a siege; or to one who has not found himself, along with dear friends and brave fellow-countrymen, exposed to the risk of a cruel death."

If there was unbounded joy prevailing among the besieged, the event that caused it lessened, in the same proportion, the hopes of the besiegers. Nevertheless, the frigate just arrived might be an isolated vessel! and the latter would not yet give up all hope. "It was only two days before, that their batteries opened fire on the city!" May 15, two other British war ships entered the port. Then De Lévis decided on raising the siege, being apprehensive of having his retreat cut off, and losing his magazine stores; for the enemy were stronger on the flood than the French, who had only two frigates, both ill armed and without proper crews. M. de Vauquelin, who commanded them, fell, sword in hand and covered with honourable wounds, into the enemy's power, after an heroic combat of two hours, maintained against several frigates, opposite Pointe-aux-Trembles. Almost all his officers were killed or wounded, as well as most of the scanty crew of l'*Atalante*, aboard which vessel he had hoisted his flag, and would not strike it.*

---

* Brave as he proved himself to be, captain Vauquelin was ill received (at court) when he returned to France. The *Moniteur de la Flotte* of 1857, in an article on this mariner, recounts the following touching particulars:—

"It is well known that Jean Vauquelin, the celebrated naval captain, highly reputed for his rare merit and admirable intrepidity, after distinguishing himself greatly in defending Louisiana, and, afterwards, the city of Quebec, was, through some dark intrigues, disgraced and put in prison. Despite his reclamations, and those of his family, he died in the year 1763, without having had his case tried. Some authors even say that he was assassinated in his prison, but this report seems not to be sufficiently attested.

"He left behind him a son, Pierre Vauquelin, who devoted himself at an early age to the study of African history and geography; his researches in which obtained for him a prize, in 1771, from the Academy of Lyons.

"This young *savant*, highly recommended by a brave officer who knew his connexions (the marquis de Vaudreuil), was, in 1774, placed, by Turgot, in the Admiralty-office, where he occupied his leisure time in drawing up a memorial, narrating the career and services of his father, (in hope of his merits being acknowledged and his memory cleared of blame by *réhabilitation*). A circumstance, occurring fortuitously, came in aid of this work of filial piety.

"In 1775, queen Marie-Antoinette was present at the first communion by some young girls of the commune of Meudon; and, after the ceremony was over, one among them, chosen by the others, presented to her Majesty a fine nosegay of white roses; reciting, at the same time, a complimentary address, prepared beforehand, thanking the queen for the honour she had done the rural parishioners, by condescending to come among them.

"The young girl charged with this duty was Miss Elizabeth Vauquelin, then aged 13, who lived with one of her aunts at Meudon. She pleased the queen greatly; who, after embracing her, asked whether she could do any thing for her.

"The youthful lady, not disconcerted, but the tears starting to her eyes, replied, 'I make bold to solicit your Majesty that you would cause justice to be rendered to the good name of my grandfather.'

"The noble heart of the queen was softened on hearing this appeal. She again embraced the girl, and promised that her request should not be neglected. Nor was it; for, that very day, she informed the king of

The French army raised the siege of Quebec during the night of May 16-17, after throwing into the flood, below the cliffs of the Foulon, a portion of its artillery. It was not pursued in its retreat. Thus terminated this short but spirited (*audacieuse*) campaign; which, proportionally to the number of the combatants, involved unusual labour, caused much bloodshed, and finished by exhausting the whole material resources of the Canadian army. From this time the French cause among us became desperate indeed.

De Lévis, being no longer able to keep his troops in hand for want of provisions, dispersed most of them about the country to seek their subsistence. He retained, however, 1,500 men; posting them, under charge of M. Dumas, at intervals between Pointe-aux-Trembles and Jacques-Cartier river, to observe any movements the enemy might make from Quebec. Such was the situation of the gulfward region of Canada, at the close of June, 1760.

Up to this time, nothing of importance had occurred at its opposite extremity. Early in April, M. de Bougainville repaired to the Isle aux Noix, being charged with the command at Lake Champlain frontier; and captain Pouchot, taken prisoner at Nia-

---

what had passed. Louis XVI, ever good, ever just, ordered M. de Sartines, then minister of marine, to make inquiries regarding Jean Vauquelin, and let him know the result.

"The inquest was entered upon at once. Among the witnesses examined were Lapeyrouse, the marquis de Vaudreuil, and members of the family of the marquis de Montcalm, the Hero of Canada. The inquiries made were eminently favourable to the memory of Vauquelin; they attested the glorious services he had performed as a French naval officer, and proved the injustice of the accusations brought against him in his latter years.

"Louis XVI caused the son of the deceased to be presented to him; and, letting M. Vauquelin know the result of the inquest, told him that his father's services would not be forgotten. The latter presented to the king a copy of his Memoir on the geography of Africa. Some months afterwards, Louis sent him on an important mission to Morocco, in which he acquitted himself admirably. In 1777, the ministry having decided to establish permanent relations in the farthest Orient, Vauquelin, appointed king's-consul in China, obtained an *exequatur* as such from Kien-Long, its reigning emperor. This fact has never obtained publicity till now. M. Vauquelin rendered great services, and left a good personal repute, in China."

VOL. II.—T

gara but since exchanged, replaced M. Desandrouins at Fort de Lévis; the latter acting as an engineer in the Quebec expedition. After this finished, 500 men were sent to strengthen the force at Champlain; and 500 more to the Upper St. Lawrence rapids, where La Corne commanded. At this date, the French remanent forces embodied were thus distributed: 800 to 900 men defended the rapids above Montreal; 1,200, posted near lake Champlain, &c.; and 1,500 in observation of Quebec as aforesaid. The other Canadians, seeing that all was thenceforth lost, betook themselves sorrowfully to their homesteads, there to dispute with the famished soldiers billeted upon them the possession of such scraps of food as might still be had. Decimated, ruined by a long war, their latest hopes were crushed by the intelligence, that not only all further military succour from France was denied, but also that the royal treasury of France itself, incapable of meeting home calls, was in no condition to repay the advances the Canadians had made to the government: in short, that payment of the colonial bills drawn upon it was suspended for the time. Vaudreuil and Bigot were apprised of this measure by an official circular; in which they were assured, however, that the exchequer bills (*lettres de change*) drawn in 1757 and 1758 would be paid, in three months after the anticipated peace, with interest; that those drawn in 1759 would be discharged, in like manner, 18 months after a peace; and as for the intendant's promissory-notes (*ordonnances*), they would be liquidated as soon as convenient (*aussitôt que les circonstances le permettraient*). This news startled those concerned, like a thunderbolt: there was owing by France to the colonials, more than 40 million francs (say £1,600,000 sterling); and there was scarcely one of them who was not a creditor of the state. "The paper-money among us," wrote M. de Lévis to the minister, "is entirely discredited, and the people are in despair about it. They have sacrificed their all for the conservation of Canada (to France). Now they find themselves ruined, resourceless: but we do our best to restore their confidence." It was in this letter the French general informed the minister that he was no longer able to keep the field; that provisions, ammunition, all kinds of stores, were used up; and that the regulars, whose battalions had been thinned of their officers and veteran soldiers (through casualties), did not exceed 3,100 combatants, including the colonial stipendiary corps, 900 strong.

De Lévis having personally inspected the Champlain frontier, sent thither an additional battalion, and, promenading the country, profited by the confidence the people publicly manifested towards him, to revive their zeal and courage, and to calm their fears regarding the paper-money; also to persuade them to furnish some few supplies. There was now no gunpowder in store for the troops, at a time when the British were about to take the field with three large armies; which were to move, one from Quebec, on Montreal, a second to advance direct from Lake Champlain, thither; while a third was coming down on that city from Oswego.

The British corps earliest in the arena was a detachment led by general Murray. The arrival of the three British vessels at Quebec, in mid-May, was followed by that of Lord Colville's fleet; and the naval force now before the city comprised six ships of the line, with 8 smaller vessels of war; but the land-force sent, under Lord Rollo, did not arrive till early in July. On the 14th of that month, Murray, leaving a strong garrison behind, embarked the rest of the troops and his army stores in 32 sailing-vessels, about 250 barges, and nine floating batteries, in order to ascend the St. Lawrence. He passed by without assailing Jacques-Cartier fort, in which were 200 men, under the marquis d'Albergotti; a post which was not surrendered till September ensuing, when colonel Fraser advanced against it with 1,000 men. At Sorel, Murray was joined by two regiments, under Lord Rollo. In the last days of August, he was still at Varennes. Become very circumspect since the affair of April 28, he resolved to stay there till the arrival of general Amherst and brigadier Haviland. He was informed that De Lévis had re-united the detachments, which were posted from Jacques-Cartier upwards (they falling back, to avoid the chance of being outflanked); and that the chevalier was only watching for a favourable opportunity in order to attack any British corps separately. When on his way, he received submission from the people of several parishes : that of Sorel (where there was a petty intrenched camp, which he did not think fit to attack) and some others, he subjected to conflagration. At Varennes, he announced that he would burn all villages whose inhabitants did not disarm, and that the Canadian regulars would be transported to France along with the French soldiers. The army of Amherst, and Haviland's brigade, were then approaching Montreal. This menace had the effect desired; and 400 men, out of Boucherville alone, came in and took the oath of fealty. From all parts the militiamen, seeing that the colony was lost to France, gave up their arms; while, concurrently, the regulars, famished and despairing, deserted in great numbers. Sept. 7, Haviland's army came up; and this served as a signal for the few savages who still held to the French, to depart all together.

Haviland had left fort St. Frederic, Aug. 11, with 3,500 men. Bougainville retired before him, quitting successively the Isle-aux-Noix, St. John's, and other posts; so that the former reached Longueuil without striking a blow, and was free to join his forces to those of Murray.

The principal army was that of Amherst, who arrived from Schenectady at Oswego, July 9, with a part of his forces; and was joined, soon thereafter, by his rear-guard, under Brig.-Gen. Gage. This army, 11,000 strong, descending the St. Lawrence, halted before fort de Lévis. M. Pouchot, deserted by the savages, had only 200 men in garrison. He resisted stoutly, however, and even repelled an assault: it was only when he saw his entrenchments destroyed, the batteries ruined, all his officers and a third of the garrison killed or wounded, that he would surrender; having had spirit enough to stay the progress of an army 11,000 strong, during twelve days, with barely 200 men.

Amherst resumed his descent, Aug. 31. The passage of the rapids was a perilous operation; but he chose to brave the danger in order to bar every route against the French; who spoke of retreating, if occasion arose, from Montreal to Detroit, and from Detroit into Louisiana. He lost, at the Cedars' rapids, 64 barges and 88 men; and attained (driving La Corne before him) the village of Lachine, 3 leagues from Montreal. He landed on the island Sept. 6, and invested the city, on its eastern side, the same day. He received, on his way thither, the submission of the inhabitants of the neighbouring country. The two other British armies which he had expected to join his, beleaguered the opposite side of the place on the 8th: so that Montreal was surrounded by a collective army more than 17,000 strong, provided with numerous cannon.

Montreal, built on the southern shore of the island of that name, between a remarkable woody height and the St. Lawrence, was encircled by a mere enclosing wall some 2 or 3 feet thick, run up to keep out savages, and unfit to withstand the shock of artillery. This wall, protected by a fossé, was mounted with six small pieces of cannon. A battery, containing six rusty guns, topped a hillock within the walls. Such were the defences behind which were sheltered the wrecks of the French army! which, including inhabitants still under arms, was now reduced to about 3,000 men in all; exclusive of 500 soldiers who guarded Sainte-Helen's island, situated opposite to the city. The forces had provision in store only for fifteen days, and as much ammunition as one encounter would exhaust.

During the night of Sept. 6–7, M. de Vaudreuil called a council of war. Intendant Bigot thereat read a memorial on the state of the colony, and a project for capitulating. All present expressed an opinion that an advantageous capitulation would be preferable for the people and more honourable to the troops, than a resistance which could defer the entire reduction of the colony only for a few days: accordingly, next morning, Colonel Bougainville was directed to propose to the enemy a truce for a month. This being refused, he was sent again with the articles of surrender above mentioned, 55 in number. Amherst agreed to nearly all of them; excepting indeed, but two, viz. one stipulating perpetual neutrality for the Canadians, the other demanding " all the honours of war " for the evacuating garrison. The latter denial much piqued De Lévis, who threatened to retire to Sainte-Helen's, and defend it to the last extremity; but De Vaudreuil ordered him to disarm, and the capitulation was signed September 8th, 1760.

By this celebrated act, Canada passed finally under British domination. Free exercise of the Catholic religion was guaranteed to its people. Certain specified ecclesiastical brotherhoods, and all communities of *religieuses*, were secured in the possession of their goods, constitutions, and privileges; but like advantages were refused (or delayed) to the Jesuits, Franciscans (Recollets), and Sulpicians, until the king should be consulted on the subject. The same reservation was made as to the parochial clergy's titles. In respect of Canadian jurisprudence (*les lois, usages, et coutumes du pays*) asked to be preserved intact, it was replied, that the inhabitants were now subjects of his British Majesty (and would be treated as such). Article 37 was inserted to tranquillize the minds of those possessed of real property (*les fortunes particulières*); and the feudal landholders (*seigneurs*) had the address to obtain the intercalation therein of terms conservative of their rights of every kind: at least the words thus inserted, read as if they secured their seignorial privileges.

The British took possession of Montreal the same day. The governor-general, Chevalier de Levis, the troops, the officers, both military and civil, all embarked for France. Before setting out, M. de Vaudreuil sent an order to M. de Belestre, commandant of Detroit (where 300 to 400 Canadian families were settled), as well as to the chiefs of other posts in the lake countries, to surrender them to Major Rogers, a famous partisan, or to his deputies. There re-passed into Europe about 185 officers, 2,400 soldiers valid and invalid, and fully 500 sailors, domestics, women and children. The smallness of this proved, at once the cruel ravages of the war, the paucity of embarkations of succour sent from France, and the great numerical superiority of the victor. The most notable colonists, at the same time, left the country. Their emigration was encouraged, that of the Canadian officers especially, whom the conquerors desired to be rid of, and whom they eagerly stimulated to pass to France. Canada lost, by this self-expatriation, the most precious portion of its people, invaluable as its members were from their experience, their intelligence, and their knowledge of public and commercial affairs.

Thus, by the year 1761, French domination existed no longer in any part of Canada, after a duration of a century and a half. When quitting the country, M. de Vaudreuil paid this homage to its people in a letter to the ministry: "With these beautiful and vast countries, France loses 70,000 inhabitants of a rare quality; a race of people unequalled for their docility, bravery, and loyalty. The vexations they have suffered for many years, more especially during the five years preceding the reduction of Quebec, —all without a murmur, or importuning their king for relief,— sufficiently manifest their perfect submissiveness."

As for the French army of Canada, the mere recital of its deeds is its best eulogium. Never had France more intrepid or more devoted soldiers. Ten weak battalions, oftenest recruited in that country itself for want of men from Europe, had to defend that immense territory which extends from Acadia to lake Erie and beyond, against tenfold numbers of foes.

Very few of those brave men returned to that native land, in which their ex-chief did this justice to their merits: "They have performed prodigies of valour," wrote he to the minister on his return; adding, "they, like the armed Canadians, gave repeated proofs (especially on April the 28th) that the conservation of Canada were ensured, had it depended on their zeal and courage alone; and it was the last of a series of misfortunes and fatalities, which, for some time past, befel the country, that the hoped-for succours from France were not sent at the critical moment. However scanty they might have been, these would, in connection with our latest victory, have ensured the re-capture of Quebec."— In the same despatch De Lévis reported of the governor-general, that he had, to the latest moment, done all for the colony's well-being that prudence and experience could suggest.

The chevalier himself, after a short stay in France, had a command assigned him in the French army then campaigning in Germany; where he fought in the battle of Johannisberg, gained in 1762 by the Prince de Condé, over the famous William duke of Brunswick. After the war concluded, he was appointed governor of Artois, nominated a marshal of France, and created a duke in 1784. Three years afterwards he died at Arras, whither he had gone to preside at a convocation of the several orders (*états*) of the province. The latter caused his remains to be buried in that city with great observance, and set up a funereal monument in its cathedral, to honour his memory.

His military career in Canada, especially after Montcalm's death, favourably manifested his courage in action and his skill in the art of war. His very presence in the field seemed to ensure success; for every fight he took part in became a victory: and we dare almost assure ourselves, that had he been present at Quebec on the 13th of September, the result of the day would have been very different; for he would have had influence enough over Montcalm to hinder him from combating till all the troops could have been got together. De Lévis was perhaps the only man in the colony capable of saving it to France. His prudence, moreover, always prevented him from taking part in the unfortunate quarrels which disunited Vaudreuil and Montcalm; and, if he had not the vivacity of the latter, he had qualities far more precious for commanding an army, viz. sound judgment, firmness, and quick soldierly perceptions of whatever were needful to be done: to these endowments he owed his unvaried success in war.

M. de Bourlamaque died, in 1764, while governor of Guadaloupe. As for Colonel Bougainville, it is well known that he played a glorious part, as a leading naval commander, in the French navy, when her fleets were combating for American independence; and that he afterwards made his name yet more illustrious by his voyage around the world, and by his geographical discoveries.

The news of the submission of all Canada was followed in Britain by a repetition of the demonstrations of joy at the fall of Quebec. The king handsomely rewarded the officers who brought the despatches to London announcing the desired event.—In France, the government had been long prepared for such a result, and had sent instructions to the colonial officials to obtain the best terms they could for the inhabitants, the chief victims of this great national disaster. But the French people, who knew not the wretched state of their country's colonies, were sensibly affected by the loss of the finest and oldest transmarine dependency of France. Shame flushed their faces, chagrin gnawed their hearts, on learning the subjugation of 60,000 of their fellow-subjects,—a race speaking the same language, living under the same laws as they; and who had in vain made every sacrifice, during seven years of trials and suffering, to escape a fate which a good government would have found means to save them from. But, in the face of Europe, the ministry took matters quite composedly; and sought a pretext for veiling its own dishonour, by prosecuting with blind vindictiveness almost all the colonial administrators— some of these being notoriously corrupt indeed, many prevaricating, but others entirely innocent; yet nearly every chief functionary from Canada, soon after landing in France, was cited to appear as a criminal before a judicial inquest, holden at the Châtelet in Paris.

When Bigot presented himself at Versailles, M. Berryer received him with indignity, and showered reproaches on him. "It is you," he exclaimed, "who have ruined the colony! your expenditure has been enormous; you became a trader, and have amassed a large fortune............your administration has been unfair, your conduct criminal." A universal cry arose against this officer, among all who took an interest in colonial matters: every Canadian, it was asserted, was ready to bear witness against the ex-intendant for his malversations. Bigot tried, but in vain, to plead his own justification. He retired, at first, to Bordeaux, and hearing, some months later, that there was an intent to arrest him, he returned to Paris, hoping to conjure the storm; but found every avenue to the ministerial presence barred against him; and, four days afterwards (Nov. 17 1761), he was thrown into the Bastile, and there lay 11 months with all access denied to him. Concurrently, a score of others, accused as his accomplices, shared the same treatment; while 30 more, who did not come forward, were ordered to be arrested wherever found. Meanwhile, the council of state ordained the Châtelet court to put all upon their trial.

Even the ex-governor-general did not escape the disgrace of being *Bastilled*. This affront he owed perhaps as much to the (criminating) insinuations of Montcalm's partisans, as to the more perfidious calumnies of Bigot. The process of all was carried on briskly, by ministerial desire; yet it lasted from Dec. 1761 till the end of March 1763. The accused obtained, in Oct. 1762, liberty to employ counsel to prepare their defences.—The Marquis de Vaudreuil had to govern Canada during the most thorny time of its history. He repaired to France a poor man, after serving the king 56 years; the earliest part of that long public career as governor of Trois-Rivières, and the middle period as chief in Louisiana. While governor in the latter, he became a proprietor of some plantations, which he was forced to sell for the support of his rank in Canada. He had even sacrificed, like Montcalm and De Lévis, his salary, in order to supply towards the close of the war, what the state did not furnish. Thus, all his fortune, as he said himself, consisted in hopes founded on the king's beneficence. His defence was dignified: he repelled the insinuations of the really guilty, and disdained attempting to justify himself by accusing others, rather exculpating indeed those Canadian officers whom Bigot slandered. "Brought up in Canada myself," he said, "I knew them every one, and I maintain that almost all of them are as upright as they are valorous. In general, the Canadians seem to be soldiers born; a masculine and military training early inures them to fatigues and dangers. The annals of their expeditions, their explorations, and their dealings with the aborigines, abound in marvellous examples of courage, activity, patience under privation, coolness in peril, and obedience to leaders, during services which have cost many of them their lives, but without slackening the ardour of the survivors. Such officers as those, with a handful of armed inhabitants and a few savage warriors, have often disconcerted the projects, paralysed the preparations, ravaged the provinces, and beaten the troops of Britain when eight or ten times more numerous than themselves. In a country with frontiers so vast, such qualities were priceless." And he finished by declaring, that he "would fail in his duty to those generous warriors, and even to the state itself, if he did not proclaim their services, their merits, and their innocence." In corroboration of this testimony, we would observe, that all the military officers who remained in Canada after the final capitulation, were found to be much poorer after the war than before; and that, among the civil functionaries, only the outlawed Deschesnaux, intendant's secretary, and some obscure tools of his, who fattened on the public wants, had their names in Canada rightly branded with ineffaceable marks.

At length (Dec. 10, 1763), the president of the commission, assisted by 25 councillors of the Châtelet, rendered his final decree regarding the parties accused. De Vaudreuil (who died next year, less from old age than vexation of spirit) was, with five more, relieved (*déchargés*) from the accusation.* Bigot and Varin were sentenced to exile for life, their goods to be confiscated. Several of the accused were condemned to minor banishments, and to modified

---

* This form of semi-acquittal was doubtless intended to be dishonouring. It was equivalent to a Scots verdict of *not proven.*—B.

confiscations, or to make various restitutions, to a collective amount of 11,400,000 francs. Commissary-general Cadet, alone, was mulcted in six millions. In regard of others of the accused, further process was stayed.*

It is certain that great dilapidations did take place; but the reports of them were exaggerations of facts, as any one may be convinced of, by comparing the public expenditure in Canada with that of the Anglo-American colonies during the war. The raising and maintaining of 7,000 men in 1758, cost Massachusetts £180,000 sterling; besides £30,000 for defence of the frontier, or 5¼ million francs in all. In the very first year of the war, Canada had as numerous a force as this to subsist, not reckoning a portion of the Acadians then on its hands. That army, not much augmented up to the year 1759, had to confront the far superior forces of the enemy, often marching to and fro between whiles, at distances widely apart, in order to defend frontiers extending from the Gulf of St. Lawrence to the Mississippi. The cost attending transports, in the then state of our roadways, would of necessity be enormous. Very soon, scarcity of provisions and goods, caused on one hand by the mastery of the enemy on the high seas, which caused interruptions of communication with France; and, on the other, the suspended tillage of much of the cleared land through the military service imposed on its cultivators, decupled state outlay; for, owing to the exorbitant rise in price of all commodities, public expenditure,—all this rapidly mounted up. From 1,700,000 livres, its totality in 1749, it rose by successive yearly leaps to 2,100,000–2,700,000– 4,900,000–5,300,000–4,450,000 (*sic*)–6,100,000–11,300,000– 19,250,000–27,900,000–26,000,000 francs; and, for the eight earlier months of 1760, to 13,500,000: in all, a total of 123½ millions.

Of this sum, there remained due by the state 80 millions, for 41 of which it was in debit to Canadian creditors; namely, 34 millions unpaid of intendant's notes-of-hand (*ordonnances*), and 7 millions in exchequer-bills (*lettres de change*). These state obligations (*créances*) held by the Canadians, an immense amount for

---

† Thus we, juridically rather than literally, interpret the words, *le jugement fut remis jusqu'à plus ample informé.*—B.

such a country, became to them almost valueless in the end. Traffickers and British officers bought up, at low rates, parcels of these paper-moneys, and re-sold portions of them to French factors on 'Change, in London, for cash. Through personal influences, a stipulation was made in the treaty of 1763, granting a compensation of 3,600,000 francs for the reduction, operated in France, of a moiety on the exchequer-bills, and of three-fourths on the intendants' notes; but the Canadians, to whom that reduction had caused a loss, at one stroke, of 29 millions on their *créances*, derived little profit from the above-mentioned compensatory stipulation. The paper they still had in hand, remained long valueless; at last, in 1765 they were invited to make declarations of the items and amount of it, in schedules (*bordereaux*), which vouchers they were to send to commissioners charged to pass audit accounts (*états*) in Britain.* There were 1639 of those schedules deposited, proving for a considerable amount; but almost the whole sum becoming a subject for brokerage, the claims got into speculators' hands, at merely nominal prices. In March 1766, a new convocation was signed between French and English state-agents, for liquidating all the paper money then remaining in Canada. It was decreed that it should be paid off in receipts for stock (*reconnaissances de rente*) at $4\frac{1}{2}$ per cent. interest; said receipts to be as valid as any other evidents of the national debt. It may be concluded from what has just been detailed, firstly,—That the war in Canada did not cause the exhaustion of the king's exchequer, to which his ministers attributed the misfortunes of France, as a justification (for abandoning the colony), since a very small part of the war's cost was reimbursed at the time; and, secondly, that the accusations brought against the colonial functionaries had for their chief intent that of diverting public odium from the ministers and directing it against their agents: the former being the real authors of the disasters, rightly responsible therefor, and, as such, all-worthy of national indignation, for the ministry could easily have cashiered its unfaithful functionaries.

After the year 1758, evil fortunes seemed never to remit for

---

* General Recapitulation of *les bordereaux*: the registry of which is reposited in the Provincial Archives, Quebec.

France, which experienced constant reverses, on land and sea, in all parts of the world. The French ministry at last tried, but in vain, to open negociations with the British cabinet. Choiseul, war-minister, and virtually premier, drew Spain into a warlike alliance with France against Britain in 1761,—that treaty being known as the "Family compact,"—but military disasters and other public calamities continued none the less. Spain lost Cuba, Manilla, 12 vessels of the line, and 100 millions value in prizes to the enemy. As for France, scarcely a colony remained to her, and in Europe she made no way. Thanks to the mediation of Sardinia, the pacific character of Lord Bute (who contrived to eliminate Pitt from the British cabinet, which the latter previously no longer led), —and to a diversion made against Britain's ally, Portugal (which Spain and France together attacked, in view of making her a handle for compensations), the preliminaries of a peace were signed at Fontainebleau, Nov. 3, 1762, between the courts of France, Spain, and Britain. A definitive treaty was concluded in Paris among the three powers along with Portugal, on 10th February ensuing. France ceded to Britain, along with other territories, Canada and all the Laurentian isles, except St. Pierre and Miquelon, reserved for behoof of the French fisheries. To Spain was ceded Louisiana, in exchange for Florida and the bay of Pensacola, which the Spaniards gave up to Britain, to recover Cuba. The only other stipulation in the treaty regarding Canada, was that by which Britain bound herself to allow the Canadians the free exercise of their religion. Silence was maintained on the subject of our people's laws, probably because, in becoming British subjects, they were made participant of legislative power ; whereas colonial catholicity, reprobated as it then was by the very principles of the British constitution, needed an express stipulation for its immunity from penal interdictions.*

Louisiana had a like fate with Canada, although not conquered. That province, indeed, enjoyed a pretty tranquil existence during nearly the whole time of the war then ended. From the date at which we left off in our brief annals of that country,

---

* We subjoin the concluding words of this sentence, copied literally from the author's text ; " .... le catholicisme, frappé de réprobation par la constitution de l'Etat, avait besoin d'une stipulation expresse pour devenir un droit."—*B.*

the object of so much hopefulness, it really began to prosper. The war against the Natchez finished by beggaring the West India Company created in 1723, and obliged it to demit to the king its rights over Louisiana, the trade of which was then rendered free. That fine country, enjoying thenceforth more liberty, saw its population, its settlements, its commerce augment at first slowly, but afterwards rapidly, despite the changefulness which again affected it. France willed to realize the project, formed in the preceding century, of binding together Canada and Louisiana, in order to bar the western regions against the British, and confine them to the Atlantic seaboard. Paucity of inhabitants, physical impracticabilities, vast regions with savage populations separating the two countries, rendered the project inexecutable. After the peace of 1748, France seemed to occupy herself more seriously with the colonization of Louisiana. Although her measures were not always fortunate, and notwithstanding the mistaken policy of most of the administrators whom she sent to govern the colony; despite the disorders they created in commerce and finance, by imprudent emissions of notes-of-hand (*ordonnances*) and paper-money, which soon fell into discredit and became a prey to brokerage; maugre all these drawbacks, we say, Louisiana made rapid progress by favour of the peace reigning within. But the calm it enjoyed was deceitful. At the moment when the colony attained the greatest prosperity it had known since its foundation, it was stricken by the most grievous infliction a community can endure, subjection to an alien race, and a partition of its territory among rival nations.*

When the French governor, M. d'Abadie, received, in 1764, the order from Louis XV to communicate the treaty of Paris to the colonists, it pained him so much that he died of chagrin. His successor, M. Aubry, next charged with the sad mission, let time run on. The appalled Louisianians made representations in France (against the transference) in the most pressing and even pathetic terms; and when some Spaniards came, in 1768, led by Don Antonio d'Ulloa, a sage and moderate man, to take possession, the

---

* New Orleans, though situated on the left bank of the Mississippi, inhered, as far as Lake Pontchartrain, to the territory ceded to Spain.

colonists constrained him to re-embark, pretending that France had no right to cede its power over them without their consent. Louis XV was then obliged to advise them, that the cession made was irrevocable. Next year, General O'Reilly arrived, with 3,000 men. The people opposed themselves to his landing; but their magistrates succeeded in appeasing them; and the procurator-general, M. Lafrenière, went to receive the Spaniard, and assure him of the submission of the inhabitants. O'Reilly manifested, at first, much benignity, maintained the ancient laws, and captivated the multitude by his conduct; but these appearances of justice had no other aim than to conceal his own evil designs or the stern instructions of his court; for he soon changed the laws he seemed at first to respect, and upset the whole interior administration. Lafrenière and the tribunals protested against these mutations. "O'Reilly took advantage of this opposition," says Barbé-Marbois, "to commit acts of violence and ferocity, which he mistook for those of wise firmness." He called together twelve deputies of the people, to fix a code of laws. These delegates met in his house, and were waiting to deliberate, when the doors of the room were suddenly opened, and O'Reilly appeared at the head of a company of soldiers, who seized the deputies, chained them, and thrust them into prison-cells. Six of them were shot, by his orders. Lafrenière, before dying, protested his innocence, and encouraged his five compatriots to suffer with firmness. He charged M. Noyan to send the scarf he wore to his wife, for the use of his son when he came of age; and gave himself orders to the soldiers to fire! abandoning to the stings of remorse the soul of the perfidious Spaniard who had set a snare for his victims. The surviving six deputies were transferred to dungeons in Cuba.

Such were the tragical events which attended the passing of Louisiana under alien domination. There now remained to France, of all North America, only some befogged and sterile rocks, scattered on sea-margins, in the vicinity of Newfoundland.

"Since the treaty of Bretigny," says Sismondi, "France had concluded no treaty so humiliating as that just signed in her name at Paris, to put an end to the Seven-Years' War. Now-a-days, that we know better the nature and extent of the regions she gave up in America; now that we therein behold a great nation arise and expand; noting how much the people of her race, whom she left behind, have prospered at Quebec, Montreal, and New Orleans, each living testification of the importance of the colonies she renounced—that abandonment of territories of a destiny so exalted, appears all the more disastrous. Still this is no reason why we should blame the ministers who negociated and signed the treaty of 1763. That peace was wisely entered into; it was needful, and as favourable as the circumstances of the time would allow. The French had succeeded in nothing of all they had proposed to themselves to do, by entering into the Seven-Years' War, for they suffered the bloodiest defeats; and, had they persisted in continuing the contest, there was every reason to expect that discomfiture still more signal would follow. Never did her generals seem to be so utterly destitute of talent; at no time were her soldiers, naturally brave, so poor in muscle, so ill equipped, so materially wretched; never had they less confidence in their chiefs, nor ever, from their indiscipline, was their confidence less in themselves than now: in a word, at no previous time was France so little redoubtable to her enemies. By imploring the assistance of Spain, she had only led her neighbour upon the same road to ruin with herself, and one campaign more in common would have reft her ally of her most important colonies.

"However disastrous that peace might be, we do not find, in the memoirs of the time, that the writers felt at all humiliated; Bachaumont seems to have seen in the event only wherewithal to supply poets with a subject for verses of felicitation and theatrical divertisements. At each page one feels, while reading those memoirs, how much the *élite* of France had become indifferent to her national polity, power, and glory. Even those Frenchmen who took the greatest interest in public matters, were oblivious of their compatriot race in Canada and Louisiana, 'who multiplied slowly in the woods, who associated with savages; but who furnished no returns to the exchequer, no soldiers to the royal host, no colonial merchandise for home traders!' The petty settlements, for fishing cod, at St. Pierre and Miquelon, the small islands of Grenada, St. Vincent, Dominica, and Tobago, appeared in the eyes of the shippers of St. Malo, Nantes, and Bordeaux, far more important than all Canada and entire Acadia.

"Besides, the nation was accustoming itself, more and more, to a want of sympathy with its government, the alienation increasing in proportion as French writers took to studying political questions. It was at this epoch that the sect of Economists were most stirring; and after the marquis de Mirabeau had published (in 1755) his "Friend of Mankind" (*l'Ami des Hommes*), the clique of Encyclopedists manifested itself with yet greater power, and the appearance of its gigantic repertory became an affair of state. Finally, Jean-Jacques Rousseau, who, as early as the year 1753, had sapped the bases upon which society rests, in his Discourse on the Origin of Inequality among Mankind, published afterwards his "Emile," and next his "Social Compact" (*le Contrat Social*): all minds were then commoved regarding the highest questions of public organization. But the French were not able to cogitate on subjects of such high import, without being struck with the unreason, the absurdities even, abounding in their own administration throughout all its parts: for example, the exclusion of all but the noble class from every superior grade in the army, which deprived the soldiery of all emulation; the crushing burdens of *taille* and *corvée*,* which sterilized the soil and paralyzed agriculture; the tyranny of intendants and sub-delegates in the provinces; the barbarities of criminal penality, initiated by seclusion in the cell, with torture for its middle term, and finishing with breakings on the wheel—such horrible punishments being inflicted, not seldom, on the innocent; finally, disorders in the financial departments, with attendant perplexity of accompts, which the most skilful could not unravel. It was thus that every Frenchmen capable of reflection or of feeling aright, especially those accustomed to direct the public mind, were beginning to cherish a hope of fundamental reforms being effected; they assumed for all France the credit of this noble aspiration, and they imputed to the government, or rather to the king, the disgrace of those reverses, as being the unavoidable con-

---

* There are no equivalent terms in our freedom-breathing vernacular, to interpret, except by periphrasis, the sense of the above two baleful words.—*B.*

comitants of the system under which the nation groaned ; at the core of which nestled the vices of a reckless voluptuary, who, being without honour himself, disregarded it in others; a crowned sybarite he was, who looked upon regality only as a means for satisfying to the utmost his own gross appetites and the avidity of his mistresses." *

There were persons, again, who looked upon the loss of Canada with complacency, as facilitating the descent to perdition of an inert and sensual despotism. The fall of the olden monarchy they allowed was certain, but it might be only looming in the distance : now a damaging event such as that which had just taken place in America, might precipitate the coming catastrophe ; while the thoughtful, who longed for a radical reform of social organization, but who wished to found that reform on the bases of freedom, were too oblivious of the intermediate evil plight of the nation, and shocked the sense of the multitude by their applauses of anti-patriotic demonstrations. For example, Voltaire, in his retirement at Ferney, celebrated the Triumph of the British at Quebec by a banquet, not indeed as if exulting over French humiliation, but as a victory Liberty had gained over Despotism. He foresaw that the loss of Canada to France would eventuate the enfranchisement of the Anglo-American colonies; and this, in turn (he thought) would be followed by that of all the European populations of our two continents. That banquet over, the company retired into an elegant private theatre, where was played " The Island Patriot " (*le Patriote insulaire*), a dramatic piece full of aspirations for Liberty ; in which Voltaire himself played a leading personage. This representation finished, the slides of the scenery unclosed, and a spacious court, illuminated and ornamented with Indian trophies, met the spectator's view. Brilliant fireworks, accompanied by military music, concluded the fête. Among the pyrotechnic devices, was "the star of St. George" which emitted rockets; and underneath was represented, the Cataract of Niagara. †

---

* "One is startled here," wrote the British ambassador from Paris Feb. 21, 1765, "at the visible disorder in public affairs, and the evident decline of the royal autnority." Raumer, Bertroyc, &c.—*Hist. of the French.*

† *Public Advertiser* (London daily paper), Nov. 28, 1759.

BOOK ELEVENTH.

CHAPTER I.

MILITARY DESPOTISM—ABOLITION AND RESTORATION OF THE ANCIENT LAWS.

1760–1774.

Cessation of hostilities; the Canadians return to their homesteads.—Military government and courts martial.—Emigration of Canadians to France.—The French laws discontinued, but the catholic religion tolerated.—Governor Murray replaces Amherst as generalissimo.—An executive, legislative, and judicial council constituted.—Division of Canada into two districts, and introduction of English laws. Murmurings of the people.—The British colonists demand an elective chamber, or representative assembly, from which Canadian members were intended to be excluded; and accuse Murray of tyranny: that general quits the colony on leave, but does not return.—Risings of the western savages.—Gen. Carleton, appointed Murray's successor, makes changes in the governing council.—The people continue their opposition to the new laws.—Official reports of five British crown-lawyers (Yorke, De Grey, Marriott, Wedderburn, and Thurlow) on the grievances of the Canadians.—A Legislative Council finally established, in 1774.

Those Canadians who did not leave the army after the siege of Quebec, quitted it entirely after the capitulation of Montreal, and the most profound peace soon reigned in all the colony. Small appearances now would there have been of a long and sanguinary struggle, but for the devastations left behind it, especially in the district of Quebec, where nought could be seen but wreck and ruin. This region had been occupied, for two years, by contending hosts; its capital had been twice besieged, twice bombarded, and almost annihilated; its environs, having been the theatre of three battles, bore all the traces of a desperate armed struggle. The ruined inhabitants, decimated in so many battle-fields, thought of nothing now but to take refuge on their lands, hoping thence to derive wherewithal to repair their losses; therefore, isolating themselves from their rulers, they gave themselves up entirely to rural pursuits.

The victors, on their part, took fit measures for making sure of their precious conquest. Amherst chose troops for guarding it, and sent the rest to Europe or into other colonies. He divided Canada into three departments, corresponding to the old divisions, and put them under martial law. General Murray was located at Quebec, general Gage at Montreal, colonel Benton at Three Rivers. Each of these chiefs was supplied with a secretary, of French-Swiss origin, as a lingual medium between the ruler and the ruled. The latter gentlemen were, M. Cramahé for Quebec district; M. Bruyères for Three-Rivers; and M. Mathurin for Montreal. Amherst, after giving final instructions to the three governors respectively, left Canada for New York.

Murray constituted a military council for his district, composed of seven army officers, as judges of the more important civil and criminal pleas. This council held bi-weekly sederunts. Murray reserved to himself the jurisdiction, without power of appeal, over other cases; or left them to the care of military subalterns in the country parts. General Gage, in his district, rather attempered the system; for he authorized the parochial captains to settle any differences amongst the people according to their own discretion, but dissatisfied clients had a power of appeal to the nearest British commandant or to himself. At a later period, Gage divided his district into sub-districts, in each of which he established a justice court, composed of seven, six, or five (Canadian) militia officers. These bodies held fortnightly sessions, and were subordinated in authority to one or other of the three councils of war, composed of British military officers, located at Montreal, Varennes, and St. Sulpice. There lay an appeal, in last resort, from the decisions of all these tribunals, in every disputed case, to Gage: at the same time, none of their penal sentences could be executed, without being first submitted to him, for approval, reversal, or commutation. Thus, through their militia officers, the Canadians of Montreal district at least shared in the administration of justice. In the district of Quebec, also, they participated somewhat in its jurisprudence, through the agency of two of their compatriots, who were appointed public procurators and legal commissaries before the military tribunal of Quebec city: one being Jacques Belcourt de Lafontaine, ex-member of the sovereign council, for the country on the right bank of the St. Lawrence; the other, Joseph Etienne Cugnet, seigneur of St. Etienne, for that on the left side of the river. At Three-Rivers, almost the same arrangement was made.

This martial system was adopted in violation of the capitulations, which guaranteed to the Canadians the rights of British subjects; rights by which their persons were not to be disposed of by any but their natural judges, unless by their own consent. It fell out, that when they hoped to enjoy legality under peaceful sway, they saw their tribunals abolished, their judges repelled, and their whole social organization upset, to make room for the most insupportable of all tyranny, that of courts martial. Nothing did more to isolate the government and alienate the people from it, than this conduct, long since repudiated by the law and custom of nations. Ignorant as they were of the speech of their conquerors, the Canadians spurned the booted and spurred legists placed amidst them; and, without complaining, for they were little used to soliciting, they settled their differences with each other; or they applied to the parish clergy or local notables as arbitrators: by having recourse to whom, the influence over the people of these classes, in the several parishes, was greatly increased. By a happy effect of circumstances seemingly adverse, pastor and flock had thus become as one in sentiment; and, under the theoretical sway of the sword, clerical intermediation became the rule practically followed by and for each and all.

The military organization adopted, attested the fear Canadian resistance to alien domination had inspired, and its existence was approbated in Britain: only under this condition, however, that it was to cease as soon as a state of amity should supervene between her people and those of France; that time once come, regular civil government was to take its place. Yet the colony remained four years under martial law. This epoch in our annals is designated as the "Reign of the Soldiery" (*le règne militaire.*)

During all this time, the Canadian people hoped that France would not abandon them, but reclaim her own as soon as hostilities ceased. The clergy, not so confident as the laity, drew up two memorials on ecclesiastical affairs in Canada, one for the Duke de

Nivernois, the other to the Duke of Bedford—these nobles being the two chief diplomatists employed for settling terms of pacification between France and Great Britain. A claim was preferred by the memorialists, that a warranty should be given for the bishopric and seminary of Quebec. "The titular bishop," said they, "holds his powers and jurisdiction from his see itself; as soon as he is confirmed by the pope, the charge (*place*) becomes irrevocable." It was proposed that the bishops, in future, should be elected by the chapter, with a royal concurrence in the choice made—as was once the custom in the Church universal, and as is still done in Germany.

After three years passed in a state of alternate hope and fear, the Canadians had perforce to renounce their latest illusion. Their destiny was bound irrevocably to that of the British people by the treaty of 1763. Consequent upon this event, a second emigration took place: numbers of commercialists, lawyers, ex-functionaries, with most of the leading men still remaining in the colony, left for France, after selling or abandoning estates, titles to which became subjects of after litigation, even down to the present times, among their descendants. None now lingered in the towns, but here and there a few subaltern placemen, some artisans, scarcely one merchant. The members of the different religious confraternities, with the rural populations of course remained.

The mother country of those immigrants was touched at heart by the love for her which had drawn them to her shores. Her rulers showed them special favour; and, for several of them, places were found in the government offices, in the navy, in the army, &c.— Some of those who had already filled high charges, were appointed to like posts in distant French dependencies. Thus M. de Repentigny, created marquis and become a brigadier-general, was appointed governor, first of Senegal, then of Mahé, in French India, where he died in 1776. M. Dumas became governor of the Mauritius and Isle of Bourbon. M. Beaujou accompanied Lapeyrouse, as aid-major-general against the British Hudson's Bay settlements, in 1782. The Marquis de Villeray, made captain in the royal guards, may also be noted; also M. Juchereau (Duchesnay) commandant of Charleville. M. LeGardeur, Count de Tilly, Messrs. Pellegrin, de l'Echelle, La Corne, became post-captains in the French navy.

The Count de Vaudreuil, as admiral during the American war for Independence, distinguished himself. Jacques Bedout, a native of Quebec, became a distinguished rear-admiral. Joseph Chaussegros de Léry, military engineer, was made a baron by Napoleon I for his great services. Other Canadian officers, not actively employed, yet pensioned by the government, lived together in Tadousac. Canadian and Acadian refugees in France were succoured even by the republicans of 1792.

Those of them who remained in Canada, trusting to the promises of the British that civil rule should obtain, sent agents to London to proffer homage to George III, and defend their interests. When chevalier de Léry and his wife, Louise de Brouages, one of the finest women of the time, were presented at court, the young king was so struck with madame's beauty that he said, " If all the Canadian ladies resembled her, we may indeed vaunt of our *beautiful* conquest."

After the series of mournful scenes which we have had to unfold to our readers' view, it is refreshing to be able to adduce a graceful trait like the foregoing.

One of the Canadian agents, Etienne Charrest, who was charged to negociate on the article of religion, as expressed in the Treaty of Paris, wrote several times on that subject to Lord Halifax, secretary of state. He demanded the maintenance of the colonial church establishment, and the restoration of French jurisprudence; he complained against martial law, and deferred justice; he recommended that the paper-money difficulty should be regulated, and that more time should be accorded for liquidation, as that fixed was too short for Canadian holders of state notes and bills; many, pressed as they had been for cash, having parted with them for whatever money-dealers chose to give. (*See Manuscripts in episcopal archives, Quebec; especially letters, dated* 16*th and* 17*th Jan.* 1764.)

The churchmen's agents also made renewed demands for the maintenance intact of the Quebec see. They offered to lodge the next bishop at the Seminary, of which he might be the Superior; its members acting as canons, to constitute his chapter. " It is an established usage everywhere," they said, " that there is no seated bishop without a chapter."

The British government made objections, and refused to recognize a bishop, but cared not to put any obstruction in the way of one. The former was now occupied in organizing a regular colonial administration. The Canadians, meanwhile, felt all the chagrin arising from subjection to alien sway. The evils they had previously endured seemed light to them, compared to the suffering and humiliations which were in preparation, they feared, for them and their posterity. First of all, the British wished to repudiate whatever was Canadian, and to deprive the *habitants* even of the natural advantages Canada offered to them by its extent. The colony was dismembered. Labrador, from St. John's river to Hudson's Bay, Anticosti, Magdalen Island, were annexed governmentally to Newfoundland; the two isles, St. John's (Prince Edward) and Cape Breton, to Nova Scotia; the lands of the great lakes to the neighbouring Anglo-American colonies. Soon afterwards, a slice of territory was detached from Canada, and took the name of New Brunswick, with an administration apart.

From parcelling out territory, the British passed to re-legislating. Their king, by his sole authority, without parliamentary sanction, abolished those laws of olden France, so precise, so clear, so wisely framed, to substitute for them the jurisprudence of England—a chaos of prescriptive and statutory acts and decisions, invested with complicated and barbaric forms, which English legislation has never been able to shake off, despite all the endeavours of its best exponents; and the above substitution was effected, merely in order to ensure protection and the benefit of the laws of their mother country to those of the dominant race who should emigrate to Canada. In an ordinance dated Sept. 17, 1764, it was assumed, that " in the supreme court sitting at Quebec, his Britannic Majesty was present in the person of his chief-justice, having full power to determine all civil and criminal cases, agreeably to the laws of England and to the ordinances of this province."

This was to renew the outrage (*attentat*) perpetrated on the Acadians; if it be a verity to say, that a man's civism (*la putrie*) is not limited to the space of a city's site, or to the boundaries of a province; but is inherent to human affections, forms family ties, is incorporated with the laws, abides in the manners and customs of a people. No one in Britain raised his voice against so tyrannical an act, which deprived a country of its laws in view of an immigration scarcely begun, and which might never make headway. The Canadians were not deprived of their implied rights in this respect alone : for in becoming British subjects, they, as such, ought to have acquired *all* constitutional rights inhering to that quality. Yet their king declared, that representative assemblies for Canada should be convoked only when circumstances allowed! This was at once to deprive them of a positive right, the full enjoyment of which would have ensured to them a continuance of others they specially enjoyed.

An order had been given, in royal instructions dated Dec. 7, 1763, to exact an oath of fealty from the Canadians. Mr. Goldfrap, the governor's secretary, wrote to the parish priests, three years thereafter, that if they refused to take that oath, they might prepare to leave Canada; while all other Canadians were also to be expelled if they too neglected to take the oath, or refused to subscribe the declaration of abjuration. It was ruled, likewise, that they were to renounce the ecclesiastical jurisdiction of Rome; also to repudiate the Pretender's claim to the British crown, of whom or respecting which they previously knew nothing whatever! Afterwards, they were required to give up their defensive arms, or swear that they had none.—Schedules were drawn up of the landed estates of divers religious communities, and particulars demanded as to the nature of their constitution, rights, privileges, amount of property, &c.; with lists of the several churches, the number of clergy, amount of their incomes, &c.

While these measures were in progress, General Murray was appointed governor-general in place of Sir Jeffery Amherst, then in England, on leave, but whence he did not return. The latter was, in reality, the first British governor-general of Canada; Gage, Murray, Burton, and next Haldimand (the last replacing Burton at Three Rivers, who was advanced to the charge of Montreal district), being all sub-governors only. Murray, become second governor-general, in obedience to his instructions formed a new executive council; in which was vested, along with himself, all executive, legislative, and judicial functions : the power of taxing, alone being excepted. This body, it was ordered, should be composed of the two lieutenant-governors (of Montreal and Three Rivers), the chief justice, the inspector-general of customs, and eight persons chosen from among the leading inhabitants of the colony. In the selection of the latter, only one native was admitted; the exceptional man being a person of no mark, and his name added merely to complete the requisite number. A hateful spirit of jealous exclusiveness had dictated the "Instructions" sent from London upon this occasion; and in the sinister document containing them we may find the embodiment of that deeply seated antipathy of race, which served Lord Durham, in our own day, with a pretext for revoking the constitution of 1791, and effecting the reunion of all Canada under one government; viz., an intent to swamp the French-Canadians by means of a British majority.

What remained undismembered of the country was subjected to a new division; abridged Canada being parted into two districts, separated by the rivers St. Maurice and St. François. As there were no protestants at Three Rivers to make magistrates of, that circumscription was annexed to those two districts, to enable justices of the peace resident in Montreal and Quebec to hold quarterly sessions in the former. The whole legal administration was now remodelled, and called "the court of king's bench;" a subordinate tribunal was also created, for the adjudication of petty causes, denominated "the court of common pleas": each of these tribunals being reputed as of similar constitution to the supreme courts of the same name in England; and both were bound to render decisions based on the laws and practice of England: except as regarded pending suits between Canadians, commenced before October 1, 1764. The judges for those courts were nominated by a majority of the councillors, but their appointment was subjected to royal confirmation or disapproval. The executive council itself could sit as a court of appeal from decisions passed in the king's bench and common pleas; and the awards of the council were, in turn, liable to revision in the sovereign's privy-council, which thus judged in the last resort.

The Canadians, to a man, repudiated the jurisprudence thus imposed upon them. In effect, English legislation has only served to favour over-centralization of landed estate in the mother country. The executive council, which was the medium employed in making those changes, discussed and passed a great number of ordinances:

such as, regulations regarding the currency and bills of exchange; with others for obliging landlords to register the original titles to their estates; for disallowing the right of any one to leave the colony without official permission; for fixing the period of majority (coming of age); for defining the crimes of high treason and felony; for regulating the police, &c.

There was a project, at this time, for authorising a great lottery with 10,000 tickets, representing an aggregate value of £20,000, for re-constructing Quebec cathedral, which was destroyed during the siege of that city. By way of interesting the leading notables of Britain in the project, it was proposed to send copies of this lottery-scheme to the lords of the treasury, the prelates of Canterbury and London, also to the Bible Society.* Such a proposal intimated, clearly enough, an intent to appropriate (for secular or protestant uses), Canadian church property. The Board of Trade nominated, at the same time, a Mr. Kneller, as administrator of the estates of the Jesuits.

The people of the colony were vigilantly observed, their comings and goings seeming to be subjects for distrust; but the colonial authorities did not venture to execute rigid law upon them, such as pressing the test oaths, or the yielding up of defensive arms, &c.

Ever since the death of M. de Pontbriant, the episcopal throne of Quebec see had remained vacant. When hostilities ceased, the grand-vicar and clergy applied to General Murray, demanding that the bishop and his chapter should be invested with the like rights possessed by bishops and chapters in all catholic countries. Murray commended this application to the favourable attention of the British ministry; and in 1763, sent his secretary, M. Cramahé, to London, to sustain the application. In 1765, all the documents relative to this subject were submitted for consideration to the attorney and solicitors general for the time, Sir F. Norton and Sir W. de Grey, who expressed their opinion (*in limine*), that, keeping in view the stipulation in the treaty of 1763 regarding the church of Canada, the catholics of that (now British colony) were not liable to the operation of the dis-

---

* There was no "Bible Society" in existence at that time; nor for forty years afterwards, namely, till A. D. 1803-4.—B.

abilities, imposed by statutory law, on their co-religionists in Great Britain. During the latter year the chapter assembled and elected as their bishop M. de Montgolfier, superior of the Seminary of St. Sulpice at Montreal; but the government, taking exception to this nomination—perhaps because the nominee was *too French* at heart—Montgolfier declined the charge, by a formal renunciation, made at Quebec, in 1764. He designated, at the same time, M. Briand, a Breton by birth, one of the canons and grand-vicar of the diocese, to fill the vacant episcopal chair. M. Briand was elected in 1764; and; that same year, repaired to London. In 1764, he received, with the concurrence of George III, his bulls of investiture from Pope Clement XIII, and was consecrated in Paris as bishop; upon which, he returned to Quebec.

Early in 1765, Messrs. Amiot and Boisseau, having demanded for certain of their compatriots permission to assemble together, the executive council consented; but on condition that two of its own members should be present, with power to dissolve such assemblies if they thought fit; and that no concourse should be holden anywhere but in Quebec. In 1766, a similar demand, made by M. Hertel de Rouville, in name of the seigneurs of Montreal, was accorded with the like restrictions. At a meeting which once took place in Montreal city, Governor Burton, who had not been previously consulted, wrote premptorily to the magistrates about the affair; who thereupon informed him that all had been done in due order. This assurance, however, did not quite dispel the general's uneasiness; as he observed in rejoinder, " In case you should stand in need of (my) assistance, I am ready to supply it."

There was small cause for wonder, that under such a system of tyranny and overturnings, its agents should tremble lest the prostrate victims might desperately rise up against it. An unquiet feeling began, in fact, to take possession of the public mind; presently, murmurs deep if not loud supervened, and were currently breathed. Even those who knew the Canadians to be so submissive at all times to authority, began to have fears as to what might result from the reigning discontent; especially when at length they heard the acts of the government loudly censured, with a freedom never known before. If General Murray were a stern, he was also an honorable and good-hearted man: he loved such Canadians as were docile under his sway, with the affection that a veteran bears to his faithfullest soldiers; and suchlike were the *habitants*, so brave in war, yet so gentle-tempered in times of peace. A soldier-like sympathy inspired him with favour for those who had bravely fought him in the battle-field; their depressed situation too, under domineering English masters, being not unlike that of the mountaineers of his native Scotland, ever so faithful to their princes; this similarity strengthened his partiality for a race akin to his own in that regard. In order to relieve the general anxiety of mind, Governor Murray issued a proclamation, intimating, that in all legal process affecting the tenure of land and successions to property, the laws and customs which had been in use under the French domination were to be followed. This was reverting at once to legality; for if the British ministry had a right to alter the laws of the country without consulting the wishes of its people, it could only be done (at worst) by an act of parliament: a consideration which afterwards caused attorney-general Masères to observe, while adverting to the consequents of the invasion of England by William the Norman, and to the conquest of Wales by Edward I, that the English laws had never been *legally* introduced to Canada; seeing that king and parliament together, but not the king alone, could exert rightful legislatorial power over that colony: hence it followed, that (the British parliament having as yet taken no part in the matter) the accustomed French laws must be recognized as existent *de jure*, if abolished or in abeyance *de facto*.

The governor-general, however, was trammelled in his beneficent tendencies by a knot of resident functionaries, some of whose acts made him often ashamed of the administration he was understood to guide. A crowd of adventurers, veteran intriguers, great men's menials turned adrift, &c., came in the train of the British soldiery, and swarmed after the capitulation of Montreal; as we learn, from Murray's own despatches, that broken-down merchants, tradesmen of bad repute, with blackleg taverners, chiefly made up the band of Brito-Canadians earliest in the field of promise. Disrespectability was the rule, good character and probity of conduct were exceptional qualities among them.* Then, as respected the government,

---

* This depreciating account of the composition of the earlier immigrations, must be taken with a due allowance of errors excepted. We

all its functionaries, as well as the judges (and even jurymen) were to be of British race and professors of some protestant faith.

The first chief-justice, named Gregory, who had been let out of prison to preside on the bench, was ignorant alike of civil law and the language of the country; while the attorney-general was but indifferently fitted for his place. The power of nominating to the situations, of provincial secretary, of council recorder, of registrar, of provost marshal [?], was given to favourites, who set them up for sale to the highest bidder!

The governor was soon constrained to suspend from the exercise of his functions the chief-justice, and to send him back to England. A garrison-surgeon and a half-pay officer (M. Mabane and Captain Fraser) sat as judges in the court of common pleas. As these gentlemen had other employments also, their conjoint emoluments were necessarily very considerable.

Murray, disgusted with his charge, could not contain himself when expressing his sentiments regarding such a state of things to the British ministry. "When it had been decided to reconstitute civil government here," wrote he, " we were obliged to choose magistrates and select jurymen out of a community composed of some 400 or 500 traders, artisans, and husbandmen, whose ignorance unfits them therefor, and causes them to be despised. It it not to be expected that such persons can help being intoxicated with the powers which have been, unexpectedly even by themselves, put into their hands; or that they will not hasten to manifest (in their peculiar way) how skilful they are in exercising it! They cherish a vulgar hatred for the Canadian noblesse, on account of their titles to public honour and respect; and they detest other colonists, be-

---

have drawn the following more favourable notice of some of the incomers, from one of our best statistical authorities :—

" A wide field was now opened for the attention of interest, and for the operations of avarice. Every man who had credit with the ministers at home, or influence with the governors in the colonies, ran for the prize of American territory. And many landowners in Great Britain, of no small importance, neglected the portions of their fathers, for a portion of wilderness beyond the Atlantic." G. CHALMERS' *Estimate*, &c., p. 123.—*B*.

cause the latter have contrived to elude the illegal oppression to which it was intended to subject them."

Notwithstanding large concessions made to the pretensions of those New Colonists,* they were not yet satisfied: they aimed at having a representative government, in order to possess, in all their fullness, those native rights which inhered to their quality as Britons, and which they had a right to vindicate, they asserted, wherever the union flag waved over their heads,—not forgetting to denounce the colonial government as despotic. Nevertheless, while thus reclaiming political franchises for themselves, they refused to extend them to their fellow-colonists of French race. Men of British blood alone were fit to elect or be elected! They insisted, also, that English law and practice were (or ought to be) as valid in Quebec as in London; and considered the recognition of Canadian catholicity, in an article of the treaty of 1763, as one of those illusory conventions which might be violated without dishonour. In a word, they willed that Canada should be no better treated than Ireland was by the Anglo-Normans, as described by M. de Beaumont.

In order to conform to the instructions given him, Murray convoked, merely as a formality however, a representative assembly; for he knew, beforehand, that the Canadians, as catholics, would refuse to take the test; and as it had been decided that a chamber entirely protestant would not be recognized, the project fell to the ground. Leading British residents, none the less, got up accusations against the governor and council, which they transmitted to London; and also excited dissensions in the colony itself, leading to disorders in the capital and other towns. Murray was charged with showing too much partiality for the military; while the Canada traders in London presented a petition to the Board of Trade and Plantations, against his administration, and asking for an elective assembly. Matters were carried to such a length in opposition to Murray, that the home government was forced to recal him. This act was really more owing to the sympathy he seemed to show for the Canadians, than to any real abuse of his powers.

---

* The British residents called themselves discriminatingly the "old colonists," and the French-Canadians the " new colonists."—B.

In his reply to a complimentary address presented to him by the members of council at his deparure, he "hoped the government of his successor would not be disturbed by a feeling of resentment against the authors of the odious calumnies that had been heaped on his own." When he reached London, he had only to show the estimate he drew up, in the year 1765, of the population of Canada, which comprised scarcely 500 protestants in all (there being but 36 families of them residing outside the town), to convince the home authorities of the impossibility there would be to exclude the representatives of nearly 70,000 catholics. At that time, according to official returns, there were only 136 protestants in the whole district of Montreal. A committee of privy council, appointed to investigate the charges against Murray, absolved him entirely; but Canada was to know him no more.

The protestant party in the colony (notwithstanding the ruling of Maseres), still insisted that the penality oppressing the Catholics of the three kingdoms should be extended to their Canadian co-religionists. Noting the close attachment of the latter to their faith, its more cautelous enemies in Britain wished to temporise, all the more surely to bring about its abolition. Thus an English university * proposed the following adverse tactics: " Never declaim against the pope or catholicity, but undermine the latter secretly; engage catholic females to marry protestant males; never hold disputations with Romish churchmen, and beware of controversy with the Jesuits and Sulpicians; delay pressing oaths of conformity upon the colonists; cause the bishop to lead a life of penury; foment dissidences between him and the clergy; exclude any European priest from the episcopal seat; discourage those inhabitants who have worthiness in them, from keeping up the old ideas; if a clerical college be retained, climinate from it the Jesuits and Sulpicians; also, all Europeans and their pupils, in order that, no longer having foreign

---

* There were but two universities in England at that time,—those of Oxford and Cambridge. It would not have been difficult to point out, were the accusation found to be a true bill, in which of the two it was this web of protestant jesuitry was woven. The author not having done so, we beg his leave to insinuate, that the university in question (and very much in question too) must have been located in some cloudy region of "Utopia," *i. e.*, the land of *No-where.*—B.

scholastic support, Canadian Romanism may be buried in its own ruins; hold up to ridicule those religious ceremonies which most impress the public mind; prevent or obstruct catechising; caress those clergymen who neglect their flocks, and allure such persons into dissipation, and raise in their minds a disgust at hearing confessions; cry up parish priests who live luxuriously, who maintain a good table, drive about, and frequent loose society; excuse the intemperance of such, induce them to break their vow of celibacy, devised as that was to impose on the simple; finally, expose all (earnest) preachers to ridicule."

The garrison chaplain of Quebec, who ministered to the protestants of that city, speaking more plainly than had been done before, formally advised the executive council to take possession of the temporalities of the see for the bishop of London, so as to be enjoyed by the latter and his successors. With respect to the estates of the religious communities, the lords of the treasury, whose regards were always attracted by this bait, wrote to receiver-general Mills, as part of their Instructions for the year 1765: "seeing that the lands of these societies, particularly those of the Jesuits, were being united, or were about to be united, to the crown domains, you are to strive, by means of an arrangement with the parties interested in them, to enter into possession thereof in name of his Majesty; at the same time, however, granting to those parties such annuities as you shall judge proper; and you are to see that the estates in question are not transferred, and so be lost to the crown, by sequestration or alienation."

Before governor Murray left Canada, the savages of the western territory showed signs of a general rising against the whites. Scarcely had the French domination ceased in Canada, when the Indians felt the truth of an observation often made to them, that they would lose their political importance and independence as soon as they had to deal with one European nation only. Ponthiac, an Ottawa chief, noted for his bravery, warlike talents, and deadly enmity to the British, whom he had desperately fought against during the last war, projected their expulsion from the upper lake regions; and brought into his scheme, besides the Ottawas, the Hurons, Chippawas, Pouatatamis, and other tribes, whom the British had neglected to court as the French had done. He tried to capture Detroit, and blockaded it for several months. He intended that the place, once in his hands, should become the headquarters of a powerful confederation of native nations, which were to hem in the Anglo-American provinces, so that they should not overpass Niagara or the line of the Alleghanies. His allies got possession of Michilimackinac, and massacred the garrison.* Seven or eight British posts—Sandusky, St. Joseph, Miâmis, Presqu'île, Venango, &c., fell into the hands of the savages, who ravaged the Pennsylvanian and Virginian frontiers, and defeated a detachment of troops at Bloody-Bridge. Two thousand whites were slaughtered by the savages, or taken captive; as many were obliged to flee the back settlements and seek the interior. But the project of Ponthiac was too extensive for his means to realize. The confederates, beaten at Bushy-Run by colonel Bouquet, and repeatedly afterwards, had to make peace at Oswego, before the ar-

* "During the year 1763, a famous chief of the Ottawas called Pontiac by the French, after fort Michilimackinac was surrendered to the British, got possession of it by a stratagem showing the ingenuity of the man, and characteristic of the crafty nature of the Indians generally. Pontiac being an inveterate enemy of the British, his being so near the garrison ought to have put the commandant on his guard. The fort was then on the mainland, near the southern part of the peninsula. The Ottawas in the neighbourhood prepared for a great game at ball, to which the officers of the fort were invited. While engaged in play, one of the parties gradually inclined towards the fort, and the other pushed after them. The ball was once or twice thrown over the pickets, and the Indians were suffered to enter and procure it. Nearly all the garrison were present as spectators, and those on duty were alike unprepared or unsuspicious. Suddenly, the ball was again thrown into the fort, and the Indians rushed after it; but not to return this time, to resume their suspended play. Mastering the sentries, they took possession of the place, while their companions massacred every one of the garrison, with the exception of the governor, whose life was saved, much at the intercession of M. de Langlade, a Canadian gentleman, who was esteemed by the savages."—W. H. SMITH'S *Canada, &c.;* BIBAUD'S *Hist. Can.*, ii, 17-18. The former relates the event, without assigning a date, and makes a French garrison to be the victims of Pontiac's guile; the latter assigns the above date, which, if correct, proves that the garrison must have been British; for M. de Vaudreuil, before he left Canada, sent orders to Belestre, the last French commandant of the fort, to give it up to Major Rogers, a partisan officer, of some note in his day.—*B.*

rival of 600 Canadians, sent by general Murray to the relief of
the French settlers at Detroit. Ponthiac retired, with his family,
into the wilderness. In 1769, he came among the Illinois: at
that time, there was much agitation among the aborigines. The
British suspecting the intents of Ponthiac, a bush-ranger, named
Williamson, caused that chief to be assassinated, in the forest of
Cahokia, opposite Saint-Louis.

It was during Murray's administration, that the first printing-
press used in Canada was imported, and that the publication of
the earliest newspaper known to it began. No. 1 of the *Quebec
Gazette*, with matter half French half English, appeared June 21,
1764. This journal, started with a subscription-list of only 150
names, was, for a long time, a repertory of events merely, without political comments, which as the printers of it were commanded
to abstain from, there cannot be obtained, in searching its early
files, even a glimpse of public opinion during the remainder of the
18th century.

Meanwhile the British parliament passed a fiscal measure sure to
cause an intense sensation among the old colonists, and which became the means of arming the people of the Anglo-American provinces against their mother country. Under a pretext that the
late war had obliged the British people to contract great debts, the
provincials were to be taxed without their consent; and a stamp-
duty, with other imposts, were enacted in regard of all the colonists of
British America. The whole thirteen provinces protested against
the new tax. The Canadians and Nova Scotians remained passive
upon the occasion.

When this matter took a still more serious a turn, the British ministry was forced to follow less oppressive courses in Canada. The
instructions sent for its governance were modified, and the chief men
in place were changed for other functionaries. In 1766, Brigadier-
general Carleton was appointed lieutenant-governor, along with a
new chief justice (Hay), and a new attorney-general (Maseres); the
latter was descended from a Huguenot family settled in England.
Carleton was Murray's successor; but major Irving, after the latter's departure, performed *ad interim* the gubernatorial duties.
One of Carleton's earliest official acts was to erase Irving's name
from the council roll, and that of surgeon Mabane, another coun-

cillor favoured by Murray. One Gluck, recorder in the common pleas, was cashiered for extortion about the same time. These changes were of good augury.

For a long time ere the present, the Canadians had been complaining to the British home authorities; but nothing short of an apprehension of what might betide from the serious troubles arising in the neighbouring colonies would have caused British ministers to deviate from the usual polity pursued in Canada. They now transmitted the memorials of the Canadians to the Board of Trade, by which these were submitted to the attorney-general (Yorke) and the solicitor-general (De Grey). Pending official reports thereupon, the governmental ordinance of 1764 was disclaimed by an order of privy council, and another was substituted giving the Canadians a right to act as jurymen in specified cases; also allowing Canadian advocates to plead, under certain restrictions.

The report of the above-mentioned English crown-lawyers was presented in April 1766. The writers admitted the defectiveness of the system of 1764, and imputed the evils resultant therefrom to two chief causes: namely, 1. administration of justice in new forms and a foreign language, without the concurrence of the Gallic Canadians, who in the courts understood neither the pleas advanced, nor the decisions pronounced—the judges and barristers not speaking French, and most clients not comprehending English. This was found oppressive; as parties to suits were exposed to the evil chances of ignorance and corruption, or, what was nearly tantamount, they had no confidence in the enlightenment and probity of the English judges and practitioners. 2. The alarm caused by the interpretation given to the proclamation of 1763, an interpretation which induced a belief that the intention of the government was to abolish the established jurisprudence of the colony. The [apparent] reason for abolishing which was not so much to extend the [supposed] advantages of English laws to the Canadians, or to protect more efficaciously their persons, property, and franchises, as to impose upon them, without any necessity therefor, arbitrary and novel rules, which would tend to confound and subvert rights instead of supporting them.

Messrs. Yorke and De Grey also expressed their general approval of a new system of judicature proposed by the lords commissioners, one point being excepted. The latter wished to divide the province into three districts, and to establish a court of chancery, composed of the governor and his council; which chancery should also be a court of appeal, its decisions being liable to revision by the privy council of the king. Second, a supreme court, composed of a chief-justice and three puisne judges, one of them, at least to be cognizant of the French language and laws; it being held incumbent on all of them to confer, from time to time, with the most able Canadian advocates, in order to inform themselves of the olden jurisprudence.

After recommending the nomination of some Canadians to the magistracy, the reporters, on the understanding that the laws of England were to be retained, observed, "It is a maxim of the law of nations, to allow the old laws of a vanquished people to subsist at least, till their conquerors substitute new, while it is oppressive and violent to change, suddenly, the laws of any country; hence wise conquerors, after having provided for the material security of their acquisitions, will innovate slowly, and let their new subjects retain all such usages as are indifferent in their nature, especially those which regard the rights of property. In the case of Canada, cautious policy is especially needed, it being a great country, long in possession of French colonists and improved by them......We cannot introduce among them, at one stroke, English laws of property, with its forms of conveyancing, alienation, fines, its modes of shaping deeds and interpreting contracts, or our laws of succession, without committing manifest wrong, or at least occasioning the greatest confusion. Englishmen, who buy property in Canada, both can and should conform themselves to the laws regarding it therein, even as they already conform, in other parts of the empire outside of England, to local law and practice. English judges sent to Canada may easily, with the help of able Canadian practitioners, become acquainted with its laws, and be guided in their decisions by the legal practice they find established: just as, in the Channel Islands, our judges decide according to the legislation of Normandy." Finally, the reporters advised that the Gallo-Canadian laws, for civil procedure, should be restored, and proposed that the judges should make rules for the guidance of all the functionaries in the various courts.

Ignoring the considerations of enlightened policy upon which the renderings of the crown-lawyers were founded, their recommendations were not adopted. The home government, next year, directed Carleton to form a commission of inquiry regarding the administration of justice in the colony. A prolonged investigation took place, which merely served to confirm what was already too apparent,—the incurable faultiness of the existing system; the most able lawyer not being able to find his way out of a labyrinth of legal uncertainty and perplexed practice. The proposals for curing the evil only tended to embarrass the authorities who had the power of applying a remedy. The favourite idea always recurred of dividing the province into three districts. It was proposed to appoint, in each of those an English chief judge along with a Canadian assistant-judge, to explain the law, but not to decide it; a sheriff, and a public prosecutor. Several expedients were adduced for putting an end to the prevailing incertitude, in legal practice; but the suggestors did not venture to intimate a distinct preference for either English or French jurisprudence *per se*. Thus it was proposed, either to compile a new code, and abolish both English and French legism; or to restore the latter, yet to engraft upon it those parts of English criminal law the most favourable to personal freedom; or, lastly, to establish the laws of England, with exceptional leanings toward the accustomed laws and usages among the Gallo-Canadians. The governor-general did not recommend any of those expedients, in his report to the ministry, but proposed the adoption of a system more conformable to Canadian wishes; namely, that English criminal procedure and penality should supersede French, and that the old civil laws of the colony should be restored without any modification. Chief-justice Hay and attorney-general Mascres each made a report on the subject; in which they advised the retention of all the old colonial laws concerning tenure of land, alienations, dowry, inheritance, and distribution of the property of persons dying intestate.

The whole of those reports, with their appendices, were transmitted to England. In 1770, the members of privy council, to whom they had been submitted, referred them to a special committee of their own number; which select body, after deliberating on the documents before them, and taking into consideration a report on the subject made by the lords commissioners in 1769, also petitions from the Canadians,—the committee of privy council recommended, we say, that all the papers should be placed in the hands of the king's advocate (Marriott), the attorney-general (Thurlow), and the solicitor-general (Wedderburne), with orders to compile a civil code and a criminal code, suitable to the colony's wants; hinting, that, as the governor-general was then in London, advantage should be taken of his presence to call him into council on the occasion. General Carleton, in effect, had gone to England, along with M. de Lotbinière, to be examined on the affairs of Canada; leaving M. Cramahé president of the executive council, as chief, *pro tem.*, of the colonial administration. Messrs. Hay and Maseres were also summoned to London.

The three English crown lawyers above named, two of whom became lord chancellors, finished their labours as official referees, in 1772–73. Two of the reports, severally accordant in all but minor points, arrived at a common conclusion, if by different routes; but in the third report (that of the king's advocate) a conclusion diametrically opposite was come to.

Marriott opined, that a representative assembly was unfitted for an uneducated people, "even though a jesuits' college was established among them." What the colony needed, he urged, was a legislative council, the members to be crown nominees and all protestants— not composed of catholics partly, as the Board of Trade suggested. He proposed that English criminal law and practice should be maintained; but that the use of the French language, in legal procedure, might be tolerated; also that all public acts ought to be promulgated in French as well as English. In terms of the 36th article of the Capitulation of Montreal, he admitted, that the British were bound to respect the property and laws covered by the terms employed in its stipulations: by consequence, land tenure as then existent, with everything thereunto appertaining, ought to be upholden: the silence of the Treaty of Versailles did not, inferentially, annul said article 36, because the latter formed part of a national paction concluded by the British with the people of another country, certain demands being accorded, on condition that the latter should cease all further resistance.

Yet, while thus recognizing the validity of the titles to which the Canadians trusted, Marriott declared that the British parliament * had a right to change their laws: a most illogical conclusion from the premises, and stultifying his own argument. Supposing the "*coutume* (jurisprudence) of Paris" were to be restored, Marriott was for changing its name to *coutume du Canada*, to efface from the minds of the Gallo-Canadians any lingering attachment they might otherwise cherish for their mother country; and with the same intent perhaps, he proposed to change parts of the (obnoxiously named) *coutume*, and assimilate it to English law, since all ought to tend towards *anglification* and foster protestantism. Again: if catholicism were to be admitted, *i. e.* recognized as lawfully existing, certain doctrines of it ought to be renounced or disavowed, for its professors in Canada had no superior rights to those in Britain. No catholic bishop was wanted (he thought) for the colony: the diocese could be governed by a grand-vicar, whom the cathedral chapter and the parish clergy might elect to perform episcopal functions, or an ecclesiastical superintendent [with nobody to superintend], to be nominated by the king [George III], might be vested with the faculty, but no other power, of ordaining to the priesthood. Marriott was for abolishing all the religious communities, both of males and females, as soon as their surviving members died out; their estates and revenues to be restored to the crown, and afterwards employed in educating all the young without distinction of communions; chief parochial clergy (*curés*) not to be removable at will; lastly, he would allow the chapter of Quebec to continue, although the Board of Trade wished its abolition.

The chapter, however, soon died out of itself, for all the canons remaining in the country were aged men; and the bishop nominated no others, under the pretext that there were not enough priests; that it was difficult to get them, in the parishes, to hold capitular assemblies; and that the episcopal treasury, deprived of

---

* "Parlement impérial" is the term used, here and elsewhere, by M. Garneau; but the British legislature did not become an "Imperial" parliament till Jan. 1, 1801; when the incorporating union with Ireland first came into operation.—*B*.

its best revenues by the conquest, could not bear the cost attendant on maintaining such a body. Marriott advised the keeping it up if only for the purpose of enabling the government to bestow canonries upon such priests as were zealous for British interests.

His report closed with recommendations to forbid all religious processioning in the streets; to relegate the estates of St. Sulpice seminary to the crown domain; to cause all (obligatory) church festivals to cease, except those of Good-Friday and Christmas; the tithes to be levied as then, but handed to the receiver-general for distribution in equal proportions, between the members of the protestant clergy and those of the catholic clergy who should subscribe to the doctrines of the Anglican Church. [?] In fine, Marriott's system was just that imposed on Ireland; for tyranny may be exercised in the name of God and religion, as well as on the plea of necessity. The lords-commissioners of the Board of Trade had already made the same suggestion; they adding, that the existing ecclesiastical edifices ought to accommodate all, by alternating the respective services, Anglican and Catholic: a double use of them which Marriott thought unsuitable, except for the parochial churches in the towns. General Murray had received an order, previously, to admit protestant ministers to the collation of urban benefices; but, from policy, had not put it in execution.

In the whole of his report, Marriott dropped no word, breathed no wish, for any amelioration of the lot of the Canadians: it was one continued call of proscription against their usages, their laws, their religion: his hostility being restrained, in some few particulars only, by certain rules of prudence or necessity, but which he could not help recognising for the moment; in expectancy, however, that their non-observation some day should become possible, and hence justifiable also.

Solicitor-general Wedderburne (afterwards lord-chancellor Loughborough) was guided in his report by principles of a higher and more philosophic order, and manifested far more equity and moderation in his proposals. He expatiated upon the twofold subject of the government and religion of French Canada; because, in his opinion, those being intimately connected, they were to be taken into primary account for properly determining what its future civil and criminal laws ought to be: and, while pronouncing that it would be imprudent to grant the Canadians a representative constitution, he intimated that they had rights which ought to have, but had not been respected : and that an equitable government ought to be ensured to them. " The government established after the treaty of 1763," he observed, " was neither military nor civil; it evidently was not made or meant to endure. A council ought to be formed with power to make ordinances for the proper government of the country, but not with power to impose taxes, a right which the British parliament should be bound to reserve to itself alone. Free exercise of the catholic religion ought to be allowed; but in temporal things, no potency incompatible with the sovereignty of the king or the authority of his government, ought to be allowed to interpose between rulers and ruled—such as the ecclesiastical jurisdiction of Rome. The parish clergy (*curés*) ought to be irremovable, and their collation to benefices rightly vested in the crown. Confraternities of *religieux* ought to be abolished, but communities of *religieuses* had better be tolerated." The civil code of France, and the criminal laws of England with modifications —a system of mixed judicature (almost the same as that the executive council recommended)—were approved of for Canada by Wederburne; who advised that, while the prejudices of neither the Canadians nor British immigrants should be entirely disregarded, " yet still," he added, " for policy's sake, more attention is due to the Canadian than to British immigrants, not only because the former are most numerous, but because it is not for the interest of Britain that many of her natives should settle in Canada." Finally, he urged, that " every Canadian also has a claim, in justice, to as much of his ancient laws regarding private rights, as is not inconsistent with the principles of his new government ; for, as property is by the former secured to him, which it defines, creates, and modifies, that much must be retained : otherwise property is reduced to the mere possession of what one can personally enjoy."

Attorney-general (afterwards Lord) Thurlow, although reputed to be more of a conservative than a liberal in his political opinions, and thus likely to be hostile to colonial freedom, yet showed himself to be the most generous of Britains political legists to the Canadians. Without making special recommendations in their behalf, he embodied in his report more elevated and just principles than those of any other British statesman of his day. Sustaining cogent arguments by that sage philosophy which repudiates the law of force and recognizes the claims of justice and reason, he appealed to such sympathies as human nature has for the oppressed and detestation of their oppressors, while vindicating all that was just, humane, and politic in the proposals which had been made, subsequent to the year 1764, on the subject of the form of government, the religious system, and the laws best suited for Canada.

After passing in review those schemes, and the several changes which were wished to be introduced, along with the conflicting opinions existing even upon the fundamental principles involved, he intimated, that, although he did not know how His Majesty meant to act in the matter, and consequently that he (Thurlow) was not warranted to make any special proposition, yet he would not quite abstain from indicating the course which ought to be followed, if the accustomed legislation of Canada were to be properly dealt with. He reasoned thus:—

"The Canadians seem to have been strictly entitled by the *jus gentium* to their property, as they possessed it upon the capitulation and treaty of peace, together with all its qualities and incidents, by tenure or otherwise, and also to their personal liberty; for both which they were to expect your Majesty's gracious protection.

"It seems a necessary consequence that all those laws by which that property was created, defined, and secured must be continued to them. To introduce any other, as Mr. Yorke and Mr. De Grey emphatically expressed it, tends to confound and subvert rights, instead of supporting them.

"When certain forms of civil justice have long been established, people have had frequent occasions to feel themselves, and observe in others, the actual coercion of the law in matters of debt and other engagements in dealings, and also in the recompense for all sorts of wrongs. The force of these examples goes still further, and stamps an impression on the current opinion of men and puts an actual check on their dealings; and those who never heard of the examples or the laws which produced them, yet acquire a kind of traditional knowledge of the legal effects and consequences of their transactions, sufficient, and withal absolutely necessary, for the common affairs of private life. It is easy to imagine what infinite disturbance it would create, to introduce new and unknown measures of justice, doubt and uncertainty in each transaction, with attendant disappointment or loss for consequences.

"The same kind of observation applies with still greater force against a change of the criminal law, in proportion as the examples are more striking and the consequences more important. The general consternation which must follow upon the circumstance of being suddenly subjected to a new system of criminal law, cannot soon be appeased by the looseness or mildness of the code.

"From these observations, I draw it as a consequence that new subjects acquired by conquest have a right to expect from the benignity and justice of their conqueror the continuance of all their old laws, and they seem to have no less reason to expect it from his wisdom. It must, I think, be the interest of the conqueror to leave his new subjects in the utmost degree of private tranquillity and personal security, and in the fullest persuasion of their reality, without introducing needless occasion of complaint and displeasure, and disrespect for their own sovereign. He seems, also, to provide better for the public peace and order, by leaving them in the habit of obedience to their accustomed laws, than by undertaking the harsher task of compelling a new obedience to laws unheard of before. And if the old system happens to be more perfect than anything which invention can hope to substitute on the sudden, the scale sinks quite down in its favour."

Thurlow said in conclusion: "Although the foregoing observations should be thought just, as a general idea, yet circumstances may be supposed under which it would admit some exceptions and qualifications. The conqueror succeeded to the *sovereignty* in a title at least as full and strong as the conquered can set up to their private rights and ancient usages. Hence we infer the legality of every change in the form of government which the conqueror finds *essentially necessary* to establish his sovereign authority and assure the obedience of his subjects. This might possibly produce some alteration in the laws, especially those which relate to crimes against the state, religion, revenue, and other articles of police, and in the form of magistracy. But it would also follow, that such a change should not be made without some such actual and cogent necessity, which real wisdom could not overlook or neglect; not that ideal necessity which ingenious speculation may always create by possible supposition, remote inference, and forced argument; not the necessity of assimilating a conquered country, in the articles of law and government, to the metropolitan state, or to the older provinces which other accidents attached to the empire, for the sake of creating a harmony and uniformity in the several parts of that empire, unattainable, and, as I think, useless if it could be attained: not the necessity of stripping from a lawyer's argument all resort to the learned decisions of the Parliament of Paris, for fear of keeping up the historical idea of the origin of foreign laws: not the necessity of gratifying the unprincipled and impracticable expectations of those few among your Majesty's subjects * who may accidentally resort thither and expect to find in force the several laws of all the different places from which they came; nor, according to my simple judgment, does any species of necessity exist, that I have heard urged, for abolishing the laws and government of Canada." In presence of the troubles in the thirteen Anglo-American provinces, this reporter's cogent representations and sarcastic logic powerfully aided the Canadian cause.

The king's privy council, by the year 1773, had placed before it all these reports, &c. During nine years, Britain had been casting about, on all sides, for means of justification, in the eyes of other nations, and to satisfy the public conscience, for abolishing the laws and religion which she had sworn, in treaties, to maintain for the Canadians. The justice due to them, as pointed out by Thurlow, would have had no effective recognition, and Canada would have passed under the yoke of a handful of aliens, with a religion and language, laws, and usages differing in toto from those of its people, but for the dawnings of the

---

* Therefore merely intimated here, that the expectations of the parties alluded to were founded on no reasonable basis; whereas, by mistranslating his actual words thus, "les espérances impossibles de cette poignée d'Anglais *dépourvus de tout principe*," M. Garneau has put a gloss upon them of an unfair and even slanderous character.—*B*.

American revolts. The British government deferred, till the year 1774, yielding the points at issue; and it may be said that the revolution which saved the freedom of the United States, obliged Great Britain to leave the Canadians the enjoyment of their institutions and laws; in other words, to act justly by them, in order to be able to retain for herself at least one province in the New World.

For some time previously, the patience of the natives and the violence of the English party of Canadian residents,—among the latter of whom Americanism was not quite absent,—formed a contrast which called up serious reflection in the British ministerial mind. The British filled all our municipal offices; and the magistrates of Montreal, as turbulent as the rest of their compatriots, had been summoned to appear before the governor and executive council at Quebec, to answer certain accusations made against them. One of them, named Walker, far from excusing himself, protested against the whole proceeding, so much in the American style, that the colonial attorney-general (Suckling) characterised his audacity as criminal.

The Canadians, on their side, never slackened in their efforts to escape from the oppression under which they groaned. They complained to the government against the tyrannical and odious modes of corporation rule in Montreal. The executive council was constrained to write (July 12, 1769), to the magistrates of Montreal district, that it appeared, from facts, become too notorious to be denied, that the king's subjects generally, the French-Canadians more especially, were made the daily objects of suffering and oppression to an intolerable extent, and which, acting for the public interest, the government could no longer tolerate. A multitude of abuses were attributed to those magistrates; for example, they were accused of "circulating papers in the different parishes signed by only one justice of the peace, to be filled up afterwards, under the form of writs, summons, arrests, taking property in execution, or other purposes, according to the circumstances of each case; the parties entrusted with serving such irregular documents not being proper officers: a practice so illegal in itself, so pernicious in its consequences, and so dishonouring to the magistrates who authorized it, that the governor and council were unwilling to believe that such practices could exist, till the proofs brought forward left no room for doubt about the matter."

The governor directed a committee of council to make an inquest on the subject; which reported, Sept. 11, 1769, that the unduly extensive powers over real estate granted to justices of the peace by the ordinance of 1764, had been exercised in an arbitrary and oppressive manner, especially in Montreal district; that the magistrates thereof had exceeded their powers in many cases, and taken upon themselves a jurisdiction not assigned them by the royal will, and never entrusted to any tribunal judging summarily; that one magistrate, in particular, had assumed an authority conferred only upon a quorum of three justices sitting in quarter sessions; that, owing to an omission in decreeing, the magistrates exercised a dangerous authority, the result of which had been to fill the prison with the unfortunate, and bring their families to want. Finally, that the authority arrogated by those magistrates of selling landed estate at the lowest price, or else arbitrarily incarcerating debtors when insolvent, were acts of the most oppressive nature.

The committee of council recommended that the portion of the ordinance of 1764 which gave justices of peace the right of deciding questions affecting real estate, should be abrogated; that each justice of the common pleas should sit and adjudge in cases when the *chose* litigated did not exceed £10 sterling value; lastly, that no writ of bodily caption or of seizure and sale, should take effect in any case where the amount of debt and costs, collectively, did not exceed 40 piastres.

A time was arriving when the English government, better informed of the true interests of Great Britain, was about to announce a change of policy and make known the course it intended to follow in the affairs of Canada. The disputes with the New-Englanders and other provincials becoming more violent daily, this circumstance became a most urgent reason for dealing more tenderly with the Canadians. The governor-general favoured that course of action; he believed that the surest means for acquiring the confidence of our race was, to restore French jurisprudence. He had often evinced a desire that the *Coutume de Paris* should be regularized, and reduced to a form better suited to the colony's wants. In this view, he now called in aid several native practitioners, such as Messrs. Cugnet (seigneur de St. Etienne), Juchereau, Pressard, and others, who were charged with the difficult task. Their labours having been revised, in England, by Marriott, Thurlow, and Wedderburne, were published in duplicate (French and English), under this title: " Abstract of those parts of the [juridical] customs of the viscounty and provostship of Paris, which were received and practised in the province of Quebec in the time of the French government; drawn up, by a select committee of Canadian gentlemen well skilled in the laws of France and that province, by desire of the Hon. Guy Carleton, Esq., captain-general and governor-in-chief of the said province. London: 1773."

The ultra-party for Canadian proscription were furious on being made aware of the new polity of the home government, and set up loud cries against it. Maseres, who returned to London, three or four years previously,* and was appointed a judge in exchequer, became the confidant and agent of this party. He, whom the Canadians had regarded as one of their protectors when he first came among them; this man, descended from a family which religious fanaticism had proscribed in France, consented to become, like Marriott, an advocate of the Canadian proscriptionists in his adopted country; and, in our affairs, played a double part which history has not yet cleared up. On one hand, in a report on Canadian matters published while their regulation was pending, he made a favourable review of the French laws; and during interviews with those charged to press their restitution, he defended the Canadian cause (according to Du Calvet) with great warmth; on the other hand, among numerous papers printed under his direction, forming several volumes, if he did not manifest entire hostility to our civil and religious institutions, he showed little zeal for the preservation of those

---

* Canadian Attorney-general Mascres did not leave finally till 1773, the year when he was appointed cursitor baron of the court of exchequer. He died at Reigate in Surrey, May 19, 1824, aged 92 and some months.—B.

conditions which seemed so essential to their well-being. Among other contradictions, one party, seeking for a solution of this enigma in his voluminous writings, and especially in the "Canadian Freeholder," may think that he wished to lead the fanatics whom he served—by a chain of reasonings which they did not see the end of, but by which they could not help being bound—to a conclusion often the opposite of that they wished to arrive at: while another party can only see, in his contradictions, the underhand dealings of an intriguer or a traitor.* However this may be, Maseres informed those persons whose representative he was [?] of the coming decisions of the home government. At this news, noting the turn affairs were taking, and learning the king's desire to attach the Canadians to his rule while the contest for independence was preparing in America, the protestant party in Canada thought the time was come for making vigorous de-

* The memory of Francis Maseres is still fragrant in England; thus it will be something novel for the few survivors among the many who knew and honoured him while living, to find him thus stigmatized as a double-dealer, and even denounced as a TRAITOR! While reproducing the French passage, in Saxon vernacular, we cannot help expressing some surprise that any respectable author, candidly writing as he would wish to be written of, should deliberately or heedlessly build so heavy a charge on such light foundations against one of the highest-minded legists of his age and country,—against the intimate friend and earnest coadjutor of Sir Samuel Romilly, that other enlightened and most philanthropic of all legislators (in whose veins, too, as in Maseres' there circulated the best blood of two noble races); in disparagement, we say, of Baron Maseres, the friend of the genial-minded Charles Lamb, and patron of the great-hearted Thomas Noon Talfourd, names united in life and death, both "to England's memory dear." No! we cannot believe that the man venerated in life by such as these, was or could be a "traitor;" or even would condescend to be the sordid agent of any selfish party.

Baron Maseres had the reputation, which no such "railing accusation" as the above is likely to impair, of being a single-hearted and self-denying as well as a most accomplished man. He spent his inherited fortune and acquired income, mostly in acts of public utility and private kindness. His munificence, in both regards, seemed, in fact, to know no bounds, as the present writer has been assured by some who had personal experience of his worth. A regard for justice to the memory of the great and good departed has alone dictated these lines.—*B*.

VOL. II—X

monstrations, and demanding at last the fulfilment of the promises, made in 1763, of constituting a representative government in the colony. In this view, several meetings were called, at the first of which forty persons attended. The associators nominated two committees of their body, one for Quebec, the other for Montreal; and they invited the French-Canadians to join with them in obtaining the boon desiderated. But the English ultra party used dissimulation, on the capital point of religion, in its proceedings. The representative assembly, convoked by General Murray in 1764, never acted, because the catholic deputies would not subscribe the oath of abjuration, and persons otherwise eligible as members for another, feared that the same test would be applied again : thus subjecting them virtually to Anglican political ostracism. As in the petition to the crown for calling a free assembly, nothing was said in the foregoing regard. The catholics, cognizant as they were of protestant wishes although not expressed, demanded that any memorial they were willing to subscribe should embody a request for catholics as well as protestant deputies being called to sit in the proposed colonial parliament. The petitioners, thus forced to intimate their intents, refused to join in the demand ; and it was owing to this refusal that the Canadians who really desired to see a representative government established, generally if not universally declined to proceed any further in the matter. Some few, perhaps, would have concurred ; but most others absolutely refused, persuaded as they now were, more than ever, that the aim of the chief petitioners was to maintain the principle of exclusion, while yet profiting by the subscription of catholic names : a persuasion which the events justified, since Maseres, acting afterwards in name of the same party, opposed himself to the admission of catholics into the legislative council established by the act of 1774.*

---

* This assumption is illogical, and, tried by the rules of constitutional law, involves a direct *non sequitur*. The choice of a catholic, made by catholics, for their representative, is an act which British legislation, either home or colonial, does not, cannot prevent; but the selection of catholic members for a deliberative and executive council, by a *protestant* government, is a measure of a different, and would be considered by many (*was* by Maseres, perhaps) of a compromising character.—B.

After catholic refusals, the protestants addressed memorials to M. Cramahé, lieutenant-governor,* asking him to convoke an assembly of representatives. He replied, that the demand was of too important a nature for him or the council to concede; but he would transmit it to those members of the British cabinet who took charge of colonial affairs. The protestants, obliged to act without catholic aid, drew up a petition, on their own behalf, in the matter, and sent it to London, for presentation to the king. It bore 148 signatures only; two of the subscribers being Canadian-born protestants; and it demanded, in general terms, the convocation of a representative assembly. The petitioners, at the same time, addressed a memorial to Lord Dartmouth, colonial secretary, asking his influence in their favour; and intimating that the colonial administration passed ordinances opposed (in principle) to the law of England; that the country lacked protestant ministers; that the Quebec Seminary had opened classes for the education of the young; and that (more alarming still!) only catholic teachers were employed therein. These remonstrants wrote, also, to the chief merchants of London, to engage them to take up the cause pleaded for; while in the province itself, councillor Finlay was so strong for *anglification*, that, some years afterwards (1782), he proposed to establish English schools in the different parishes, and to prohibit the use of French in the law courts after a certain term of years.

Meanwhile, in presence of such hostility among the English colonists against the catholics, the British ministry did not venture to give a representative assembly to Canada. For the moment, they limited the mutations in contemplation to a legislative council, to be nominated by the king. Then Maseres suggested that it should be composed of 31 irremoveable members; that it should assemble only after public convocation; proposing to allow the members to initiate laws, and to vote at discretion, but without a right to impose taxes. Lastly, to admit into it protestants only.

* Mr. Cramahé being, not lieut.-governor, as we have seen, but merely *locum tenens* during the absence of Sir Guy Carleton, it was strangely absurd to proffer such a request to one who, even if he had been the chief functionary whose place he temporarily filled, had no power to grant it.—*B.*

While the protestant party thus demanded bondage for the catholics, the latter never ceased trying to remove English prejudices against them; prejudices which their enemies sought ever to envenom by their writings and discourses. They also had their eyes directed to what was passing in the neighbouring provinces. They could judge correctly of their situation and of the mother country's American interests, as is proved in a Memoir cited in the Introduction to this work. That production exposed, with great force of logic, that if Britain were anxious to keep Canada, she ought to accord to its people all the rights of freemen; that she ought to favour its religion, and not to undermine it by a destructive system of exclusiveness; and that there was no real religious liberty for catholics, if, in order to enjoy secular franchizes, they were obliged to renounce or tamper with their faith.

A number of French-Canadians, on their part, held meetings; and, December 1773, signed a petition to the king, asking for the restitution of their ancient laws, and claiming the rights and privileges of other British subjects. This demand, which passed for an expression of the sentiments of a majority of the Gallo-Canadians, yet was subscribed only by a few of the seigneurs and some burgesses of the towns. There is reason to believe that the clergy concurred in the views of the petitioners, although, as is their wont, if they did make similar applications, they made them apart. The masses did not stir at all in the business; and a belief (once current) that certain remonstrances then made in their name were actually theirs, is quite unfounded: they made no demonstrations whatever. In the depth of their distrust, they believed, with reason, that they would obtain no concessions from Britain; since the whig or liberal party—although that which, through its parliamentary leaders, Britons usually relied on for obtaining redress of the wrongs of the subject—was the political section which called out most loudly for the abolition of everything French in Canada, scarcely even excepting their religion. Our people, therefore, let the petitioning seigneurs and their friends demand, unsanctioned from the home government and legislature, what they would have asked for themselves; the seigneurs, on the other hand, hoping that their cause ought to meet with some sympathy in the tory party, which possessed most political power and was formed chiefly of the privileged classes in Britain, whose compeers, in some sort, our colonial feudalry were.

The language of the latter, in their address to the throne, was redolent of profound respect. *They* at least did not seek, they said, to despoil the protestant townspeople of their rights, while seeking their own freedom; *they* did not crave the proscription of an entire race, because its religion was not the same: all that the Canadians wished to enjoy, said they, like the other subjects of his Majesty, was their rights and immunities as Britons: which the common law of England, indeed, assigned them. This requisitory was accompanied with a memorial in which the applicants claimed a right to participate in all public employments, military and civil: a claim against which Maseres, in name of his party [?], had strongly pronounced. They took occasion to remark, also, that the Canadian limitary parallel of latitude 45° N., being fixed at 45 miles only from Montreal, straitened the province on that side, and deprived it of its best lands; that western Canada, embracing the regions about Detroit and Michilimackinac, ought to be restored to eastern Canada as far down as the left bank of the Mississippi, for the needs of the peltry trade; and that the Labrador seaboard ought to revert to Canada likewise, for the sake of its fisheries there. The applicants added, that the colony, through the calamities of war, famine, disease, and other adverse vicissitudes it had long to sustain, was not in a state to repay the cost of its government, and still less able to be at the charge of maintaining an elective assembly; that a numerous council, composed of British and Canadian members, would be far more suitable in present circumstances; lastly, the applicants expressed a hope that their suit would be received with all the more favour, as the Gallo-Canadians possessed more than 5-6ths of the seigniories, and almost all the copyhold lands (*terres en roture*).

The disclamation of a desire for a representative assembly, has since been made a matter of reproach against the subscribers to the above petition. But, seeing that it was impossible to obtain a legislature in which (accordant to the British constitution itself, as it then stood) catholics would be eligible for election to seats; those requisitionists acted wisely, while seeking the preservation of their religion and laws, to demand, simply, a legislative council of royal nomination. What advantage, in effect, could the Canadians have derived from an elective assembly, whence they were excluded? from a conclave sure to be composed of the declared foes of their language and all their dearest institutions; from men, in fine, who, at that very time, willed to quite deprive them of public employment; and who would, without doubt, have signalized the advent of a representative system by the proscription of all that was dearest and most venerable amongst men,—religion, law, and nationality?

The demands of the parties were met as favourably as could have been expected, considering the circumstances in which Britain was then placed; and those conceded served as bases for the law of 1774; which formed part of a plan far more vast, since it was meant for all British America. The growing power of the thirteen Anglo-American provinces was becoming more and more redoubtable to their mother country; and a due consideration of the determined antagonistic attitude they now assumed, will further develop the true motives for the unwonted concessionary policy of the British government at this time.

The lieutenant-governor, M. Cramahé, in 1772, tolerated the consecration of a coadjutor to the catholic bishop; the burden of the episcopate, in so wide a diocese, being too great for one prelate to bear: this alone constrained M. Briand to ask for a helper.— M. d'Esglis, born in Quebec A. D. 1710, was elected, by a capitulary act of the chapter, in 1770; but the difficulties attending this nomination caused a delay of two years before it took full effect. These being at length surmounted, by the aid of governor Carleton, Clement XIV, with the assent of the king, granted the requisite bulls of confirmation; and the coadjutor-elect was recognized, Jan. 22, 1772, as Bishop of Dorylæum, *in part. inf.*, with right of succession to the see of Quebec.

The chapter of Quebec became extinct soon afterwards. Its latest capitulary act took place in 1773, and the last surviving canon died in 1776.

Meantime, despite the ardent wishes of Britain for the extinction of catholicism (such is the inconstancy of all mundane things!) that the Jesuits, driven out of Paraguay, and expelled from France ever since the year 1762, still maintained their position in Canada;

and it required a papal decree, issued in 1773, to abolish that order in our country. It was not till this took place, that the British government thought of appropriating their estates; forgetting, as it did, that the Jesuits were only the depositaries of that property, since it had been given to them by the kings of France for educating the people, and the instruction of the savages, of New France.

The same administrator, M. Cramahé, also recommended, in 1773, the home government to treat the Canadians with liberality and justice in religious matters; and Lord Dartmouth promised to follow a generous course with them (in all things). By way of consoling the party bent on proscription, Maseres wrote to its members, that he "hoped the colonists would be more happy, in six or seven years' time, under the government established by the act of 1774, than under the influence of an assembly..." composed of Catholics.

It was in the year 1776, that the government, true to its first instincts, transformed the Jesuits' college into barracks for the garrison of Quebec. These good fathers had been obliged to discharge their pedagogues during the siege of 1759; and were not able to re-open the primary schools after the war was over. In 1778, the government took possession of the episcopal residence, granting in compensation, however, a yearly allowance of £150 to the bishop.

The past acts of the reigning powers (upon the whole) allowed of no favourable augury as to their dispositions in our regard for the future; and they allowed it to be understood that it was only pressure of external circumstances which constrained the British ministry to abate the rigour of their system of colonial polity, trusting to obtain thereby the good graces of the Canadians; the concessions made for special purposes being fairly attributable neither to the high principles nor enlightened liberality of those who made them.

CHAPTER II.

AMERICAN REVOLUTION.

1775.

Disputes between Great Britain and her ancient colonies.—Divisions in the British parliament regarding that subject.—Advent of Lord North to the ministry.—Troubles at Boston.—Coercive measures applied by the mother country, which seeks to gain Canada by concessions.—Petitions and counter-petitions of the Canadians and Anglo-Canadians; reason for delays in deciding between those two parties.—The Quebec Act of 1774; debates in the house of commons.—Congress of Philadelphia; it classes the Quebec Act among American grievances.—Addresses of Congress to Britain and Canada.—General Carleton arrives in Canada.—Feelings of the Canadians regarding the coming struggle.—First hostilities.—Surprise and capture of Ticonderoga, Crown-Point, and St. John's.—Civil war.—Battle of Bunker's Hill.—General Invasion of Canada by the United States troops.—Montgomery' and Arnold march on Quebec; they take Montreal and Three Rivers.—The governor re-enters the capital as a fugitive; the Americans lay siege to it.

All the American colonies were now at open war against Britain, and marching with rapid strides towards the revolution which was to achieve their independence. Ever since 1690, a year which operated changes so considerable in provincial constitutions, Britain ceased not to restrain American privileges, especially those of trade. We have seen, in another part of this work, which were the causes of those changes, and what was the character of the British colonials, whose sentiments and principles were mainly those of the English republican party in Cromwell's time. It is not to be wondered at, therefore, if we find them repelling, in 1775, the pretensions of a mother country monarchic in its constitution.

After passing the Navigation Act, to restrain the colonial trade, Britain prohibited, in 1732, the export of hats and woollens from one province to any other; in 1733, the importation of sugar, rum, and molasses was subjected to exorbitant duties; and in

1750 a law passed against erecting saw-mills, or cutting pine and fir-trees in the forests. Finally, she claimed absolute authority over all the colonies. "It would be a strange abuse of human reason to gainsay that right," said one M.P.; adding, that treason and revolt were indigenous to the New World. Public opinion in Britain, on this point, had varied according to times and circumstances. New England, not to seem as if acting under British compression, when acquiescing in any act passed by parliament, gave to each new law a local colour while promulgating it, thus giving it a semblance of American origin. The other provinces, inspired by a like feeling, had always held British pretensions in aversion; and if they submitted to them occasionally, it was because they did not think themselves potent enough to resist; but their strength was daily increasing. The total Anglo-American population, which, about A.D. 1700, numbered 262,000 souls, had risen to three millions by the year 1774. Britain, recognized sole mistress of North America by the treaty of 1763, became more exacting than ever. She determined to draw a direct revenue from the Americans, to aid her in paying the interest of her public debt, which the recent Canadian war greatly augmented, notwithstanding that the Americans had expended two and a half million pounds sterling to defray its cost. The project of taxing the latter was (long before) suggested to Walpole, who replied, " I have the whole of Old England against me; would ye that I should have New England too for my enemy?" Secretary Grenville, who cared more to keep his ministerial place than did his predecessor, proposed in parliament, against his own desire, but to please George III, a series of (declaratory) resolutions, serving as the basis of a Stamp Act; and these were adopted, without opposition, in March 1764.

All the colonists entered protests against the principles thus laid down. The austere Massachusetts-men observed, that if Britain's power to tax the colonies, at her own discretion, were recognised by them, there would result a system of oppression which would soon become insupportable; for, once let such asserted right be acknowledged, there would thenceforth be an impossibility to abolish or even modify any impost which the British might find it convenient to lay on. " We are not represented in the British parliament," they said. "What will prevent the house of commons from trying to load our shoulders with burdens, too heavy for the people at home to bear? As British subjects (no matter where located) we assert, that we are not imposable except through our own representatives."

The Anglo-Americans had other grievances besides to complain of. The presence of a standing army, in their midst, they found undesirable; augmentations of their judges' salaries they considered an insidious means of making them subservient; and the provincial governors, no longer popularly chosen, as they once were, ever manifested arbitrary dispositions.

Despite all opposition made to the taxing project, the British legislature passed a law in 1765, extending the provisions of the existing acts imposing stamp duties in Britain, to all its colonies. Franklin, resident agent in London for Massachusetts, wrote to his constituents, "The sun of liberty has set; we must trim the lamps of industry and economy." Although Franklin received from the government, about this time, a large grant of land on the Ohio,* he adhered to the most advanced opposition party in the colonies. The Americans had resolved to buy no goods from Britain; this measure caused the mercantile classes there to take part with them in the dispute. The Virginians, inspirited by Patrick Henry, began their resistance to the American stamp act. By resolutions he proposed in assembly, and which passed after long debates, it was declared that provincials were not bound to obey any taxation-laws but those passed by their own representatives; and that every man who inpugned this truth was a public enemy. As the discussion grew warmer, Henry's patriotism became more fervid. Making allusion to the evil fate of tyrants, he said, " Cæsar had his Brutus, Charles I his Cromwell; and George the Third ..." (here the orator was interrupted by cries of *Treason! treason!!* when he continued)—"...and let George the Third, I say, take warning from those examples. If such a caution smell of treason, I would fain be informed wherein it consists!" Several riots took place, but chiefly in Boston, where the people destroyed the stamp-office lately opened there. At Phila-

---

* E. B. O'CALLAGHAN: *Documentary History of New York.*

delphia, when the vessel freighted from England with stamped paper entered the port, all the other shipping displayed their colours half-mast high, in sign of mourning; and the church bells, muffled, tolled all day, as if for a funeral. Forthwith a congress of deputies, from all the provinces, met at New York, and voted petitions to the British parliament against its proceedings. Opposition became so general, that the British stamp-masters were obliged to shut up shop and return to England. Traders, lawyers, &c. met and agreed to suspend the exercise of their callings, rather than use stamps. Bales of these were seized and burnt by rioters, amid the people's huzzas. The colonial merchants dropped their trade with Britain for the time. Presently local manufactures sprang up, concurrently with a stagnation of industrial pursuits in Britain; all which greatly embarrassed the ministry, some of whom were for employing exertion against the colonists, while others inclined for temporising with existing difficulties.

The parliamentary session of 1766 opened most inauspiciously; suffering and discontent were rife even in the three kingdoms. Menaced with a revolution, they proposed, Pitt and Burke aiding, to annul the stamp acts which had outraged colonial feeling; but that any act rescissory should, in its terms, vindicate absolute British rights over the provincials. The debates upon this proposal were long, and many of the speeches against it admirably eloquent, but the ministry outvoted their opponents. In order to regain popularity, the cabinet caused several measures to be taken, favourable to colonial trade; and obtained from France a liquidation of its paper obligations to Canada, which had remained in abeyance ever since the war of the conquest.

The abrogation of the colonial stamp act was joyfully received in America, and for some time softened provincial hostility; but quickly other troubles arose, the first being mutual disaccord between the governor and assembly of Massachusetts. The Grenville ministry had fallen; and Pitt, created Earl of Chatham, was at the helm of power. By one of those inconsistencies due to human ambition or weakness, the new ministers, several of whom had strongly opposed British right to tax America—Chatham himself, more than any other—in 1767, initiated taxes on tea, paper, glass, &c. for export to the colonies. Parliament concurred, the king assented, and the measure became law. To awe the colonists, the sittings of the New York provincial Assembly were suspended, as a penalty for repudiating British (fiscal) jurisprudence. Here was a new proof that philo-colonials in the mother country of any dependency, are often less animated by a regard for justice, than by a spirit of opposition to the cabinet of the day.

Soon afterwards, the Grafton ministry, composed, according to "Junius," of deserters from every party, succeeded to the cabinet of Lord Chatham; but who kept his situation, nevertheless, in Grafton's, though he was no longer popular. The new project of colonial taxation was yet more odious in America than the stamp act. Massachusetts was the first province which overtly resisted it, and proposed a general convention. The arrival of General Gage, with four regiments and some artillery, put a stop, for a time, to those demonstrations; but discontent was not extinguished, it only smouldered, and was reproduced in all the other provinces. New measures in Britain precipitated a crisis. Parliament addressed the king to send a special commission to Boston, to try all parties accused of high treason. British parliamentarians and American loyalists trusted thereby to intimidate the patriotic party. Sir W. Johnson thus wrote to Lord Hillsborough, in 1769: "I humbly intimate that I respectfully approve of the king's speech and the address, both just received from London. The firmness of the one, the unanimity of the other, afford me great satisfaction, and give me hopes that the unhappy dissensions, excited by turbulent fanatics of this country, will end in a way compatible with the dignity of the crown and the true interests of the people."* Thus, in every age, is the future misinterpreted. Despite Johnson's expressed hopefulness, the Americans again resorted to trading non-intercourse with Britain. This step renewed the alarm of her merchants; and the ministry announced an abrogation of all the lately imposed duties, except the article of tea, which was retained as a vindication of home sovereignty. This was at once to confess its weakness, and to leave a door open for added discord.

Meanwhile, Lord North (1770) taking the ministerial helm in

---

* E. B. O'CALLAGHAN: *Documentary History of the State of New York*, ii. 933.

charge, carried out the polity of his predecessor. Concurrently, skirmishes took place in Boston, between the citizens and soldiers. Alarm spread to every province, and among all classes; every one was apprehensive of what might follow; but most of the colonists determining to vindicate their rights by force of arms, an organized system of resistance was formed. The malcontents, however, were guarded in their expressions, though firm in an intent to make every sacrifice, if needful, to secure success. Massachusetts took the lead, directed by Hancock, Otis, and Adams. It soon became apparent that neither Old nor New England would bate a jot of their respective pretensions, and that the sword alone must decide the quarrel. In 1773, parliament passed an act authorizing the British India company to transport tea to America, on payment of the duties imposed by a previous act, of 1767. Forthwith, some consignees to whose address the first cargoes were sent, had to refuse to receive them, under popular constraint. At Bostons parties who warehoused the tea when landed, were tarred and feathered. Three cargoes of tea were spilt in the harbour. Like outrages were committed in other places. Lord North, indignant at these audacities, and setting himself to punish the Bostonians, got an act passed (but not without parliamentary opposition) to close their port; *i. e.* no vessels were to load or to discharge cargoes there till further orders. " Let us root out that wasp's nest," said an approving British legislator. Two other laws, of coercive kind, were presented by the ministry: one, abridging the franchises of Massachusetts, and prohibiting sederunts of assembly if not authorized by the governor; the other, according immunity from the action of criminal procedure, to all functionaries engaged in suppressing riots, even should death ensue in any case. Such a law as this, under the ingeniously fictitious name of " an act of indemnity," was passed, to give a colour of legality to tyranny, during the troubles of 1838, in Canada. The passing of those two laws was as much opposed as the Boston port bill. Fox, Col. Barré, Burke, and Lord Chatham protested against them. " We have crossed the Rubicon," said one peer; " the watchword now is, *Delenda Carthago.*" Barré exclaimed, " Take heed what ye do! the finances of France are now flourishing; see if *she* do not intervene in our quarrel with the Americans." In fact, Choiseul had skilfully prepared means for taking signal vengeance on Britain for the loss of Canada. Another parliamentary orator vehemently exclaimed, "I trust the Americans *will* resist these oppressive laws; I desire at least, that they may. If they do not, I shall regard them as the most abject of slaves!" Lastly, the British ministry introduced a fourth law, intituled "A Bill for Re-constituting the Government of the Province of Quebec," as all Canada was then called. This measure was the complement of a plan for administering the whole affairs of British America; and as it imposed a system of absolutism upon us, it served to convince the older colonists of the after designs of Britain being inimical to their liberties: especially when they adverted to the past, and thought of her illiberal polity, so retrogressive ever since the revolution of 1689–90. The passing of such a law was indeed ominous of a still more evil future. Accordingly great outcries arose among the objects of it. They protested, more especially, against the recognition of catholicity as the spiritual establishment of Canada: but perhaps there was more craft than conscientious feeling in their remonstrances thereupon, as well knowing Old England's prejudices against our religion; for, soon afterwards, the provincials, become republicans, allowed the Catholics the same franchises as themselves in every respect.

We all know the plans successively proposed, after the Conquest, for governing the Canadians; that, in 1764, it was hostile to their freedom, whereas, in 1774, British jealousies were diverted from us for the time, and directed against the American people and their legislative assemblies. Self-interest thus triumphed over ignorance and passionateness. The abolition of the language and laws of the Canadians would inevitably cause them to take part with their malcontent neighbours; and therefore it was that Britain postponed the settlement of the Canadian question, from year to year, till the time was come when she felt impelled to resort to repressive measures against her old colonists. The decision of the home government as to the establishment of French law and usages in Canada, long depended on the result of the ministerial determination to tax the southern provincials; and their stern opposition to it decided the cabinet to turn a favourable ear to Canadian representations. By so doing, a double end was attained: the clergy and upper classes being gained over, our people were induced to recognize British taxing supremacy; for, in Canadian estimation, this acquiescence was regarded as a small matter in itself, compared with its welcome accompaniment,—the conservation accorded to cherished institutions which the Anglo-Americans had willed to be abased, or even annihilated.

The Earl of Dartmouth, colonial secretary of state, introduced the bill of 1774 to the lords, who passed it without any difficulty. Its provisions greatly enlarged the boundaries of the province of Quebec, as defined in 1764. On one side, they were extended to the frontiers of New England, Pennsylvania, New-York (province), the Ohio, and the left bank of the Mississippi; on the other, to the Hudson's Bay territory.* The bill preserved to the catholic colonists the rights assured to them by capitulations, and relieved them from the operation of the British test act; French civil procedure was to be maintained, but English criminal law, and the English law of successions to property, were to be substituted for French. Finally, the bill gave to the province a governing council of 17 to 23 members,—part catholics, part protestants; in whom were vested, in name of the sovereign, but subject to his veto, all needful regulations of government and police; they not to have power to levy any imposts except those indispensable for constructing and maintaining roads and public edifices. For the king was reserved the right of founding all tribunals, civil and ecclesiastical. The bill passed unanimously in the upper house, but was violently opposed in the lower house; the commons debating the questions raised upon it for several days. Certain London traders,† excited by their compatriots in Canada, made urgent

---

* In 1775, a project for a pacification of the colonies was proposed to the British ministry by Franklin. He stipulated that the Quebec Act should be rescinded, and a free government established in Canada. It was replied, that the act might be so far amended, as to reduce the province to the limits fixed by the proclamation of 1764.—RAMSAY: *History of the American Revolution.*

† Why many of the upper and most of the substantial middle classes, with a majority of the clergy of London, should be denominated *marchands* in M. Garneau's text here, we cannot say; except that men of French race, tacitly adopting a Napoleonic sneer, affect to account us all "a nation of shopkeepers."—B.

remonstrances against the bill and even employed stipendiary advocates to "show cause" why it should not pass. The friends of the bill, on the other hand, demanded that witnesses should be examined in its favour. Governor Carleton was summoned for that purpose, and gave excellent testimony as to Canadian deservings: Chief-Justice Hay, Messrs. de Lotbinière, Maseres, and Marriott were also interrogated. The latter found himself anomalously situated. Not being able, as attorney-general, to express direct dissent from a ministerial bill, he eluded most of the questions addressed to him, so as not to say anything inconsistent with opinions formerly expressed by him in his report on Canadian affairs, for consideration by the privy council,—which clashed, in many particulars, (as we have seen) with the Quebec Act. He extricated himself with much dexterity, however, from the difficulty; but the occasion served to shew how liable general interests are to be compromised, through personal exigencies, for the convenience of men in place.

Among the members in opposition to the measure, were Messrs. Townshend and Burke, also Col. Barré. Most of the dissentients spoke against the restoration of French laws and the free exercise of the Catholic religion in the colony. They wished that a representative chamber should be established, but with such studied reservation, that it was plain they would admit no catholics into it. Continuance of protestant domination, not general franchises, was the kind of political delegation alone meant to be conceded. Such were the inconsistencies in the men of the time; for the upholders of Anglo-American claims, when in the house, were even foremost in wishing that Canadian catholics should have no political franchises. Fox stood forth, however, a noble exception to most others of his party. He said: "From all that I have heard, it appears to be right to give a representative assembly to the Canadians. It is in behoof of that people I now speak, for is it not chiefly in their interest that the bill has been drawn up? How that interest is to be secured but by free representation, I know not...... I have not yet heard one valid reason adduced why the Canadians should not be represented by their own delegates. Much has been said, indeed, as to the peril of intrusting with political power men of alien race and manners; but as the great bulk of the colonists are attached to French laws and usages, if we repose that power solely in the hands of a legislative council, shall we not be confining it to parties the most likely to be obstinate in employing it exclusively for partisan legislation? Nobody has said that the Romish belief naturally disqualifies a man for becoming politically unfranchised; and I, for one, will never listen complacently to such an assertion. No man, intimately acquainted with the catholic mind, will say that there is anything in it opposed to the principles of political freedom. Its aspirations, though repressed by rulers in catholic countries, exist in the breasts of the people, catholics and protestants alike. If any danger there be, it is more likely to come from among the higher than the lower ranks." The premier, Lord North, immediately replied, " Will Britain be safe (for her interests are paramount in the case) when her chiefest powers are entrusted to an assembly representative of catholics? I do not deny that such may be honest, capable, worthy, intelligent, and have just political appreciations; but I still say, that it would not be wise for a protestant government to delegate its powers to a catholic assembly." It is certain, that distrust of catholicism was a chief motive for preventing Britain from according an elective chamber to the Canadians; just as a fear of the Americans became a reason for inducing the British to restore the civil jurisprudence of lower Canada.

Restoration of our laws and free exercise of our religion were two capital points so just, so natural in themselves, that the opposition could not attack them overtly. "What you ask," said Thurlow, " will bring about the subserviency of the Canadians. Here is what I should propose to do: Let such laws as have reference to superseded French sovereignty be replaced by such as arise out of British domination; but in regard of all other legislation, in itself indifferent, and not affecting the relative position or mutual obligations of king and people,—humanity, justice, wisdom, all conjoin in impelling us to leave this community even as we found it... But it is said that Britons carry along with them their political franchises whithersoever they go, and that we should be unjust to the new colonists did we subject them to unaccustomed laws...... I say that if a home-born Briton enter a colony conquered by his race, he does *not* take thither his country's laws.

VOL. II.—Y

It is absurd to pretend, for example, that if any Englishman find it convenient to settle in Guernsey, the laws which prevail *here* (London) shall be administered for his convenience *there*." The opposition, generally, manifested much political chicanery on the occasion. In regard of a legislative council of royal nomination, instead of an assembly, most of the leading members, being hampered by their religious prejudices, spoke under great embarrassment; and when Lord North opined that a catholic assembly were undesirable, Mr. Pulteney, a leading oppositionist, imprudently exclaimed, "It does not thence necessarily follow, that Canada should have no representative chamber at all !" He thus intimated a wish to put the French-Canadians on an inferior political level to British colonists, being protestants. This was the weak point of the oppositionists to the bill; for those among the latter, in all the American provinces, were in an overpowering majority, and fiercely contesting the supremacy of the mother country. As for the assertion, that by countenancing catholicism in any part of British America, the Anglican church incurred danger, it was unworthy of any formal refutation.

Finally, the bill passed the houses, after receiving a few amendments in both, despite the opposition of Lord Chatham; who characterized it as " an oppressive and odious law." Vainly he called on the occupants of the episcopal benches to side with him in resisting the establishing of popery in a country more extensive than insular Britain itself.—Thenceforward, therefore, were our language and laws to arise from their temporary abasement; even as those of Saxon Britain in time overtopped the institutions forced upon it, for a season, by the Normans.

No sooner did the Quebec Act pass, than the Londoners reassembled, and voted an address to the king, praying he would refuse his assent to it. It was alleged that the provisions of the act struck at the fundamentals of the British constitution; that French laws gave no security to person or property; that the bill violated the promise, embodied in the proclamation of 1763, of establishing English jurisprudence in the colony; that popery was a bloody and idolatrous religion : a monition being superadded, that the reigning family had superseded the Stuart dynasty solely from regard for the meritorious potestantism of the former, and the disqualifying popishness of the latter. Among other objections to the measures was this, that it placed legislative power in the hands of revocable crown-councillors, &c.

The lord-mayor, along with several aldermen and fully 150 notabilities, went in procession to St. James's palace, to present this address; but on arriving there, they were informed by the lord chamberlain that the king could, according to usage, take no recognition of the decried bill till it were presented to him in due form. His Majesty, in fact, was at that moment in the house of peers, proroguing parliament, after assenting to the Quebec Act along with other bills of the session: he singling out the former for special commendation, as being "founded on the plainest principles of justice and humanity;" adding that, he doubted not, "it would have the best effects, by calming the inquietudes and promoting the well-being of our Canadian subjects." This official declaration greatly soothed the irritation caused by the stinging depreciations of colonial worth by the parliamentary oppositionists. A supplementary bill, which became law at the same time, abolished the colonial customs-dues—,those sole imposts levied by the French government; and substituted for them duties on strong drinks, to provide means for supporting the civil and judicial administrations of Canada.

Maseres forthwith advised the British or Protestant colonials of all that had been done and said. A meeting of them immediately took place, and resolutions passed demanding that the Quebec Act should be annulled. The agitation raised on the occasion spread to the Gallo-Canadian population, meetings of whom took place, in which counter-resolutions were passed.

About this time an unsigned letter appeared, which made some sensation; sufficient, indeed, to induce Maseres to refute it at length in one of a series of papers published by him in 1775, to support the pretensions of his party. The letter itself, artless in style but sincere in tone, circulating largely among the Canadians, made a deep impression. "Certain of the British among us," thus it ran, "are doing their utmost to indispose us to give acceptance to the late acts for regulating the government of this province. They declaim especially against the restoration of French laws, which they represent as favouring tyranny. Their emissaries would fain persuade the uninstructed, that we shall yet see royal warrant-arrests (*lettres de cachet*) in use by the authorities; that our property will be arbitrarily taken from us whenever the executive thinks fit; that will drag us into the army, and dungeon us if we resist impressment; that we shall be oppressed with imposts; that law we may have, but justice will be denied; that our governors are despotic, and the British laws unfavorable in our regard: but the falsehood of these imputations, is it not plain at first blush? What necessary connexion did we find between our olden institutions and Bastilings, enforced conscriptions, and governmental despotism? Under restored French laws, indeed, we have no jurymen brought in to decide litigation by the votes of men (suddenly called on), too often ignorant or biassed; but is this really an evil? Is British law-process less costly than our own? Do we desire to adopt the law of primogeniture—its principle being all things to one, nothing for all—instead of our present equitable system of succession to real property? Are those among you who wish to enter on wild land as cultivators, willing to obtain it accompanied with British rack-rents and burdened by English manorial exactions? Would you be content to give up the tenth sheaf, as every English farmer (of the Anglican faith or not) is forced to do for the support of the parson and his family? French law, is it not written in a language known to you? our own legism, therefore, is suitable to us in all ways; and judicious Britons, of whom there are many in the colony, own that you cannot rightly be deprived of it.

"But that is not the chief circumstance the most distasteful to those envious men in the acts they wish you to assist them in abrogating. Here is the sore point, which they strive to hide, but it is plainly apparent:—one of the vituperated acts not only allows the exercise of your religion, but frees you from all religious tests contrary thereto; thus a door is opened to admit you to public situations. Hence the wrath of these people! Thus it is, that they print in their newspapers diatribes against what they designate as a detestable law; an abominable measure, 'one which recognizes a sanguinary religion, the professors of which spread abroad doctrines redolent of impiety, murder, and rebellion.' The violence of the language thus used is indicative of the malign sentiments it expresses; it discloses chagrin at not obtaining from parliament the privilege of sitting in an assembly whence you were to be excluded, by the mere administration of oaths which, they well knew, your religious conscience would prevent your taking; thus did the party treat the French Grenadians." Logic so cogent as the foregoing proved irresistible at the time.

Nevertheless, Earl Camden, in May 1775, presented the Canadian protestant petition against the Quebec acts to the house of lords; it was, however, rejected at the instance of Lord Dartmouth. A duplicate of the same, presented by Sir George Savile to the commons, met a like fate.

While the law of 1774 thus tended to reconcile the Canadians to British domination, that which closed Boston port infuriated the southern provincials to the utmost. The assembly of Massachusetts appointed a committee to convoke a general congress of deputies from all the Anglo-American provinces, to confer together, and direct the people in their opposition to the home government; but for the time, to give "recommendations" only, these to be interpreted as so many orders. The colonists were advised to discontinue the use of tea and all other articles imported from Britain, until colonial wrongs should be redressed. The congress thus convoked met at Philadelphia early in September, and sat till October 26. Twelve provinces were therein represented, by delegates from nearly 3 millions of collective population. Only Canada and Georgia did not enter into this new confederation, composed of most the people of British-America.

The congress initiated its proceedings by a Declaration of the Rights of Man,—the indispensable preliminary of all revolutions. This was followed by a series of resolutions, debated and passed, detailing the grievances (real and alleged) of the colonies, among which figured the passing of the Quebec acts; a law which, it was declared with affected solemnity, "recognized the catholic religion, abolished the equitable jurisprudence of England; and, ignoring the antagonistic faith of the old colonies, their laws and government, set up civil and spiritual tyranny in Canada, to the great danger of the neighbouring provinces; those provinces which had so much aided Britain to conquer our country!" "Nor can we suppress our astonishment," it was added in conclusion, "that a

British parliament should ever consent to establish in that colony a religion that often drenched your island in blood *; and has disseminated impiety, bigotry, persecution, murder, and rebellion, through every part of the world." This strain of language we should designate as fanatical, had it been sincerely conceived; but it was simply insensate, as proceeding from men then about to call upon the Canadians to join them in achieving colonial independence. That part of the Philadelphian demonstration became a dead letter in Britain, yet perhaps was the means of losing Canada to the confederation ; such a declaration against French laws and catholicism necessarily armed against the congress the Canadian people; while it violated those rules of eternal justice on which the Americans professed to base their recognition of the " rights of man."

The congress afterwards caused three addresses to be drawn up, one, to George III; another, to the British people, to justify themselves for the adverse position they had taken up; and a third, directly addressed to the Canadians, in which were expressed quite different sentiments from those already cited, when speaking of the same people. The Canadians were now (at wearisome length) informed of the advantages attending the enjoyment of a free constitution, and of the defects of the new system our people were then living under. The testimony of Montesquieu the addressers evoked, in condemnation of it. Finally, the addressed were adjured to join the people of the other colonies, to vindicate the rights common to all; and they were invited to send delegates to another (constituent) congress soon to meet. " Seize the opportunity thus presented to you by Providence, " it was urged. " If you will to be free, free you must necessarily become...We are too well acquainted with the liberality of sentiment distinguishing your nation, to imagine that difference of religion will prejudice you against a hearty amity with us. You know that the transcendent nature of freedom elevates the minds of those who unite in the cause, above all such low-minded infirmities. The Swiss cantons furnish a memorable proof of this truth; their Union is composed of catholic and protestant states, living in the utmost concord and

---

* This document, it is to be noted, was addressed "To the people of Great Britain." It was dated Sept. 5, 1774.—*B*.

peace with each other; and they are thereby enabled, ever since they bravely vindicated their freedom, to defy and defeat every tyrant that has invaded them."

This second address of the congress was sent to a rich Montreal merchant, named Cazeau. He was an influential man, not only with the Canadians, but also among the savages, through his trade with them and the numerous persons he employed in business. Cazeau, who was a Frenchman by birth, had been ill used by the British government; he consequently, took part readily with the insurgent colonials. As soon as Thomas Walker, another Montreal merchant, who had taken upon him to represent Canada at the American congress, brought copies of the address of the Congress, the former set himself to spread them about all parts of the country. Although the document probably expressed the real sentiments of the congress, it could not efface the impression from the Canadian mind of the previous insult offered to catholicity. Firm in their just distrust, most of the best friends of freedom refused to join in the impending struggle. Many other Canadians, gained over by the law of 1774, promised fidelity to Britain, and kept their word. Thus a few words of proscription, emitted heedlessly, were the remote cause why the American confederation now sees the redoubtable power of its repudiated mother country consolidating in the north, and ever ready to come down heavily upon it with her warlike legions!

Carleton, made major-general and created knight of the Bath for his good conduct, returned to Canada in 1774, and inaugurated the new constitution. He formed a legislative council of 23 members, of whom 8 were catholics. This council sat twice or thrice, and then adjourned. Several Canadians were placed in offices which had, till then, been filled exclusively by British or Swiss,— the posts of chief inspector of highways and French secretary excepted. The pay for these being small, they ever required men versed in the language and habitudes of the colonials. Colonial feudality was respected; and the Seminaries were recognized, in accordance with the rules of their foundation.* But the Canadians knew it was only from motives of policy that they were thus allow-

---

* Royal Instructions of 1774.

ed to take a share in governing the country; they were perfectly certain that, whatever changes took place, no chief place would ever be open to any of them; and as for the smaller charges put within their reach, only docile aspirants would be selected, whose submissiveness to the ruling powers could be well ascertained beforehand.

Meanwhile, scarcely did the governor find time to make a survey of the state of the colony, from which he had been absent for several years, or to complete the arrangements necessitated by the law of 1774, when his attention was drawn towards the frontiers, and upon the propagandism the Americans were striving to maintain against British sway in Canada, into which copies of the congress' address had penetrated by several ways simultaneously.

The fine names of "liberty" and "national independence" have always a charm for noble minds; a generous spirit is ever moved at their very sound. The polished Parisian, the Swiss herdsman, feel the sacred influence, in common, of proclaimed freedom. The address of the congress, therefore, despite the recklessness of parts of its strain, caused a great sensation among the Canadian rural populations and the British townsmen. The latter, now no longer hopeful of dominating their fellow colonists of French race, mostly became American partisans. The situation of Carleton was a difficult one at this crisis. Happily for him, the Canadian clergy and *seigneurs* had become firmly bound to British interests through the confirmation of feudal tenures and the recognized right of tithing, two institutions which they could not hope to preserve if a levelling revolution supervened; and with these two orders of men marched the burgess class in the towns, which was as yet, however, neither numerous nor opulent.

Through a fear of jeoparding their religion and nationality by entering into a confederation both protestant and alien in blood,— an apprehension not groundless, for the men of that confederation had already incorporated the French settlements of Louisiana,— the clergy and seigneurs resolved to resist every assault of the Anglo-Americans, and to retain our country for monarchic Britain, 3,000 miles distant; a patroness all the less likely, for that remoteness, to become perilously inimical to Canadian institutions.

Besides, even had the Canadians not been outraged by the declaration of congress against catholicism and French jurisprudence, they ever preserved in their hearts that hatred for the British race, wherever born or located, which they had contracted during long wars; they thus made no distinction, in their minds, between those of it mingled with themselves, in Canada, and men of kindred blood dwelling beyond: viewing both alike as one body of turbulent and ambitious oppressors. Knowing this common feeling, the governor might and did rely on a majority of the population following the lead of the superior classes in rejecting American invitations to revolt; his own popularity, also, counting for something in the matter. Upon the whole, then, his least favourable expectation was, that if the Canadians would not take up arms for Britain, neither would they fight against her. Several *seigneurs*, on the other hand, promised to Carleton that they would march against the rebels at the head of their tenants (*censitaires*). The sequel proved, however, that they undertook to do more than they were able to realize, for, when they did assemble their tenants and explain to them the questions at issue, with an intimation added, that the government looked to the Canadians for warlike support, the latter refused to fight the Americans; these "neuters," as they were called, observing, "We know neither the cause nor the likely result of the differences between the contending parties. We shall manifest our loyalty to the government we live under by a quiet and submissive life, but we will take no side in present quarrels." In certain districts, some ardent youthful seigneurs, trying the effect of menaces to constrain tenants to follow their lead, were obliged themselves to flee precipitately.

Meanwhile, affairs were assuming a graver aspect, day by day, and, far from being able to attack the revolting provincials on their own ground, as he wished to do with the troops and Canadians (had the latter been consentient), the governor was startled by an invasion from the other side. Blood had already been shed, in April 1775, at Lexington and Concord, where the British lost nearly 300 men in battle against the Americans. The latter were now arming everywhere, also taking possession of forts, arsenals, and government stores. Colonels Ethan Allen and Arnold fell, unawares, on fort Ticonderoga, garrisoned by 100 men, and captured 118 cannon,—the latter a great prize for the insurgents. Colonel

Warner got hold of Crown Point, and obtained the mastery of lake Champlain, without any loss of men. Fort St. John's next fell; but was retaken, the day after, by M. Picoté de Belestre, leader of 80 Canadian volunteers.

The American congress met at Philadelphia, June 10. As the home government decided to carry out its polity by force, the most energetic measures were promptly adopted for resistance to it. A new parliament had been called, in order to test the opinion of the British people as to coercion for the Americans. The response to the address from the throne returned no uncertain note; the parliament undertook to sustain the monarch in vindicating its own assumed supremacy of legislation over the colonies. The martial spirit of the Americans was contemptuously spoken of by one minister, who, when asking for a vote of men sufficient to make General Gage's army at Boston 10,000 strong, observed, "This corps will assuredly suffice to bring the cowardly colonists to their senses." Franklin, after making vain efforts in London to persuade the British ministry to adopt a pacific policy, returned to his own country, and prepared to assist, by wise counsels, his compatriots to carry on successfully a war he had done his utmost to prevent. Shortly thereafter, Generals Howe, Burgoyne, and Clinton arrived in America with reinforcements.

The congress now directed the several provinces to be put in a defensive state. The British forces in Boston were blockaded by the provincial militia; while a "continental army" was brigaded with General Washington as generalissimo. The congress, at the same time, voted another address to the Canadians, exposing the evil tendency of the Quebec Act, and justifying the seizure of Ticonderoga and Crown Point, as a needful measure for the security of all the colonies.

While the congress was sitting, the battle of Bunker's Hill was fought (June 16), during which Gage was twice repulsed, while attempting to take the entrenchments of the provincials by assault, but gained his end in the third effort, his army being more numerous than their forces by a moiety. This battle, wherein the British lost many men, was the bloodiest and most obstinate of the whole war; but, if lost, it made the Americans confident in their powers of resistance, avenged the parliamentary slightings of their prowess, and taught the British regulars to respect a courage which they found so deadly to encounter. Colonel Arnold, who had assisted to capture Ticonderoga, proposed to the congress to invade Canada; promising that he would take and hold the colony with 2,000 men only. The congress, menaced by Carleton with an attack on that side, thought the best mode of averting it would be to march an army against Quebec, the water-ways to which lay open ever since the Americans became masters of lake Champlain. So hardy an enterprise would thus make the war offensive instead of defensive. The congress was all the more inclined to this course, that they believed all the Canadians to be (their nobles and clergy excepted) malcontent under the new order of things, and would meet the armed Americans rather as friends than foes.

General Schuyler was named, by the congress, chief of the army of the north; with orders to take St. John's, Montreal, and some other places in Canada—provided the inhabitants offered no obstruction. He foresaw that Carleton would leave Quebec with his troops, to defend the assailed frontiers: the conquest of the capital and key of the colony would thus become easy, for it was not likely that Britain could send succour before winter set in, when the navigation of the flood would necessarily cease. If these fond expectations so indulged should be realized, though but in part, it was intended to make a lateral descent unawares on Quebec, by a detachment directed along the course of the rivers Kennebec and Chaudière. On the other hand, supposing the invaders could not take Quebec, still a leaguer of it would oblige Carleton to return; thus leaving the Canadian middle frontier again open to invasion by the corps of Schuyler and Montgomery.* In fact, these generals disembarked under fort St. John's, in September, with a detachment 1,000 strong, but, finding the place formidable, and being harassed by a band of savages, led by the brothers Lorimier, the Americans retired to the Isle-aux-Noix. When entering our coun-

---

* The latter was the same Montgomery who served under Wolfe in 1759, and commanded the British detachment sent to burn St. Joachim. After the war he married an American woman and settled in New York. When the troubles between Britain and her colonies burst into open war, he sided with the insurgents, was welcomed as an ex-officer, and attained high grades in the revolutionary army.

try, they addressed a proclamation to its people, announcing that the congress wished to extend to them more than the full franchises of British subjects, parts of which even they had been unjustly deprived of; that the congress' army was embodied to act only against the royal troops, and that the persons, goods, civil freedom, and worship of the Canadians would be religiously respected. This proclamation was widely circulated in the colony.

On the first report of invasion, Carleton directed troops to lake Champlain. There were but 800 regulars in all at his disposition. The people of the lower districts, indifferent to events, remained in their parishes; those of the upper districts, being nearer to the scene of action, were diversely affected; some inclining to side with the invaders, but, in general, from motives expressed, as we have already learned from themselves, resolved to stand neuter. As for the Anglo-Canadians, who weighed so heavily in the balance when the agents of the mother country were distributing her favours! they now counted for little, their numbers being so few: besides, most of those few were, openly or secretly, partisans of the congress,* and the governor was well aware of the secret meetings these held at Quebec and Montreal. Such was the state of things when martial law was proclaimed, June 9; the government having called out the militia previously, to repel invasion and maintain order in the province. This double measure, new to Canada, did not work well. Some parishes, put under constraint by M. de la Corne, rose in resistance at the portage of Lachenaye. By prejudicing opinions, and recourse to threats, the indifferent were alarmed, and those who wavered were forced into open enmity to the government. The latter now called the clergy in aid. The bishop of Quebec addressed an encyclical lettter to his flock, exhorting the faithful to be true to British allegiance, and to repel the American invaders. He strove to prove, at the same time, that their religion would not be respected by puritans and independents if these obtained the mastery in the struggle going on, and that it would be folly to join them. These sentiments were more widely developed by him afterwards, in a lengthy pastoral letter (*mandement*)

---

* MS. of Sanguinet, a Montreal barrister; Journals of the provincial congress; ditto of the provincial convention; of the committee of safety, &c. of New York state, vol. II.

published next year. Meantime, neither the proclamation, nor the encyclical, was able to move the Canadians from their state of apathy.

Finding the people deaf to his calls, the governor proposed to raise a body of volunteers, to serve so long as the war should last: offering tempting conditions; namely, each unmarried private to receive 200 acres of land, if married 250, besides 50 more for each of the children: the land to be holden free of all imposts for 20 years. Yet these offers attracted few recruits, and Carleton had to look further afield. He bethought himself of Indian combativeness; and sent emissaries among the native tribes, especially the Iroquois, to enlist savage warriors. Fifteen years of peace were understood to have strengthened the Iroquois' confederation, and the Five Nations were resuming their supremacy over all the other native races; it seemed probable, therefore, that their example, if they acceded, would be followed, and Britain thus be well supplied with an auxiliary force. But much address, and potent stimulation, were needed to engage the Iroquois chiefs to take part in a war which regarded them not. Their elders looked upon the anti-fraternal struggle among the whites as a kind of providential expiation for the ills that both belligerents had made the Indians endure. "Behold!" said they, "war now raging between men of one race; they are contending which shall possess lands they have ravished from us. What have we to do with either party? When *we* go to war, do any white men join *us*? No: they look on contentedly, and see us weaken ourselves by mutual slaughters; ever ready to step forward, the battle once finished, and enter upon lands bedewed with our bloodshed. . *Their* turn is now come; let us imitate their past example, and look on complacently while they strive to exterminate each other. If they succeed in this, we shall again possess the forests, prarie lands, and waters which belonged to our ancestors."

Cazeau, on his part, to deter the savages he traded with or influenced from taking part with the British, told them, "This is a family quarrel: once made up, you will be viewed as enemies by both the brotherhoods of Britain." Sir W. Johnson, and Messrs. Campbell and De St. Luc, agents among the tribes, laboured in an opposite direction, and not without success among the younger chiefs. Campbell loaded them with presents; Johnson cajoled or harangued; and, at length, many of the Indian chiefs were induced to descend to Montreal, to " take up the war hatchet." They bound themselves to enter the field early in spring, or as soon as the British should be ready to begin their next campaign. While the governor was at Montreal, a troop of the Iroquois arrived, led by Colonel Guy Johnson, who impressed upon Carleton the necessity there was for employing those savages at once, as what they could least endure was a state of inaction. The governor replied, that his regular forces were too few for campaigning; that the defence of the country depended entirely on its militia; but that he hoped to be soon able to collect a respectable force: meantime, that the savages must have their attention taken up, in some other way than that proposed,* for he did not think it would be prudent, as yet, to overpass the Canadian boundaries.

The governor desired to succour St. John's, by means of the armed rural populations of Trois-Rivières and Montreal; but, from what we have said above, it may be easily imagined such persons would not be very ready to go thither. The Chambly parishioners, at first all indifferent to the British cause, were now, many of them, actively hostile to it; and had even sent emissaries into other parishes, to induce their people to do the like: intimating that the time was propitious for the Canadians to cast off the yoke of Britain. Nearly the whole militia of the district of Trois-Rivières refused to march at command of the governor. Some few hundreds of royalists, responding to his call, assembled at Montreal; but, perceiving that Carleton was dubious of their fidelity, most of them returned to their homes. The Chambly villagers joined an American detachment, under Majors Brown and Livingston, whom Montgomery sent to take a small fort there, which was disgracefully yielded up, after 36 hours' investment, by Major Stopford; the walls being intact, the garrison relatively large, no man of it hurt, and stores of every kind abounding. Stopford struck his flag, and gave up his sword to the lucky Americans; who found in the fort 17 pieces of ord-

---

* Extracts from the records of Indian transactions under the superintendence of Sir Guy Carleton, during the year 1775.

nance, and much gunpowder—a warlike munition of which Montgomery was all but destitute previously, and whose acquisition now enabled him to press the siege of St. John's vigorously, the men of Chambly taking part therein. Thus did the frontier contest, through the partisanship of some Gallo-Canadians, take the colour of a civil war. Most of the British in Canada, also, became during the autumn, openly or secretly, favourable to the American cause; while many among the rural populations near the seat of war either joined the insurgents, or prayed they might be successful; while the rest remained quite neuter. Only the clergy and seigneurs, with a portion of the men in towns, stood up firmly for the reigning power, and their influence finally induced a majority of the Canadians to observe neutrality at least. It may be fairly assumed, then, that to the clergy of Canada, at this juncture, was Britain indebted for the conservation of the dependency now her greatest colony.

The governor still persisted in his design to relieve the besieged garrison of St. John's, a part of whom had only planking to shelter them from the enemies' fire, although the fort itself was the key of the frontier line on the Champlain side. Accordingly, he ordered Colonel Maclean, commandant of Quebec, to call up his militiamen and ascend the flood to Sorel, where he would meet with the royal forces. Maclean led 300 men to Sorel, but found no governor there; and, tarrying only a little, his own men began to desert. Meanwhile the governor, with 800 more, led by M. de Beaujeu, did set out for Sorel, but instead of directly descending the St. Lawrence to that place, chose to cross the flood to Longueuil on its right bank, where he was confronted by a petty American corps well posted. He was about to disembark, but was suddenly restrained by apprehensions that the men under De Beaujeu would join the enemy. This determined him to hold off; but he did not quit the shore all unscathed; several parting cannon-balls and shot from small arms reaching his boats, while some Canadians and savages, who landed too precipitately, were left behind.

Maclean was to march, simultaneously, towards St. John's, and did reach St. Denis, the first stage thither; but finding the bridges broken and the parishioners up in arms, he returned perforce to Sorel, where nearly all his men, being gained over by

Chambly emissaries, abandoned his standard. This desertion forced him to retreat to Quebec, after loading the return barges with arms and munitions in store at Sorel and Trois-Rivières. Fort St. John, the garrison despairing of being succoured, was surrendered after a siege of 45 days. The victors there took 500 prisoners; but they allowed the officers of the regulars and all the Canadian volunteers to keep their arms, out of a (feigned) respect for the courage they had manifested.*

The unexpected successes which thus illustrated the American arms at the outset were gained at small cost of men, even reckoning those casualties attendant on a contemporary attempt to take Montreal by surprise, through the aid of confederates within that city. This daring enterprise, adventured by Colonel Allen and Major Brown, failed for want of proper concert in its parts. Allen alone, with 110 men, was to traverse the island of Montreal, and reaching the city, communicate with partisans inside; but being encountered, at Longue-Pointe, by Major Carden, with 300 Canadian volunteers and 60 British soldiers,† he was surrounded, discomfited, and taken prisoner with most of his people. During the combat, the governor-general and General Prescott were ensconced (*se tenaient*) in the city barrack, the troops being formed in its square, knapsack on back, all ready to embark for Quebec, had the royalists been defeated. The victory suspended Carleton's retreat, however, only for a few days; as, no sooner was Montgomery master of St. John's, than he despatched troops, by forced marches, toward Montreal, Sorel, and Trois-Rivières. The defection of the inhabitants, and Maclean's retreat, left Carleton almost without an escort. Thus abandoned, he jumped aboard a small vessel in Montreal harbour, and, with 100 soldiers and a few civilians, set out for Quebec; but winds proving adverse to further sailing progress, he landed at Lavaltrie, a few leagues below Montreal, disguised himself as a villager, and went on

---

* Journal kept during the siege of Fort St. John, by one of its defenders (M. Antoine Foucher.)

† Memoirs of Colonel Ethan Allen. "About thirty of the British traders agreed to march against the enemy; all the others refused." *Mémoires de Sanguinet* (*MS.*).—"Now was the time," says this royalist, "that the traitors showed themselves in their proper colours."

board the row-barge of a coasting-trader called Bouchette, with intent to drop down the flood by nocturnal stages. Arrived thus at Trois-Rivières, he was just in time to witness the ingress of the American invaders; and he was fain to leave the perilous locality even as a fugitive, just as Maclean, his town-major, did shortly before.* While the governor was thus fleeing, Montreal opened its gates to Montgomery; the people of its suburbs declaring themselves sympathisers in the American revolutionary cause.

Trois-Rivières, now ungarrisoned, followed the example of Montreal; the townsmen only asking to be as well treated as the Montrealers had been by the Americans. Montgomery said he was sorry they could suppose for a moment their lives or property would be unsafe in his hands; expressing a pious wish that if Providence continued to favor him, &c. the province would soon be enabled to achieve its freedom. Part of the British townspeople joined the Americans; and most of the Canadian inhabitants, following suit, disarmed the resident loyalists. The Americans who descended to Quebec in the flotilla which had followed the governor to Lavaltrie, and which they took without striking a blow, conjoined themselves to Arnold's corps at Pointe-aux-Trembles. This Arnold, who afterwards betrayed his country's cause, had been a horse-dealer. He was of a robust bodily make, of ardent temperament, and a stranger to fear. Having had an extended experience of men and things, he was an acute observer of both, and his natural tact compensated for his want of scholastic training. His great repute for courage and military skill caused Washington to select him as leader of the detachment drafted from the Bostonian army, to make a sudden descent on Quebec by the Kennebec and Chaudière, as above-mentioned. His instructions, similar to those given Montgomery, enjoined him to be very careful in his dealings with the Canadians, and even to humour their prejudices. He was to show respect for their religion, to pay them liberally for whatever supplies he obtained, and to punish severely all maraudings. He set out, and it took him six weeks to clear the Alleghanies and pass from Cambridge to Quebec. He

---

* Journal (MS.) kept at Trois-Rivières, in 1775-6, by M. Badeaux, a royalist notary.

arrived by the St. Lawrence at the Fuller's (Wolfe's) Cove; encamping, Nov. 13, with 650 men only, on the Plains of Abraham. Forced to travel through a rugged wilderness, following the courses of rivers vexed with rapids, and penetrating interspaces full of obstructions, he was enabled finally to surmount the natural obstacles in his way only by sacrificing most of his ammunition and baggage, and by subsisting chiefly on such wild fruits, &c. as the country produced. Arrived at the Kennebec head-waters, he sent back the sick and all others who were knocked up, or whose hearts failed them. Too weak in numbers to attack Quebec without aid, he ascended the left bank of the flood to Pointe-aux-Trembles, to effect a junction with Montgomery. Although their collective force, even then, did not exceed 1200 men, the twain descended to Quebec with their corps, and invested it early in December.

The governor had re-entered the city Nov. 13, after having narrowly missed being taken prisoner at Pointe-aux-Trembles, where he desired to land. He was only just able to quit the village, as Arnold's troops entered it. He found most of the citizens of the capital divided into two antagonistic camps, while a third party was undecided which standard to join. There had been several public meetings holden, to discuss and determine this matter. The very day the governor returned, a meeting was in progress in a chapel; the question being mooted, whether the city should or should not be defended. One Williams, the first signer of the petition the British traders in the place addressed to the king the year before, and who had mounted the rostrum to persuade the townspeople to surrender the city to the army of congress, was so doing when Colonel Maclean ordered him to come down; then the latter dissuaded his auditors from following counsel so cowardly, and caused the assembly to disperse. A rumour arose, that the British in the place had proposed terms of capitulation for the consideration of Arnold. As soon as the governor resumed his charge, he set about putting the defensive works in proper order, and encouraging the citizens to do their duty by king and country. He assembled the trained bands (*milice bourgeoise*), passed along their ranks, beginning with the native Canadians, ranged on the right, to whom he put the question, Whether they were resolved to comport themselves as true men and loyal subjects? when all responded to the appeal by affirmative acclamations. The British-born militiamen responded in like manner. But as there still remained a number of known or suspected malcontents, who wished, at least, the invading enemy to be successful, the governor ordained, on the 22nd day of November, that all those who would not take up arms for the common defence should quit the city. A number of British merchants, Adam Lymburner at their head, retired into the island of Orleans, to Charlesbourg, or to other places where they had villas, to await the result of the leaguer, and hail it with a cry of *God save the King!* or *The Congress for ever!!** according to circumstances.

---

* In the author's text, "Vive le roi! *ou* Vive la Ligue,"—antagonistic expressions of popular preferences not intelligible to readers unconversant with French religio-civil wars during the middle and latter decades of the 16th century.

END OF VOLUME II

CONTENTS.

CHAPTER I.

LA SALLE, M. DE LA SALLE in Texas.

Chevalier de Tonty.—Chipewa village—La Salle—
Tonty last visits to the western posts—Tonty's voyage
down the Mississippi to Fort Louis on the Illinois—1685-1712.

Fortunate addition to La Salle's party—Facts developed which heighten the
peril of his unfortunate shipwreck and misfortune—His treachery
and intrigue—He winters and intrigues with the natives. Misfortune continues—Enters the country of the Mississippi, and is
lost in Matagorda bay, Texas—unsuccessful conduct of Beaujeu,
who leaves La Salle and the colonists to their fate—La Salle
builds two forts, and calls one St. Louis.—He explores several
parts of the country, to no good end, during several months,
and loses many of his men.—Description of setting the Mississippi
—he sets out for the Illinois in view of obtaining succors from
France—Part of his companions murder him and his nephew.
—His assassins fall out, and two of their number killed by the
others—Joutel and six of the party, fearing the compunctions
behind, reach the Illinois—sad end of most of the party of the
Texas colony—arrives at Fort St. Louis, where De la Hogue arrives and joins a colony at Detroit.—War fleet to Japan, etc.
Louisiana further settled—Means of Indian trade for his
colony—Illusive meeting under a false pretence.—The Illinois
removal to Mobile in 1714.—Lonley's progress apace.—Death
of M. d'Iberville.—As it is carefully explained, and its evil results.
—Louisiana ceded to M. de Crozat, 1712.) . . . .

CHAPTER II.

TREATY OF UTRECHT.—1701-1713.

A French colony settled at Detroit—Bear-meat scarce.—"War of
the Succession."—Operations in America—Mutuality in the
western region; hostilities continued . . . . . provinces . . . .
—Tribal state of Acadia.—Quarrels among the western savages.—

CONTENTS.

BOOK SIXTH.

CHAPTER I.

ESTABLISHMENT OF LOUISIANA.—1683–1712.

PAGE

Province of Louisiana.—Louis XIV puts several vessels at the disposal of La Sale to found a Settlement there.—His departure with a squadron; and misunderstandings with his colleague, M. de Beaujeu.—He misses the sea-entry of the Mississippi, and is landed in Matagorda bay, Texas.—Shameful conduct of Beaujeu, who leaves La Sale and the colonists to their fate.—La Sale builds two fortlets, and calls one St. Louis.—He explores several parts of the country, to no good purpose, during several months, and loses many of his men.—Despairing of finding the Mississippi, he sets out for the Illinois, in view of obtaining succour from France.—Part of his companions murder him and his nephew.—His assassins fall out; and two of their number killed by the others.—Joutel and six of the party, leaving the conspirators behind, reach the Illinois.—Sad fate of most of the party left in the Texas territory.—D'Iberville undertakes to re-colonise Louisiana, and settles a colony at Biloxi (1698-8).—Appearance of the British on the Mississippi.—The Huguenots ask leave to settle in Louisiana, but are refused.—D'Iberville demands free trade for his colony.—Illusive metallic riches of the country.—The Biloxians removed to Mobile in 1701.—The colony progresses apace.—Death of M. d'Iberville.—An intendancy appointed, and its evil results.—Louisiana ceded to M. de Crozat. (1712).................. 3

CHAPTER II.

TREATY OF UTRECHT.—1701–1713.

A French colony settled at Detroit.—Four years' peace.—" War of the Succession."—Operations in America.—Neutrality in the western region: hostilities confined to the maritime provinces.—Trinal state of Acadia.—Quarrels among the western savages.—

Raids in New England by the French and the Abenaquis.—Destruction of Deerfield and Haverhill (1708).—Colonel Schuyler's remonstrances on these acts, and M. de Vaudreuil's defence of them.—Captain Church ravages Acadia (1704).—Colonel Marck's two sieges of Port-Royal; is repulsed in both (1707).—Notices of Newfoundland : hostilities in that island; M. de Subercase fails to take Fort St. John (1705).—M. de St. Ovide captures St. John (1709).—Further hostilities in Newfoundland.—The Anglo-American colonists call on the British government to aid them to conquer Canada : promises made in 1709, and again in 1710, to send the required aid, but none arrives.—General Nicholson besieges and takes Port-Royal.—The articles of its capitulation diversely interpreted. Resumption and termination of hostilities in Acadia.—Third attack meditated on Quebec, and double invasion of Canada; the Iroquois arm again.—Disasters of the British maritime expedition.—The Outagamis at Detroit; savages' intents against that settlement; their defeat, and destruction.—Re-establishment of Michilimackinac.—Sudden change of ministry in England, its consequences.—Treaty of Utrecht; stipulations in it regarding New France.—Reflections on the comparative strength of France at this time and at the death of Louis XIII... 18

CHAPTER III.

COLONIZATION OF CAPE BRETON.—1713-1744.

Motives of the French Government for founding an establishment at Cape Breton.—Description of that island ; its name changed to "Isle-Royale."—British jealousies excited.—Plans of the Messrs. Raudot, for colonizing the island and making it a trading entrepôt (1706).—Foundation of Louisbourg.—Notices of the island's later colonization; its trade, &c.—M. de St. Ovide succeeds M. de Costebelle.—The Acadians, being aggrieved, threaten to emigrate to l'Isle-Royale.—Abortive attempt, in 1619, to colonize St. John's (Prince Edward's) Island.—A few notices of that isle... 33

BOOK SEVENTH.

CHAPTER I.

LAW'S SYSTEM—CONSPIRACY OF THE NATCHEZ.—1712-1731.

Notices of Louisiana and its inhabitants.—M. Crozat's monopoly.—Civil government re-constituted.-*La Coutume de Paris* introduced as a legal code.—Abortive attempts to originate a trade with New

Mexico.—Traffic among the aboriginal tribes, shared with the British colonists.—The Natchez tribe exterminated by the French. —M. Crozat throws up his trading privileges in disgust; they are transferred to the Western Company, as re-instituted in favour of John Law and others.—Notices of this adventurer; rise, progress, and fall of his banking and colonizing schemes, known as the Mississippi System.—Personal changes in the colonial administration.—New Orleans founded, in 1718, by M. de Bienville. —New organization of the provincial government.—Immigration of the West India Company's colonists; the miserable fate of most of them.—Notices of divers French settlements.—War between France and Spain; its origin and course.—Capture and re-capture of Pensacola.—At the peace, the latter restored to Spain.— Recompenses to the Louisianian military and naval officers.— Treaties with the Chickasaws and the Natchez.—Hurricane of Sept 12, 1722.—Charlevoix recommends missions, and his advice is adopted.—Louisianian trade transferred to the Company of the Indies, after the collapse of Law's company.—M. Perrier, a naval lieutenant, appointed governor of the province.—Most of the aboriginal tribes conspire to exterminate all the French colonists.—The Natchez perform the first act of this tragedy, with savage dissimulation and barbarity, but too precipitately happily for the remainder of the intended victims.—Stern reprisals of the French.—A few concluding words on the polity of the West India Company in Louisiana; which is fain to render up its modern privileges therein to the king........................ 41

CHAPTER II.

Discovery of the Rocky Mountains.—1713-1744.

State of Canada; reforms effected and projected by M. de Vaudreuil.—Rivalry of France and Britain in America.—The frontier question; uncertain limits of Acadia.—The Abenaquis' territories. —Hostilities between that tribe and the New-Englanders—Murder of Père Rasle.—Frontiers of western New France.—Encroachments on the Indian territories.—Plans of Messrs. Hunter and Burnet.—Establishments, one at Niagara by the French, one at Oswego by the British, are followed by complaints from the former, and protests from the latter.—Fort St. Frederick erected at Crown-Point; a deputation from New England vainly remonstrates against this step.—Loss of the *Chameau*, French passage-ship, in the Laurentian waters.—Death of M. de Vaudreuil; his character.—M. de Beauharnais appointed governor-general, with M. Dupuis as intendant.—Death of M. de St. Vallier, second bishop of Quebec; dissensions among his clergy about the interment of his corpse—these lead to a complication of troubles, in which the civil authorities take part; the governor betraying his duty to the state, the clergy come off with flying colours.—Recal of M. Dupuy, who is thus made a scape-goat by the French ministry.—M. Hocquart nominated intendant.—Intolerance of the clergy of the cathedral of Quebec.—Mutations in the episcopate for several years; nomination of Messrs. de Mornay, Dosquet, de l'Aube-Rivière, as third, fourth, and fifth bishops; appointment and settlement of M. Pontbriant as sixth prelate.—The Outagamis' hostilities avenged on their allies.—Travels and discoveries of the Messrs. Vérendrye, in search of a route to the Pacific Ocean:—they discover the Rocky Mountain range.—Unworthy treatment experienced by the family.—Appearances of war being imminent, M. de Beauharnais takes precautionary measures, and recommends more to be adopted by the home authorities: the latter (as usual) repel or neglect his warnings.—Anecdote, affecting the reputation of M. Van Renselaer, of Albany......... 57

BOOK EIGHTH.

CHAPTER I.

COMMERCE, INDUSTRY.—1608–1744.

Canadian trade; evil effects of war upon it.—Its rise and progress: cod fisheries.—The peltry traffic the main branch of the commerce of Canada. From an early date, the fur traffic a monopoly.—Rivalry of Canadian and Anglo-American fur-traders.—Policy of governors Hunter and Burnet.—Non-intercourse laws of 1720 and 1727; their evil effects upon French colonial interests.—Various branches of Canadian industry in former times.—Canadian Exports, their nature.—Ginseng, notices of.—Mining and Minerals. —Quebec the great entrepôt.—Manufactures; salt-works.—Posting commenced, in 1745.—Formation of an admiralty court; exchange for merchants opened.—Negro slavery in Canada.—Money of the colony, its nature, and various depreciations,.......... 81

CHAPTER II.

LOUISBOURG.—1744–1748.

Coalitions of European powers for and against the empress Maria-Theresa, which eventuate in a war between France and Britain.—First hostilities in America.—Cape Breton; Louisbourg, and its defensive works.—Expedition of Duvivier to Canso, &c.—Governor Shirley proposes to attack Louisbourg.—His plans disapproved of by the council, but welcomed by the people of New England, and adopted.—Colonel Pepperel and admiral Warren, with land and sea forces, invest the place.—Mutiny in the garrison.—Mr. Vaughan makes a bold and successful night assault, and destroys garrison stores.—Capitulation of Louisbourg; the settlers taken to France.—Project for invading Canada.—The duke d'Anville's expedition, and the work cut out for it to perform.—Of the disasters which attended it from first to last; the duke dies of chagrin, and his successor in command kills himself.—M. de Ramsay menaces Annapolis.—Part of his men attack and defeat colonel Noble and a corps of New-Englanders, at Grand-Pré-aux-Mines.—The American frontiers invaded in many places, and the country ravaged.—Sea-fight near Cape Finisterre, and another at Belle-Isle; the French defeated in both.—Count de la Galissonière appointed interim governer of New France; the previous nominee, M. Jonquière, being a prisoner in England. —Troubles with the Miâmis.—Treaty of Aix-la-Chapelle, and its conditions.—Concluding reflections on the past war............ 99

CHAPTER III.

THE FRONTIERS' COMMISSION.—1748-1755.

The peace of Aix-la-Chapelle only a truce.—Britain profits by the ruin of the French war-marine to extend the frontiers of her possessions in America.—M. de la Galissonière governor of Canada.— His plans to hinder the neighbouring colonies from aggrandizing themselves, adopted by the court.—Pretensions of the British.— Rights of discovery and possession of the French.—The limitary policy of Galissonière expounded and defended.—Emigration of the Acadians; part taken in their regard by that governor.—He causes several forts to be raised in the west; founding of Ogdensburgh (1749).—The Marquis de la Jonquière succeeds as governor; the French ministry directs him to adopt the policy of his predecessor.—De la Corne and Major Lawrence advance to the Acadian isthmus, and occupy strongholds thereon; *i.e.*, forts Beauséjour, Gaspereaux, Lawrence, Des Mines, &c.—Lord Albemarle complains, at Paris, of French encroachments (1749); reply thereto of M. Puyzieulx.—The French, in turn, complain of British hostile acts on sea.—The Acadians take refuge in St. John's (Prince Edward's) Island; their miserable condition there.— Foundation of Halifax, N.S. (1749).—A mixed commission, French and British, appointed to settle disputes about the frontier lines;

first conferences, at Paris, on the subject.—Pretensions of the parties stated and debated ; difficulties found to be insurmountable.—Affair of the Ohio ; intrigues of the British among the natives of the regions around that river ; intrigues of the French among those of the Five Nations.—Virginian traffickers arrested, and sent as prisoners to France.—French and British troops sent to the Ohio to fortify themselves in the country.—The governor-general at issue with certain Demoiselles and the Jesuits.—His mortal illness, death and character (1752).—The Marquis Duquesne succeeds him.—Affairs of the Ohio continued —Colonel Washington marches to attack Fort Duquesne.—Death of Jumonville.—Defeat of Washington by M. de Villiers at Fort Necessity (1754).—Plan of the British to invade Canada ; assembly of Anglo-American governors at Albany—General Braddock sent from Britain with an army to America.—Baron Dieskau arrives at Quebec with four battalions (1755).—Negociations between the French and British governments on the frontier difficulties.—Capture of two French ships of war by admiral Boscawen.—France declares war against Great Britain............................ 110

BOOK NINTH.

CHAPTER I.

THE SEVEN YEARS' WAR.—1755-1756.

Dispositions of mind in Britain and France at the epoch of the Seven Years' war.—France changes her foreign policy in forming an alliance with Austria ; which mutation only flattered the self-love of Madame de Pompadour.—Warlike enthusiasm in Great Britain and her colonies ; their immense armaments.—Small number of the Canadian forces.—Plan of the first campaign ; zeal of the Canadian people.—First operations.—Troops from Boston scour Acadia and capture Fort Beauséjour, &c. ; exile and dispersion of the French Acadians.—General Braddock advances towards Fort Duquesne ; M. de Beaujeu marches to meet him ; battle of the Monongahela ; the British defeated, and Braddock killed.—A panic ensues in the American colonies.—The Canadians and savages commit great ravages, and take many prisoners.—British corps formed to attack Niagara and Fort Frederic.—Colonel Johnson encamps at the head of Lake George.—Baron Dieskau attacking him, is defeated and taken prisoner.—General Shirley delays the siege of Niagara.—Results of the campaign of 1755.—

Bad harvest in Canada; a dearth ensues.—British preparations for the campaign of 1756.—State of Canada; succour solicited from France.—General Montcalm, sent with a reinforcement of troops, arrives at Quebec in spring, 1756—Plan of operations.—Disproportion of the forces of the two belligerent parties; invasions projected by the British.................................... 136

CHAPTER II.

Capture of Oswego and Fort William-Henry.—1756-1757.

Alliances with the savages; the Iroquois affect a neutrality.—Military preparations.—Canadian bands afoot the whole winter of 1755-6.—Fort Bull razed, and an enemy's convoy of 400 bateaux dispersed.—Disaccord begun between the governor-general and Montcalm.—Siege of Oswego; The garrison capitulates; booty gained by the victors; The savages kill many of the prisoners; the works of the place razed; joy at its fall in Canada.—The British suspend all further operations in the field for the year; the savages ravage their provinces.—The Canadians capture Grenville.—Dearth in Canada; an arrival of famished Acadians, to make matters still worse.—Aid demanded from France.—Rapid increase of colonial expenditure.—Montcalm proposes to attack Acadia, rather than forts Edward and William Henry.—Pitt obtains ministerial power in Britain.—Renewed efforts made by the British government and people, in view of achieving American ascendancy in 1757.—Abortive enterprise against Louisbourg.—Canadian bands afoot again during the winter of 1757-8; exploits of M. Rigaud.—Succours arrive from France; the alliance of the savages secured.—Siege and capture of Fort William Henry;—massacre of many of the prisoners taken, by the savages; the works of the place razed.—The dearth in Canada becomes a famine; the troops murmur at the privations they endure.—Disagreements become notorious among the colonial chiefs.—Varying fortunes of the French forces in Europe, Asia, &c.—The British raise an army 50,000 strong, for their American campaign of 1758... 169

CHAPTER III.

Battle of Carillon (Ticonderoga).—1758.

The Canadians, left to their own means of defence, determine to fight to the last.—Plan of the British campaign: proposed simultaneous attacks on Louisbourg, Carillon, and Fort Duquesne.—Capture of Louisbourg, after a memorable siege, and invasion of the island of St. John (Prince Edward's); the victors ravage the settlements of Gaspé and Mont-Louis.—Defensive measures in Canada.—General Abercromby advances, with 16,000 men, on Carillon, defended by scarcely 3,500 French. BATTLE OF CARILLON, fought July 8: defeat and precipitate retreat of Abercromby.—Colonel Bradstreet captures and destroys Fort Frontenac.—General Forbes advances against Fort Duquesne.—Defeat of Major Grant.—The French burn Fort Duquesne, and retreat.—Vicissitudes of the war in different parts of the world.—Ministerial changes in France.—Dissidences between Montcalm and the governor.—The French ministry takes Bigot to task.—Intrigues for superseding M. de Vaudreuil.—The ministry accept the self-proposed recal of Montcalm; the king opposes it.—Conciliatory despatches sent to the rival chiefs, with knightly orders, &c. for them, and promotions of their subalterns; but accompanied by no soldiers or other substantial succours.—Defection of the French Indians, who at Easton adopt the British side.—The British decide to advance upon Quebec, with three armies, to rendezvous under its walls.—Amount of Canadian force in hand to resist this triple invasion.. 197

BOOK TENTH.

CHAPTER I.

VICTORY OF MONTMORENCI, AND FIRST BATTLE OF ABRAHAM.—SURRENDER OF QUEBEC.—1759.

Invasion of Canada.—Defensive means adopted.—The French army entrenches itself at Beauport, &c., below Quebec.—The British troops land on the Isle d'Orléans.—Proclamation addressed by General Wolfe to the Canadians.—That General, judging an attack on the French camp to be too hazardous, determines to bombard the city and ravage its environs.—The former set on fire.—Attack on the French lines at Montmorenci.—Wolfe being repulsed, returns dispirited to his camp, and falls ill.—He vainly attempts to put himself into communication with General Amherst at Lake Champlain.—His officers advise that he should take possession, by surprise, of the Heights of Abraham, and thus force the French to quit camp.—General Montcalm sends troops to guard the left bank of the St. Lawrence, above Quebec, up to the river Jacques-Cartier.—A great number of the Canadians, thinking all danger past, quit the army to attend to field labour.—On the Lake Champlain frontier, M. de Bourlamaque blows up forts Carillon and St. Frederic, and retreats to the Isle-aux-Noix, followed by General Amherst with 12,000 men.—The British generals Prideaux and Johnson, operating towards Lake Erie, take Fort Niagara and force the French to retire to la Présentation, below Lake Ontario.—The British scale the Heights of Abraham, Sept. 13.—A drawn battle ensues; defeat of the French and death of Montcalm : capitulation of Quebec.—General de Lévis takes command of the army, and intends to offer battle instantly; but learning the surrender of the capital, retires to Jacques-Cartier and entrenches his troops.—The British army, enclosed in Quebec, prepares to winter there.—Proper succours asked in vain from France, for re-capturing the city............................ 230

CHAPTER II.

SECOND BATTLE OF ABRAHAM AND LAST VICTORY OF THE FRENCH.—CESSION OF CANADA TO BRITAIN, AND LOUISIANA TO SPAIN.—1760-1763.

Diverse impressions which the capture of Quebec causes in Britain and France.—The ministers of Louis XV leave Canada to its fate.—The British organize three armies to finish the conquest they have begun; measures taken in the colony to resist this triple invasion; respective French and British forces.—General de Lévis marches towards Quebec.—Second battle of Abraham: complete defeat of the British army, which shuts itself up in the city; the French lay siege to it, in expectation that the succour they demanded will come from France.—Common belief in the colony that, of the antagonistic armies in Canada, the one first to be reinforced will have the mastery of Canada.—Arrival of a British relieving fleet.—De Lévis raises the siege of Quebec and begins his retreat towards Montreal; deficiency of provisions forces him to disband the militia and disperse his regulars.—State of the frontiers towards Lakes Champlain and Ontario.—The enemy sets out to attack Montreal.—General Murray leaves Quebec with 4,000 men; brigadier Haviland, with a corps nearly as numerous, descends Lake Champlain, and General Amherst sets out from Lake Ontario with 11,000 soldiers and savages; the French fall back and rendezvous at Montreal 3500 strong.—Impossibility of longer useful resistance becoming manifest, a general capitulation follows.—Triumphal demonstrations thereat in Britain.—Trial and condemnation of Canadian dilapidators at Paris. —Situation of the Canadians; immense losses they sustained through the depreciated state paper-money.—Continuation of the war in other parts of the world.—Peace of 1763, by which Canada is ceded to Britain, and Louisiana to Spain.—State of France at the time of this too-famous treaty, as depicted by Sismondi..... 269

BOOK ELEVENTH.

CHAPTER I.

MIILITARY DESPOTISM.—ABOLITION AND RESTORATION OF THE ANCIENT LAWS.—1769-1764.

Cessation of hostilities; the Canadians return to their homesteads.—Military government and courts-martial.—Emigration of Canadians to France.—The French laws discontinued, but the catholic religion tolerated.—Governor Murray replaces Amherst as generalissimo.—An executive, legislative, and judicial council constituted.—Division of Canada into two districts, and introduction of English laws.—Murmurings of the people.—The British colonists demand an elective chamber, or representative assembly, from which Canadian members were intended to be excluded; and accuse Murray of tyranny: that general quits the colony on leave, but does not return.—Risings of the western savages.—Gen. Carleton, appointed Murray's successor, makes changes in the governing council.—The people continue their opposition to the new laws.—Official reports of five British crown-lawyers (Yorke, De Grey, Marriott, Wedderburn, and Thurlow) on the grievances of the Canadians.—A Legislative Council finally established, in 1774.

CHAPTER II.

AMERICAN REVOLUTION.—1775.

Disputes between Great Britain and her ancient colonies.—Divisions in the British parliament regarding that subject.—Advent of Lord North to the ministry.—Troubles at Boston.—Coercive measures there, of the mother country; but which seeks to gain Canada by concessions.—Petitions and counter-petitions of the Canadians and Anglo-Canadians; true reason for delays in deciding between those two parties.—The Quebec Act of 1774; debates in the house of commons.—Congress of Philadelphia; it classes the Quebec Act among American grievances.—Addresses of Congress to Britain and Canada.—General Carleton arrives in Canada.—Feelings of the Canadians regarding the coming struggle.—First hostilities.—Surprise and capture of Ticonderoga, Crown-Point, and St. John's.—Civil war.—Battle of Bunker's Hill.—General Invasion of Canada by the United States troops.—Montgomery and Arnold march on Quebec; they take Montreal and Three Rivers.—The governor re-enters the capital as a fugitive; the Americans lay siege to it...................................... 344

www.ingramcontent.com/pod-product-compliance
Lightning Source LLC
Chambersburg PA
CBHW030356230426
43664CB00007BB/615